J.L. Austin's Concept of "Performative Word"

European University Studies
Europäische Hochschulschriften
Publications Universitaires Européennes

Series XXIII
Theology

Reihe XXIII   Série XXIII
Theologie
Théologie

Vol./Bd. 928

PETER LANG
Frankfurt am Main · Berlin · Bern · Bruxelles · New York · Oxford · Wien

Alexander Chukwujindum Uzoh

J.L. Austin's Concept of "Performative Word"

A Systematic Theological Analysis in Sacramental Theology and in Igbo Traditional Religion

Its Impact on the Use of Igbo Language for Effective Evangelization in Igboland

PETER LANG
Internationaler Verlag der Wissenschaften

Bibliographic Information published by the Deutsche Nationalbibliothek
The Deutsche Nationalbibliothek lists this publication in the Deutsche Nationalbibliografie; detailed bibliographic data is available in the internet at http://dnb.d-nb.de.

Zugl.: München, Univ., Diss., 2011

D 19
ISSN 0721-3409
ISBN 978-3-631-63608-4

© Peter Lang GmbH
Internationaler Verlag der Wissenschaften
Frankfurt am Main 2012
All rights reserved.

All parts of this publication are protected by copyright. Any utilisation outside the strict limits of the copyright law, without the permission of the publisher, is forbidden and liable to prosecution. This applies in particular to reproductions, translations, microfilming, and storage and processing in electronic retrieval systems.

www.peterlang.de

Dedication

To my late mother Mrs Margaret Mary Uzoh, my late brother Mr Eddy Uzoh and my late sister Mrs Sabina Megbuzie.

I also dedicate this work to all men and women who for the purpose of evangelization work tirelessly in order to make the proclamation of the gospel message in our land more acceptable to our people.

Table of contents

Acknowledgement	13
Forword	15
0 General Introduction	17
0.1 The genesis of this research	17
0.2 The aim of this research	17
0.3 The method used in the study	19
0.4 The division of work	20
0.5 Sources and Bibliography	22
1 Analysis of the key concept: "performative word"	23
1.1 Introduction	23
1.2 The history of the concept of performative word	24
1.3 The concept of performative word	25
1.4 Criteria for performative word	27
1.4.1 The Doctrine of Misfires	28
1.4.2 The Doctrine of Abuses	29
1.5 Forms of performative word	30
1.5.1 Explicit performative word	30
1.5.2 Implicit performative word	33
1.6 Performative word versus speech act theory	34
1.6.1 Aspects of speech act theory	35
1.6.1.1 Locutionary act	35
1.6.1.2 Illocutionary act	36
1.6.1.3 Perlocutionary act	37
1.6.2 Comparative analysis of speech act theory	38
1.6.2.1 Similarities in the speech acts	38
1.6.2.2 Dissimilarities in the speech acts	39
1.6.2.3 Illocutionary act versus perlocutionary act	39
1.7 References	40
1.7.1 Performative symbols	40
1.7.2 Performative identities	41
1.7.3 Performative magic	41
1.7.4 Performative theater	42
1.8 Conclusion	43

2 Performative word and sacramental theology 45
　2.1 Introduction 45
　2.2 The concept of performative word in sacramental theology 45
　2.3 The form of performative word in sacramental theology 47
　　2.3.1 Explicit performative word 47
　2.4 Criteria for performative word in sacramental theology 48
　2.5 References to performative word in sacramental theology 49
　　2.5.1 Performative identities 50
　　2.5.2 Performative theater 51
　　2.5.3 Performative symbols 51
　2.6 Performative word: the hermeneutic of the sacraments 52
　　2.6.1 The sacrament of the eucharist 52
　　2.6.2 The sacrament of penance 57
　2.7 Performative word and the scriptures 58
　　2.7.1 The Old Testament 59
　　2.7.2 The New Testament 61
　2.8 Performative word and the church's doctrine 63
　　2.8.1 The Doctrine of Incarnation 63
　　2.8.2 The Doctrine of Inspiration 66
　2.9 Performative word and the contributions of some theologians 68
　　2.9.1 St Augustine's theory of language 68
　　2.9.2 Odo Casel's treatise on cultic mystery 71
　　2.9.3 Dietrich Bonhoeffer's treatise on ecclesiology 72
　　2.9.4 Thomas Cranmer's Book of Common Prayer 73
　2.10 Conclusion 75

3 Performative word and igbo traditional religion 77
　3.1 Introduction 77
　3.2 What is Igbo? 77
　3.3 Who are the Igbo people? 78
　3.4 Nature and content of Igbo traditional religion 83
　3.5 Igbo Language: Formation and Interpretations 93
　3.6 The concept of performative word in Igbo traditional religion 96
　3.7 Forms of performative word in Igbo traditional religion 99
　　3.7.1 Explicit performative word 99
　　3.7.2 Implicit performative word 100
　3.8 Criteria for performative word in Igbo traditional religion 101
　3.9 References to performative word in Igbo traditional religion 102
　　3.9.1 Performative identities 102
　　3.9.2 Performative symbols 103
　　3.9.3 Performative theater 103
　　3.9.4 Performative magic 104
　3.10 Agents of performative word in Igbo traditional religion 105
　　3.10.1 Chief priest 105

    3.10.2 Family head 106
    3.10.3 The Downtrodden 107
  3.11 Performative word and the celebration of various rites in
     Igbo traditional religion 108
    3.11.1 The rite of initiation 108
    3.11.2 The rite of purification 109
    3.11.3 The rite of healing 110
    3.11.4 The rite of the Igbo traditional priesthood 111
    3.11.5 The rite of the Igbo traditional marriage 115
    3.11.6 The rite of kolanut (Iwa Oji) / sacrifice (Ichu Aja) 123
    3.11.7 The rite of oath taking – Inu iyi 127
    3.11.8 The rite of covenant making – Igba Ndu 130
  3.12 Additional References 131
    3.12.1 Performative word in Igbo folktales 131
    3.12.2 Performative word in Igbo traditional songs 135
    3.12.3 Performative word in Igbo proverbs 145
  3.13 Conclusion 148

4 Performative word in sacramental theology and in igbo traditional religion:
    towards a comparative analysis... 151
  4.1 Introduction 151
  4.2 Similarities 151
    4.2.1 The concept: Performative word 151
    4.2.2 The form: Explicit performative word 153
    4.2.3 The criteria for performative word 154
    4.2.4 The reference: Performative identities 154
    4.2.5 The reference: Performative symbols 155
    4.2.6 The reference: Performative theater 158
  4.3 Dissimilarities 159
    4.3.1 The conceptual analysis 160
        4.3.1.1 Performative word as a sacred word 160
        4.3.1.2 Performative word as scripture-oriented 161
        4.3.1.3 Performative word as sacrament-oriented 163
        4.3.1.4 Performative word as theology-oriented 164
        4.3.1.5 Performative word as incarnate word 165
        4.3.1.6 "Ex Opere Operato" 166
    4.3.2 The form: Implicit performative word 167
    4.3.3 The reference: Performative magic 169
  4.4 Conclusion 169

5 Performative word versus use of igbo language
    for effective evangelization in igboland... 171
  5.1 Introduction 171
  5.2 Performative word versus Igbo word 172

5.3	Infelicities	172
	5.3.1 Misinvocation	173
	5.3.2 Misapplication	173
	5.3.3 Misexecution	174
	5.3.4 Abuse	174
5.4	Explicit performative form versus Igbo word	175
5.5	How does the word perform in today's Igbo church?	176
	5.5.1 Prayer ministry	176
	5.5.2 Crusade	182
	5.5.3 Family ministration "olu ezi na ulo"	185
	5.5.4 Parish annual retreat	187
	5.5.5 Parish weekly adoration	188
	5.5.6 Charismatic renewal prayer group	190
	5.5.7 Homily	195
	5.5.8 Catechism classes	196
	5.5.9 School apostolate	198
	5.5.10 Counselling	199
5.6	Scriptural Background to evangelization	200
5.7	What is evangelization?	201
	5.7.1 The goal of evangelization	202
	5.7.2 The methods of evangelization	203
	5.7.3 The evangelizer and the evangelized	204
5.8	Early evangelization among the Igbo natives	205
5.9	Evangelization in the new vision of the church	207
5.10	Evangelization by means of implimenting the language of the people	211
5.11	The call to evangelize is a call to inculturate	212
	5.11.1 Inculturation	214
	5.11.1.1 The Historical Background	214
	5.11.1.2 The meaning of inculturation	215
	5.11.1.3 Principles of inculturation	217
	5.11.1.4 Inculturation as a means of evangelization	218
	5.11.1.5 Problems of inculturation of christianity	220
	5.11.1.5.1 The system in formation houses	221
	5.11.1.5.2 Western-oriented nature of church doctrines and rites	222
	5.11.1.5.3 More rationalizations	223
	5.11.1.5.4 The indigeneous ecclesiastical hierarchy	224
	5.11.1.5.5 The dependent nature of the Igbo church	225
	5.11.2 Dialogue	226
	5.11.2.1 Interreligious Dialogue	227
	5.11.2.1.1 The church in dialogue with other religions	229
	5.11.2.1.2 The church in dialogue with African (Igbo) religion	231
	5.11.2.1.3 The necessity of Interreligious Dialogue	233

5.12 Recommendations 235
    5.12.1 The right disposition of the agents of evangelization 235
        5.12.1.1 Priests and religious 235
        5.12.1.2 Lay faithful 236
    5.12.2 Specific areas of inculturation 239
        5.12.2.1 Prayer books 240
        5.12.2.2 Liturgical books 241
        5.12.2.3 Use of Igbo names and titles 242
        5.12.2.4 Use of local compositions 244
        5.12.2.5 Use of local symbols 246
        5.12.2.6 Use of traditional narratives 247
        5.12.2.7 Use of traditional proverbs 249
        5.12.2.8 Use of traditional folktales 250
        5.12.2.9 Use of traditional terminologies 252
5.13 Conclusion 253

Evaluation and General Conclusion 255

Abbreviations 265

Bibliography 267

Acknowledgement

Blessed be the holy and undivided Trinity: Father, Son and Holy Spirit, for the divine providence which I have experienced all through my life, and especially, during my stay and studies in Germany.

I express my profound gratitude first of all to my Bishop, Most Rev Hilary Paul Odili Okeke for his fatherly care towards me, and for offering me the opportunity to study overseas. I thank the Archdiocese of Munich and Freising in Germany for accepting to sponsor my studies. I am most grateful to the management and staff of Ludwig-Maximilians-Universität München, Germany, whose assistance facilitated my studies. May I express my sincere and hearty gratitude to my moderator Prof Dr Andreas Wollbold for his critical and constructive reading of the entire work which gave it a master touch, and for his constant encouragement and availability. Indeed, he is an efficient scholar and a competent moderator. Similarly, I thank Prof Dr Martin Thurner and Frau Dr Katharina Karl for reading this work and for offering relevant suggestions which helped me to improve the quality of this work. I thank the supervisors Prof Dr Bertram Stubenrauch and Prof Dr Roland Kany for their various contributions. My sincere regards to Prof Dr Peter Neuner for reading this work and for his corrections and advice.

I am grateful to my brother priests from Nigeria who have in one way or the other contributed to the success of this work. My special thanks go to Rev Fr Prof Dr Ignatius Obinwa, Rev fr Dr Dr Celestine Uzondu, Rev Fr Dr Moses Nnajiofor, Rev Fr Dr Joe-Barth Abba, Frs. Edwin Udoye, Fidelis Kwazu, Stephan Oranuba, Fabian Eke, Michael Ukpong, Gerald Njoku, Augustine-Ben Onwubiko and Paul Nwandu. I wish to thank the priests, the religious men and women, and the entire lay faithful of the catholic diocese of Nnewi as well as host of other priest-friends outside the diocese.

I am highly indebted to my German benefactors and friends who indeed were very helpful to me throughout my sojourn in Germany. In particular, I thank Fr Dr Oratio Bonasi, Fr Berislav Grgic (now Bishop of Tromso in Norway), Fr Rüdiger Karmann, Fr Josef Schlossnikel, and the entire parishioners of St Bartholomäus and St Stephan Pfarrverband Deisenhofen/Oberhaching. I sincerely thank Ernst Schlossnikel, Angela Schaller and Wolfgang Hering, Gertrude and Herbert Schlicht, Sigrid Zielmann and the family of Giorno for their benevolence. I thank Fr Christoph Nobs and the entire parishioners of St Magdalena Ottobrunn, especially, Maria Wehrheim, Renate Dürr, Christa Remig and Roswitha Krieger. Sincere regards too to Fr Andreas Heck and the entire parishioners in Marktsteinach, Waldsachsen, Löffelsterz, Abelsfeld and Rednersdorf. I thank especially the families of Gehard and Emma Werner, Mechthilde and Werner Möller, Oswald Seufert, Gabi and Gehard Rost, Hans and Rainer Biegner, Ferdinand Friedrich, and the family of Peter Schwarz.

I wish to thank the members of my family, especially, my late mother Mrs Margaret Mary Uzoh, my late brother Mr Eddy Uzoh and my late sister Mrs Sabina Megbuzie whom I fondly remember in my prayers and Holy Masses. My special thanks to my father, all my sisters and brothers, relatives, friends and well-wishers for their constant support and prayers in all my endeavours.

Uzoh Alexander Chukwujindum
Germany, 2011.

Forword

Everyone of us possesses an amazing power to uplift, encourage, bless, motivate, strengthen, and even heal others with words that come out from our mouths! **What a gift!** And hence, the Igbo tribe of Southeastern Nigeria say: "Ire oma ka ejula ji aga n'ogwu !" which can be interpreted as, With kind and gentle words, one frees himself from his difficulties.

On the flip side, we also have the power to tear down, hurt, malign, meddle, criticize, and judge. That is the power of words! Hence the Ibo people say: "Onu sel'ogu!" which means that a spoken words can cause war. "Okwuoma enwero usa" and it is explained as – A well spoken word deserves no criticism.

Jesus says in John 6:63 that, His "words are Spirit." And they are life. Anybody's words can be interpreted in the bible as "Spirit" and "Life." **Words** generate emotional, attitudinal, and behavioral reactions. They can induce and compel powerful reactions, such as murder, on the bad side, peace or joy, on the good side. What actually happens in **Word** is, – spirit passing from one person to another. We say in Ibo, 'Okwu ekwulu n'onu bu obi afulu anya.' ie, a spoken word brings to light, the mind or intention of the speaker. We can cite an example from a text in the Bible, where Jesus, during his passion was questioned by the Jews about his identity: Lk. 22:63–71.

The Jewish guards began mocking and beating him. They blindfolded him and demanded, "Prophesy! Who hit you?" And they said many other insulting words to him. At daybreak the council of the elders of the people, both the chief priests and teachers of the law, met together, and Jesus was led before them. "If you are the Christ, they said, tell us "Jesus answered, "If I tell you, you will not believe me, and if I asked you, you would not answer. But from now on, the Son of Man will be seated at the right hand of the mighty God." They all asked, "Are you then the Son of God?" He replied, "You are right in saying I am." What irritated them was the affirmative word of his being the Son of God. They then said, "Why do we need any more testimony, we have heard it from his own lips, what further witness do we need?"

Every spoken **'word'**, no mater how brief, has unlimited impact. For instance, a person who appears before mourners in a funeral service of a person whose death cause was unknown, and with microphone says beating his chaste **"I"** This is a single **word** but it has unlimited meanings. It may land him in prison if luckily he is not mobbed by the mourners.

Nothing touches us but the meaning of a **word**, a disposition, or an attitude that is communicated.The extent to which we grasp and believe the truth of doctrines determines our desire to be holy. By this holiness created within us we become sanctified. The gospel is the power of God unto salvation. The gospel's power lies or resides in its **words** produced in our minds. That is all that the gospel is, – **words** spoken by God. **"The words that I speak unto you are spirit, and they are life"** (John 6:63).

This said, any body who reads through this doctoral work of Rev. Fr. Dr. Alex. Uzor, his analysis of the concept, **"Performative Word"** the impact it bear in the celebration of Sacraments and in the Evangelization, will get to appreciate the dept of research and the scientific presentation put into book. The work also creates a deeper awareness to the impact of man's utterances whether as written or spoken words. Dr. Alex. made his readers to appreciate the role, the fruits or the effects which **word** played in creation. Through His Word, God created the world and all that are in it. He said, "Let there be Light, and there was Light. We appreciate the **"Performative word"** in the celebration of Eucharist which is the highest praise we can give to God. The words of Consecration at Holy Mass brings down the divine presence of Christ's Body and Blood, that is the **"Transsubstantiation"**. The original sin which man inherited from our first parents, Adam and Eve, is totally removed from a newly baptized with he words. "... I baptize you, in the name of the Father, and of the Son, and of the Holy Spirit".

His message to us is that the 'word' creates, it sanctifies, it protects, it gives and preserves life. We learn from this that because of the sensitive nature of the word, one should strive apply his words in such a manner that it creates, builds and promotes peace in the world.

Dr. Alex argues that the 'Word', which he discussed as 'Performative', because of its power to effect a negative or a positive results, it should be preferred as a powerful instrument of evangelisation among the Igbos who value the use of proverbs in discussing very important matters, and in the church, as a means should continue to utilize it in order to produce rich fruits of Faith, Love and Holiness of producing fruits of Faith, Love and Holiness through the celebration of Sacraments.

I am impressed about the copious research that went into his work, his scientific presentation, and his courage to delve into the topic which I consider very demanding because of the wide scope which the study covers. I have no hesitations to urge our reading public to benefit from the interesting content of this book.

Rev. Fr. Dr. Chukwuemeka Moses Nnajiofor.

0 General Introduction

0.1 The genesis of this research

It was my encounter with J.L.Austin's "How To Do Things With Words," which is the product of his "The William James Lectures" in 1955 at the Harvard University that inspired me to investigate into how words perform in sacramental theology and in Igbo traditional religion of south-east Nigeria, and how the product of this investigation can be of pastoral relevance in evangelizing mission in Igboland.

Not satisfied with the presumption of the philosophers that word is used for descriptive purposes only, J.L.Austin went into discussing a more plausible way in which word can be used. Prior to his investigation there was already this feeling among the linguistic philosophers or as J.L.Austin would prefer to call them – Grammarians – that after all human language cannot be associated with the philosophical realism in which the concept of word has its real separate existence. These grammarians went further to argue that after all there are also statements that express wish or command or are used as questions. Immanuel Kant (1724–1804) attempted to mediate between the philosophical realism and the teaching of the grammarians and insisted that the traditional philosophy of realism would lead to illusions, and instead maintained that reality is a product of our thoughts. Neither the traditional philosophy nor grammarians nor Immanuel Kant could appeal to J.L.Austin who argues that the traditional distortions of the facts and of our language have been due fundamentally to certain central errors in the theory of knowledge which have been pervasive in philosophy from Plato to the present day. Having carefully studied the role word plays, J.L.Austin arrived at the conclusion that human language is action-oriented, and that our act of saying something or in our saying something or by our saying something a certain effect is achieved. This is what J.L.Austin meant by performative word.

0.2 The aim of this research

In what may seem as a comparative religious studies, this work intends to undertake theological investigations in contemporary Black Africa with the Igbo tribe of south-east Nigeria as a case-study. This theological investigations are based on J.L.Austin's concept of performative word, and to be analyzed in the context of sacramental theology and the Igbo traditional religion, and then to give this concept a pastoral relevance in such a way that the use of Igbo word would be performative in evangelization among the Igbo themselves.

The performative role words play in sacramental theology cannot be denied. Word and sacrament, although recognized by the church as two different concepts are acknowledged by the church as interrelated: the word brings about sacrament, and sacramental celebration offers opportunity for proclamation of the word. Since sacrament is recognized as fruit of the word, sacramental word is considered to have an efficacy that can come from God alone. The efficacy of the sacramental word, therefore, is faith-oriented. The word brings along with it a new and revitalizing action that influences the hearer out of faith. This means, in order to experience the performative power of word in sacraments, faith is a necessary condition so that the word can be likened to a seed falling onto fertile ground, bearing the Holy Spirit's life-force within it. So, in the celebration of sacrament, word plays the important role of preparing and disposing the minds and hearts of the participants. It does not stop on this, rather, goes ahead to act on the elements in order to bring about sacrament. Word, therefore, is efficacious within the frame-work of sacramental celebrations. This means, word is performative because it is sacrament-oriented. The sacrament gives value to the word and makes its performative character to assume sacred value, as well as, ritualistic.

Likewise, Igbo traditional religion is an element that is at the basis of the culture itself, and therefore, necessary for African christian theology. The spiritual system of the Igbo people is one of the oldest on earth. The roots of Igbo spirituality is the same as the roots of every other African one. Igbo spirituality predates Islam, Christianity, Judaism, and every other – ism that one can think of. If there are any similarities between the traditional practices of the Igbo and those of other religions, it is because they were borrowed from our ancestors, and not the other way round. It is pertinent here to mention that in Igbo traditional society there were no atheists. This is because religion in the indigenous Igbo culture was not an independent institution. It is an integral and inseparable part of the entire culture. Religion for an Igbo man was practical in the sense that one's entire action is reflective of one's religious concepts and practices as is seen in the ordering of society – social morality is dependent on religion. Within the context of the total belief system of the Igbo traditionalists, there are private worship and public worship. We shall consider this aspect later in our discussions.

When discussing the performative character of Igbo word, therefore, it should not be separated from the cultural values of the Igbo people with particular respect to their ritual practices and religious beliefs. Although there exist today, numerous literatures on Igbo religious belief system, little attention so far has been paid to studying how word performs in the rites and rituals of this great religion. According to Igbo traditional religion, the situation before the utterance is no longer the same after the utterance. This means, performative words can be explored not only for their meanings but also for the effects they have on the lives of the adherents. So, performative words in Igbo traditional religion are believed to have the power to effect meaningful transformations. In Igbo traditional society, therefore, one does not tamper with the spoken word. To tamper with a spoken word is one of the greatest felonies in Igboland and the consequence is great. The meaning and interpretation of performative words in Igbo traditional religion, nevertheless, should not be understood in the sense of self-suggestion or auto-suggestion because these terms have to do with self presumption. Such presumptions are dangerous whenever and wherever they are allowed in any religion. Rather, the culture of the Igbo people helps to build a favourable ground on which the performative power of words are genuinely experienced in rituals and religious acts. So, verbal words in Igbo traditional religion are considered sacred because they are ritual words, and are uttered within the framework of religious rites and rituals. The religious convictions of the Igbo people, therefore, empower the ritual words and make them performative and elevate them to be sacred and no longer ordinary.

Since there are certain similarities in the way performative word is conceived in both religions (dissimilarities notwithstanding), it implies that a healthy relationship can develop in which the actions of the sacramental words are properly understood by the Igbo christian because similar actions of the words are already recognized in the traditional religious environment where he comes from.

In the light of J.L.Austin's concept of performative word, therefore, this research work aims at studying the various ways through which proper use of Igbo language can be effective means of evangelization in Igboland. In other words, I will try to reconcile my findings in such a way that it will show how much pastoral impact J.L.Austin's performative word has in the use of authentic Igbo word in the church's missionary purpose of evangelization in Igboland, whereby the gospel message, presented in authentic Igbo language, would be able to perform in such a way that it will lead to sincere conversions and better formation of authentic Igbo christians within the Igbo cultural milieu. This will not only add to the gradual development of a systematized traditional theology for Igbos but will make christianity not to be a stranger on Igbo soil.

0.3 The method used in the study

Our study approach would be deductive, namely: from the already established J.L.Austin's concept of performative word, we engage on a fact-finding mission. It would be based on the principle that allows nothing to remove the reader's interest from the theme of this research to the factors extraneous to it. This does not imply that we are myopic and narrow-minded, but instead, while concentrating on the theme, we shall try as much as possible to reach out to other necessary factors that have to do with our theme of investigation. In discussing performative word in Igbo traditional religion, therefore, it would not be out of place to begin by discussing the Igbo people themselves, their beliefs and practices as an introduction to the subject matter. Likewise, discussion on performative word in sacramental theology should not be done in isolation but in relation to other existing theologies of sacrament. Through this approach we equip our reader with a comprehensive and necessary information he needs in order to appreciate the theme and the aim of our research.

0.4 The division of work

This work is systematically divided into five chapters, and each chapter has its own short introduction and conclusion.

Chapter one analyzes the key concept "performative word." This chapter traces the historical origin of the concept, and how J.L.Austin had successfully launched it as a new thought in which word is valued in a totally different dimension, quite different from the way it had been perceived. Under this new concept, emphasis is shifted from the constantive or metaphysical use of word to performative use. By citing practical examples, therefore, J.L.Austin was able to prove that certain utterances result to actions, and that situations before the utterances change after the utterances. In this way, he showed the relationship between words and actions. On a broader discussion on this concept, this chapter goes on to study different forms of performative word, its various aspects, as well as, the criteria that regulate it. It extends its scope to include the speech act analysis and the contributions from philosophy to our theme.

Chapter two discusses performative word in relation to sacramental theology. It analyzes the concept "performative word" in the light of the church's teaching on sacrament. As a systematic inquiry, it builds on the scriptural foundation and extends to some aspects of the church's doctrines, and does not ignore the various contributions of some theologians. This work presents the sacraments of the Holy Eucharist and Penance as examples to prove this relationship between word and actions in the sacramental celebrations.

Chapter three studies performative word in relation to Igbo traditional religion. It articulates both the concept, the forms, the aspects and the criteria for performative word in the context of Igbo traditional religion. Furthermore, this chapter goes on to explain how Igbo words perform in Igbo religious rituals and rites. While discussing certain agents of performative word in Igbo traditional society, it presents folktales, traditional songs and proverbs as various areas where performative word is applied.

Chapter four teaches that the application of J.L.Austin's concept of performative word in sacramental theology and in Igbo traditional religion has some similarities as well as some dissimilarities. Our study reveals that our key concept relates similarly to both sacramental theology and to Igbo traditional religion in terms of definition, in terms of criteria, and in terms of the use of explicit form. Besides, the present chapter presents also the basic differences in the way the J.L.Austin's concept of performative word is interpreted in sacramental theology and in Igbo traditional religion. For example, in sacramental theology, every performative word is sacred because it is uttered within the context of ritual ceremonies. The Igbo cosmology does not totally agree to this because of its inseparability of cultural, social and religious life of the people from one another. It may, therefore, not totally be correct to say that all the performative words within the context of Igbo traditional rituals are sacred. Again, the teachings of sacramental theology implies that performative word is scripture-oriented, sacrament-oriented and theology-oriented. Bible, of course, is the major source upon which the teachings and practice of sacramental theology is based. Likewise, the word constitutes the sacrament through its performance within the context of sacramental celebrations. The actions of the word is geared towards realization of sacraments. Again, in sacramental theology, performative word has a defined theology that sustains it, which, as it were, may be referred to as the theology of the word. It is this theology of the word that compliments the theology of the sacrament. On the contrary, Igbo traditional religion is not a religion of the book, and therefore, there is no association of performative word to any written source within Igbo traditional religion. Although there are some sacramental realities in Igbo religious rites and rituals, it will be totally wrong to say that performative word in Igbo traditional religion is sacrament-oriented. It may not be logically accepted that performative word in Igbo traditional religion is theology-oriented. This is because Igbo traditional religion itself has not yet got a commonly defined and standardized theology of its own. Sacramental theology in its doctrine of incarnation, personifies performative word to be Jesus Christ, whereas, there is no such personification in Igbo traditional religion. Furthermore, our present chapter shows that the teaching of sacramental theology on "ex opere operato" is in sympathy with J.L.Austin's concept of performative word, whereas, the "ex opere operato" has no place in Igbo traditional religion.

In chapter five, the pastoral impact the J.L.Austin's concept of performative word has on the use of Igbo language for effective evangelization in Igboland is unfolded. In other words, it is the chapter that channels our discussion to an end that will be a great benefit in the work of evangelization in Igboland. Along this line of thought, this chapter begins by focusing on the impact the concept of performative word has on the use of Igbo language for effective evangelization in Igboland. It goes on to highlight the various infelicities in the light of Igbo traditional society and thereby giving them pastoral interpretations. It discusses explicit form of performative word and stresses its pastoral relevance. It enumerates concrete situations where word performs among the present day Igbo Christians, viz: prayer ministry, crusade, Family ministration, parish retreat, parish weekly adoration, charismatic prayer group, homily, catechism classes, school apostolate and counselling. Because the whole issue of giving pastoral relevance to our key concept hinges on evangelization, we took a step further to analyse the term "evangelization." Evangelization, according to our discussion, is a biblical term rooted in both Old Testament and New Testament. The term evangelization could, therefore, be understood to mean proclamation of the Gospel message. To be an evangelizer is synonymous with being a proclaimer of this Gospel message, and the evangelized is taken to be all the nations and peoples everywhere. The goal of evangelization is conversion and to arrive at this conversion, the evangelizer must adopt certain methods that he considers most suitable to any given circumstances. This chapter listed some of these methods to include christian witness, person to person encounter, catechesis, mass media, proclamation, and most importantly, the proper use of the local language.

Ours is a changing world and the church must introduce a new vision in its evangelizing mission. Thus, this chapter proposes a new vision that should be totally disposed to all cultures. In this new vision, the language of the evangelized should play a leading role in order to make the Gospel message original to the evangelized. This means, inculturation should be an essential aspect of evangelization. Proper evangelization cannot be achieved when the Gospel message is not incarnated in the people's culture. The process of inculturating the Gospel is not a matter of choice since Christ himself has commanded it (Mt.28,19; Mk.16,15; see also Acts 15,1–33). Inculturation should be based on the very principles: that God wills that all men should be saved; and that Christ himself though he was inform of God accepted to take a human nature and be born into a culture. Therefore, various obstacles that might be encountered in the process of inculturating the Gospel message, namely: the system in formation houses, western-oriented nature of the church's doctrines and rites, more rationalizations, the dependent nature of the church, among others, should not frustrate this process. Instead, they should be overcome through sincere dialogue. This dialogue would boost the relationship between Gospel and Culture and make the light of the Gospel be more far-reaching to certain areas that urgently need attention. Our present chapter in its recommendations lists then the areas where the effective use of Igbo language is needed, they include: right disposition of the agents of evangelization, prayer books, liturgical books, use of Igbo names and titles, use of local compositions, use of Igbo symbols, use of traditional narratives, use of traditional proverbs, use of traditional folktales, use of traditional terminologies, to mention but a few.

0.5 Sources and Bibliography

This work is a product of field work, personal interviews and works of other scholars, and articles and books written by theologians of proven orthodoxy. I also made use of the Holy Scriptures and christian tradition. I also cited documents of ecumenical councils. I made references to some liturgical and canonical texts, papal encyclicals and addresses.

As we can see from our discussions, J.L.Austin's concept of performative word has exposed us to the fact that proper use of Igbo language is performative within the context of Igbo religious rituals, and therefore, can be effective instruments and necessary guide in the pastoral work of evangelizing the Igbos. What this would mean to the Igbo christians is that they could then be motivated by the word of God as it is being presented to them in their original Igbo language either by proclamations or by songs or by any other verbal means. It is hoped that this work would be a mind-set. It might be a further invitation for more researches by future generations who would be expected to critically lay bare the deficiencies of this work and to bring into completion what has been started.

1 Analysis of the key concept: "performative word"

1.1 Introduction

According to J.L.Austin: "It was for too long the assumption of philosophers that the business of a 'statement' can only be to 'describe' some state of affairs, or to 'state some fact', which it must do either truly or falsely".[1] There arose later this feeling among the linguistic philosophers or as J.L.Austin would prefer to call them-Grammarians-that after all not every word describes since there are also statements that express wish or command or are used as questions.[2] The above differences brought about "Kantian Revolution" in which Immanuel Kant (1724–1804) insisted that the traditional philosophy in which word serves descriptive purposes would lead to illusions. Not satisfied by neither traditional philosophy nor by grammarians nor by Immanuel Kant, J.L.Austin argues that the traditional distortions of the facts and of our language have been due fundamentally to certain central errors in the theory of knowledge which have been pervasive in philosophy from Plato to the present day. J.L.Austin himself rather acknowledged a new approach to human language, totally different from the approaches of his predecessors, in which to say something or in saying something or by saying something an action is performed, and this he called performative word.

I decide to write on this J.L.Austin's "Performative Word" because of my interest of investigating how much relevance it has to the church's teaching on the sacraments, as well as its relevance to the beliefs and practice of Igbo traditional religion. At the end of my investigation, I will try to reconcile my findings in such a way that it will show how much impact the use of authentic Igbo word can have in the church's missionary purpose of evangelization in Igboland, whereby the Gospel message, presented in authentic Igbo language, would be able to perform in such a way that it will lead to sincere conversions and better formation of authentic Igbo christians within the Igbo cultural milieu. This chapter, therefore, is an investigation into the J.L.Austin's teaching on performative word. We shall trace the history of the concept of performative word; the concept of performative word; criteria for performative word; the explicit and implicit forms of performative word; performative word versus

---

[1] Austin, John Langshaw, How To Do Things With Words; The William James Lectures delivered at Harvard University in 1955, Oxford 1962, 1; see also Austin, John Langshaw, Philosophical Papers, Oxford 1961, 220.
[2] Cf. Austin, How To Do Things With Words, 1.

speech act theory in which we shall discuss the three aspects of speech act theory and the comparative analysis of speech act theory. Finally, we shall make references to performative linguistic symbol, performative identity, performative magic and performative theater.

1.2 The History of the concept of Performative Word

The Lecture delivered by J.L.Austin[3] in 1955 "The William James Lectures" at the Harvard University marked the historical beginning of the philosophical investigation on "performative word." In this 1955 lecture titled "How To Do Things With Words," Austin embarked on a mission of proving how a language can be seen as a form of social action. This is in direct opposition to the way Philosophy and philosophers have treated "word" for descriptive purposes. In the words of J.L.Austin: "It was for too long the assumption of philosophers that the business of a , statement' can only be to ‚describe' some state of affairs, or to, state some facts,' which it must do either truly or falsely."[4]

But the fact remains that sentences are not only for descriptive purposes. Grammarians would rather emphasize that word serves in expressing wishes or commands, in asking questions, as well as, for command, and so on, and the philosophers themselves "have not intended to deny this."[5] Both philosophers and grammarians, however, failed to distinguish between what might be called ordinary statements and expression of commands or wishes or questions. But then, this failure of philosophy and its dogmatic concept of word could no longer easily be accepted in the modern times. J.L.Austin himself reiterated this point by saying: "But now in recent years, many things which would once have been accepted without questions as , statements' by both philosophers and grammarians have been scrutinized with new care."[6] Under this new wave, every statement which would have been simply accepted without any

---

3   John Langshaw Austin was born in 1911 in Lancashire, England, the son of an architect. During World War II he served in British intelligence; a lieutenant colonel by the end of the war, he was instrumental in planning the Normandy landings. His entire academic career was at Balliol College, Oxford, both his undergraduate studies and, from 1952 till his death from cancer (at the early age of 48) in 1960, as White's professor of Ethics. Austin was a popular teacher, and his irrepressible wit and sense of the absurd which made him popular with students is everywhere evident in his writing as well: his book How To Do Things With Words is one of the funniest books on philosophy ever written. Austin published very little during his lifetime, but what he did publish – and what was published of his writing after his death – has been astonishingly influential. How To Do Things With Words revolutionalized the study not only of language but of drama as well: the field of performance studies is heavily indebted to Austin's thoughts about speech acts. An article of his on meaning is often cited as one of the early seminal statements of what would become cognitive science. See also Yan Huang, Pragmatics, New York 2007, 93.
4   Austin , How To Do Things With Words, 1.
5   Austin, How To Do Things With Words, 1.
6   Austin, How To Do Things With Words, 2.

problem was subjected to thorough investigation "and this led to the view that many ‚statements' are only what may be called pseudo-statements."[7] Most of the statements were, as Kant would qualify it, "nonsense." In addition, it was discovered that "many utterances which look like statements are either not intended at all, or only intended in part, to record or impart straightforward information about the facts."[8] So, J.L.Austin refers to the views of philosophers on word as "descriptive fallacy," and would later prefer to call it "constantive."[9] He concludes that "many traditional philosophical perplexities have arisen through a mistake-the mistake of taking as straightforward statements of fact utterances which are either (in interesting non-grammatical ways) nonsensical or else intended as something quite different."[10] Disgusted with the way word has been conceived, J.L.Austin intended to give a new concept to word with utterances "which are not nonsense, and which contain none of those verbal danger signals which philosophers have by now detected or think the have detected [...] all will have, as it happens, humdrums verbs in the first person singular present indicative active."[11] These humdrums of verbs, according to J.L.Austin, would contain the following features:

> A. they do not 'describe' or ‚report' or constate anything at all, are not 'true or false' ; and
> B. the uttering of the sentence is, or is a part of, the doing of an action, which again would not normally be described as, or as 'just,' saying something. [12]

So, Austin J.L prefers to call this type of utterance "a performative sentence or a performative utterance, or, for short, a performative."[13] Although J.L.Austin delivered these lectures in 1955, the views which underlie these lectures were already conceived as far back as 1939 as evident in his article on "Other Minds" published in the , Proceedings of the Aristotelian Society, Supplementary Volume XX ,1946, 173 f. He had earlier delivered similar lectures in Oxford in the years 1952–1954 under the title : "Words and Deeds." The next question is what then is performative word?

1.3 The Concept of Performative Word

Etymologically, the concept of performative word is derived from the verb "perform" which is usually associated with the noun-action.[14] This means that "the issuing of the utterance is the performing of an action."[15] J.L.Austin, therefore, defines performative utterance as an utterance "in which to say something is to do something; or in

---

7   Austin, How To Do Things With Words, 2.
8   Austin, How To Do Things With Words, 2.
9   Austin, How To Do Things With Words, 3.
10 Austin, How To Do Things With Words, 3.
11 Austin, How To Do Things With Words, 5.
12 Austin, How To Do Things With Words, 5.
13 Austin, How To Do Things With Words, 6.
14 Cf. Austin, How To Do Things With Words, 6.
15 Austin, How To Do Things With Words, 6.

which by saying or in saying something we are doing something."[16] Thus, there exist three senses in which performative utterance is understood. These three senses do not stand in isolation from his "speech act theory" in which human language performs its action under three usages: locution (corresponding to "act of saying"), illocution (corresponding to "in saying") and perlocution (corresponding to "by saying"). Later in this chapter, we shall still relate our investigation on performative utterance to his speech act theory. J.L.Austin continues his teaching on performative utterance and comments: "They will be perfectly straightforward utterances, with ordinary verbs in the first person singular present indicative active, and yet we shall see at once that they couldn't possibly be true or false."[17]

J.L.Austin cautions that the concept of the performative is not a simple one because its application is not all that easy but rather places further demands on an adequate analysis of the term and on the assessment of its applicability. Thus, the performative as a concept needs to be understood in relation to its application because when a person makes performative utterance "we should say that he is doing something rather than merely saying something."[18] One of the examples given by J.L.Austin in order to clarify this point is the Christian marriage in which he explains "when I say, before the registrar or altar,&c., 'I do', I am not reporting on a marriage: I am indulging in it." [19] Pronouncing 'I do', therefore, does not tell the couple that they are married, it marries them instead. So, this word performs action of marrying. So, when words perform the actions, they are called performative words.

Performance here is about the concrete use of language and refers to the realisation of expressions in a specific situation by an individual speaker. In this way, J.L.Austin teaches that language does not only have a referential function but also a performative one. According to him, performative realises what it characterises – speech act. This means that there is a strong relationship between action and language. The relevant analytic judgement of performative expressions is, accordingly, not based on their level of truth or false, but rather on their level of being considered as happy or unhappy (success or failure of their intended meaning). Performative is thus understood as the constitution of a meaning through an act or a certain practice. It accounts for situations where a proposition may constitute or instantiate the object to which it is meant to refer. Similarly, it is an utterance that performs an act or creates a state of affairs by the fact of its being uttered under appropriate or conventional circumstances. Performative word as speech act, therefore, concerns itself to proving various ways in which to say something is to do something. Similarly, it concerns itself with the ways in which people using language are doing things with words. J.L.Austin himself calls for the following precautions to be made:

> It is always necessary that the circumstances in which the words are uttered should be in some way, or ways, appropriate, and it is very commonly necessary that either the speaker himself

---

16   Austin, How To Do Things With Words, 12.
17   Austin , Philosophical Papers, 222.
18   Austin, Philosophical Papers, 222.
19   Austin , How To Do Things With Words, 6.

or other persons should also perform certain other actions, whether physical or mental actions or even acts of uttering further words.[20]

But J.L.Austin realizes that not all utterances can be performative. He observes that some utterances may seem not to be descriptive and not to be valued based on their being judged as true or false. But the very nature of such utterances does often imply that certain things are true and not false. He illustrates this further by giving marriage contract as an example. The "I do take this woman as my lawful wedded wife" presupposes that the speaker is not already married and not at the present living with any other lawfully married woman as his wife.[21] In order to avoid any confusion about which utterances are performative, J.L.Austin came up with a set of criteria regulating performative utterances.

1.4 Criteria for Performative Word

J.L.Austin proposed the following three criteria to regulate performative utterances:

1. There must exist an accepted conventional procedure having a certain conventional effect, that procedure to include the uttering of certain words by certain persons in certain circumstances, and further the particular persons and circumstances in a given case must be appropriate for the invocation of the particular procedure invoked.
2. The procedure must be executed by all participants both correctly and completely.
3. Where, as often, the procedure is designed for use by persons having certain thoughts or feelings, or for the inauguration of certain consequential conduct on the part of any participant, then a person participating in and so invoking the procedure must in fact have those thoughts or feelings, and the participants must intend so to conduct themselves, and further must actually so conduct themselves subsequently.[22]

To violate any of these above mentioned conditions is to make any performative word unhappy.[23] The extent by which our utterances can be made unhappy varies just as these conditions themselves do not have the same veracity. The first two rules are grouped together, and are in opposition to the third rule. A violation of the first rule and the second rule makes the performative act not to be achieved. This is in the understanding that either the formular is incorrect or the speaker is not in the position to perform the act. In this situation one says that the act is purported but void. Taking marriage as an example, contraction of a new marriage by someone who is already successfully married is not accepted because he is already married, therefore the new marriage is rendered void and not achieved. A violation of the first rule and the second rule is referred to as "Misfires". Under Misfires, the acts are purported but

---

20 Austin, How To Do Things With Words, 8.
21 Cf. Austin, Philosophical Papers, 224.
22 Austin, How To Do Things With Words, 14–15.
23 The various ways in which a performative utterance may be unsatisfactory we call, for the sake of a name, the infelicities: and an infelicity arises-that is to say, the utterance is unhappy-if certain rules, transparently simple rules, are broken; Cf. Austin, Philosophical Papers, 224.

have no effects, and that is why they are not achieved and can further be described as "attempted" or "went through" Although purported acts under Misfires are not achieved, they are bigamous and have their consequences and results. However, there are some distinctions between the first rule and the second rule. Violation of the first rule in particular is called "Misinvocations" and "Misapplications" Misinvocation either because there is no such procedures or that the procedure cannot be applied in the concrete situation-Misapplications. On the other hand, offences against the second rule are regarded as "Misexecutions", – the purported act is applied but marred with flaws or hitch in the way it was performed.

When the third rule is violated, the act still remains achieved although insincerely. A violation of the third rule is referred to as "Abuses." Under the third rule, acts are not "purported", they are instead "professed and not consummated or implemented". For example, a Youngman tells a lady: I love you-but in himself does not mean what he said. In this situation, the Youngman has in actuality professed his love for the lady, and nothing prevents him from making such a profession. That he does not mean it is something else. We shall now turn our attention to a more elaborate explanations of what we mean by "Misfires" and "Abuses".

1.4.1 The Doctrine of Misfires

Misfires refer to the infelicities arising from the first and the second rules which are such that the act for the performing of which, and in the performing of which, the verbal formular in question is designed or purported but not achieved. In discussing Misfires, certain terminologies are used to distinguish between cases pertaining to any of these rules. With regard to cases pertaining to the first rule, they may be called Misinvocations because there is no such existing procedure. In a situation, however, where the procedure does exist but only cannot be applied in a given situation, it is called Misapplications. On the other hand, cases pertaining to the second rule, in contrast to the cases pertaining to the first rule are called Misexecutions.

The first rule: "that the convention invoked must exist and be accepted"[24] insists that there must exist an accepted conventional procedure having a certain conventional effect which include the uttering of certain words by certain persons in certain circumstances. It is not enough that a word is uttered , there must be acceptance on the part of the person it is meant for. The key words in this formular are "exist" and "accepted". Here, the emphasis is more on "accepted," because it gives meaning to "exist", and makes the performative purposes be realized. So an existed utterance can become a "Misfire" when the procedure involved is not "accepted". This is "Misinvocation". In this case, no performative utterance takes place. For example, when a priest in a social gathering takes a glass of wine and says "This is my blood", and none of those in the audience believes him because they know that he (the priest) did not observe the conventional procedure. In this case, because there is no acceptance,

---

24 Austin, Philosophical Papers, 224.

the performative utterance is not realized. There are also situations where there exists the conventional procedure but cannot be properly applied in a given circumstance. Any attempt to apply the conventional procedure in the unfavourable circumstance would mean "Misapplication". In which case it is no longer accepted either generally or by anybody. By and large, the fact remains that "acceptance" plays the greatest role here as the key word.

The second rule: "that the circumstances in which we purport to invoke this procedure must be appropriate for its invocation"[25] insists that the particular persons and circumstances in a given case must be appropriate for the invocation of the particular procedure invoked. When this formular is not fulfilled, there is "Misexecution", and no performative utterance takes place. We take the case of someone who gives orders when he has no capacity to do so, or when the order he gives is not to be directed to the person he gives the order to. In discussing the second rule, we have to distinguish between "incapacities", with regard to where the performer or the object is the wrong type. It is a case of incapacities where a Bishop in confirming a Christian woman in faith names her Alexander instead of Alexandra. Whereas it becomes "wrong type", when a Bishop by confirmation anoints a dog in order to confirm the dog in faith. In both cases, the acts are wrongly executed, and so, no performative utterance takes place. Again the second rule insists that procedure must be executed correctly by all the parties involved. This refers most especially to the use of implicit formulars, the use of vague formulars and the use of uncertain references. Thus, precision is needed to avoid violating this formular. So, whatever is to be said must be said correctly.

1.4.2 The Doctrine of Abuses

Abuses refer to the violation of the third rule which are such that the act for the performing of which, and in the performing of which, the verbal formular in question is designed, is achieved. They are "insincerities" and "infractions" or "breaches" because the purported cases are insincerely achieved. The performance is not void, although it is still unhappy.

The third rule: "A good many of these verbal procedures are designed for use by people who hold certain beliefs or have certain feelings or intentions"[26] insists that where, as often, the procedure is designed for use by persons having certain thoughts, feelings, or intentions, or for the inauguration of certain consequential conduct on the part of any participant, then a person participating in and so invoking the procedure must in fact have those thoughts, feelings, or intentions, and the participants must intend so to conduct themselves. Dominant words in this formular are: Feelings, Thoughts and Intentions.

Taking "feeling" for example, we examine the case of someone who sings praises of his enemy. When the feelings he has for the enemy is quite opposite of the praises he

---

25 Austin, Philosophical Papers, 224.
26 Austin, Philosophical Papers, 224.

sings, in this circumstance, the act is performed although insincerely. Or in the words of J.L.Austin: "if I say 'I congratulate you' when I'm not pleased or when I don't believe that the credit was yours, then there is insincerity. Likewise if I say I promise to do something, without having the least intention of doing it or without believing it feasible. In these cases there is something wrong certainly, but it is not like a misfire. We should not say that I didn't in fact promise, but rather that I did promise but promised insincerely; I did congratulate you but the congratulations were hollow."[27] In considering "thought", we think of the suggestions someone gives to another person when he infact harbours an opposite idea in his mind. It is also a case of insincerity although the performed act is achieved. In describing what we mean by "intention", we have a look at those commitments we pronounce when we truly know that we do not intend to fulfil what we pronounce. Here, the utterance is performative even though we are insincere.

Sometimes, feelings, thoughts and intentions are so closely related that in every given case, one finds them interplaying. For example, in one singing praises of his enemy he does so as a mere lip service because he thinks the enemy does not merit sincere praises, and in doing so, he fulfils what he intends. So, feelings, thoughts and intentions interplay. The third rule insists further that the participants must so conduct themselves subsequently. This subsequent conduct of participants are very essential to determine when the third rule is violated. By and large, Abuses happen in those circumstances that we describe as insincere but retaining the purported acts as not void. J.L.Austin's effort to assign certain verbs to performative utterances leads him to the discussions on the two important forms of performative word: explicit performative word and implicit performative word.

1.5 Forms of performative word

Explicit performative word and implicit performative word are the two forms of performative word. Let us examine the meaning of these terms.

1.5.1 Explicit Performative Word

J.L.Austin introduces explicit performative utterance by saying:

> Language as such and in its primitive stages is not precise, and it is also not, in our sense, explicit: precision in language makes it clearer what is being said-its meaning: explicitness, in our sense, makes clearer the force of the utterances, or how it is to be taken.[28]

Explicit performative word clarifies the force of the utterances and makes explicit what action it is that is being performed in issuing the utterance.[29] This means that

---

27 Austin, Philosophical Papers, 226.
28 Austin, How To Do Things With Words, 73.
29 Cf. Austin, How To Do Things With Words, 69; see also Austin, Philosophical Papers, 232.

making an utterance explicit is not the same as describing or stating what one is doing.[30] Explicit performative utterance, however, is a successful speech device which has always been used with greater success to arrive at performative action. It follows the formular: Subject + Active + Present. Reducing performatives only to this formular is also not appropriate. As a compliment, J.L.Austin emphasizes that explicit performative utterance also is a commendable invention that clearly distinguishes the different forces in any performative utterances.[31] We now consider this statement : "I shall come". This statement alone lacks qualification. It needs to be interpreted in order to be clear on how it is to be understood. To obtain this clarity one may ask – what type of statement is that? For example, is it a promise? If it is a promise, a clearer statement is needed to prove that the statement is a promise. So, the same statement may read: "I promise that I shall come". This is what we mean by explicit performative word, because the action is clearly exposed as a promise.

Most of the times, explicit performative utterances make use of "That-clause". J.L.Austin cautions that this should not be confused with the "That-clause" associated with indirect speech. In other words, being explicit is not the same as indirect speech. Indirect speech is understood as a reported speech about what an individual or a group of persons have said: "I said that ..." is another use of "that" as an indirect or reported speech quite different from explicit formular.[32] Austin cautions that it is not always the case that "That-clause" must follow performative verbs. There are some other situations where performative verbs are followed by "To-clause" – "I promise to buy you a car" or simply "I promise" without any clause.[33] In the history of the evolution of language, one discovers that explicit form is a late comer in comparison with implicit form, and as J.L.Austin himself would say it, "historically, from the point of view of the evolution of language, the explicit performative must be a later development than certain more primary utterances, many of which at least are already implicit performatives, which are included in most or many explicit perform-

---

30   Cf. Austin, How To Do Things With Words, 69.
31   Cf. Austin, How To Do Things With Words, 72.
32   "When we say 'I promise that [...]', the case is very different from when we say 'He promises that [...]', or in the past tense 'I promised that [...]' For when we say 'I promise that [...]' we do perform an act of promising-we give a promise. What we do not do is to report on somebody's performing an act of promising-in particular, we do not report on somebody's use of the expression 'I promise.' We actually do use it and do the promising. But if I say 'He promises', or in the past tense 'I promised ' I precisely do report on an act of promising, that is to say an act of using this formular 'I promise'-I report on a present act of promising by him, or on a past act of my own. There is thus a clear difference between our first person singular present indicative active, and other persons and tenses. This is brought out by the typical incident of little Willie whose uncle says he 'll give him half-a-crown if he promises never to smoke till he's 55. Little Willie's anxious parent will say , of course he promises, don't you, Willie? Giving him a nudge, and little Willie just doesn't vouchsafe. The point here is that he must do the promising himself by saying , I promise', and his parent is going too fast in saying he promises" (Austin , Philosophical Papers, 229).
33   Cf. Austin , Philosophical Papers, 71.

atives as parts of a whole".[34] This means, for example, "I shall come" is older than the later addition – "I promise that I shall come".

Caution must also be given that explicit utterances are not descriptive. We will always remember that performatives are differentiated from the constatives by the fact that the former refer to the cases which are happy or unhappy, and the later the cases which are true or false. Descriptive utterances are constantives, and therefore, should not be confused with explicit performatives. Taking a step further, J.L.Austin identifies certain verbs that are associated with explicit performatives, and these verbs "make explicit what precise act it is that we are performing when we issue our utterance".[35] He classifies them into behabitives, expositives, verdictives, commissives and Exercitives.

Behabitives refer to performatives that are related to human behaviour in terms of responses towards others. They include "the notion of reaction to other people's behaviour and fortunes and of attitudes and expressions of attitudes to someone else's past conduct or imminent conduct".[36] Feelings play a great role here. Examples of such verbs are:

I approve that
I apologize that
I criticize that
I censure that

Expositives are often referred to as expositional performatives. Expositives, as it were, "are used in acts of exposition involving the expounding of views, the conducting of arguments, and the clarifying of usages and of references".[37] This explicit performative verb determines how the statement is to be fitted into the context of conversation, interlocution or dialogue. Examples of such verbs are:

I testify that
I admit that
I argue that
I conclude that
I prophesy that
I predict that

Verdictives refer to judgements that are uttered in a given situation. It is "a judicial act as distinct from legislative or executive acts."[38] Examples of verdictive verbs are:

I declare that
I date it that
I pronounce that

---

34 Austin, Philosophical Papers, 71.
35 Austin, Philosophical Papers, 232.
36 Austin, How To Do Things With Words, 153.
37 Austin, How To Do Things With Words, 161.
38 Austin, How To Do Things With Words, 153.

I rule that
I hold that
I make it that

Commisives are a binding force to what is being uttered. In other words, their aim is "to commit the speaker to a certain course of action".[39] For example:

I undertake to
I dedicate myself to
I guarantee to
I commit to

Exercitives are associated with decisions as opposed to judgement, but "arbitrators and judges make use of exercitives as well as issuing verdictives".[40] Examples include:

I appoint
I choose
I dismiss
I decide

In uttering an explicit statement whether behabitives, expositives, verdictives, commisives or exercitives the performative speech is clearly defined. However, J.L.Austin admits that the introduction of the explicit performative verbs does not remove all our troubles associated with performative utterances.[41]

1.5.2 Implicit Performative Word

Implicit performative word is sometimes referred to as primary utterance.[42] According to J.L.Austin, in the implicit performatives the explicites are in "contrast with merely implicit performatives".[43] He goes further to say: "Primitive or primary form of utterance will preserve the ambiguity or equivocation or vagueness of primitive language in this respect; they will not make explicit the precise force of the utterance".[44] The performative utterances are considered implicit when they are unclear and the meaning they convey are doubted. In such a situation, there arises such questions as: What does the speaker mean by that? What type of utterance is that? In a statement : "I shall fight him", the person addressed still waits to know if the utterance is, for example, a promise or a threat. Admittedly, implicit utterances are the oldest form of performatives that existed. It is in giving answer to such above questions created by implicit performatives that explicit performatives were invented.

---

39   Austin, How To Do Things With Words, 157.
40   Austin, How To Do Things With Words, 155.
41   Cf. Austin, How To Do Things With Words, 77.
42   Cf. Austin, How To Do Things With Words, 69.
43   Austin, How To Do Things With Words, 32.
44   Austin, How To Do Things With Words, 72.

We cannot successfully study J.L.Austin's performative word in isolation from his speech act theory because it was in trying to find a set of explicit performative verbs that he realized the need to go back to the very fundamentals, viz: the speech acts in which to say something (locution) or in saying something (illocution) or by saying something (perlocution) an action is achieved.[45] What I intend to do now is to investigate into his speech act theory to see how his treatise on performative word eventually traces back to his earlier discussions on speech act theory.

1.6 Performative word versus speech act theory

J.L.Austin's speech act theory is a teaching quite different from his discourse on performative word. Despite their different interests, it is later to be discovered by J.L.Austin himself that his treatise on performative word cannot but be related in some way to his earlier teaching about his speech act theory. This relationship between J.L.Austin's performative word and his speech act theory can be better understood in terms of two different theories that have special link despite their varied teachings. J.L.Austin's speech act theory is older than his theory about performative word. Although in his speech act theory the three acts of speech: locution,illocution and perlocution, were not concerned with the performance of speech, J.L.Austin's later teaching on performative word in which he concentrated on performance of speech, and his classification of performative utterances into three senses led him to acknowledge that in his speech act theory the classification of the speech-act into three basic groups had already given a favourable condition to which the three senses of performative word correspond. Furthermore, J.L.Austin discovered that while discussing performative word, not every verb can be performative. So, the need to outline the list of performative verbs made him to realize that his earlier teaching about speech act theory has an influence on his teaching on performative word, and in which case the verbs associated with speech act theory cannot be said to be different from the verbs associated with performative word. For instance, in performing a locutionary act, we are at the same time performing such acts as asking or answering a question, giving some information or an assurance or a warning, announcing a verdict or an intention, pronouncing sentence, making an appointment or an appeal or a criticism, making an identification or giving a description, and the numerous like.[46] Performative word is interpreted to mean action, and whenever we utter any word we are performing an act of speech which can be locutionary or illocutionary. Our utterance, according to J.L.Austin, may lead to perlocutionary act because "statements do take effect".[47] In this way, we continue to notice the relationship between speech act theory and performative word.

---

45   Cf. Austin, How To Do Things With Words, 94.
46   Cf. Austin, How To Do Things With Words, 98–99.
47   Austin, How To Do Things With Words, 139.

Although speech act theory is not directly concerned with studying how speech performs, there are traces of its interest about performative nature of language with regard to how language is operative, and the effect it has when it occurs in face-to-face personal conversation or in any communicative action. Our discussions on performative word, on the other hand, is considered from the ground up on how many senses there are in which to say something is to do something, or in saying something we do something, and even by saying something we do something,[48] which correspond to the three senses in which we discuss J.L.Austin's speech act theory, viz: locutionary act, illocutionary act and perlocutionary act. Since the J.L.Austin's performative word cannot be discussed in isolation from his speech act theory, let us now further discuss and understand more what he means by speech act theory.

1.6.1 Aspects of speech act theory

J.L.Austin's speech act theory is a teaching that in general every speech act is an act of communication, and that communication is an expression of a certain attitude whereby the type of speech act performed corresponds to the type of attitude being expressed. For example, apology expresses regret, command expresses authority, and so on. In his speech act theory, J.L.Austin categorizes the uses of language into three senses: locutionary act, illocutionary act and perlocutionary act.

1.6.1.1 Locutionary Act

Locutionary act is a speech act of saying something (locution) with a certain meaning. In locutionary act, we have utterance acts and propositional acts. Utterance acts are where something is said or a sound is made, and which may not have any meaning. Propositional acts are where a particular reference is made. J.L.Austin himself recognizes three types of locutionary act: phonetic act, phatic act and rhetic act. He explains each of these terms in the following way:

> The phonetic act is merely the act of uttering certain noises. The phatic act is the uttering of certain vocables or words, i.e. noises of certain types, belonging to and as belonging to, a certain vocabulary, conforming to and as conforming to a certain grammar. The rhetic act is the performance of an act of using those vocables with a certain more-or-less definite sense and reference.[49]

These three aspects of locutionary act inter-relate in most cases because in performing one we perform the other. Thus, when we perform locutionary act we make use of speech, but in what way? For it matters whether we use them as command or as promise or as advice, and so on. J.L.Austin, therefore, accuses philosophers of confusing locutionary act with descriptives. While descriptives describe some state of

---
48 Cf. Austin, How To Do Things With Words, 94.
49 Austin, How To Do Things With Words, 95.

affairs or state some facts which must either be true or false and hereby not recognizing the fact that certain sentences can be questions or exclamations and that they oftentimes express commands or wishes or concessions,[50] locutionary act performs such an act as: asking or answering a question, giving some information or an assurance or a warning, announcing a verdict or an intention, pronouncing sentence, making an appointment or an appeal or a criticism.[51] J.L.Austin goes on to say:

> It may be said that for too long philosophers have neglected this study, treating all problems as problems of locutionary usage, and indeed that the descriptive fallacy mentioned in Lecture 1 commonly arises through mistaking a problem of the former kind for a problem of the later kind.[52]

The study of locutionary act is the same as the study of locutions or utterances or full units of speech.[53] Performing a locutionary act, therefore, refers to things we perform in the act of saying something, which is roughly equivalent to uttering a certain sentence with a certain sense and reference, which again is roughly equivalent to "meaning" in the traditional sense.

1.6.1.2 Illocutionary Act

It would be said that locutionary act gives birth to illocutionary act. Illocutionary act can be defined as performance of an act in saying something.[54] An interesting type of illocutionary speech act is that performed in the utterance of performatives. For example:

I promise to pay back
I urge you to marry her
I order you to leave
I nominate you to be president

In these typical, rather explicit cases of performative sentences, the action that the sentence describes (promise, urge, order, nominate) is performed by the utterance of the sentence itself. Illocutionary acts are utterances which have a certain conventional force "an act done as conforming to a convention".[55] Explaining further J.L.Austin writes:

> Speaking of the use of language for arguing or warning looks just like speaking of the use of language for persuading, rousing, alarming; yet the former may, for rough contrast, be said to be conventional, in the sense that at least it could be made explicit by the performative formular; but the later could not. Thus we can say 'I argue that' or 'I warn you that' but we cannot say 'I convince you that' or 'I alarm you that.'[56]

---

50   Cf. Austin, How To Do Things With Words, 1.
51   Cf. Austin, How To Do Things With Words, 98–99.
52   Austin, How To Do Things With Words, 100.
53   Cf. Austin, How To Do Things With Words, 94.
54   Cf. Austin, How To Do Things With Words, 98.
55   Austin, How To Do Things With Words, 105.
56   Austin, How To Do Things With Words, 103–104.

Illocutionary act is happily and successfully performed only when a certain effect is achieved. This is not to reduce illocutionary act only to the achievement of a certain effect. For example, I cannot say to have ordered an individual unless he hears what I say and accepts it by carrying out the order. So, effect gives meaning to illocutionary act, and completes it. The effect to illocutionary act can be judged as a response to the utterance or sequel. For example, an order provokes obedience; promise demands fulfilment. On the other hand, "I got him to obey", has the implication that other extra means were involved to produce a consequence. This may amount to duress. Waving stick at someone is understood as a sign of warning in illocutionary act. But strictly speaking there cannot be illocutionary act unless the means employed are conventional. Many illocutionary acts cannot be performed except by saying something. Therefore, illocutionary acts favour: assertives, commissives, expressives, directives and declaratives, rather than exercitives and commissives.[57] In summary then, illocutionary act is a speech act whereby in saying something, an effect is realized. There are various kinds of possible insufficiencies of illocutionary acts but not all of these insufficiencies are sufficient to vitiate the act in its entirety. In some cases, a condition may indeed be intrinsic to the notion of the act in question and not satisfied in a given case, and yet the act will have been performed nonetheless. J.L.Austin calls such insufficiencies infelicity.

1.6.1.3 Perlocutionary Act

Perlocutionary act is a speech act that has an effect on the feelings, thoughts or actions of either the speaker, or the listener. It is understood as the consequence of

---

57 The primitive assertive in English is "assert", which names the force of assertion. It is sometimes used in the stronger sense of positively asserting as opposed to denying, in which case it is a strong assertive relative to its primitive use. Our list of assertives contains: assert, reassert, negate, deny, correct, claim, affairm, state, disclaim, tell, suggest, prophesy, vaticinate, report, retrotict, warn, forewarn, advise, alert, alarm, remind, describe, inform, reveal, divulge, divulgate, notify, insinuate, sustain, object, recognize, criticise, praise, blame, accuse, reprimand, denounce, boast, complain, lament. Our list of commissives contains: commit, pledge, undertake, engage, promise, hypothecate, guarantee, threaten, vow, avow, swear, assure, certify, accept, agree, consent, acquiesce, abide, reject, refuse, renounce, offer, counter-offer, bid, rebid, tender, dedicate, bet, wager, contract, covenant, subscribe. Expressives name forces whose point is to express mental states of the speaker such as joy, approbation or discontent which are important in our social forms of life. Our list of expressives are: approve, compliment, praise, land, extol, plaudit, applaud, acclaim, brag, boast, complain, disapprove, blame, reprove, deplore, protest, grieve, mourn, lament, rejoice, cheer, boo, condole, congratulate, thank, apologize. Directives are generally used in the passive form. Our list of directives include: direct, request, ask, question, inquire, interrogate, urge, encourage, discourage, invite, petition, convoke, convene, tell, instruct, demand, require, claim, order, propose, permit, recommend, allow, authorize, intercede. Most declarative verbs name declaration that require a position of authority of the speaker in an extra–linguistic institution. Declarative verbs are: declare, renounce, disclaim, veto, adjourn, decree, condemn, sentence, abolish, revoke, baptize, excommunicate.

the utterance. In other words, it seeks to change minds. Examples of perlocutionary act include:

He inspired me to write
He persuaded me to marry her
He deterred me from smoking

Thus perlocutionary act is understood as what we bring about or achieve by saying something, such as, inspiring, persuading, deterring.[58] Perlocutionary act may be achieved by either perlocutionary object (inspire, persuade, deterred) or by the production of a perlocutionary sequel. For example, the act of warning may achieve its perlocutionary object of alerting and also have the perlocutionary sequel of alarming. This means, what is the perlocutionary object of one illocution may be the sequel of another.

1.6.2 Comparative analysis of speech act theory

Locutionary act, illocutionary act and perlocutionary act are in certain areas related to the concept of performative word, and as well not related in some other areas. Let us in summary discuss these similarities and dissimilarities.

1.6.2.1 Similarities in the speech acts

The three senses under which J.L.Austin categorizes human language in his discussions on speech act theory/performative word: locutionary act (act of saying something), illocutionary act (act in which we say something) and perlocutionary act (act by which we say something) have certain similarities associated with them. First and foremost: locutionary act, illocutionary act and perlocutionary act, just like performative word, are defined with a common concept "senses or dimensions of the use of a sentence or of the use of language".[59] Secondly, the speech acts and performative word are oriented towards actions, and J.L.Austin simply identifies from each of them "three kinds of actions".[60] Thirdly, they share the same problems associated with actions. J.L.Austin again identifies the problems as "subject to the usual troubles and reservations about attempt as distinct from achievement, being intentional as distinct from being unintentional, and the like".[61] Fourthly, these three aspects of speech act, just like in performative word, compliment each other. So in performing one, we are performing the other. Illocutionary act presupposes locutionary act, and according

---

58 Cf. Austin, How To Do Things With Words, 109.
59 Austin, How To Do Things With Words, 109.
60 Austin, How To Do Things With Words, 110.
61 Austin, How To Do Things With Words, 110.

to J.L.Austin "to congratulate is necessarily to say certain words".[62] He cautions that this does not mean that illocutionary act is the consequence of locutionary act. Again, talking about illocutionary act and perlocutionary act, J.L.Austin writes: "I cannot be said to have warned an audience unless it hears what I say and takes what I say in a certain sense".[63] So, it is necessary that a certain effect must be achieved in the audience in order to show that illocutionary act had taken place. Since illocutionary act and perlocutionary act have special relationship, we shall still have time in this chapter to focus on the two of them specially.

1.6.2.2 Dissimilarities in the speech acts

The most distinguishing dissimilarity among these three aspects of the speech act in correspondence with performative word lies in their mode of operation "modus operandi". It is true that each of them is action-oriented but locutionary act achieves this, for example, through "act of saying something", and illocutionary act does the same "in saying something", while perlocutionary act performs "by saying something". J.L.Austin writes:

> We distinguished the locutionary act (and within it the phonetic, the phatic, and the rhetic acts) which has a meaning; the illocutionary act which has a certain force in saying something; the perlocutionary act which is the achieving of certain effects by saying something.[64]

It follows that the variation in these names of the speech acts is also a basic difference. This means, locutionary act cannot be identified as illocutionary act, and neither can illocutionary act be identified as perlocutionary act, and so on. Since illocutionary act and perlocutionary act present more difficult distinctions, it will be necessary, at this juncture, to discuss briefly on their distinctions.

1.6.2.3 Illocutionary act versus Perlocutionary act

As J.L.Austin himself would acknowledge "it is the distinction between illocutions and perlocutions which seems likeliest to give trouble".[65] We begin to distinguish by emphasizing that illocutionary act is conventional whereas perlocutionary act is not conventional.[66] Conventional act, as it were, is "an act done as conforming to a convention".[67] So, illocutionary act is conventional because it could, at least, be made explicit by the performative formular but perlocutionary act could not.[68] For example, the illocutionary verb "decree" has the explicit performative formular "I

---

62   Austin, How To Do Things With Words, 114.
63   Austin, How To Do Things With Words, 116.
64   Austin, How To Do Things With Words, 121.
65   Austin, How To Do Things With Words, 110.
66   Cf. Austin, How To Do Things With Words, 110.
67   Austin, How To Do Things With Words, 105.
68   Cf. Austin, How To Do Things With Words, 103.

decree that..." and cannot be applied to the perlocutionary verb "convince". It is then wrong to say "I convince that... ."
Illocutionary act referred to as "in" formular "is often used to account for my doing something".[69] When we make the utterance: "in writing a book I became an author". In accounting for my being an author I state the effect. This can as well be contrasted by saying: In accounting for my writing a book I state the purpose. Perlocutionary act, the "by" formular, on the other hand indicates the means or manner or method of an action as well as indicates the criterion that defines an action: By drinking ten bottles of beer I was drunk (indicates means or manner or method of my action); By attending Sunday masses I was trying to be a good Christian (indicates a criterion). Verbs that are associated with illocutionary act "seem to be pretty close to explicit performative verbs".[70] Warning, advising, pronouncing, for instance, are illocutionary acts, and are adopted by the explicit performatives: "I warn that... or I pronounce that...", and so on. The perlocutionary verbs cannot be adopted by the explicit performative formular.

1.7 References

By careful study of J.L.Austin's performative word, it becomes obvious that this concept refers to many fields of human endeavours. For examples, there are evidences of performative word in the use of symbols, in identifications, in theater and even in magic. I hereby make brief explanations of what I mean.

1.7.1 Performative symbols.

Symbols are as well performative, and in this case, I would rather prefer to use linguistic symbolism to demonstrate how J.L.Austin's performative word can also be derived from symbols. As bedrock of human language, symbols should not stand in isolation but dependent on the conventional interpretations they receive. There are direct symbols that have to do with material images. We have also indirect symbols that concern themselves with material objects. But then, linguistic symbolism is verbal and is the third form of symbolism according to this ranking. It is the most difficult form of symbolism to comprehend because it is sophisticated and to understand it requires deep reflections and adequate knowledge of the world-view of the speaker or the speakers. J.L.Austin presents the two linguistic symbols "Hurrah" and "Damn" to show how linguistic symbols can be performative. By "Hurrah, the speaker is performing the act of cheering".[71] Likewise, by "Damn", "the speaker is performing the

---

69 Austin, How To Do Things With Words, 127.
70 Austin, How To Do Things With Words, 137.
71 Austin , Philosophical Papers, 233.

act of swearing".[72] There are some other situations where linguistic symbols are performative. For example, by "Hi" the speaker performs the act of greetings, and so on.

1.7.2 Performative Identities

Performative identities explain how words define who we are, thereby making us what we are. Take for instance that I am named "Alexander". It is then the case that the uttering of this name by anyone performs in me. What do I mean by this? Assuming that I am in a given situation where there are many other people or walking along a street and someone from a near distance shouts the name "Alexander", it follows that I automatically react by answering or looking at the direction from where this name is mentioned without knowing yet whether it is my own "Alexander" or not. In this way, my identity as "Alexander" performs in me whenever it is uttered. J.L.Austin explains this point by giving an example with a ship named Queen Elizabeth in which he says "I name this ship the Queen Elizabeth has the effect of naming or christening the ship".[73] Performative identity, therefore, must be a group action in which, for instance, I must have Alexander as my name, and then, someone else must call this name to my hearing. Both the bearer and the caller combine to make performative identity a team work. The actions of both the bearer and the caller are necessary to avoid pretences and false identities. So, in performative identities, the actions of both parties compliment each other.

1.7.3 Performative Magic

The practice of magic is upheld by anthropologists and sociologists as performative. By uttering certain words, something assumes a particular fake reality. Some anthropologists go further to assume that performative magic is the origin of language. Thus, language is born out of performative necessity. We must understand it that this presumption, however, is a mere speculation. The origin of language is not formally traced to performative magic. In performative magic also, both the actor and the audience have important role to play. The actor by uttering certain words transforms a thing into a particular seeming reality. For the utterance to have performed, the audience must confirm the quasi reality, that is when a performative magic has taken place. Let us portray this point clearer by a magician who picks up some pieces of stone and covers them in a particular container. He tells the audience that after uttering some words the pieces of stone turn into packs of sweet. If at the end the actor successfully makes those pieces of stone to become packs of sweet through his utterances and the audience confirms this reality, performative magic has taken place.

---

72   Austin, Philosophical Papers, 233.
73   Austin , How To Do Things With Words, 117.

J.L.Austin, however, refers to such performance as marred with pretences, and concludes that "it is a not unimportant point that it is usually obvious when someone is pretending".[74] Words used in performing magic may be strange to the audience. What is important in this circumstance is not whether the people understand the words, but whether the words perform.

1.7.4 Performative Theater

Performative thinkers have argued in favour of languages used in theater as performative. This is at the background that although theater has a lot to do with imaginations, words themselves do have power over imaginations. Imaginary existence itself is made real in a drama by the use of words which are performative in character. Performative words, therefore, helps to shape the way we imagine situations, bringing these situations into being. This means that the actions of performative words are not limited to normal situations only, but perform even when they are acted. In a drama, for instance, that the chief actor says to the subordinate "I command you to sit down", and the subordinate sits down cannot be differentiated from the same command in a normal situation even though the former is only acted. Performative words do not only help actors to represent already pre-existing reality, they also help to create a reality that has not existed before. This is what we call dramatic improvisation, and it is performative.

A further inquiry into how words operate in drama explores the question of how words moves, and how movement talks. Take the case of an actor shouting "danger! danger!! danger!!!". Of course, the people to whom those words are being addressed will take necessary precaution and that is performative. It is performative because when we ask of what does the speaker mean by his utterance we may say that he is warning somebody or some people. So, we may arrange the utterance under the explicit performative formular: "I warn that there is danger…". Play writers, therefore, are primarily interested in creating utterances that will move both the actors and the audience into performing. That means, play writers are interested in the people. The actors speak in order to create realities for the audience. The spontaneous reaction of the audience by either clapping, ovation, cheers are all signs of these realizations, and a proof of the fact that the words from the actor has performed in the audience.

The power of theater helps to elucidate how words do perform in the audience: to understand how things work in the social world; and how they could be changed by the power of the word. We must, however, acknowledge the basic problem that is encountered in an effort to make words perform in theater. This problem is identified as the problem of the language and the form of communication. In some situations, there are lack of appropriate words in a given language to realize the action the actor has set out to achieve. This is blamed on the fact that while words are finite, the things they perform on are infinite. Another serious challenge in the performative theater

---

74 Austin, Philosophical Papers., 201.

is that the dramatist should know that sometimes, he must act the role of a translator while the audience plays the part of an interpreter. What do I mean by this? When, for example, a dramatist is presenting what happened at the time of the initial encounter between native Africans and the whites, the dramatist is dealing with chiefs and commanders of the colonial era, the time when the local people could not speak English, yet these characters are presented speaking in the English language. So, the actor is translating into a language in which the original African native did not speak, and the audience is to interprete by imagining that the characters in the play are speaking their original language. Performatives can then be properly active in theater when these two great roles are successfully played.

1.8 Conclusion

Our attention in this chapter is centered on J.L.Austin's concept of performative word. In order to grapple with the analysis of performative word, it becomes necessary to begin by tracing the history of the concept of performative word. Indeed, it was the lecture delivered by J.L.Austin in 1955 titled "The William James Lecture" at the Harvard University that marked the official historical beginning of the inquiry into the concept of performative word. I used the phrase "official historical beginning" because the views that underlie these lectures were already conceived as far back as 1939 in his articles on "Other Minds", and on "Words and Deeds" of 1952–1954.

How does this chapter define the concept-performative word? Etymologically the concept performative word is derived from the verb "perform" and is associated with action now. J.L.Austin, therefore, defines performative word as an utterance whereby to say something is to do something; or in saying something we are doing something; or by saying something we are doing something. J.L.Austin teaches that language has performative function. In this way, he was concerned with revolutionizing the way philosophy had used language only for description, and cautions that the validity of an utterance is not judged based on whether it is true or false but on whether it is happy or unhappy.

In order to properly arrange his teachings on performative word so as to avoid any confusion about which utterances are performative, J.L.Austin came up with a set of criteria regulating performative utterances, namely: that there must be a conventional procedure; that the procedure must be executed by all participants both correctly and completely; that the same emotion regulating the feelings and thoughts of the audience must guide the speaker. Violation of the above criteria would make any performative utterance unhappy. Violation of the first criterion are called "misinvocation" and "misapplications". Misinvocation either because there is no such procedures or misapplications because the procedures cannot be applied in the concrete situation. Violation of the second criterion is called "Misexecutions" in which the purported act is applied but marred with flaws in the way it is performed. Violation of both the first and the second criteria is referred to as "Misfires" in which the acts are purported but have no effects. A violation of the third criterion is referred to as "Abuse". When the third criterion is violated the act still remains achieved despite the falsification of feelings, thoughts and intentions. J.L.Austin discovered that there might exist the problem of which verb to be considered performative. This led him to discussing the two forms of performative word: explicit and implicit forms. Explicit performative word clarifies the force of the utterance and defines the action that is being performed. Verbs associated with explicit perfomative word are classified into behabitives, I apologise that ...; expositives, I admit that ...; verdictives, I pronounce that ...; commisives, I understand that ...; exercitives, I appoint that ... . Implicit performative word does not clarify the force of the utterance and makes the utterance unclear, and therefore, doubtful. In implicit performative word, one needs to ask: what type of utterance is that? What does the speaker mean by this utterance? In implicit performatives, these questions are necessary in order to clear any doubt.

We cannot successfully study J.L.Austin's concept of performative word without going back to his treatise on speech act theory because J.L.Austin himself came to acknowledge that the concept of performative word could not be isolated from his speech act theory. J.L.Austin had earlier in his speech act theory proposed three acts of speech to be: locution, illocution and perlocution. The three senses in his concept of performative word could not but be associated to the three acts of speech to mean: saying something (locution); in saying something (illocution); by saying something (perlocution). By careful study of J.L.Austin's concept of performative word, it becomes obvious that this concept refers to other fields of endeavour, namely: there are evidences of the concept of performative word in identities, symbols, theater, and even in magic. In performative identities performative word explains how word defines who we are. Linguistic symbolism is performative within the context of convention. Performative theater helps actors both to represent already pre-existing reality and to create a reality that has not existed before. Incantations employed in performing magic are performative since through such words an effect is produced.

We have up to now been presented with the analysis of the J.L.Austin's concept of performative word. Our immediate task is to consider whether the J.L.Austin's treatise on performative word is of any interest to sacramental theology, and if yes, how? This question and subsequent clarifications will be the focus of our next chapter which is chapter two.

2 Performative word and sacramental theology

2.1 Introduction

In the first chapter we have established the concept of J.L.Austin's performative word in which we were able to shed light on how word should be considered in the three senses of saying something is doing something or in saying something is doing something or by saying something is doing something, and no longer the pre-existed notion of the use of word for descriptive purposes in which the value of word was judged based on its veracity as true or false. In this chapter we are setting out to establish how the J.L.Austin's performative word is of interest to sacramental theology. In order to do this properly we shall begin by discussing the concept of performative word in sacramental theology. This will be followed by forms of performative word in sacramental theology; aspects of performative word in sacramental theology; performative word as the hermeneutic of the sacraments with special emphasis on the sacraments of the eucharist and penance; performative word and the scriptures; performative word and the church's doctrine especially the doctrines of incarnation and inspiration. Most importantly, we are to study how the contributions of certain theologians of various christian faith aided our subject matter. Let us now examine in details each of these proposals that are just listed.

2.2 The Concept of performative word in Sacramental theology

Discussion on the concept of performative word in sacramental theology emphasizes the role the word plays in the sacramental rites; it is the action of the word that constitutes the sacrament, and the sacrament provides the occasion for the word to act. Anyanwu C.C.U, therefore, was right by saying that "in the world of the Christian liturgy, the intrinsic connection of word to rite stands out significantly. The working together of word and rite in a community ritual context inaugurates already a celebration".[75] In what may seem as an acceptance of J.L.Austin's treatise on performative word, the church's magisterium never relents in teaching that the sacramental words are efficacious. Its efficacy implies that it is not to be regarded as an ordinary word but as a proclamation of God's revelation to us which has a transforming effect

---

75 Anyanwu, Cyprain Chima Uzoma, The rites of initiation in christian liturgy and in Igbo traditional society: towards the inculturation of Christian liturgy in Igboland, Frankfurt am Main 2004, 299.

in what is being celebrated and in the individual hearts and minds of the participants. The language that arises as a result of the celebration of the sacramental rite is what I prefer to call performative word or language. It is performative word because it concerns itself in establishing a situation in which to say something is to do something or in saying something we do something or by saying something we do something. It affirms a situation in which people in using language or by using language are doing things with words, and thereby manifesting the relationship between word and action. We cannot comprehend the meaning of sacrament without localizing it in the context of a language in order that its practice and celebration be properly manifested.

Celebration of sacrament is a ritual process, and therefore, demands a ritual language. In order words, performative word can be ritual word in Sacramental theology. This means, in Sacramental theology, performative word is sacred. This word is not to be compared with other words that are mundane, but because it is sacred, it is divine, and as it were: "the Holy Spirit, through whom the living voice of the Gospel rings out in the church- and through her in the world- leads believers to the full truth, and makes the Word of Christ dwell in them in all its richness".[76] So, ritual language informs us of what happens in the sacramental celebrations. In other words, one can fully and deeply understand the sacrament that is being celebrated when one is able to articulate the language that is employed. In sacramental theology, performative word is an action language. It is a symbolic action that establishes interaction between God and man, as well as the consequences of such relationship. The action is symbolic because the ritual language is expressed in the action that accompanies it. The meaning of the investiture of a newly baptized infant in a white garment, for instance, is imbedded in the ritual language that is proper to this very action:

> N., you have become a new creation, and have clothed yourself in Christ. See in this white garment the outward sign of your christian dignity. With your family and friends to help you by word and example, bring that dignity unstained into the everlasting life of heaven.[77]

Sacramental theology, therefore, does not consider performative word as an abstract language. On the contrary, it is a concrete language, and it is characterized by action expressed in symbolic mode. As an action language, its words are performative and arouses faith in the hearers, and motivate them to live in accordance to what they have heard for the sole purpose of sanctification and salvation. Performative word functions as a determining factor both for what is being celebrated and for the adherents. The words of the epiclesis (invocation of the Holy Spirit at the Liturgy of the Eucharist), for instance, inform one that the minister is at the point of the consecration of Host and Wine. The words of the exchange of consent at the celebration of the Holy Matrimony bind the couple into husband and wife. In these ways, the performative word is specific in determining the meaning of what is being celebrated, and determines too the status of the participant as catechumen, baptized, confirmed, married,

---

76 D V, no. 8.
77 The Pocket Ritual. Rituale Parvum, Collected and edited by The National Liturgical Center, Bangalore 1988, 13.

ordained minister, and so on. Sometimes it would appear as if performative word, in Sacramental theology, is programmed. This is in the sense that ritual languages are traditional – oriented. Instead of being more modern in the choice of the sacramental words, ritual languages are limited to the original words of the institutions. This exposes ritual languages to the dangers of being misinterpreted as routine, formalism and legalism. If one understands ritual language as being programmed, it is because it acts in accordance to the will of the founder, Jesus Christ. This is why the sacramental action is a re-enactment.

The sacred character of the performative word empowers it to effect actions as it is being uttered in liturgical celebrations. In the celebration of the Holy Matrimony, the man and the woman exchange their consent with the following words: "I, N., take you, N., to be my wife (husband). I promise to be true to you in good times and in bad, in sickness and in health. I will love you and honour you all the days of my life".[78] When this exchange of consent is performed within the context of the sacramental celebration of marriage, it becomes binding. It is no longer common, and no longer an ordinary language that could have been uttered in a Beer parlour that has no binding force. Thus, what we utter in sacramental celebrations becomes an utterance of faith in action. We are no longer left with any doubt that in Sacramental theology, performative word or if you may choose to call it, ritual word, is action language or word. What nature or form does performative word assume in sacramental theology?

2.3 The form of performative word in sacramental theology

There are two forms of performative word: Explicit and Implicit forms of performative word. I would insist on Explicit form of performative word as the only form of performative word that is associated with Sacramental theology.

2.3.1 Explicit Performative word

Explicit performative word does not put anyone in doubt about the clarity of the utterance. It does not lack qualification, rather it is definite about what it implies. One does not need to ask „what type of statement is that?" The statement is self explanatory.[79] The statement "I presume that he is a good man" has already interpreted itself that it is a presumption. Explicit performatives can be behabitives when they refer to human relationships with one another: "I vow that ...". Explicit performatives can also be expositives because they are not clumsy: "I agree that ...". Again, Explicit performatives can be verdictives because they pass judgements: "I pronounce that

---

78 The Pocket Ritual. Rituale Parvum , 52.
79 Cf. Austin , How To Do Things With Words, 69.

...".[80] It is very important to note that explicit performatives are normally in the first person present tense, active voice, indicative mood. Contrary to Explicit performative word is Implicit performative word in which the utterance is unclear and the meaning it conveys is doubtful. In relation to sacramental theology, it is the explicit performatives that are mostly implied when referring to the performative function of the word in bringing about sacramental realities. I maintain this opinion for the following reasons:

i. Self explanatory utterances: It is said that explicit performative is self explanatory and defines by itself what is meant by the utterance. The statement "I suggest that we eat" is very clear that it is only but a suggestion. Therefore, one does not need to ask "what type of utterance is that?" for it clarifies and qualifies itself. Likewise in Sacramental theology, the words that perform in the celebration of sacraments do not put anybody in doubt about the type of statement for it is self explanatory. That means, at the Eucharistic celebration, for example, the words of consecration: "Take this and eat it ... Take this and drink from it ..." imply in themselves "command". The words the priest-confessor speaks over the penitent at the confessional in the celebration of the Sacrament of Penance imply in themselves that they are "absolution". In this way, the performative words in sacramental theology prove to be explicit.

ii. Verdictive Utterances: Verdictive utterances are aspects of explicit performatives that are concerned with making pronouncements based on the judgement of situations. Likewise, performative words in the celebration of sacraments are verdictives because they pronounce, they declare. Again, using the sacraments of Eucharist and Penance as examples, we consider the words of consecration and the words of absolution as pronouncements of transubstantiation and declarations of forgiveness respectively: I absolve you ..., I baptize you ..., I pronounce you husband and wife... . In this way, the performative words in sacramental theology prove to be explicit. It does not, however, mean that implicit performative word is totally absent in the celebration of the sacraments.

2.4 Criteria for performative word in Sacramental theology

For a word to perform, certain conditions must be fulfilled on the part of the speaker, the audience, and even the word itself.[81] These criteria can be summarized in the following way:

i. There must be a conventional procedure.
ii. The procedure must be executed by all participants both correctly and completely.
iii. The same emotion, feeling and intention of the speaker must operate in the hearer.

---

80   Cf. Austin, How To Do Things With Words, 88, 151,153.
81   Cf. Austin, How To Do Things With Words, 14–15; see also Austin, Philosophical Papers, 224–225.

Performative word is described as 'unhappy' and fails to achieve its aim if any of the above-mentioned conditions is not met. In this case, the act is purported but void. This offence is referred to as "misfire". When the procedure used in a purported act is non-existent, the purported act despite being void is regarded as "misinvocation". When the purported act has an existing procedure but only that this procedure cannot be applied in the given situation, then, the purported act is regarded as "misapplication". The purported act is regarded as "misexecution" when it is characterized by flaws in its execution. There is still a situation in which an act is achieved but insincerely, and such a purported act is not void but achieved, and because it is done without sincerity, it is regarded as "abuse".[82] The same criteria regulate the celebration of the church's sacraments. The performative word in sacramental celebration must follow the conventional procedure determined by the church's guiding principles. The situation in which the sacrament is celebrated plays a vital role in validating the sacramental celebration, and there must be unity of intention between the speaker and the audience. We make an example with the sacrament of Holy Eucharist. The law of the church states: "The only minister who, in the person of Christ, can bring into being the sacrament of the Eucharist, is a validly ordained priest" (c.900,1CIC). About the recipient of the Eucharist, the law says: "Any baptized person who is not forbidden by law may and must be admitted to holy communion" (c.912CIC). The proper words of consecration are carefully contained in the ritual. These are the conventional procedures that regulate the church's sacrament of eucharist. Inadequacy in these procedures affects the way the celebration will be interpreted. For example, when an individual who is not an ordained priest or not validly ordained priest wilfully celebrates Mass, he has not only committed impersonation but his act is purported, and what he has done is both invalid and illicit. This is in accordance with the doctrine of "misfire". For a non-baptised who, in a validly celebrated Holy Mass, receives Holy Communion out of insincerity, the Holy Communion itself which he has received is valid but the recipient has acted illicitly. Again we can associate this act with the doctrine of "abuse". So, there is proper adaptation of the criteria regulating performative word in the church's celebration of her sacraments. In discussing the relationship between performative word and sacramental theology further, let us make some references to the various aspects of human endeavours where the actions of performative word can be compared with sacramental celebrations.

2.5 The references to performative word in Sacramental theology

Performative identities, performative theatre and performative symbols are the various aspects of performatives that are contained in Sacramental theology. We now make a brief discussion on each of these aspects.

---

82 Austin, How To Do Things With Words, 17–18.

2.5.1 Performative identities

This is the aspect of performative word that clarifies how word defines our identity. The definition of one's identity can be a two-way process. Psychologists affirm this position by insisting that "a person possesses identity in relation to others".[83] Suppose I give myself the name "Alexander", my identity as "Alexander" is actualized when people call me with that name. Likewise, whenever, may be, on the street and someone from a near distance mentions the name "Alexander" to my hearing, reflexively the tendency is my automatic response either by answering or by looking at the direction from which the call is being made. In this way, both I, the bearer, and the caller contribute to make my identity "Alexander" to perform.[84]

Performative identity is very much applicable in Sacramental theology. Sacraments offer the opportunity for identifying a christian or offer the opportunity through which a christian tries to create identity for himself. What do I mean by this? Take the case of the sacrament of Baptism as an example. Before a child is presented for Baptism, he is not identified with any name. He is then baptised with a christian name, for example, Peter: "I baptize you ...". From this moment forth he grows up with this name and people associate him with this name as his identity. Anywhere and at anytime this name is mentioned he consciously or unconsciously responds to it in whichever way is the case. In a similar instance, an individual christian, because he is a communicant or is baptized, and because he is confirmed or properly married in the church presents himself as "a good Christian". But because performative identity is a group action, the individual alone cannot successfully impose this identity upon himself but must need the testimony of people before he can be identified as "a good Christian" : "If anyone thinks he is religious, and does not bridle his tongue but deceives his heart, this man's religion is vain. Religion that is pure and undefiled before God and the Father is this: to visit the orphans and widows in their affliction, and to keep oneself unstained from the world [...] So faith by itself, if it has no works, is dead" (Js 1,26–27; 2,17). Likewise, the acknowledgment of the identity of a christian member can first come from the members themselves. For example, the dedication with which a parish priest discharges his priestly ministries among his members makes the parishioners to identify him as "a good parish priest". The Bible testifies also that the identity of Nathanael as a true Israelite did not first come from him. Rather, it was Jesus Christ Himself who identified him with the following words : "Behold, an Israelite indeed, in whom is no guile" (Jn 1,47). Bishop William B.Fried, the Bishop of the Diocese of Shreveport, Louisiana, demonstrates this point further with the story of a young lady he prefers to call Linda, and according to him, "Linda gives about five hours a week to helping other people and is a ready Volunteer [...] Linda's friends describe her as self-giving and generous almost to a fault".[85] So, performative identity is an important factor in Sacramental theology.

---

83 Fried, William, Evangelization, Culture and Catholic identity: proceedings of a symposium for catholic leaders, Florida 1996, 29.
84 Cf. Austin , How To Do Things With Words, 117.
85 Fried, Evangelization, Culture and Catholic identity, 29.

2.5.2 Performative theater

The performative power of words extends to theater. Actors act to create imaginations and imaginary scenes, and we should know that words do direct and control these imaginations, and often words do present these imaginations as if they were real. Performative word does not only help to make present a reality that is absent but help to create an imaginary existence of what in reality does not exist. That is the power of performative word in theatre. Actors speak in order to create a reality in audience, and the reactions of the audience confirm the performative power of the word in theater. Thus, every play writer has the interest of the audience in mind while he writes, and the actor does the work of a translator–translating the situation that the play writer creates in his work, while the audience does the work of interpreting by imagining in order to understand the situation the actor is presenting. The celebration of sacraments can be associated with what happens at the theater. The world in which we live is the theater and the altar is the stage; Jesus Christ is the performative word of God; the ordained ministers are the actors; the people of God (the lay faithful) are the audience; God Himself is the play writer. The ordained ministers who are the actors have the duty of making Jesus Christ-the performative word of God, to be realized in the lives of the faithful who are the audience. The confirmation that the word has performed in the lives of the audience is by their conversion of hearts and reception of divine grace, and this is done by the help of the Holy Spirit: "No one can say that Jesus Christ is Lord except under the influence of the Holy Spirit" (1 Cor 12, 3).

2.5.3 Performative symbols

Symbolic languages are performative. They are, however, difficult to understand because of their sophistication. In order to understand symbolic languages, a good knowledge of the people's world-view is required. J.L.Austin presents the two linguistic symbols "Hurrah" and "Damn" to show how linguistic symbols can be performative. By "Hurrah", the speaker "is performing the act of cheering".[86] Likewise, by "Damn", the speaker "is performing the act of swearing".[87] There are some other situations where linguistic symbols are performative. For example, by "Hi" the speaker performs the act of greetings, and so on. Because Hurrah, Damn or Hi are circumscribed within a particular world-view, they would only perform on a foreigner if the foreigner understands the world-view in which they are uttered.

So, symbolic languages should not stand in isolation but needs convention in order to have a uniform interpretation and to perform, and to ignore the people's linguistic symbolism is to put their world-view into crisis. In the celebration of sacraments, symbols are very essential elements. Certain representations of sacramental reali-

---

86   Austin, Philosophical Papers, 233.
87   Austin, Philosophical Papers, 233.

ties in symbolic forms carry along with them powerful messages that influence the thoughts of the hearers and direct their responses. Linguistic symbolism, therefore, is an important aspect of symbolism in the church's sacramental theology. For example, the expression "praise be to Jesus Christ-now and forever" is a symbolic utterance, and when one asks about the type of utterance it is, we may say that it is "a praise": "I praise that ...". This presents the speaker to be a christian, and it takes another person to know the christian world-view in order to understand the expression. So, performative symbol is part of sacramental theology.

2.6 Performative word: the hermeneutic of the sacraments

Since man cannot realize his vocation by his own powers alone, Christ instituted the sacraments as means to empower man in his struggle to be holy. Christ actualizes this solely by the power of his word:

> In katholische Perspektive wird den Sakramenten ein gewisses Eigenleben gegenüber dem Wort dadurch zugestanden, dass ihm ein aus dem Wortgeschehen nicht ableitbares essentielles plus hin- sichtlich seiner seinshaften Qualität zugesprochen wird.[88]

The sacramental words are the words of Jesus Christ. The words and works of Jesus Christ are considered as words and works that are pronounced and fulfilled with the authority of God the Father and in the power of the Holy Spirit (Mt 11,27; Jn 3,34;14,24;17,8). In the sacramental word, God in His mysterious way addresses himself to humanity, and communicates His plan for salvation. The sacred scriptures and tradition contain this word; the preaching of the Church transmits it; the liturgy celebrates and actualizes it. In the sacraments, one experiences these in details. The sacraments of the Holy Eucharist and Penance will serve as our case-study in determining how word performs in the sacraments of the Church.

2.6.1 The Holy Eucharist

The proclamation of the word is very essential in the first part of the Eucharistic celebration. Hence, in the celebration of the Holy Eucharist the saving word resounds with performative efficacy. So, there is an irreversible and dynamic relationship between the word proclaimed and the sacrament that is realized. One cannot celebrate the liturgy of the Eucharist before the liturgy of the Word, because of the pre-existence and hence primacy of the Word "Verbum sine carne". Again, one cannot celebrate the Eucharist without the liturgy of the Word because of the irrevocability of the incarnation of the Logos, but one can celebrate the liturgy of the Word alone without the Eucharist, because

---

[88] Klöckner, Stefan, Sakrament im wort, christologische Fundamentierung, eschatologische Ausrichtung und ekklesiale Vermittlung wortsakramentalen Geschehens als Gegenstand ökumenischer Konvergenzbestrebungen, Inauguraldissertation, Tübingen 1991, 128.

of the value of the pre-incarnate Logos or the validity of the "Verbum sine carne". Also, one cannot separate the liturgy of the word and the liturgy of the Eucharist, celebrating them in different times and places, because of the indissociability of the hypostatic union. In the quest to make the church's teaching on the Eucharist more admirable in our time, we recall one of the teachings of Pope John Paul II on the Eucharist:

> In his homily at the World Youth Day Mass in Paris, Pope John Paul II put forth these words on the Eucharist: "Rabbi, where are you staying?"each day the Church responds: Christ is present in the eucharist, in the sacrament of his death and resurrection. In and through the eucharist you acknowledge the dwelling place of the living God in human history. For the eucharist is the sacrament of the love which conquers death. It is the sacrament of the covenant, pure gift of love for the reconciliation of all humanity. It is the gift of the real presence of Jesus the redeemer [...][89]

The Church, therefore, appeals that all Christians, when present at the celebration of this great mystery of faith, should not be there as strangers or passive participators, but should rather be actively and devoutly involved. The Eucharist forms the Church. The eucharistic words are not proclaimed if there is nobody to announce them. The memorial is in- turn not celebrated if there is no one to do it in obedience to the Lord's mandate, and the proclaimed word is not fulfilled if there are nobody on whom it will act on. Word and sacrament, therefore, require the ministry of the Church, the service of proclamation, of the celebration of the sacrifice, and of the regathering of the human family into the unity of the holy people of God. The eucharistic Church is totally ministerial. The Church's emphasis on the words as the key-players in bringing about the Eucharistic presence is evident even in the way they are presented in the liturgical books. In the liturgical books, the words of consecration are printed in block letters to distinguish them from the other words used in the liturgy, and to underline their irreplaceability. The words of the institution are pronounced by the priest himself who is acting "in persona Christi et nomine ecclesiae", by virtue of his ontological configuration to Christ through ordination whereby he is constituted minister of God to the people of God. These words of Christ should be spoken clearly and distinctly as their meaning demands:

On the night he was betrayed,

He took bread and gave you thanks and praise. He broke the bread gave it his disciples, and said:

TAKE THIS; ALL OF YOU; AND EAT IT: THIS IS MY BODY WHICH WILL BE GIVEN UP FOR YOU.

When supper was ended, he took the cup. Again he gave you thanks and praise, gave the cup to his disciples, and said:

TAKE THIS ALL OF YOU AND DRINK FROM IT: THIS IS THE CUP OF MY BLOOD, THE BLOOD OF THE NEW AND EVERLASTING COVENANT. IT WILL BE SHED FOR YOU AND FOR ALL MEN SO THAT SINS MAY BE FORGIVEN.
DO THIS IN MEMORY OF ME.

---

[89] Carter, Edward, ed., Shepherds of Christ Newsletters, volume 2, New York 2002, 125–126.

The Eucharistic words of consecration: "This is my body ... This is my blood ..." are performative. Although they do not follow the explicit performative formular, we can say that they are pronouncements: "I pronounce that this is my body; I pronounce that this is my blood". The literary genre of the account of the institution of the Eucharist is aetiological: "For the tradition I receive from the Lord and also handed on to you is that on the night he was betrayed, the Lord Jesus took some bread, after he had given thanks, he broke it, and he said, 'This is my body which is for you; do this in remembrance of me.' And in the same way, with the cup after supper, saying, 'This cup is the covenant in my blood'. Whenever you drink it, do this as a memorial of me" (1 Cor 11,23–25).

The two gestures of Jesus accompanied by words in the institution of the Eucharist: "body broken and given (for you)"; blood shed for you (Lk 22,20) or blood shed for many (Mk 14,24; Mt 26,28), symbolically announced his immediate passion and death. The words over the chalice re-echo two Old Testament references. The first "blood shed" recalls the famous text of Genesis 9,6 which is synonymous to violent death. The second "for many" comes from the fourth song of the Servant of Yahweh: "By his sacrifice, delivering himself to death, he takes away the sins of many" (Is 53,12).

The efficacy of the words of consecration [90] derives from the divine "I" of Jesus which is the implied subject of the words: "This is my body", "This is my blood", and from the Holy Spirit who inspired them. It is not the power of man but the divine power and operation that changes the bread and wine into the body and blood of Christ. Surely the words of Christ, which could make out of nothing that which did not exist, can change things already in existence into what they were not, for it is no less extraordinary to give things new natures than to change their natures. These words which have no parallel among the literary genres of the Scripture are not to be taken metaphorically but literally and realistically as they sound. They effect the transsubstantiation of the bread and wine into the body and blood of Christ. The bread and wine become truly really the body and blood of Christ such that the celebrant genuflects both after the consecration of bread and after that of wine to pay tribute of adoration to Jesus Christ present under the sacred species.

The Eucharistic bread and wine are traceable to Jesus Himself. These two elements are preserved in the different accounts of the institution of the Eucharist. Hence the elements, like the form, have their origin not from the apostles but from Jesus. By identifying these earthly elements with His body and blood, Jesus considered them

---

90   The Council of Trent upholds that it has always been the convinction of the Church of God that by the consecration of the bread and wine a change takes place in which the entire substance of the bread is changed into the substance of the body of Christ our Lord and the entire substance of the wine into the substance of His blood. This definition became necessary due to certain heresies that were experienced in the church of the middle ages. The church's protection of this precious inheritance, therefore, led to the various arrangements in the celebration of the Eucharist, and in the words of the consecration, of which the result is the present formular in today's Eucharistic celebration. See also , H. Dezinger, Enchiridion symbolorum, Freiburg 1963, 1642.

adequate to express the offer of His life which He accomplished the following day on the cross. This may explain why the church has never changed the Matter and Form of the Eucharist down the centuries unlike in other Sacraments. This ecclesial practice has been challenged by different groups who rejected or substituted one or the other element. It is still under controversy in our times, especially in those places where these elements are scarce or inexistent. In Africa, Bishop Dupon of Pala (Chad) experimented with Millet and Beer as Matter of the Eucharist between 1973 and 1975. He was promptly retired. A Nigerian liturgist proposed Millet and Palm Wine. The seminar of the Association of the Member Episcopal Conference of Eastern Africa, held in Nairobi – Kenya (16 – 28 September, 1991) criticized the retention of a wheaten Eucharist. These objections to the traditional Matter of the Eucharist are refuted in the light of sound doctrine. The use of bread from wheat (Jn 6,9) and wine from vine (Mk 14,25; Mt 26,29; Lk 22,18; Jn 15,1) by Jesus Himself during the institution of the Eucharist established a tradition of which the Church is no inventor but guardian. Therefore, fidelity to this tradition brings the Christian community in worship, its geographical location notwithstanding, in contact with the mystery of Christ. In addition Ralph J. Lawrence writes:

> The tradition of the Church has always recognized that the sacramental rites themselves are rooted in the very words and deeds of the historical Jesus. For this reason Christians are led to reject the so-called relevant appeals for "trans- culturalism" in the Church's sacred signs. Perhaps a good argument can be made for substituting beer for wine in certain cultures, and rice for bread in others,when the Eucharist is celebrated. If Christianity had been born of some trans-cultural myth, open to a mult national flexibility, such changes might be cogently argued. But christianity is an historical religion. The mind of the Founder is the mind of a real Jew who lived in the Near East almost two thousand years ago. The stamp of his time, his Jewishness, His human will shows; the Church that he founded will bear this stamp even as it spreads to the utmost corners of the earth. His authority to institute a Church and its sacraments derived from His divine form; but it was in His human state that He taught His disciples, worked His signs, and fulfilled His paschal mysteries.[91]

The use of elements of nature as sacramental matter in the liturgy confirms their intrinsic goodness (Gen 1,31) and shows the unity between the order of creation and the order of redemption. Unlike Manichaeism which despises matter, regarding it as evil, christianity upholds the goodness of creation. By using the elements of nature in the liturgy, the Church elevates the entire cosmos in gratitude to its Creator. This elevation constitutes the highest appreciation of created realities. These elements so to say are incapable of conferring grace, but by virtue of the Word, they confer the grace which they signify "Accedit verbum ad elementum et fit sacramentum". Just as the glorified humanity of Christ is full of grace and confers grace because of its substantial union with the Logos, in a similar manner, sacramental matter can confer grace only because of its union with the word. In the dispensation of the sacraments, the sacramental matter is the visible channel through which invisible grace passes to man by virtue of the sacramental form. The diadic structure of the Eucharistic

---

91   Gratsch, Edward, Principles of Catholic Theology, A synthesis of Dogma and Morals, New York 1981, 168–169.

celebration, that is, the liturgy of the word and the liturgy of the Eucharist, derives its origin from the diadic constitution of the Incarnate Word. But since the Logos pre-existed His flesh, the liturgy of the word necessarily precedes the liturgy of the Eucharist. Again, the inseparability of the liturgy of the word and the liturgy of the Eucharist derives from the inseparability of the hypostatic union which results from the incarnation. According to Alexander of Hales:

> The union of the divine and human nature...was a miracle entirely above nature both in its mode and in the species of activity involved; it belongs to the first type of miracle, which differs from a second type whose species of activity is according to nature, but whose mode is above nature [...] man can come to a knowledge of God through God's operations in the world; but, he adds, no human reason is able without grace to attain, through any operation of God, a knowledge of the Trinity or of the Incarnation.[92]

The same God-man Jesus Christ who is the effect of that union of the Word of divine nature with the flesh of human nature (enhypostatic union) and of the divine nature of the Word and the human nature of the flesh (hypostatic union)[93] by the Holy Spirit which is called incarnation, is also the effect of that pronounciation of the very words of Christ as He spoke them at the Last Supper over the visible earthly bread and wine by the priest (consecration) and the consequent change of the whole substance of the visible earthly bread and wine into the substance of the invisible heavenly body and blood of the celestial Christ by the power of the invoked Holy Spirit inherent in the words pronounced over the bread and wine (transsubstantiation) which is called the celebration of the Eucharist. Humanly speaking, it is difficult to interprete these words to determine the concept in which they act. To portray how difficult this may be, Colman E. O'Neill writes: "When it comes to systematic theology, general hermeneutics, presuppositions, abound, though it is often difficult, even for those who are influenced by them, to discern their structure".[94]

The event that is being celebrated in the sacrament of the Eucharist as we know is a mystery, and normally mysteries are beyond human comprehension. In order that the church might shade some light to help human comprehension, philosophi-

---

92   Principe, Walter, The Theology of the Hypostatic Union in the Early Thirteenth Century, Volume II, Alexander of Hales' Theology of the Hypostatic Union, Toronto 1967, 73.
93   In patristic writings the word hypostasis was first used about the Trinity. Origen speaks of three hypostases in God–the Father, the Son, and the Holy Spirit. Dionysius of Alexandria, writing against Arius and Sabellius, says that there are three hypostases in the unity of the divine monarchy. Gradually hypostasis came to be distinguished from "ousia",-being, reality, which was reserved for what was common to the three persons, the divine nature. Hypostatic union, therefore, is the union in one person, or hypostasis, of the divine and human natures. Anyone who says that the Son of God is from a different hypostasis or ousia (than the Father), him the catholic church anathematizes. See also H. Dezinger, Enchiridion symbolorum, Freiburg, 1963, 126. Enhypostasis is a response by Leontius of Byzantium to the monophysite objection that nature without hypostasis is nothing, and hence one hypostasis in Christ means one nature, by saying that the human nature of Christ is neither uncentered (anhypostasis) nor self–centered, but encentered in God (enhypostasis).
94   O'Neill, Colman, Sacramental realism: A General Theory of the Sacraments, Theology and Life series 2, Delaware 1983, 163.

cal or rather metaphysical interpretations become unavoidable. This has in no small measure contributed to the difficulties that Colman E.O'Neill is talking about, and has as well produced a lot of heresies. In interpreting the words of the Eucharistic consecration "This is my Body, This is my Blood", it is not to be understood in terms of Jesus being represented in the Eucharistic bread or wine, rather on the contrary: "He (Jesus) identified himself with bread (my body) and wine (my blood) ... and in the commemorative meal they (the faithful) proclaim his presence, and actualize it and celebrate it and unite themselves to him as already present".[95] This is based on the background that what is being celebrated is a re-enactment of an event in which Jesus himself is both the priest and the victim. By the pronouncement of "This is my Body, This is my Blood" at the Eucharistic celebration, the same sacrifice of the calvary by which Jesus paid for our sins and by which he bought our salvation is represented at the sacrifice of the altar. The two sacrifices of the Calvary and the Altar are the same; the former in bloody form and the later in unbloody form.

2.6.2 Penance

The words of absolution at the sacrament of penance are performative: "I absolve you from your sins ...". The explicit performative verb shows clearly that the act performed is absolution. Penance is the sacrament that reconciles the sinner with God in virtue of the sins committed after Baptism. On the part of the penitent, three essential conditions must be fulfilled: contrition, confession and satisfaction. Contrition is understood in terms of remorse, confession in terms of accusation of oneself and satisfaction in terms of relief. These three essential conditions required of a penitent may be categorized under matter of the sacrament. Our objective is to focus on the performative role words play in this sacrament. This is experienced in the words of the priest confessor and is known as absolution:

> God, the Father of mercies, through the death and resurrection of his son has reconciled the world to himself and sent the Holy Spirit among us for the forgiveness of sins. Through the ministry of the church may God give you pardon and peace. And I absolve you from your sins in the name of the Father, and of the Son, and of the Holy Spirit.[96]

The authority by which the words of the minister performs absolution is based on the mandate received from Christ himself: "Receive the Holy Spirit. If you forgive the sins of any, they are forgiven; if you retain the sins of any, they are retained" (Jn 20,22–23). Under the power of the key, Peter received from Christ the authority to bind and to lose: "I will give you the keys of the kingdom of heaven, and whatever you bind on earth shall be bound in heaven, and whatever you you loose on earth shall be loosed in heaven" (Mt 16,19). We must, however, not limit the power of binding and

---

95 Lawler, Michael, Symbol and Sacrament: A Contemporary Sacramental Theology, New York 1987, 152.
96 Lawler, Symbol and Sacrament, 121.

loosing to Peter alone, but is indeed extended to the twelve apostles: "Truly, I say to you, whatever you bind on earth shall be bound in heaven, and whatever you loose on earth shall be loosed in heaven" (Mt 18,18). Although the power of binding and loosing may imply various interpretations, in this context, we apply it to mean the power to excommunicate the sinner and the power of reconciling him back with God:

> As early as his Second Letter to the Thessalonians Paul gives instructions that one who has been excommunicated from the church is not to be looked upon "as an enemy" but warned "as a brother " (3:15). And in his Second Letter to the Corinthians he explains how the repentant sinner is to be dealt with. He is to be forgiven and, in later language, to be reconciled.[97]

The apostles carried out this command in obedience to Jesus himself: "What I have forgiven, if I have forgiven anything, has been for your sake in the presence of Christ, to keep Satan from gaining the advantage over us; for we are not ignorant of his designs" (2 Cor 2,11). Thus, in humble obedience of carrying out this wish of Christ, the church keeps on with this practice handed down by the apostles, and in accordance with the practice of St Paul in his excommunication and reconciliation of Corinthian sinners. Our interest here is not to go into various interpretations and practices this sacrament has gone through in different periods of the church's history, and the various heresies associated with it. Rather, we are concerned with the efficacy of the words of absolution which in effect forgives not only the sins committed after Baptism whether mortal or venial, but as well, the punishments due to them. The eternal damnation is completely averted, and the temporal punishment that may await the penitent after death may be avoided depending on whether the penitent by his acts of penance is completely exonerated. Again, by the power of the words of absolution, the sinner is once more restored to grace which is lost to sin, and the fruits of the new state of life which are happiness and peace are enjoyed. There is as well scriptural background to affirm that in Christianity our faith depends a lot on the actions of the word as it is divinely communicated in various times and by different means. On this note, it would be necessary that we spare a little time and see how the word performs in both Old and New Testaments.

2.7 Performative word and the scriptures

In emphasizing the importance of the Scripture as the source of the divine word, and the bedrock of theology Vat. II writes:

> She (the church) has always regarded, and continues to regard the Scriptures, taken together with sacred Tradition, as the supreme rule of her faith. For, since they are inspired by God and committed to writing once and for all time, they present God's own word in an unalterable form, and they make the voice of the Holy Spirit sound again and again in the words of the prophets and apostles. It follows that all the preaching of the church, as indeed the entire Christian religion should be nourished and ruled by sacred scripture. In the sacred books the father who is in heaven comes lovingly to meet his children, and talks with them. And such is

---

97   Lawler, Symbol and Sacrament, 106.

the force and power of the Word of God that it can serve the church as her support and vigor, and the children of the church as strength of their faith food for the soul, and a pure and lasting fount of spiritual life. Scripture verifies in the most perfect way the words: " The Word of God is living and active" (Heb 4,12), and "is able to build you up and to give you the inheritance among all those who are sanctified" (Acts 20,32; cf. 1 Th 2,13). [...] Sacred theology relies on the written Word of God, taken together with sacred Tradition, as on a permanent foundation. By this Word it is most firmly strengthened and constantly rejuvenated, as it searches out, under the light of faith, the full truth stored up in the mystery of Christ. The Sacred Scriptures contain the Word of God, and , because they are inspired, they are truly the Word of God. Therefore, the "study of the sacred page" should be the very soul of sacred theology.[98]

The council fathers go further to make a deep and reflected clarification when they said that John at the beginning of his Gospel calls Jesus "The Word" (Jn 1,1). Beginning with the Old Testament, and moving across the New Testament, let us consider what the scripture teaches about word of God.

2.7.1 The Old Testament

The Old Testament begins by the story of the creating power of the Word of God: "It is God's own creative intervention that is the word and that also transforms itself into concepts, ideas, thoughts, and visions in those to whom it comes".[99] All that came to be was by the performative power of the word : "And God said, 'Let there be light , and there was light' ; [...] And God said, 'Let there be a firmament in the midst of the waters, and let it separate the waters from the waters... and it was so'; [...] And God said, 'Let the waters under the heavens be gathered together into a place, and let the dry land appear, and it was so' ; [...] And God said, 'Let the earth put forth vegetation, plants yield seed, and fruit trees bearing fruit in which is their season each according to its kind, upon the earth, and it was so' ; [...] And God said, 'Let there be lights in the firmament of the heavens to separate the day from the night and let them be for signs and for seasons and for days and years, and let them be lights in the firmament of the heavens to give light upon the earth, and it was so' ; [...] And God said, 'Let the waters bring forth swarms of the living creatures, and let birds fly above the earth across the firmament of the heavens' ; [...] And God said, 'Let the earth bring forth living creatures according to their kinds, cattle and creeping things and beasts of the earth according to their kinds, and it was so [...]' (Gen 1,1–25). The "Let there be …" in the creation account could be interpreted to be a command. We can make this phrase to be more explicit by saying: "I command that there be …". Creation account, therefore, "expresses an activity, a personal will to effect that which lies in the being of God. It creates what it names".[100] God also made manifest the performative power of his word through his angels. When Hagar, Abram's Egyptian maid conceived for

---

98 D V, nos 21 and 24.
99 Sigmund, Mowinckel, translated by Reidar B.Bjornard, The Old Testament as word of God, Oxford 1960, 43.
100 Sigmund, The Old Testament as word of God, 42.

him as a result of the mutual understanding between him and his wife Sarai, Hagar was looking with contempt on her mistress Sarai. This made Sarai to deal harshly with her and Hagar fled from her into the wilderness. The angel of God found her in the wilderness and said to her : "Hagar, maid of Sarai, 'where have you come from and where are you going?' She said, 'I am fleeing from my mistress Sarai'. The angel of the Lord said to her, 'Return to your mistress, and submit to her'; I will so greatly multiply your descendants that they cannot be numbered for multitude.' And the angel of the Lord said to her, 'Behold, you are with child , and shall bear a son , you shall call his name Ishmael, because the Lord has given heed to your affliction. He shall be a wild ass of a man, his hand against every man and every man's hand against him, and he shall dwell over against all his kinsmen [...]. And Hagar bore Abram a son, and Abram called the name of his son whom Hagar bore 'Ishmael' (Gen 16,7–16). We could interpret the words of the angel in a more explicit way to mean a promise: "I promise that you shall bear a son ...".

Prophets are another people through whom God showed how performative his words can be. We take an encounter between Prophet Elijah and the prophets of Baal as a case study: "Then Elijah said to all the people, 'come near me' ; and all the people came near to him. And he repaired the altar of the Lord that had been thrown down; Elijah took twelve stones, according to the number of the tribes of the sons of Jacob, to whom the word of the Lord came, saying, 'Israel shall be your name,' and with the stones he built an altar in the name of the Lord. And he made a trench around the altar, as great as would contain two measures of seed. And he put the wood in order, and cut the bull in pieces and laid it on the wood. And he said, 'Fill four jars with water, and pour it on the burning offering, and on the wood.' And he said, 'Do it a second time' ; and they did it a second time. And he said, 'Do it a third time'; and they did it a third time. And the water ran round the altar, and filled the trench also with water. And at the time of the offering of the oblation, Elijah the prophet came near and said, 'O Lord, God of Abraham, Isaac, and Israel, let it be known this day that thou art God in Israel, and that I am your servant, and that I have done all these things at thy word. Answer me o God, answer me, that this people may know that thou, o Lord, art God, and that thou hast turned their hearts back'. Then the fire of the Lord fell, and consumed the burnt offering, and the wood, and the stones, and the dust, and licked up the water that was in the trench. And when all the people saw it, they fell on their faces; and they said, 'The Lord, he is God; the Lord, he is God.' (1 Kgs 18,30–39). Again, the above words of the prophet Elijah could be explicitly interpreted to mean "testimony" to the mighty power of God. In other words, he could be saying: "I testify that the Lord God who answers by fire is the true God ...". Again, the prophet Elisha, the servant of Elijah and the direct inheritor of Elijah's prophetic spirit, is another witness to the performative power of God's word. His encounter with small boys on his way to Bethel is a typical example of the performative power of God's word at work : "He went up from there to Bethel; and while he was going up on the way, some small boys came out of the city and jeered at him, saying, 'Go up, you headed! Go up, you bald headed!' And he turned around, and when he saw them, he cursed them in the name of the Lord. And two she-bears came out of the woods and tore forty-two of the boys. (2 Kgs 2,23–25). The type of performative utterance here could be taken to be a pronouncement of curse: "I pronounce curse on you that...". The Psalmist confirms the performative power of the word of God when he writes: "The voice of the Lord is powerful, the voice of the Lord is full of majesty. The voice of the Lord breaks the cedars, the Lord breaks the cedars of Lebanon [...] The voice of the Lord flashes forth flames of fire. The voice of the Lord makes the oaks to whirl, and strips the forests bare; and in the temple all cry, 'Glory!.' [...] By the word of the Lord the heavens were made, 'and all their host by the breath of his mouth.' [...] Let all the earth fear the Lord, let all the inhabitants of the world stand in awe of him! For he spoke , and it came to be; he commanded, and it stood forth" (Ps 29,4–9; 33,6–9).

We may be right to say that the Old Testament presents the Word of God as expressive of the divine law (cf.Gen 14,19). It sees the Word of God as infallible and efficacious. Whether these refer to historical interventions or to God's cosmic action, once God utters his Word, it necessarily accomplishes what it contains (cf.Is 55,11). First and foremost, the Old Testament applies the efficacy of the Word of God to God's intervention in the history of Israel (cf. Dt 9,59). This Word of God later took a new dimension. Let us examine how it re-echoes in the New Testament.

2.7.2 The New Testament

In the New Testament, the Word of God becomes a distinct reality stimulated with power. It is God's turning to human beings to reveal himself, as well as calling human beings to a communication of life.[101] As we have already known, New Testament is a collection of all that Jesus said and did during his earthly ministry. The four gospels bear testimonies to Jesus numerous miracles. The miracles are of different types, but basically Jesus performed these actions by the power of his words. [102] Describing the words of Jesus, Stefan Klöckner writes:

> Das wort Jesu wird in seiner Mächtigkeit gespürt, was sich auch an den durch das wort geschehenden Wundertaten/Zeichenhandlungen erweist. Worte und zeichenhandlungen Jesu wirken aufeinander zu, gehen ineinander der über, sind dergestalt aufeinander verwiesen, dass Jesus als der charakterisiert wird, der "ein Prophet, mächtig in Wort und Tat vor Gott und dem ganzen Volk" war. In dieser Formel, die aus der Sicht der nachösterlichen Gemeinde das Wirken Jesu brennglasartig zusammenfasst, finden sich drei Elemente:
>
> 1) Jesus ist ein prophetischer Mann; er steht in der Tradition derer, die durch ihre Mahnung eine Spannung aufreißen, indem sie ein Wort in die konkrete Wirklichkeit sagen und zugleich einen Hinweis auf das mit der Verkündigung anbrechende "Noch Nicht" geben.

---

101 Cf. Dupuis, Jacques, Towards a Christian Theology of Religious Pluralism, New York 2002, 42.

102 The efficacy of Jesus words attracted many to believe in him as one who full of authorities not only over the earthly powers but that his authority goes beyond to control principalities and powers of the evil one. The Gospel accounts are full of evidences of Jesus healing and casting out devils by the command of his words. This is a testimony that the words of Jesus are full of powers.

Er ist Botschafter des d`bar YHWH, nicht Wächter der torah(wie der Priester) oder Verwalter eines Spruches (wie ein Weiser). Daher partizipiert sein Wort an der Wirkmächtigkeit dessen, der ihn sendet.
2) Seine Worte und Werke sind machtvoll. Auch das wirkmächtige Reden steht mit dem Tun auf einer Ebene, erweist sich also im Charakter der Tat. Hierbei sind beide Elemente von gleicher Wichtigkeit und nicht gegeneinander zu stellen. Das dynatos bezieht sich auf die erga Jesu genauso wie auf seine logos. Aus der alt. Tradition, in welche sich Jesus als kündender Prophet stellt, wenn er mit Rekurs auf Jes 61,1 das euangelizesthai zum Kern seines Wirkens macht, erweist sich der enge Zusammenhang zwischen Wort und Tat. Dem Wort eignet der Charakter des Geschehens, indem das Gesagte durch die Ansage beginnt, Wirklichkeit zu werden; die Tat ist Zeichen und verdeutlicht in gleichem Maße die Botschaft, wie sie sie zur Verwirklichung bringt.
3) Aus dem Zusatz „vor Gott und dem ganzen Volk" wird deutlich, wie sehr Jesus nicht nur Bote, sondern die Botschaft selbst war, so dass in ihm Gottes Wort an die Menschen zusammenfällt mit seinem die Herrlichkeit Gottes bezeugenden Schicksal, das zugleich die Antwort des Menschen an Gott darstellt.

So wie im AT das d`dar YHWH aus dem Mund des Propheten durch den Akt des biser Kunde von der anbrechenden Heilszeit gab, so zeugt die Botschaft Jesu – mächtig in Werk und Wort [...][103]

The word of Jesus has immense power. His word has the power to heal: "The official said to him, 'Sir, come down before my child dies.' Jesus said to him, 'Go; your son will live.' The man believed the word that Jesus spoke to him and went his way. As he was going down, his servants met him and told him that his son was living . So he asked them the hour when he began to mend, and they said to him, 'Yesterday at the seventh hour the fever left him.' The father knew that was the hour when Jesus had said to him, 'Your son will live' " (Jn 4,49–53). All Jesus did to heal this man's son was to speak, even though Jesus was not in the same place as where the child was lying. The performative power of his words in performing healings can be categorized as "command": "Jesus commanded that the son be healed ...". By the power of his word, Jesus raised the dead back to life. In fact, in the gospels there are several accounts of persons Jesus raised from death back to life. For example, a twelve year old girl died in her bed but Jesus came, took her by the hand and told her "child arise" (Lk 8, 54), and she got up. In a different occasion, Jesus met a funeral procession coming out of the town of Nain. The dead person was the only son of a woman who was a widow. Jesus told her not to cry. He went up and touched the coffin and told the Youngman to get up, "And the dead man sat up, and began to speak" (Lk 11,15). One of the most amazing stories is the raising of Lazarus (Jn 11,17–27; 38–44). Again, the performative word by which Jesus raised the dead can be made more explicit to mean "command": "I command you Youngman get up [...] I command you Lazarus, come out". Jesus goes further to show how sins can be forgiven by the power of his word: "And when Jesus saw their faith, he said to the paralytic, 'My son, your sins are forgiven' " (Mk 2, 5). For those who reflect on what took place, the miraculous cure is seen as the confirmation of the truth proclaimed by Jesus and perceived and opposed by the scribes, that he (Jesus) has power on earth to forgive sins. We can position

---

103 Klöckner , Sakrament im Wort, 151–152.

the performative word through which Jesus forgives sins to be explicit: "I forgive you your sins ...". After the death of Jesus, the apostles carried on their master's ministry, and their words were also confirmed by the miracles that followed. Peter for example cured a paralytic in front of the Temple. By the power of the words, many who listened to what they were saying were moved to conversion: "So faith comes from what is heard, and what is heard comes by the preaching of Christ" (Rm 10,17).

The word of God, therefore, is not only vibrant in itself but has a transforming effect through the power of its proclamation, and by its acceptance, offers illumination, sanctification and salvation. There is similarity in the way the word of God performs in both Old and New Testaments. However, Sigmund Mowinckel notes a slight difference in the following comment: "But that which the New Testament most clearly adds to the Old Testament is the knowledge that this Word of God became flesh".[104] Taking scriptures as platform, how does the church's magisterium emphasize on the efficacy of the word?

2.8 Performative word and the church's doctrines

The church in her teachings has developed strong doctrines to emphasize the efficacy of the word in every sacramental celebration. For precision, we concentrate on the doctrines of incarnation and inspiration.

2.8.1 The doctrine of incarnation

The word incarnation is a combination of two latin words "in" with the same meaning as "in" in English, and "carnis" interpreted as "flesh". Karl Barth described incarnation as "the most concrete reality (concretissimun)".[105] Although the word "incarnation" is not found in the Bible, its doctrine is associated with the second person of the Divine Trinity – Jesus Christ: "He is the incarnation of God's own proper word, he is God speaking humanly by being humanly".[106]

According to the doctrine of incarnation, Jesus Christ – the second person of the Divine Trinity, took flesh in the womb of the Blessed Virgin Mary by the power of the Holy Spirit and is both truly God and truly man in obedience to the will of the Father who sent him. It is very important to note that it is the Virgin Mary's utterance "Behold, I am the handmaid of the Lord; let it be to me according to your word" (Lk 1,38), that made this incarnation possible. Thus, Virgin Mary's verbal response brought about the divine action of incarnation. In this we witness the performative nature of the Virgin Mary's verbal acceptance to be the mother of Jesus Christ: "And

---

104 Sigmund, The Old Testament as word of God, 44.
105 Sykes, Stephen, editor, Karl Barth: Centenary Essays, Cambridge 1989, 27.
106 Cooke, Bernard, Sacraments and Sacramentality, Mystic, Connecticut 1987, 321.

the Word became flesh and dwelt among us" (Jn 1,14); "For there is one God and there is one mediator between God and men, the man Christ Jesus" (1Tim 2,5), and Thomas F. Torrance adds: "The homoousion of the Son with the Father expressed the convinction that what he was toward us in his incarnate activity he was inherently, and therefore antecedently and eternally, in himself".[107] This doctrine is widely accepted among Roman Catholics, Eastern Orthodox, Anglicans and most Protestants. It is yearly commemorated at the Feasts of Annunciation and Christmas. Although this doctrine was generally accepted by christians, there arose a problem as to the exact nature of Christ's sonship. The first four centuries of christianity witnessed a raging debate on this issue, and this led to various heresies: Docetism, Arianism, Gnosticism and Nestorianism.[108] It was at the councils of Nicaea (325), Ephesus (431) and Chalcedon (451) that the church formally adopted the definition of the doctrine of incarnation as we know it today. The church's definition of incarnation is in line with the teaching of St Athanasius, who: "Spent his later career as archbishop in Alexandria, clarifying and fighting for the principle of the Son's eternal essentia identity with the Father (one in essence, and that the same essence)".[109]

The union of the two natures in Christ (Divine and Human) is described as hypostatical under the one personhood of Jesus Christ. It is the same personhood of Jesus Christ, the second person in the Divine Trinity, who shares the same eternity, omnipotence, majesty and divinity with God the Father and the Holy Spirit, is distinctly

---

107 Torrance, Thomas, Divine Meaning: Studies in Patristic Hermeneutics, Edinburgh 1995, 344.
108 "Docetism, deriving from the Greek dokesis, to seem or to appear, is a term first used by Serapion the bishop of Antioch (190–203) to defend his view that the flesh of Jesus was spiritual" (McGuckin J.A., The Westminster Handbook to Patristic Theology, London 2004, 105).
"Arianism, one of the most extensive ecclesiastical controversies, spread through most of fourth century and shaped Christian thought decisively. It has been regarded as the archetypal heresy. It began with the theories of Arius of Alexandria, opposed by Alexander the Bishop of Alexandria, which concerned a dispute over the status of the Logos [...] as Arius believed, was the Logos the Son and Servant of God, but in no way God in the same sense as the Father was God? [...] Arianism led to the formulation of the doctrine of the Trinity of Co-equal hypostases in the single deity " (McGuckin , The Westminster Handbook to Patristic Theology, 29–30).
"The term (Gnosticism) derives from the Greek word for knowledge (gnosis) understood as secret insight into spiritual truth [...] One common factor in all the Gnostic systems, therefore, is a profound suspicion of materiality, a dichotomous view of matter and spirit; and thus a tendency to moral and religious duality " (McGuckin , The Westminster Handbook to Patristic Theology, 147).
"The doctrine (Nestorianism), ascribed to Nestorius of Constantinople, that there were two separate persons in Christ, one human and one divine. Nestorius himself did not actually teach this, but in antique rhetorical argument the positions that could be logically extrapolated from an opponent's original position statements were often assigned to that speaker, whether they had actually maintained them or not. Nestorius thought that he was representing the traditional Christology of Syria as exemplified in Diodore of Tarsus's, and Theodore Mopsuestia's christologies, where both thinkers had stressed the need o preserve the distinct intergrity of the two natures (human and divine) in the Christ " (McGuckin , The Westminster Handbook to Patristic Theology, 236).
109 McGuckin , John Mary, The Westminster Handbook to Patristic Theology, 2004, 89.

expressed with name "Logos" who is always with God. The testimony of St John confirms this: "In the beginning was the word, and the word was with God, and the word was God. He was in the beginning with God; all things were made through him, and without him was not anything made that was made. In him was life, and the life was the light of men. The light shines in the darkness, and the darkness has not overcome it" (Jn 1,1–5). This passage of the Gospel underlines the eternal existence of the Logos of God and defines his fundamental mission, namely, bringing light which displaces all darkness. The word of God which is eternal is personified in Jesus Christ, and it is through this eternal word that life came to be. Whatever is, is by him; whatever lives, lives by him:

> As a result, the works performed by God in the history of salvation show forth and bear out the doctrine and realities signified by the words; the words, for their part, proclaim the works, and bring to light the mystery they contain. The most intimate truth which this revelation gives us about God and the salvation of man shines forth in Christ, who is himself both the mediator and the sum total of Revelation.[110]

So when we talk about the Word of God we are not primarily talking about the words of a book, but about a person, the second person of the Blessed Trinity, who was made flesh and gave his entire life for us. So the church in her sacraments takes a step forward, her teachings do not only appreciate the performatives but go beyond this appreciation by personifying it. Jesus Christ is not only "the Word of God", but also "the condensed Word", "the personified Word", "the abbreviated Word of God":

> God gave himself to us and for us in the fact that the word, which had been at work since before the creation of the world, became flesh in the historical man Jesus Christ. It is through this incarnation that God entered history in all his fullness of power and essence; it is through it that the perfect revelation of God took place. God in his character of active word became historical man and identified himself with us.[111]

This stands at the core of every saving message about God, beginning with the testimonies of the prophets of the old covenant who announced the eternal presence of Christ the Messiah among the chosen people of God. The pre-existence of the Logos proves to be a stereological statement. The eternal Logos of God, Jesus Christ, began his saving work for the universal salvation of the human family from the very beginning since his mission is inseparable from his being. Through the word of God, a truly divine harmony is produced in all things be it individually or communally. There is nothing existing or created which did not come into being and subsists in him and through him:

> And in one Lord Jesus Christ, the only begotten Son of God, begotten of the Father before all worlds, true God of true God, Light of Light, being of one substance with the father, by whom all things were made; who for us men and for our salvation came down from heaven, and was incarnate by the Holy Ghost of the Virgin Mary, and was made man [...][112]

---

110 D V, no. 2.
111 Sigmund, The Old Testament as word of God, 44.
112 Torrance, Divine meaning: studies in Patristic Hermeneutics, 343.

While the word of God remains unmoved with God the Father, his inner being moves all creatures as seems good to his Father. The Logos gives every creature according to its own nature, life and subsistence. Through him a wonderful and truly divine order is made visible. Through the same Logos, human beings enter into intimate union with God, and likewise, are in unity with themselves since by the singularity of his eternal generation and his incarnation in space and time, all creatures are orderly put together, whereby, each acts in its characteristic mode of being and of living, and all produce a single common order for the perfection of all, either individually or collectively. Some theologians have oftentimes used the phrase "Voice for God" to express what we mean by "Word of God", and according to Regina Dawn Akers: "The Word of God is the Voice for God. They are one and the same, as they cannot be separated. One is an extension of the other. In this extension, sameness is contained".[113] The eternal Logos possesses a twofold function: the dynamic function of bringing salvation, and the function of instruction. Jesus spoke in the Synagogues, debated with the scribes and taught the disciples. So, the twofold functions are only but two sides of the one function of the word, which is the self-discourse of God. Jesus speaks with authority, and his authoritative words bring about the desired effects. His words were concrete, alive and convincing, but sometimes they were paradoxical, hyperbolic and provocative. It can be said that almost all the saving works of Christ took bearing from his word. By the power of his word, Jesus cures the sick, raises the dead, forgives sins, performs miracles. He descended into hell in order to preach to the dead, and by the power of his word to resurrect them to new life: "For Christ also died for sins once for all, the righteous for the unrighteous, that he might bring us to God, being put to death in the flesh but made alive in the spirit; in which he went and preached to the spirits in prison" (1 Pt 3,18–19). Infact, eternal word of God became incarnate in time and space in order to give opportunity to all humankind to hear the saving message of God who created all to know him, love him, serve him and live with him for ever in his eternal kingdom of light, life and love. The mystery of the divine incarnation is contained in the Bible, and we as christians, are obliged to acknowledge it because the Bible is inspired. Let us, as a follow up, discuss what the church teaches in its doctrine of inspiration.

2.8.2 The Doctrine Of Inspiration

A verse in one of the Pauline letters reads: "Great indeed, we confess, is the mystery of our religion: He was manifested in the flesh, vindicated in the spirit, seen by angels, preached among nations, believed on in the world, taken up in glory" (1Tim 3,16–17). St Peter in one of his epistles writes: "First of all you must understand this, that no prophecy ever came by the impulse of man, but men moved by the Holy Spirit spoke from God" (2 Pt 1, 20–21). The Old Testament is not left out in bearing testimony

---

113 Akers, Regina Dawn, The Holy Spirit's Interpretation of the New Testament: A Course in Understanding and Acceptance, London 2007, 187.

to inspiration of the Biblical messages. In fact, it testifies to both direct and indirect froms of inspiration. God's dialogue with Moses is an example of direct inspiration: "Then Moses told the words of the peole to the Lord. And the Lord said to Moses [...]" (Ex 19,9–10). On the other hand, the use of the prefix: "Thus says the Lord" (Jer 35,13; 1 Kgs 12,22–24; Ezek 2,4), introduces the indirect form of inspiration. Enlightened by these Biblical passages, the church fathers authoritatively affirmed the doctrine of inspiration understood as the action of God in infusing his spirit into the writings of the Bible. This is why the Bible is known as the word of God. The OldTestament refers to this action of God as "God's breath" (Ps 33,6). It was St Paul who in the New Testament introduced the word inspiration. Jesus Christ himself defends this doctrine in the following words: "For truly, I say to you, till heaven and earth pass away, not an iota, not a dot, will pass from the law until all is accomplished " (Mt 5,18). The Biblical texts are so important not to be neglected because they are the word of God. This means that no word of God is more important than the other, and that every word that proceeds from the mouth of God carries the same effect.

The doctrine of inspiration centers its attention on the word of God itself and not on the writers. It is the word of God that is inspired and the writers share in the dual authorship: the Holy Spirit and the human. In reading the scriptures, one observes the limitations of human account of certain events and phenomena. These human limitations, however, explain the reasons for the inerrancy[114] one observes in the scriptures. These inerrancies can be considered as the accidents that do not in any way affect the substance. The truth remains that God moved certain men in such a way that they wrote what became the word of God. The word of God performs because it is inspired, and the individual believer acts according to this word because he or she believes that as an inspired word, it is God himself who speaks through the mouth of one who proclaims the word, and this leads to acting according to what the word says. So, the relationship between faith and inspiration offers the fundamental explanation as for the reason why the word performs in the hearts and minds of the hearers.

---

114 Inerrancy is a term that explains those Biblical inconsistencies. By Biblical inconsistencies I mean those Biblical accounts, be it scientific or historic, that are simply not true when subjected under thorough investigation. For instance an Old Testament account reads, "A generation goes, and a generation comes, but the earth remains for ever" (Eccl 1:4). This suggests that the earth is stationary, and this is contrary to the discovery of the modern science. In defence of the infallibility and indefectibility of the Word of God, the Fathers of the church, various theologians and recent popes have explained that it was not the intention of the Biblical writers to teach us geography or history for this is not an essential knowledge for human salvation, and therefore, they only spoke of the physical universe as it subjectively appealed to them and according to the understanding of their time.

2.9 Performative word: the contributions of the theologians

Eminent theologians across different epochs and christian affliations have devoted most of their teachings on defending the efficacy of the word in sacramental celebrations. Below are the contributions of some of these theologians to our theme.

2.9.1 St Augustine's theory of language

The influence of the Doctor of Hippo, St Augustine (354), has been so exceptional in philosophy that also resulted to his great theological methods. Augustine was platonic in his approach to philosophical issues. He could agree with the platonic philosophers who said :

> That the true God is at once the author of all things [...] He could believe that there are three ‚natures' or kinds of substance: bodies, mutable in time and place; souls, incorporeal but mutable in time; and God, incorporeal and immutable [...] Like Plato's Form of the Good, Augustine's God is not only the cause of things' being but the cause of our knowing them. God illumines truths as the sun illumines visible things. [115]

How Augustine was able to translate these platonic philosophy into his own theological thoughts and at the same time retaining their originality to himself, is what distinguishes him as a great theologian. To portray this point clearer, we shall now consider his reflections about language which can be found in the following books of his: De Doctrina Christiana (AD 389–426) on the interpreting the Bible, De Magistro (AD 389), a dialogue with his son Adeodatus on how and whether teaching is possible, and De Dialectical (ca AD 387), a fragmentay school book containing prolegomena to logic. Augustine's theory is that language is a system of signs. According to Christopher Kirwan, this theory leads one to attribute the following propositions to Augustine:

1) Speaking is giving signs
2) Words are signs given in speech
3) A sign is a thing employed for signifying something
4) Words are things whose sole employment is for signing

> The texts leave it unclear so far whether in a passage of speech each separate word is a separate sign; they also leave it unclear whether in the employment of words for signifying the signifying is done by the words or only through them by those who speak them. [...] In order to complete the outline statement of Augustine's theory we need now to ask what kinds of thing words signify. Augustine gives divergent answers. On the one hand, his general remarks about signs in the passage already quoted from De Doctrina Christiana suggest that words will regularly signify external objects [...] and this is confirmed in a later passage of

---

[115] Honderich ,Ted, (ed.), The Oxford Companion to Philosophy, second edition, New York 2005, 66.

the De Magistro (4.8) when we learn that the nouns (nomina), Romulus, 'Roma' and 'Virtus' signify respectively Romulus, Rome and Virtue. On the other hand we have already found Augustine asserting that a speaker may give a sign of his will (Mag. 1.2) [...] This rival suggestion that words signify thoughts and wills, not external objects, is a natural corollary of the view that thoughts are conveyed by words.[116]

Thus Augustine's account in Deo Doctrina Christiana seems to commit him to the view that all given signs are, or at least are meant as, evidence; and since by saying that all words are given signs, he is committed to the view that all verbal signs are, or at least are meant as evidence. Augustine, however, quickly concludes that it is not a route to knowledge at all, but can be significative of things. Saint Augustine's theology must be seen within the broader, and in some ways loftier context of wisdom. In his theology of the sacraments, he has wisely translated his theory of language as a system of signs, thereby converting the platonic "Substance and Accident", into "Word and Element". Augustine says that the visible sacrifice is the sacrament, that is a sacred sign of the invisible sacrifice. He defines sign as a thing that in addition to the appearance it imprints on our senses of itself makes something else come into our thoughts. Saint Augustine distinguished between natural sign and sign contained in the Scriptures. He, in showing how a sacrament comes into being, established a principle that is derived from baptismal practice, that the word comes to the element and the sacrament comes into being. And so the element is this matter or this natural sign such as water in Baptism, or bread and wine in the Eucharist. And the verbum, the word, has been generally interpreted to mean the words or formular used by the minister. John Hospers has a similar view with Augustine in interpreting words as a system of signs, but unlike Augustine, he calls them conventional signs:

A word is only a sign. But it isn't a natural sign, the way a twister in the sky is the sign of a tornado or falling barometric pressure is the sign of an approaching storm. These signs occur in nature, and human beings had to discover what they are and act accordingly.We could not turn them around or change them, since they are not man–made.But words, like the notes on a musical staff, are conventional signs: This word stands for this class of things, this note on the staff stands for this class of sound pitches. In natural signs, A signifies B regardless of what human beings believe or decide; in conventional signs, human beings decide which A's will be used to stand for which B's [...] however not all words are the names of classes of things (no-uns) or even classes of actions (Verbs) or classes of qualities (adjectives). Every word in a language has some job to do, but no two of them have exactly the same job or even the the same kind of job. Words are like tools in a tool kit. Just as each tool is used to do a different job–you don't do with a hammer in the same thing you do witha wrench–so different kinds of words perform different tasks [...] To know the meaning of a word is to knowwhat kind of job it does, what its function is in the language.[117]

Again, Augustine was aware that there are different kinds of words even as he talked of inner word and the role of an inner word in human communication through language. Inner word in the sense that God's word is his deed. God effects his will by speaking it, for example, "Let there be Light" (Gen 1,3). Since God is not corporeal,

---

116 Kirwan, Collins, Augustine, London and New York 1989, 36–39.
117 Hospers, John, An introduction to philosophical analysis, fourth edition, London 1997, 12.

his words are not vocal. This is what Augustine, therefore, referred to as inner word. God uses no particular language like Latin or Greek or Hebrew, but speaks to man internally, and man in turn hears this internally spoken words of God and acts accordingly. So, St Augustine maintains that sacrament is a sign, a sacred sign since it is divinely instituted by Jesus Christ himself and not by any man. It is a sacred sign of the invisible sacrifice. It is compared to a hidden treasure since the sanctity it offers is appreciated with the eyes of faith. This sanctity can, therefore, be referred to as a sacred secret. It belongs to human nature to obtain knowledge of the suprasensible through the sensible. In this case, the use of the outward sign leads to the knowledge of the inward grace. St Augustine in explaining further what he meant by outward sign introduced the concepts "word" and "element". Thus, these concepts become synonymous with outward sign. According to him, when "word" acts on "element", a sacrament is realized. What St Augustine earlier had referred to as "verbal sign" is what he means when he talks of "word" in his sacramental theology, and as John M. Rist would put it: "Augustine's account of verbal signs is an account of the nature and information-value of words and sets of words used by a verbalizing agent".[118]

In his sacramental theology, Augustine teaches the important place of divine illumination so that the words will achieve the desired effect on the hearers.Therefore: "The christian doctrine that the Eucharist is his (the Lord's) body is, therefore, in this life, only to be believed (by faith), not known".[119] St Augustine insists that this belief must not be unreasonable for we owe to reason what we believe by faith. Faith, therefore, must be reasonable and must be followed with reason. The influence of St Augustine's thought remained strong in the medieval period so much so that: "In particular, Aquinas was careful to remain within the guidelines he (Augustine) laid down for the correct appropriation of pagan philosophy by christian thinkers".[120] The thoughts of St Augustine reflect in the teachings of leading Christian medieval thinkers that included St Thomas Aquinas. He became a standard by which these thinkers modelled their teachings, as well as the yard-stick of measuring the veracity of those teachings. St Anselm's 'a priori', for example, and its consequent ‚ratio Anselmi' have their origin in St Augustine's divine illumination and the acceptance of which is based on reason. St Augustine teaches that sacraments have always existed since the creation of the human race, hidden in the Scriptures, proclaimed by angels and prophets, and eventually instituted by Christ himself:

> The mystery of eternal life was, though signs and symbols, proclaimed by the angels from the beginning of the human race to those who were intended to know it [...] The same race has subsequently been scattered among the nations,in order to bear witness to the Scriptures in which the eternal salvation which was to come through Christ was foretold.[121]

The institution of the sacraments carries along with it the establishment of worship-pattern, the ministerial office, the sense of sacred places and the observance of feast-

---

118 Rist, John, Augustine: Ancient Thought Baptized, Cambridge 1994, 30.
119 Rist, Augustine: Ancient Thought Baptized, 32.
120 Stump, Eleonore (ed.), The Cambridge Companion To Augustine, Cambridge 2001, 257.
121 Dyson, Henry (ed.), Augustine: The City Of God Against The Pagans, Cambridge 1998, 307.

days. Sacrament by its uniting force is necessary for man's salvation. This necessity is based on the fact that man attains the supernatural knowledge through natural realities. Again, all men have sinned and are in short of God's glory because of the corporeal weakness. It is necessary that man rises to glory by corporeal assistance (Rm 5,18). So material things aid man whose nature it is to be dependent on them.

2.9.2 Odo Casel's treatise on cultic mystery

Odo Casel did not limit himself to the material and formal components of the sacraments, rather he made an expansion to include the liturgical dimension. He considered sacrament from the cultic perspective, and insisted that one understands fully the meaning of the sacraments by experiencing the rites. He laid much emphasis on the sacraments of the Holy Eucharist and Baptism to prove his point. Borrowing a leaf from the Greek church fathers of the early fifth century A.D., he acknowledged that both the Holy Eucharist and Baptism are mysterial celebrations. He, therefore, proposed a tri-partite nature of the mysterial celebrations: Easter mystery, cultic mystery and mystery of the participant. Easter mystery revolves around Christ himself: his passion, death and resurrection for the salvation of mankind. The cultic mystery is the celebration or re-enactment of the Easter mystery in the liturgical form. In the mystery of the participant, the faithful proclaim this great mystery by uniting themselves with this mystery that is being celebrated. In return, they receive the necessary graces that it offers.

Odo Casel maintained that myth, symbol and drama are central in sacramental celebrations. He likened liturgical celebrations as celebrations of a myth that continues to live in the present and experienced in the cultic rites. He presents a close relationship that exists between myth and symbol in which myth is considered as cultic symbol which expresses the reality of the saving mystery celebrated in what may seem as dramatic. I must emphasize that Odo Casel's treatise on myth, symbol and drama in the liturgical celebration has a very big concern for the church in Africa, especially, Igboland. Liturgy, as we know, should take into account, the culture of the celebrating community, thereby making use of the local symbols of this community, and dramatizing this salvific history in the way that it becomes comprehensible for the local faithful. This can only be achieved when the liturgical words, gestures and other expressions are translated in such a way that they motivate the worshipping community and make the worship not only comprehensible but also lively. It is only in this way that the gospel message can be meaningful to the Igbo whose religious experience is in dramatic form, and who express what is being celebrated in a symbolic gesture , and with appropriate words and expressions. Vatican II truly understands this need in its quest for what it calls active participation of the faithful in liturgical celebrations (Cf. SC 26). The only way to make an Igboman to actively participate in the liturgical celebrations is to make the celebrations truly Igbo by endowing them with the Igbo spirit, that is, allowing the Igbo spirit with its symbolisms, rites and expressions to prevail within the recommendations of the church's magisterium. Actualization of this condition is not only a fulfilment of the liturgical propositions of Odo Casel but the fulfilment of the spirit of Vatican II as well.

2.9.3 Dietrich Bonhoeffer's treatise on ecclesiology

Dietrich Bonhoeffer considers Karl Barth's theology as revelational positivism. Instead, he chooses the dialectical method in presenting his own theology. His theology of ecclesiology presents sacrament as synonymous with church as the body of Christ in which Christ occupies the central place between God and mankind just as he occupies the central place in each sacrament. He insists that any meaningful discussion on Christ must be within the context of the church, a place where Christ is revealed, loved and worshipped. Dietrich Bonhoeffer teaches that Christ is the church and in the church in two capacities: as and in the sacrament, and as and in the word. Christ's presence in the church is experienced on the ground of "pro me" (being for me). This means Christ's total commitment to mankind as his creator and his redeemer. Christ, therefore, is the mediator between God and man. His treatise on ecclesiology presents the word (proclamation) and the sacraments as acting inseparably whereby Christ the word is as well Christ the sacrament. Christ the word is by the sacramental preaching God's spoken word. Thus, Christ is the sacrament that speaks: "Das Wort Gottes ist für die Reformatoren das höchste Kriterium und besitzt höchste Priorität".[122] In elevating the word to the central position, Dietrich Bonhoeffer teaches that it is the word that binds the faithful together: "Die Gemeinde, die durch ein Wort verbunden ist, hört dies Wort, immer wieder versammelt".[123] Again, in refering to the word, Dietrich makes no difference between written word of the Holy Scriptures and the word as it is preached at the holy gathering of Christ's faithful: "Konkret ist Wort in der Gemeinde vorhanden als Schrift- und Predigtwort".[124] Dietrich Bonhoeffer maintains the stand that it is in the assembly of the faithful "sanctorum communion" that the effectiveness of the word is experienced. It is the gathered faithful that provides the occasion for the preaching and hearing the word. The word preached and heard brings renewal in the hearts of the faithful for the word is not a repetition of what is known, rather it comes with a new lesson as often as it is preached.

In his Christology, Dietrich Bonhoeffer teaches that the Holy Spirit has its original interpretation in word: "Geist ist ursprünglich Wort und Sprache und nicht Kraft, Gefühl und Tat".[125] It is only as word has the spirit the power to create (Jn 1,3). On the relationship between word and sacrament, Dietrich has a similar view to that

---

122 Klöckner, Sakrament im Wort, 52.
123 Bonhoeffer, Dietrich, Sanctorum Communio: Eine dogmatische Untersuchung zur Soziologie der Kirche, Dritte erweiterte Auflage mit Register, München 1960, 170.
124 Bonhoeffer, Sanctorum Communio, 175.
125 Bonhoeffer, Dietrich, Christologie, mit einem Nachwort von Eberhard Bethge und Otto Dudzus, München 1981, 27.

of Karl Barth: "Das Sakrament ist Wort Gottes, denn es ist Verkündigung des Evangeliums".[126] This means that the sacrament is at the service of the word. Christ is both in the sacrament as well as the sacrament itself. By the institution of the sacraments, he mediates between God and man. Christ as the sacrament and in the sacrament implies also that Christ is the word and in the word. Christ as the word refers to the second person of the Trinity as the son of God in which the incarnate word is the center of our salvific history. So, Dietrich Bonhoeffer argues that Christ exists in three forms: Christ as and in the sacrament, Christ as and in the word, and Christ as and in the church. It is nevertheless important to clarify that Dietrich Bonhoeffer's treatise on church led him towards a turning point in which he proposed a "religionless Christianity". In this proposal, Christ transcends above the church and becomes not only Christ "for me" but "for others". In this sense, Christ is not only limited to Christianity or Christian religion, but indeed, to the world in general as the Lord of the world. So, the world is not left on its own but under the mediating influence of Christ. This makes the church not to be a closed society but open to the world as a church "for others".

2.9.4 Thomas Cranmer's Book of common prayer

In dialogue with other reformers like Zwingli or Calvin, Thomas Cranmer developed his own independent theology of the sacraments. His theology of the sacraments is liturgy oriented and although his thought was independent its liturgical nature is not outside the Anglican tradition because:

> This emphasis on liturgical experience offers us a key to a significant aspect of the Anglican understanding of the gospel, namely, the importance of our experience of God's present action as the way in which God's work in Christ touches and is effective in successive generations of believers.[127]

It is in liturgy that the Anglican is able to express the faith which the gospel has offered. The liturgy, therefore: "celebrates the faith. It lifts up through words and signs in a corporate experience which expresses the faith which has summoned the people together".[128] In order words: "what is prayed is, as the adage affirms, what is believed". [129] The importance of Thomas Cranmer's Book of Common Prayer to our topic is to show how words in liturgical celebrations perform by nourishing the faith, energizing it and thereby transforming people into a community of believers with common faith experience. This means: "Our language of corporate prayer-both word and action-is expressive of our experience of God".[130] For example, in trying to impact on the people the belief in paschal mystery which is Christ's victory over

---

126 Bonhoeffer, Christologie, mit einem Nachwort, 31.
127 Sykes, Stephen, editor, The Study of Anglicanism, Revised Edition, Minneapolis 1988,58.
128 Sykes, The Study of Anglicanism, 59.
129 Sykes, The Study of Anglicanism, 65.
130 Sykes, The Study of Anglicanism, 60.

death and our share in this victory, Thomas Cranmer could not make this message in no better way to perform than to formulate it in his Book of Common Prayer and to be recited or sung as an anthem for use on Easter Day. So, we may be right to say that Thomas Cranmer adhered to the Pauline injunction that faith comes through hearing. Therefore, in order to create this faith among Anglicans, Thomas Cranmer resorted to making the written words of prayer to be beautifully constructed and meditatively recited or sung in such a way that they lead one to expressing this faith that one has received in the gospel. The performance of Thomas Cranmer's Book of Common Prayer is obvious in its ability to connect one to God in prayer and make him totally consumed in this divine interaction, in its vitality in the prayer life of the Anglicans, in its ability to liturgize its prayers, and in its ability to make the Anglican liturgy formidable. To put the above points clearer Louis Weil writes:

> It is in this perspective that we see why the Book of Common Prayer has played so fundamental a role [...] The Prayer Book is first of all the basis for corporate prayer [...] In addition to this essential role, and as a kind of natural overflow from it, the Prayer Book is also a formative element in the private prayer of Anglicans.Even in solitude, the use of collects or psalms, or the texts of the various rites, link the individual Anglican at prayer with the common prayer of the larger fellowship. Again, the Prayer Book is also turned to as a source for the teaching of the Church.[131]

The "Book of Common Prayer" was the official liturgical book in Anglican Communion following the break with Rome. Describing the 'Book of Common Prayer' Peter Neuner writes: "Dies war eine Zusammenfassung von Meßbuch,Rituale für die Sakramentenspendung und Brevier zum Gebrauch des Volkes".[132] It contained structured words for prayers and liturgical worship. It equally outlined various forms of daily prayers for morning and evening times. The popularity of this "Book of Common Prayer" is also due to the fact that it offered guidelines for Sunday worship, celebration of the Holy Communion, Baptism, Confirmation, Matrimony, Anointing of the sick, Holy Orders and Confession of sins. It included list of the litany, and organized various readings from the Old and new Testaments for Sunday liturgical services, as well as, for the daily prayers. In-between these readings are set of psalms and canticles that were to be melodiously sung in the atmosphere of worship and prayers. The "Book of Common Prayer" was later revised and edited in 1552 under the same Thomas Cranmer. In 1559, a new version of the book that was enriched by the combined elements of 1549 and 1552 versions came to be published and promulgated for use in the church. This approved version was again revised in 1662 and has survived the test of time until recently in this 21st century when the book "Common Worship" surfaced to replace the "Book of Common Prayer" in most of the churches of Anglican Communion. The extent the "Book of Common Prayer" has been widely acknowledged in the Anglican Communion is testified to by its introduction and use in over 50 countries of the world, and translated in over 150 different languages, and the reasons are very clear:

---

131 Sykes, The Study of Anglicanism, 60.
132 Neuner, Peter, Kleines Handbuch der Ökumene, Düsseldorf 1984, 60.

> Within Anglicanism the Prayer Book is a living expression of the profound union between what we believe and what we pray; a doctrinal document, not because it may contain such didactic materials as a catechism, or historical materials of doctrinal significance, but because it is in corporate worship that Anglicans find the common ground for their profession of faith.[133]

Its influence is not only limited to the Anglican Communion but also outside of it. The traditional Lutherans, Methodists and Presbyterians have borrowed a lot from the "Book of Common Prayer" to enrich their own prayer books.

Although, afterwards, many forms of prayer books and rituals for liturgical services followed suit, one must acknowledge that it was the contributions of Thomas Cranmer, the contributions that gave birth to the "Book of Common Prayer", that led to the publications of subsequent prayer books of worship. His theology of the sacraments that is founded in liturgy served as the background of his numerous contributions in the areas of prayers and worship. For him, therefore, sacraments cannot be comprehended outside liturgy. He insisted that it is in the liturgy that one experiences the sacraments, and therein are the sacraments celebrated.

2.10 Conclusion

Chapter two has proceeded to examine the relationship of J.L.Austin's concept of performative word to sacramental theology. This is an attempt to show if the teachings of J.L.Austin on performative word can successfully be translated within the context of sacramental theology. In other words, it is considered as an effort towards giving a theological interpretation to our key concept-performative word. The astride nature of such a contextual reflection has indeed exposed the intimate relationship between word and sacrament. This chapter testifies to the teaching of the church's magisterium that it is the action of the word that constitutes the sacrament. This means, the words employed in the celebration of the sacraments are efficacious, and therefore, performative. There is an irreversible and dynamic relationship between word and sacrament. For eample, in the sacrament of the eucharist, the words of consecration of bread and wine: "This is my body ... This is my blood ...", changes the bread and wine into the body and blood of Jesus Christ through a process known as transsubstantiation. Likewise, the words of absolution over the penitent at the celebration of the sacrament of penance forgive sins. Besides, the sacred scriptures testify to the performance of word (Gen1,1–25;1Kg18,30–39;2Kg2,23–25;Ps29,4–9;33,6–9;Jn4,49–53;11,17–27;Lk8,54;Mk2,5;Rm10,17). The church in its teachings has developed strong doctrines to emphasize the efficacy of the word in every sacramental celebrations. This chapter presents the doctrines of incarnation and inspiration as typical examples where the efficacy of word is incontestable. Concerning the doctrine of incarnation, it is the Mary's verbal acceptance of the divine message about being the mother of Jesus Christ that constitutes the conception of Jesus in her womb (Lk

---

133 Sykes, The Study of Anglicanism, 67.

1,38; Jn 1,14). Jesus Christ who in the womb of the Blessed Virgin Mary took flesh became the incarnated Word of God. This means, when we talk about the Word of God, we are not primarily talking about the words of a book, but about a person, Jesus Christ. The doctrine of inspiration explains that the word is efficacious and is able to act on the elements to bring about sacrament because it is inspired (2Pt 1,20–21; Ps 33,6). In compliance with our key concept, eminent theologians across different Christian affiliations have devoted most of their teachings on defending the efficacy of the word in sacramental celebrations, namely: St Augustine's theory of language, Odo Casel's treatise on cultic mystery, Dietriech Bonhoeffer's treatise on ecclesiology and Thomas Cranmer's Book of Common Prayer.

This chapter insists that explicit performative word is the only form of performative word that can be associated with sacramental theology because sacramental words cannot be said to be doubtful which is the case with implicit performative word. Again, the same criteria in J.L.Austin's concept of performative word regulate the efficacy of the sacramental word. Performative identities, performative theater and performative symbols are various references to J.L.Austin's concept of performative word that are reflected in sacramental theology. So, the efficacy of the word in sacramental celebrations can neither be ignored nor denied. Although word and sacrament are two different concepts, our discussion has proved that they are closely related because it is the actions of the word that bring about sacrament. This is a proof that the J.L.Austin's performative word is of an interest to sacramental theology because in the act of uttering certain sacred words or in uttering certain sacred words or by uttering certaing sacred words at the sacramental celebrations, the minister actualizes certain sacraments. Should it also be said that J.L.Austin's concept of performative word is of interest to Igbo traditional religion? Can we in any way relate the teachings of J.L.Austin about performative word to the actions of the ritual words in the celebration of Igbo religious rites and rituals? This is exactly what the next chapter, chapter three, will be discussing.

3 PERFORMATIVE WORD AND IGBO TRADITIONAL RELIGION

3.1 Introduction

The previous chapter has clarified how the J.L.Austin's performative word is related to the celebration of the church's sacraments. Our discussion in this chapter shall be focused on whether the same J.L.Austin's performative word is also of interest to Igbo traditional religion. Suffix it to mean that the Igbo words are efficacious, to what extent can we associate them with the J.L.Austin's treatise on performative word? To begin this investigation it will be necessary to understand what the word Igbo means, who the Igbo people are, and the nature and content of their religion. Then, we shall go further to discuss the formation and interpretation of Igbo language; the concept of performative word in Igbo traditional religion; the explicit and implicit forms of performative word in Igbo traditional religion; the criteria for performative word in Igbo traditional religion; agents of performative word in Igbo traditional religion; performative word and the celebration of various rites in Igbo traditional religion. We shall conclude this chapter by studying how performative word functions in Igbo folktales, Igbo traditional songs and Igbo proverbs.

3.2 What is Igbo?

The terms "Igbo" and "Ibo", says Achebe O.P: "are spelling variation of the same word. The western influenced writers prefer Ibo which offers them a simpler pronounciation but the natives use Igbo which is the original and correct word".[134] Experts are not yet certain about the original meaning of the word "Igbo". For Uchendu V.C:

> Igbo is used in three senses today to refer to Igbo territory, to the domestic speakers of the language, and to the language spoken by them. According to Greenberg's classification of African languages, the Igbo language is one of the speech communities in the kwe sub-family of the Niger-Congo family.[135]

The origin and meaning of the word "Igbo" certainly did not originally refer to the whole Igbo tribe as we know it today, for before the arrival of Europeans about a hundred years ago, there was no common name for the whole tribe, but each town or village had its particular name often taken from an ancestor. Such derivations as these have been suggested: man of the bush, forest–dwellers, or probably an abbreviation

---
134 Achebe, Okey Patrick, The Social – Religious significance of the Igbo prenatal, natal and puberty rates. Unpublished doctoral thesis in theology, Innsbruck 1972, 1.
135 Uchendu, Victor, The Igbo of Southeast Nigeria, New York 1965, 1.

of the longer name connected with an ancestor long since forgotten. Following the understanding of the natives themselves, we consider the term "Igbo" in contradistinction to "Olu" – the peoples of the river. The word "Olu" today connotes people that live by the water, and is probably derived from "Oluluelu" (it is rich harvest) and would easily connote people, who without much labour, obtain rich products in both this fertile land and water. Conventionally, "Olu" connotes people who are lax and lazy. Igbo or "Onye Igbo" would also denote "Onye ugbo aniocha" (a farmer on white soil), thus indicating a person who spends all his life toiling in his farm (Ugbo) year in, year out without, however, any prosperous results. "Olu na Igbo" denoted an entire humanity, and this is verifiable from some Igbo philosophical names given to children: Onwululigbo (death touches all Igbo, that is, death is universal) and Odezuligbo (universal fame). It means therefore, universal mankind or humanity. Having established the origin and the meaning of the name "Igbo", it is necessary to know who the Igbo people are.

3.3 Who are the Igbo people?

The Igbos are West African Negros located in South – Eastern Nigeria, and according to Uchendu V.C Igboland lies between:

> latitude 5 to 7 degrees North and longitude 6 to 8 degrees East, and they occupy an area of some 15,800 square miles. Before it enters the Atlantic Ocean through a network of distributaries which characterize its delta, the Niger River divides the Igbo country into two unequal parts. The greater Portion lies in what is now called the Eastern Region of Nigeria. While a Smaller triangular portion, is [...] the Midwestern Region.[136]

The Western Igbo are territorially marked off from the Bini and Warri, their non-Igbo neighbours. On the left bank of the Niger, the Eastern Igbo stretch from the Niger Delta, where the Ijaw and Ogoni are their southern neighbours, to the North, where the Igala and the Tiv mark the boundary. On the eastern boundary are the Yako and the Ibibio. Though separated by the Niger and thus falling into two separate political units, the Western and Eastern Igbo have retained their cultural as well as their psychic unity. According to Nigeria's census of 1963, the Igbo speaking people numbered ten million.[137] A current census will put the figure above twenty five million. This population is very unevenly distributed, the bulk of it concentrates in a geographical axis formed by Onitsha, Orlu, Okigwe and Mbaise areas. Along the Onitsha–Mbaise axis the density of population exceeds 1,000 per square mile in many places. The Igbo country is characterized by a wide variety of physical features. Dense forests cover the delta, but a great part of Owerri province as well as the part of Igboland west of Ogoja are mainly grassland with scattered forests

---

136 Uchendu, The Igbo of Southeast Nigeria, 1.
137 This figure is quoted from Eastern Nigerian population census of 1963. The Mid–Western Igbos numbered 1 million, while the Igbos of the then Eastern provinces numbered 9 million.

especially along the rivers. The chief river is the Niger. The other three main waterways comprise the Anambra, the Cross River (which does not flow through most South-eastern Igbo regions, though it helps to drain the Afikpo and Igbo areas) and the Imo. The land is low – lying except in the Awgu–Udi–Nsukka line. According to Arinze F. A, "Awgu is 1,287 feet, Enugu 1,715, and Nsukka 1,315 feet above see level".[138] Igboland has a tropical climate. The rainy and dry seasons are well marked. The rainy season is from April to November with a break in August. The rainfall varies from about 105 inches in the south to 60 inches in the north. The dry season on the other hand is from December to March with "Harmattan" (extreme dry wheather) in December and part of January. The origin of the Igbos is a subject of much speculation. According to G.C. Ikeobi: "Ethnologists have not agreed on the precise origin of the Igbo people".[139]

Some of these ethnologists have advanced the view that the Igbo people have no common tradition of origin. Strikingly enough, as professor Forde remarked, they themselves "[...] have got no general or elaborated traditions of origin or migration".[140] Floyd Barry, commenting on this particular point thus expressed the difficulty: "It is a well high impossible task to trace the history of the Ibo or the origin of their homenclature".[141] The local traditions the Igbo have do not provide clues to their origin. It is for this reason that some western authors on the colonial era treated the Igbos as "a people without history".[142] This view has evoked much criticism from people who have since come to know better. The critics argue that: "A people with a culture are a people with some form of history.The Igbo have a culture; they have also a history–an unwritten history which it is the task of the culture historian to piece together".[143] This view of an ancient origin and independent development finds its backing in the recent archaeological evidences of professor T. Shaw of the Institute of African studies, university of Ibadan-Nigeria; Professor Hartle of the university of Nigeria; and the Igbo anthropologist Dr. Onwuejeogwu. Taking their findings in order between 1959 and 1960, professor Shaw made several excavations in Igboukwu, a village group near Nri in Awka division. The Igboukwu bronze objects now in Nigeria Museum belong to the Nri complex. They have been dated A.D. 1,000 years ago. At the same time, excavated collections of Professor Hartle of the university of Nigeria's department of Archaeology, are in the Museum of the university. They were got from the site survey he did at Bende, Afikpo, Okigwe, Awka and Nsukka. It emphasized the wide distribution of Nri activities and collaborates Shaw's work. It also showed that those areas were settlement sites of some antiquity, like the Bende site which has been dated 205 A.D and its occupation con-

---

138 Arinze, Francis, Sacrifice in Igbo Religion, Ibadan 1970, 1.
139 Ikeobi, Godwin, Towards the purification of the Igbo Ozo Title in Onitsha Archdiocese, unpublished Doctoral Thesis in Theology, Rome 1970, 2.
140 Forde, Daryll and Jones, Gwilym Iwan, The Ibo and Ibibio speaking peoples of South–East Nigeria, London 1967, 11.
141 Barry, Fredrick, Eastern Nigeria, London 1969, 29.
142 Uchendu, The Igbo of Southeast Nigeria, 2.
143 Uchendu, The Igbo of Southeast Nigeria, 2.

tinues until about 50 years ago.[144] Dr Onwuejeogwu identified Shaw's and Hartle's excavated objects and collections, which he maintains, substantiate oral traditions and what people usually call folk – tales with objects now existing in Nri culture. He insists that there is a strong continuity in material between the Nri culture of antiquity and that of the contemporary time. The study of the findings of these archaeologists brings into light the fact that Igboland has been under continuous occupation for at least 3,000 years, and, as it is now being discovered, that her people developed an ancient civilisation a thousand years ago which is about half a millennium before the emergence of the kingdom of Benin.

Some authors seeing a very close resemblance between the Igbo and the Jews have insinuated that their origin might have had some link with that nation. This brings about the thought that from the presence of many ritual and cultural similarities the Igbo must have in some remote past either lived near or had very close association with the semitic races. In the light of correct reasoning, this is total phantacy, however, many trace some similaries between the Igbo and the Israelities in the rites of circumcision, marriage customs, birth rites, bloodly sacrifices, inhibitions and taboos with respect to food and drinks imposed on individuals. Both the Igbo and the Israelites have the cherished custom of respect for the aged, the observance of new moons and harvest festivals, the mourning of the dead, purification. This is the view of Innocent Okorie, the stigmatist from Owerri–Ebeiri in Imo state of Eastern Nigeria, which he holds as divinely revealed to him. Basing on the geographical data and dates from Innocent Okorie's hypothesis, Helen Chukwuma has this to say about the Igbo ancestors:

> They fled southwards through Hebron and Beersheba and arrived Cairo in 710 B.C. They soon departed Egypt and journeyed on to their present habitat where they were joined by other exiles of the Jewish province of Habatea called the Effikdonaelis or present-Day Effiks. The Igbo settlers were those exiles from Juda province called Schechenigbo, Jabborigbo is the name of their leader who led the tribe of Schechenigbo in Juda out to become a tribe in Nigeria. The name Igbo is derived from their leader Jabborigbo. The original native town of the Igbo, Scheschenigbo, is situated between Bethle-hem in the north and Hebron in the south on the road which runs through to Cairo in Egypt. Today it is a forest zone and uninhabited [...]. This migration took eighty years. They left Judah in 718 B.C. and arrived Nigeria 638 B.C.[145]

No matter how plausible this may be, it is however dangerous to conclude from cultural similarities to racial origin. Many peoples of black Africa have ritually a lot in common. In the end however, this resemblance in the cultural traits of the Jews and the Igbo could, as Basden noted: "[...] prove no more than coincidence, but it is nevertheless, an interesting subject".[146] Considering the question of Igbo identity, it seems that the Igbo are people of their own with centuries of cultural development.

---

144 Cf. Achebe, Okey Patrick , The Social-Religious significance of the Igbo prenatal, natal and puberty rates, 2.
145 Chukwuma, Helen, Igbo Oral Literature, Theory and Tradition, Abak 1994, 3.
146 Basden, George, Niger Igbos, , London 1966, 411.

Their cultural and ritual characteristics belong to them as their share of the universal cake of creation.

An analysis of demographic patterns, trait lists, and other cultural features, combined with available local traditions would throw more light on the two interrelated hypotheses of Igbo origin that there exists a core area which may be called the nuclear Igboland, and that waves of immigrant communities from the north and the west planted themselves on the border of the nuclear Igboland as early as the fourteenth or the fifteenth century. By nuclear or core Igboland is meant that the people there have no tradition of coming from any other place. This nuclear Igboland is believed to be the belt formed by Owerri, Awka, Orlu, and Okigwe divisions. It is a most densely populated area. There was an early migration from this area into the Nsukka-Udi highlands in the north and into Ikwerri, Etche, Asa and Ndokki in the south. This migration might have continued to the so-called border areas: the western Igbo, Onitsha proper, Nri and Oguta. This process was already perfected long before immigrations from the north and west of Igboland started. As a result, the first inhabitants of these border areas were originally Igbo with Igbo culture. In the course of time, a group of immigrant communities joined those Igbo original settlers, thus introducing heterogeneous culture. This was a movement that tended to homogenize Igbo culture. The main attractions for dispersion included an ever-widening frontier of the "no man's land" and the desire to found independent villages, but the most compelling reasons were the pressure of population in certain areas and natural disasters that made continued settlement in some places inauspicious. In addition to the above pattern of migration from the nuclear area, there are traditions, confirmed by intrusive culture traits, of peoples who entered Igbo territory in about the fourteenth or the fifteenth century. Of these, there are the Nri, in whom Igala influence is marked, and the Nzam and Anam, who combine Bini and Igala traits. Onitsha, Oguta, and Ezechima group of villages in western Igbo who claim affinity with Bini and have their kingship institution to show as evidence of descent. However, the fact of their Igbo originality remained unchallenged, for if all or the greater majority were originally non – Igbo how then did they come to speak still the same language (Igbo) and have the same customs and worse still forget their original language and characteristics? Even the leader of the Onitsha group had an Igbo name, Chima. Conclusively, these Ezechima people (Onitsha group) were not Bini but Igbo speaking people once under the political domination of Bini kingdom. One could also say that they were adulterated Igbo and that their so-called pride of superiority over their pure Igbo brethren could be explained by the fact of that foreign element in them. In the case of the Aro Igbo, the original Igbo mixed up with and took in certain cultural traits from their Ibibio neighbours. There is a time – honoured prevalent belief that the Igbos are descended from Nri. The reverence and precedence which is accorded to the Nri section by all the other Igbo clans proper in their vicinity is evidence in favour of this belief. Undoubtedly for centuries Nri has been the heart–centre of Igbo ritual life, but not necessarily its only origin or the beginning nor is it acceptable that a great majority of the Igbo claimed Nri town in Awka district as their ancestral home. There are no traditions of any sort in support of this. Just as we have seen from our discussion so far, in addition to Nri tradition, Igbos are believed to have also migrated from Benin, from Igala, from Ibibio. Before the emergence of Nri tradition, such ritual concepts like Chukwu (God), Igwe, Ala, Alusi, and Mmuo had always existed. This tends to confirm our view on migration. The seemingly elusive problem of Igbo identity has received a fair treatment under this topic. Amidst the speculation on the precise origin of the Igbos, it would be useful here to recall the words of an elder of Mbaise, in 1972: "we did not come from anywhere and anyone who tells you we came from anywhere is a liar. Write it down".[147]

From the above considerations, one sees that the Igbos are a people characterized by a homogeneous culture. This homogeneity in culture thus brings into sharp focus the validity of the theory of the "nuclear" Igboland, inhabited by people who have no tradition of coming from any other place. This heartland was subject to change. For as we have seen, there are traditions, confirmed by intrusive culture traits, of peoples who migrated into Igbo territory. Maintaining the validity of the theory of the "core" Igboland, the fact to bear in mind is that the Igbo heartland repeatedly built up levels of population pressure which the ecological environment was unable to sustain, and which from time to time gave rise to migrations to other parts of Igboland. In the light of these considerations it would be wrong to treat the Igbo as a people without a certain origin. As at today, there are Igbos living in every country of the world. The only place where Igbos do not live in the world is the Antarctica. In fact, if there was no global "Antarctic Treaty" prohibiting activities and mineral mining within the Antarctic region, there probably would have been some Igbos living and fishing on the ice-desert of the Antarctica today. This means, Igbos are hardworking people, deretmined and resilient.[148] Next, let us discuss their religious beliefs and practices.

---

147 Isichei, Elizabeth, A History of the Igbo people, London 1973, 3.
148 As a resilient people, Igbos are remarkable and outstanding for their resistance to injustices. This often resulted to revolts and wars. The first revolt and rebellion carried out in the Caribbean (Jamaica) by the slaves were orchestrated by a group of Igbo slaves who seized up their masters and demanded that they be given an "Ebo" king to rule over them. The first slave who seized his master's gun and shot his master in Sierra Leon as a revolt for the maltreatment he received from the master, was an Igbo. The first black man to publish a book and became the millionaire in the 18th century, was Olaudah Equino, an Igbo. The first women riot in Nigeria to protest against British oppression of the local people was orchestrated by Igbos. The Igbos are a people who fought a war in Nigeria in a quest to liberate themselves from a modern systems of governmental oppression, probably the only war in the world in which food-blockade was employed as a weapon of war against a people (the Igbos). They lost about one million people during the war. Most of their intelligent people migrated in their thousands to other parts of the world; all infrastructures within the Igboland were destroyed and an ordinary 20 pound promissory note from the Nigerian government was all they had to build from to re-establish their peoplehood once again. Igbo are the people who have suffered much in history. They suffered the loss of their brothers and sisters and relatives during the war. They have suffered the loss of their human rights and dignity within and outside their country. Inspite of this, Igbos remain the most individually and communally progressive people in Africa. (Cf. Onwu E.N., ?Z?ND? NA EZIOKWU: Towards an understanding of Igbo Traditional Religious Life and Philosophy in: 2002 Ahiajioku lecture).

3.4 Nature and Content of Igbo Traditional Religion

The Igbo traditional religion is as old as the first Igbo man.[149] This great religion is based on the experiences of the Igbo in the world and of the world. This implies that the Igboman's knowledge of God is based on what he experienced. Being observant lovers of nature and imbued with the sense of mystery and wonder, they come to have a sense of the existence of God. For an Igbo man, God simply exists. He does not worry himself into proving how God exists. Such a proof is not his priority.

The fact that he simply believes spares the Igbo traditional religion from such problems as Agnosticism, Scepticism and Atheism.[150] All these are products of doubts

---

149   Although many Igbo sons and daughters have written much about their Igbo country, none has ever paid a particular attention to the whole issue of the origin of the Igbo traditional religion. In discussing the origin of Igbo traditional religion, one observes that it is an integral part of the study on the origin of Igbo race itself. According to my source, the origin of Igbo traditional religion is closely associated with Nri town. Nri occupies a prominent position when it comes to affairs that pertain to Igbo race. Based on Nri myth ,therefore, Igbo traditional religion underwent three stages of development. The first stage is the earliest period of human existence. This is the Eri period, the age of Chukwu-when God created and dominated the earth. Here, Chukwu had fed Eri and his people directly , and Eri had intimate contact with God and worshipped him alone. It was a highly religious age. The second stage is the stage of hunting and gathering of wild edibles. This is the period Nri (the son of Eri) came into the scene. There was a shift from dependent on God for direct feeding to the dependence on human effort to feed through agriculture and iron technology. This is the time ani-earth because of its importance in agriculture became deified. This is the period that Igbo traditional religion actually began. So, one can say that Igbo religion began with the worship of ani-the earth-goddess, and the earth-goddess dominated the traditional life. The adoption of the idea of gods, spirits and deities which appear to work in controlling the Igbo world, was made at this point. There was a shift from the worship of Chukwu to the worship of created things. The worship of the earth-goddess later gave rise to the worship of other divinities such as Ibinukpabi of Arochukwu, Amadioha-god of thunder, Igwekaala of Umunoha, Agbala Awka and Oha Mmiri of Oguta. These deities were brought into their various communities and by the ministration of diviners, priests, medicine men and other ritual experts, people were able to take oaths and to make sacrifices. The third and the final stage is not pleasing for Igbo race because of the evils of slave trade. It is the era of Arochukwu oligarchy with its Ibinukpabia oracle-the famous long juju. This is the dark period in the history of Igbo race. So, we conclude that Igbo traditional religion in its earliest stage was monotheistic. Later at a stage, the loss of direct contact with Chukwu led our ancestors to focus their attention on minor spirits and deities thereby presenting Chukwu-God as "Deus Otiosus". To interpret this shift as polytheism, however, is a misrepresentation because despite the worship of these spirits and deities, the Igbo believe in the existence of one Supreme Being who is the creator.

150   Agnosticism is a proposition that the truth of certain claims whether religious beliefs or secular opinions cannot be determined, and therefore, doubtful. Although agnosticism appeared earlier in the teaching of Protagoras in 5th century B.C., Thomas Henry Huxel is acclaimed, since 1860, as the protagonist of the term. Etymologically, agnosticism is a Greek word and comprises two parts: 'a' without, and ,gnosis' knowledge. So, agnosticism is a rejection of all claims of spiritual or mystical knowledge. Scepticism is synonymous with doubt. It has the attitude of rejecting proposition or claim that lacks evidence. A sceptic subjects any claim to a systematic investigation in order to ascertain its authenticity. Atheism is a rejection of the

and negation of the human mind about God's existence. The Igbo belief in the existence of the Supreme Being explains itself in such names as "Chukwudi"-God exists. The existence, nature and attributes of God-Chukwu are freely admitted. Igbos had already believed and worshipped the Chukwu – Supreme Being prior to the advent of christianity. The reason for this is not far fetched. According to Anderson, J.F: "a spontaneous knowledge of God is common to all men including Pagans".[151] Since the origin of the world, no people have been found to have no religion, and not to have manifested a belief in the existence of God which is an innate idea. Igbos do not have a systematic doctrine on the origin of the Supreme Being, but they do have stories which tell of the beginnings of things. However, having these in Igbo religion is one thing, and systematising them into doctrines is quite another thing. Before this could successfully be done, basic theological questions bothering on God, Creation and Man must be addressed from different disciplines in order to discover and use the authentic Igbo conceptions about them. That the Igbo venerate certain objects like hills, mountains, thick forests, big trees, rivers, rocks, deserts and wild animals confirms his close relationship with nature, and that God exists as a Supreme Being who created all these objects. Through nature the Igbo approach God who alone is the creator and source of life–Chukwu Onye Okike. So an Igbo man does not attribute life to these objects, but that he receives life from God-Chukwu Onye Okike through these objects as divine media. So by venerating these media-the objects, the Igbo assert that the existence of such creatures implies the existence of a creator. Igbo traditional religion form the vital root of Igbo culture. It is the determining principle of Igbo life. The Igbo affirmation of the existence of a Creator God through the observation of nature is not only a religious act, but essentially philosophical. It is philosophical in that it is by wondering about nature and order of the existing objects that the Igbo arrive at the conclusion of a creator–the Supreme Being. The act of wonder, as we know, arising from the exercise of the human intellect, is an essential function of philosophy. Thus, Igbo religion and Igbo philosophy of life compliment each other. The Igbo philosophy of life, however, does not go into rationalization about God. This does not mean that the Igbo are not rational beings.

    It is pertinent to establish that the Igbo people are born religious. The Igbo deify time and space, objects and persons. According to the Igbo belief everybody is born with his or her personal chi-personal god or protective spirit. Igbo traditional religion is an element that is at the basis of the culture itself, and therefore, necessary for African christian theology. The spiritual system of the Igbo people is one of the oldest on earth. The roots of Igbo spirituality is the same as the roots of every other African one. Igbo spirituality predates Islam, Christianity, Judaism, and every other–ism that one can think of. If there are any similarities between the traditional practices of the Igbo and those of other religions, it is because they were borrowed from our ancestors, and not the other way round. It is pertinent here to mention that in Igbo tradi-

---

    existence of God. Etymologically, it is from the Greek ‚atheos' meaning "without gods". There are strong and weak atheism, practical and theoretical atheism.
151 Anderson, Stephen, Natural Theology, Bruce 1961, 14.

tional society there were no atheists. This is because religion in the indigenous Igbo culture was not an independent institution. It is an integral and inseparable part of the entire culture. Religion for an Igbo man was practical in the sense that one's entire action is reflective of one's religious concepts and practices as is seen in the ordering of society – social morality is dependent on religion. Contributing to this very discourse, Sigo John writing on Igbo in the wider sense of an African community says:

> In Africa, religion involves the whole of the African personality. This includes his emotional, economic, social, intellectual and spiritual integrity. Thus, Professor John Mbiti confirms: "wherever the African is, there is his religion; he carries it to the field where he is sowing the seeds or harvesting a new crop:he takes it with him to the beer party or to attend funeral ceremonies and if he is a student, he takes religion with him to the examination room, at school or in the university and, if he is a politician, he takes it to the House of Parliament". Religion gives the African the way to understand the world. It supplies the answer to many problems and questions that face him in this world. These questions may include who made you? Why am I here on earth? Where am I going? Though their answers may not be correct, they give the African a satisfactory reason to go through life. These religious answers equip Africans emotionally, culturally and intellectually to go through life effectively and face with maturity many of life experiences and vicissitudes. [...] Again, religion pays attention to key moments in the life of an individual. In Africa, these key moments include birth, initiation and puberty period, marriage and death. Thus, religion recognises the place of the individual in the society and thus it is through religion that the society celebrates these individual's key moments of life. Religion makes people celebrate life. In Africa people don't just sit down to meditate upon life. They put life into real action .Thus they dance life, sing life, ritualise life, drum life, shout life, celebrate life both for the individual and the community. For instance during naming ceremonies, the Yoruba will close main roads and declare surplus like very wealthy people. Similarly, the Maguzawa (Hausa) people of Katsina State may borrow to eat but make their son's marriage a memorable celebration. [152]

It is therefore wrong to say that the white man brought religion to Igboland. Instead, that the white man brought christianity to Igboland is a better way to put it. This follows from the very fact that our forefathers from the on–set had the correct understanding of the cosmos as an endless space of both visible and invisible realities. They not only believed in these realities but also lived it out. The much reverence and awe with which they approached divinities was a testimony that their belief sums up their life, their entire existence. So, they had practised religion before the advent of christianity.

The moral norms associated with Igbo traditional religion are greatly observed, not merely as a fulfilment, but with devotion and conviction. An Igbo man believes that every wrong he does must be rewarded with corresponding punishment, likewise his good deeds receive befitting blessings. The most important thing to note is that these punishments or blessings are instant and not delayed. It is believed that the offender does not need a witness before his evil deeds are brought to open. Instead, he is pushed by the divine force to publicly confess the very evil he committed. This is the frightening thing about it. Sometimes, this confessions come when the offender is already struck by a mysterious illness, and needs to confess as a remedy to his illness.

---

152 Sigo, John, Sharia : Blessing in Disguise, Enugu 2001, 70–73.

So the fear of these divinities already in every Igbo man helped to appreciate the Christian message about the fear of God. But Igbos had already formed community of believers before being turned into community of church–members. For this reason, subjecting Igbos to a religionless group before the arrival of the early missionaries is a misconception. Instead, the missionaries brought a new religion that aimed at replacing the already existing Igbo tradition religion through conversion. In Igboland, people acknowledge the existence of God and approach him by the worship of the lesser gods. However, when the worship of this Supreme Being is clouded with much attention to these lesser gods it creates the impression that Igbo traditional religion is polytheistic. To subject Igbo traditional religion to polytheism may be a wrong judgement. Instead, I prefer to address Igbo traditional religion as monotheism. A pantheon of forces or a large number of spirits or ancestors or some kind of divinities stand between human beings and the Supreme Being. Igbo traditional religion believes in the Supreme Being, and believes that this Supreme Being reveals himself in nature. This differs from the Christian religion which maintains that God reveals himself in his son Jesus Christ. There is this impression, however, that Igbo acknowledge the most exalted position of the Supreme Being but only revere him as a result of his transcendent nature. The Igbo instead worship the deities whose concrete existence they feel. In the words of Ogbalu F.C:

> It can be said with a little reservation that while they revered his (the Supreme Being) transcendence, immanence, omnipotence, invisibility, omniscience, justice and immortality, they do not worship Him.What the Ibos worship and offer sacrifices are idols and gods.[153]

This may explain the reason why there is no shrine dedicated to the Supreme Being in Igbo traditional religion although there are numerous shrines for various deities. The reason for worship in Igbo traditional religion is not mainly for salvation as in Christian religion, but: "A means of honouring spiritual beings or an act of veneration paid by man to such spiritual beings".[154] The worship aims towards gaining favours, thanksgiving, warding off a disaster and protection. It takes form of offerings, sacrifices, observance of certain customs and participation in certain ceremonies. The worship of this Supreme Being in Igbo religion is devoid of temples. Instead, there are shrines which serve as a place for offering sacrifices. These shrines are normally situated at the outskirts and corners of villages, and are constructed with stones and wood. There are two types of worship in Igbo traditional religion: private worship and public worship.

Private worship refers to the sacrifice the head of any family offers before the Ihu Ndiichie–family ancestral shrine for the welfare of the house hold. In other words it is: "Offered by a single person in a house or shrine".[155] The family ancestral shrine is usually located in the family Obi-Family reception hall or better still "common hall".[156] This reception hall is situated at a very conspicuous location, usually infront

---

153 Ogbalu, Felix, Igbo Institutions and Customs, Onitsha 1992, 61.
154 Awolalu, Joseph, Yoruba Beliefs and Sacrificial Rites, London 1979, 97.
155 Awolalu, Yoruba Beliefs and Sacrificial Rites, 99.
156 Lieber, Joachim, Ibo village communities, Ibadan 1971, 34.

of the family house, facing directly the main entrance, confronting whoever enters the compound from the main entrance. It is in this Obi that one sees the Ihu Ndiichie- the ancestral shrine which is located at a specific corner of the Obi, and is made of many wooden carved images representing the family ancestors. It is beautifully arranged and approached with solemn reverence. This family ancestral shrine may be translated into what christian church refers to as "altar of the saints". The revered ancestors are also seen as the custodian of the Igbo tradition and its stability. The following conditions are, therefore, necessary for a dead person to be member of the ancestral cult: he must attain a good ripe–old age; he must have been without blemish; he must be given a proper and befitting burial ceremony; he must be declared as having died honourably by the society; his good deeds must be declared by Ikoro.[157] The Igbos maintain that someone who dies out of malpractices or who committed suicide or murder should not be considered an ancestor, and therefore, deprived of any befitting burial rite.

It is correct to say that a typical Igbo family comprises of the living and the dead. Igbos belief in ancestors is related to its doctrine of life after death. Ancestor veneration is appreciated in terms of communion and communication. Ancestors are patrons of their descendants and their various clans and communities, and work closely with Ala–Earth goddess in protecting their lineage from such harms as draught, sickness, war, and so on. Despite their usefulness, one must understand it correctly that ancestors in Igbo traditional religion are venerated and revered, and not adored or worshipped. Ancestors exist in a line of succession similar to the apostles in christian religion. Nevertheless, ancestors are not in succession of representing any founder, because Igbo traditional religion has no particular founder. Igbo traditional religion stands on the foundation of the ancestors. Beliefs concerning ancestors are an important element not only in Igboland but in Africa as a whole, and are forces to reckon with in the formation of the Igbo religious life and mentality, because they are situated in the family life and springs out of the family structure. What must be

---

157 Ikoro is made of wood, artistically carved in such a way that it allows hollow that produces a deep and far reaching sound. It is used to announce important information in Igboland. It is very popular especially in Ndi- Okoroukwu, Ndi-Ugbugbo and Acha-Isiukwuato. In his 'Things Fall Apart', Chinua Achebe narrates how Ikoro is used to announce the death of Ezeudu: "Go-di-go-go-di-go. Di-go-go-di-go. It was the ekwe talking to the clan. One of the things every man learned was the language of the hollowed-out-instrument. Diim! Diim! Diim! Boomed the cannon at intervals. The first cock had not crowed, and Umuofia was still swallowed up in sleep and silence when the ekwe began to talk, and the cannon shattered the silence. Men stirred on their bamboo beds and listened anxiously. Somebody was dead. The cannon seemed to rend the sky. Di-go-go-di-go-di –di-go-go-go floated in the message laden night air [...] The wailing of the women would not be heard beyond the village, but the ekwe carried the news to all the nine villages and even beyond. It began by naming the clan [...]. Then it went nearer and named the village: Iguedo of the yellow grinding-stone! It was Okonkwo's village. Again and again Iguedo was called and men waited breathlessly in all the nine villages. At last the man was named and people sighed ‚E-u-u, Ezeudu is dead'. A cold shiver ran down Okonkwo's back as he remembered the last time the old man had visited him" (Chinua Achebe, Things Fall Apart, London 1958, 84).

affirmed is that the cult of the ancestors is a strong element in Africa in general, but it is only an element. It must be clear that the cult of ancestors outlines appropriate rites for contact with the spirit world. This explains why they are believed to be part of the family and throws light on why they are called-Living Dead. The cult of ancestors does not represent or replace religion in Igboland. The ancestors, as spirits, are believed to be present in the family in a number of ways, at times, as physically reincarnated members. The Igbos express this aspect when they say – Nnamdi, which means, my father lives again. Igbos believe on the transmission of ancestral blood from generation to generation, along the lineage. However, it is not all the ancestors that are revered and reverenced. It is only those whose lives were proved to be good and were buried according to legitimate traditional rites. Igbos manifest their belief that man lives after death by revering their ancestors. It is the duty of the family head as a routine to go to this family ancestral shrine every morning to offer prayers to his ancestors for the welfare of the family members. He takes along with him water with which he washes his hand and face. Then, he makes several long and some crossing lines with white chalk on the floor of the shrine, cuts some kola nut into pieces and throws them into the shrine for the ancestors to partake, he goes on to pray for protection, good health, progress of the family members while holding up the family Ofo (symbol of authority) stick. He rounds up the prayer by pouring some little quantity of the locally made schnapps / liquor into the shrine, and drinking some himself after he had also taken some kola nut, usually combined with some quantity of alligator pepper. Private worship can also take another dimension when it is occasional. Ocassional private worship takes place as a response to a specific situation. An example of such is when a diviner passes information or a message believed to be received from the gods, requiring the person or the family concerned to offer some sacrifices. The diviner outlines the procedures to follow. The individual or the family goes to the particular priest of the particular deity as prescribed by the diviner and offers the prescribed sacrifice which comprises usually Nwa uriom (chicken), Akwa (eggs), Mkpuru Oji (kola nuts), Ose Oji (alligator pepper), Eghu (goat), Mmanya (palm wine), and Nzu (white chalk). As usual, the intentions for such sacrifice range from protection from both the evil spirits and evil persons to asking of other favours such as the fruit of the womb.

There are also worships in Igbo traditional religion that are considered public. Such public worships refer to feasts and festivals that are not only related to an individual family alone but to the whole kindred, clan and the entire community as a whole. The performance of the public worship is often followed by heavy celebrations and feastings. In some parts of Igboland, people gather in their community squares to watch masquerades perform. In other parts of the Igboland, it can be celebrated by organising dances and wrestling competitions. There is always enogh provisions of food and drinks. New yam festival is an example of such celebration that authorizes public worship. Although this celebration is honoured in every family, there is a set out date when the community as a whole mark this festival. Because this feast is associated with the Earth goddess which is responsible for agricultural produce, a date is ear – marked when a public sacrifice is performed in the shrine of Ala –

the earth goddess with full representation of the various family, kindred, clan and community heads. Ala is the mother of other deities, and Ogbalu F.C adds: "The earth is worshipped as the sustainer of all lives and fertility, champion of justice and defender of the weak".[158] It is regarded as the earth goddess of fertility, and of the public morality. Going against public morality or traditional laws and other violations are direct offence against Ala and are referred to as Nso Ala– abomination. Kalu O.U emphasizes on this issue when he writes: "The earth sustains life and this elevates the earth goddess into great prominence, and since the offences are committed on the earth, abominations are usually affronts to her".[159] Such offences include: stealing from the barn, homicide, incest, infidelity, woman climbing palm tree, or woman wrestling her husband down in a fight. Any of these offences is viewed as moral, spiritual and social violation of the land, and a certain ritual is observed for cleansing by the offender in order to appease the earth goddess. Ala is so sacred that no Igbo man or woman and no community in Igboland could afford to trespass, offend, much less discard it. Ala is so much cherished and recognised that in some communities, for most Igbo customs and practices to be complete, ratification must be in Ala shrine, example to this is Ozo title taking, and most people go by the title Eze Ala. Ala is pre–eminent among the other divinities. It is evident that any serious study or research into the foundations and principles of Igbo ethics must derive its inspiration and support from the Igbo philosophy and theology of this earth goddess-Ala. The worship of earth goddess is not only limited to the Igbo but spreads among Africans. Awolalu J.O gives some reasons why earth is worshipped among the Yoruba tribe of western Nigeria:

> The earth is venerated in Yorubaland because it is believed to be inhabited by a spirit [...] when a new born baby comes into the world, the first landing place is the earth; when man grows old and dies, he is buried in the earth. The earth supplies food for human consumption, and so it keeps life going.[160]

It is affirmed that Ala is a collaborator with the spirits of the dead ancestors especially in matters regarding their burial rituals. Both farmers and hunters believe that Ala is behind every success in their endeavour. This explains why various seasons of the year are dedicated to Ala-Earth goddess.

In Ukpor area of the south eastern Igboland, there is also an important feast called "Igba Mgbiri" or "Asala"-thanksgiving feast. The Ukpor people celebrate this feast in appreciation to the gods for their help in protecting them in the trying moments of wars and other trial periods. At the present circumstance, this feast comes up at every ten to fifteen years. Prior to the celebration of this feast, the elders gather at the Obiukwu-the town shrine, to offer their public worship. The choice of this venue is explained by Ogbalu F.C in the following words: "Actual worship whether private

---

158 Ogbalu, Igbo institutions and Customs, 1992,52.
159 Kalu, Ogbu, Under the Eyes of the Gods: Sacralisation and Control of Social Order in Igboland, art. in The Concept of the Sacred, papers presented at the 1988 Ahiajoku Lecture (onugaotu) Colloquium, no. 4,
160 Owerri 1989, 45. Awolalu, Yoruba Beliefs and Sacrificial Rites, 45.

or public, individual or communal is usually cold and takes place in the front of the shrine or grove dedicated to the idol".[161] Cows are slaughtered and public worship is offered on behalf of the Ukpor community. Unless this public worship is performed, no celebrations will follow. There are other public worships like "Iro Mmuo", and so on, that are observed in various Igbo communities. In various Igbo communities, one observes that the elements of the public worship are unique.That the Igbo people do not offer sacrifice directly to God, but indirectly through the lesser spirits does not mean that the Igbo do not profess the existence of the "one God". Instead, Igbos understand it that the "one God"-the Supreme Being is too transcendent to comprehend, and too high to be approached directly, hence, they do so through the minor spirits in the form of "Igo Mmuo",– worship of lesser spirits. Igbos believe in the existence of spirits in general. On the one side are the spirits whose names are known and are localized, enshrined, and therefore worshipped. The most prominent ones are often owned by a community, or at times, by a kindred or family. On the other side are the spirits whose names are not known, but commonly referred to as spirits.

These unknown spirits are very awful and dreaded by humans who refer to them as bad spirits. These are not localized, that is, they are not associated with a particular community specifically and exclusively, nor are shrines erected for them anywhere. Sacrifices to them are often placed on the road sides, often on the forked roads, because they are believed to be wandering spirits and through which road they came out they would eventually meet the sacrifice. While the known spirits are considered as divinities, these unknown spirits are not considered as divinities. While some Africans have the belief that these spirits are the origin of evil or agents of evil, it must be added that among the Igbos, they are mostly considered to be ambivalent in nature. The same spirit that does man good today can turn out to be his enemy tomorrow, despite the sacrifices. As wandering spirits, specific periods in the day are very special to them. Mid–day is an example of such periods, especially when the sun is in its swing. This explains the reason why children are not allowed to visit Udala tree at this period, because it is believed that one could have the possibility of running into these spirits. Night is also recognized as the time spirits could wander. An oral story in this connection is told of Nwankwo Okeji who was coming back from a visit in the middle of the night and ran into a group of these spirits along a lonely pathway that led to his village Umuka. Nobody could explain what happened to him after it was observed the following day that he could no longer speak nor eat. It took the intervention of the Dibia-medicine man to announce that he (Nwankwo Okeji) had unfortunately run into the spirits and badly influenced.

Spirits have also possessive ability, and particular misnormer is attributed to particular spirit. For example, when an individual turns out to be intoxicated–by a particular musical rythme such as Ogene music in Igboland, and becomes attached to it to the detriment of other meaningful engagements, it is then believed that he is possessed by the spirit of Ogene music. Spirits are believed to be responsible for evils that befall man such as sickness and various forms of misfortunes. Commenting on

---

161 Ogbalu, Igbo Institutions and Customs, 62.

this A. Echema writes: "Africa peoples believe that all forms of misfortune including sickness, barrenness, mental disorder, premature death, unhappy family life, accident, absence of material well-being are caused by the activities of ubiquitous evil spirits".[162] As a people with a particular ideology, Igbos resist the malicious influences by placating the spirits. This function belongs to the traditional diviner. Among the Igbos of Nigeria, there are three types of healers as they are called: Dibia Afa (diviner), Dibia Aja (priest), and Dibia ogwu (medicine man). An individual may combine the two functions of being diviner and priest or diviner and medicine man at the same time. The diviner is a diagnostician and a diviner magician. The medicine man on the other hand is mainly a healer of both physical and psychological ailment, as well as cases relating to spiritual problems. Speaking about medicine men Kalu O.U says: "Medicinemen were very important people in the community. Some of them serve as curator priests to shrines; others engage in healing, while some provided amulets (ekike) which could be used to protect property and self".[163] When someone falls sick, the diviner (Dibia Afa) is consulted to examine the spiritual and the material factors involved. It is his duty to first diagnose and identify the source and cause of the illness and to prescribe the type of cure in the form of sacrifice to remedy the situation. The consultations are followed by sacrifice and propitiation. This then falls within the area of work of the diviner–priest (Dibia Aja). He offers sacrifices to the many spirits, among them are spirits without specific shrines. Such sacrifices are usually joyless and made to evil spirits. The purpose of such sacrifices is to drive away evil believed to be responsible for the calamity or sickness, thereby appease the malevolent spirits. As we have earlier mentioned, road junctions and the border between villages are suitable for such sacrifices. Immediately after sacrifices have been made, the medicine man sets out to bring about healing and cure. The medicine man is able to effect the desired cure only in due collaboration with the diviner and not without the necessary sacrifices. The medicine man sees to the physical cure, and the diviner takes responsibility for the symptom. This procedure in the cure of sickness is rooted in the belief of the African that nothing is purely physical or merely spiritual. That is why in critical moments like serious illness when the African says he or she is going to find out or consult; he or she is not only going to the laboratory, or to the psychiatrist or to the gynaecologist, rather, he or she is more importantly seeking to find out the evil spirit that is causing the undesirable events. The considerations so far show that sickness and other forms of misnormer and calamities were always caused by malevolent spirits. Therefore, a cure must be sought for. While christianity for instance preaches resignation to the will of God, African traditional religion explores every possible avenue to obtain the desired healing through warding off and appeasing whichever spirit that is responsible.

There are spirits that are personal to individuals. In this case, they are referred to as Akalaka–destiny. Similarly, they are also called Chi that personally guide and define

---

162 Echema, Augustine, Anointing of the sick and the Healing Ministry, The Nigerian Pastoral Experience, Frankfurt 2006, 15
163 Kalu, Under the Eyes of the Gods, 44.

the now and future of the individual, and according to Iwe N.S.S: "Chi is the divinely endowed spirit of God which functions as a guardian spirit, personal to each human beings".[164] The basis of Igbo spirituality is the concept of Chi. Ndi Igbo do not believe that they are separate from their creator, and felt that the Chi that resides within them keeps them connected. They represent this thought in the following manner:

> The man indicates where his chi is by planting an Ogbu tree in front of his house. There he offers sacrifices to it and on his death, the ogbu–chi is uprooted indicating the end of his chi on earth. Unlike men's chi, women's chi is worshipped by her children and all who discended from her.[165]

Igbos feel that their Chi is unique and personal and serve as a guide and protector to them. A person's destiny is also guided by Chi. This explains why the Igbo sacrifice to it: "Every individual has his own personal god. Sacrifices of cows, goats, sheep, fowl and fish are made to these gods at specific seasons of the year".[166] Those with a strong Chi would have prosperity, good health and good fortune, while those with a weak Chi would be prone to sickness, poverty and bad luck. It is very unfortunate that Igbo traditional religion and its practice has grossly been misrepresented and misconceived. The ancient spirituality of the Igbos, like most other traditional African systems, has been misunderstood and demonized unjustly. Churches and film industries have helped to paint a negative picture of traditional Igbo spirituality that dates back to the arrival of the europeans in Igboland. It is quite unfortunate that those who condemn Igbo traditional religion do not know much about it, and base their information from the lies of the very same people who wanted to destroy it and everything about the culture. Giving a credit to Bishop Shanahan, a great missionary to Igbo people of Eastern Nigeria, V.A Nwosu writes:

> He took a deep personal interest in peoples' lives and aspirations and saw that they were already deeply religious. He realized that what was needed was not a destruction of those religious values but a transformation of them into Christianity. This he tried to do.[167]

The misconception of Igbo traditional religion is most apparent in the terminologies wrongly applied to it. Such terminologies include primitive, native, juju, ancestral worship, polytheism, animism, and so on. Animism, for instance, is popularly adopted by many foreign mercenaries to describe Igbo traditional religion. Animism is from Latin "anima", meaning soul or spirit. The choice of the word to describe Igbo traditional religion suggests that Igbos believe that objects and animals have souls or spirits–anima, and worship them. Oliver Onwubiko insists that: "it is important to correct the notion of African Traditional Religion as animism".[168] Igbos, however,

---

164 Iwe, Nwachukwu, Igbo Deities, art. in The Igbo Concept of the Sacred, papers presented at the 1988 Ahiajoku Lectures (Onugaotu) Colloquium, no 4, Owerri 1989, 15.
165 Ogbalu, Igbo Institutions and Customs, 52.
166 Lieber, Ibo village communities, 67.
167 Makozi, Alexius and Afolabi, Ojo, The History of the Catholic Church in Nigeria, Lagos 1982, 42.
168 Onwubiko, Alozie Oliver, Echoes From The African Synod, The Future Of The African Church From Present And Past Experiences, Enugu 1994, 134.

cannot be said to believe that every object and every creature has such a spirit. Again, the idea that some objects have spirits is not perculiar to Igbos or Africans alone. So, it is simply incorrect to call Igbo traditional religion animism.[169] Having introduced the Igbo people and their religion, let us now focus our attention on Igbo language which will eventually lead us to the purpose of this chapter.

3.5 Igbo Language: Formation and Interpretations

Igbo language is the language of over 25 million Igbos of the south east and some parts of the south west of Nigeria. Just like any other language, the Igbo language is born out of the need for human interaction in various levels of interpersonal relationships, and community coexistence. We have already explained the version of the Igbo history which upholds the teaching that Igbos are migrants from various parts of Nigeria: Benin, Igala, Nri and Ibibio. It becomes, therefore, very necessary to find out how Igbo language came to exist if the early migrants have no common ancestor, which means, no common language. According to Louis-Marie Chauvet: "In order to be able to invent language, one must think of it; but in order to be able to think of it, one must already be in language".[170] It is the opinion of Louis-Marie Chauvet that language is an inseparable part and parcel of humanity, and that man from conception is a thinking being, and cannot be denied of the ability to speak out his thoughts which is innate in the thinking ability. He, therefore, traces human language right to conception.

> Consequently, with respect to language, the notion of instrument will be replaced by that of mediation, that is to say, the milieu in which the subject becomes subject. This milieu is to be regarded as a sort of womb. This term has the advantage of bringing us back to the fetal condition; from the time of pregnancy, the child is enclosed in a maternal womb which is not only biological but already cultural since the mother already speaks to her baby, shares with it, consciously and especially unconsciously, her emotions and feelings, and begins, most often without realizing it, to transmit to it the cultural heritage of the group, the mother tongue to begin with. In summary, the fact that speaking begins in the mother's womb must be considered a necessary condition of any humanization.[171]

---

169   But the word animism, which derives from the Latin word "animare", meaning an attribution of conscious life to nature as a whole or to inanimate objects. Here, we have to make a distinction between attributing life to nature as a living being or entity and attributing life to nature in terms of life originating from nature. The attribution of consciousness to nature or inanimate objects in Animism does not pertain to the source of life but to the possession of life as a living object, that is, as an object that has life in it. Igbos in particular and Africans in general do not attribute life to nature like earth or inanimate objects, as the source of life, rather they see nature as mediating life. So when an Igbo man sacrifices to these objects, for child, he means that the objects would mediate in helping him obtain child from God who is Chukwu Onye Okike–God the Creator.
170   Chauvet, Louis-Marie, The Sacraments, The Word of God at the Mercy of the Body, translated by Madeleine Beaumont, Minnesota 1997, 7.
171   Chauvet, The Sacraments, The Word of God, 7.

The stand of Louis-Marie Chauvet may sound convincing and is accepted by today's psychologists, but it may only be a theory which a common man may not be able to comprehend. It is still left to be proved logically and practically how a language of a particular tribe of migrant groups, and in this case the Igbo, came to be formed, bearing in mind that these migrants coming together are already adults from different backgrounds of various languages and cultures.

According to a source, the language of the first settlers must have played a great role in determining those of the later arrivals. By this I mean, the people who later came to settle in the Igbo territory from other areas could only relate better with the people who had already settled in this territory if they were able to speak their language. If, for example, the earlier settlers had Igbo as their language, this means that the later settlers had to adapt to the new language. This may be the answer as why there are different dialects in the Igbo language. This dialects may be as a result of the ways by which the later settlers attempted to learn the language-Igbo. Another hypothesis suggests that Igbo language may be corrupt form of the different languages of the migrants put together, resulting to a language that is later known as Igbo language. In this case, no particular migrant group can lay claim to Igbo language. Yet, there is another proposition which holds that Igbo language is neither a language of a particular migrant group nor a corruption of the different languages of the various migrant groups. Instead, these various migrants who were determined to form a community of people with a common world-view, preferred to overcome their differences, and resolved to have a common identity in which a totally new language, independent of which ever language that had existed, is formulated and learnt as a pathway to a common purpose. This new language came to be known as Igbo language.

Apart from the oral tradition which we have discussed above, there is also to it, a written tradition. The Igbo alphabets are written in the Roman script, and like some other world languages, Igbo language is a tonal language.[172] The current Igbo alpha-

---

172 Ida C. Ward has this to say about Igbo language as a tonal language: "Ibo has long been known to be a tone language in so far as the tones of individual words are concerned, and the tonal variants of words like akwa, meaning cry, bridge, egg, and cloth, isi, meaning head, smell, six, and blindness, are frequently quoted. Where two or more words are found with the same sounds and different tones, it is not difficult to realize the part played by tone in distinguishing meaning, but what is more difficult to realize is that even where such variants in meaning do not exist, the tones are an integral part of the word, and not to use them correctly constitutes a mistake in pronounciation as important as the use of a wrong vowel or consonant, and leads as inevitably to misunderstanding or lack of meaning. A tone language, therefore, is one in which every word in the language has its own individual tone or tone patter. [...] Ibo makes use of the following tones:

1. High Level.
   Nouns   ji (–) yam   isi (– -) head
   Verb roots   gbu (–) kill   kuzi (– -) teach
   Other words   ezigbo (---) true   otu (– -) as
2. Low Level.
   Nouns   ite (_ _) pot   obodo (_ _ _) town
   Verb roots   ba (_) enter   wepu (_ _) take away
   Other words   na (_) and   ka (_) that mgbe (_ _) when

bets are referred to as the "Onwu Orthography". This is a concensus between the older Lepsius Orthography and a newer orthography. There are thirty six Igbo alphabets. Below are the alphabets:

A B CH D E F G GB GH GW H I Į J K KP KW L
M N NW NY Ň O Ọ P R S SH T U Ụ V W Y Z

Out of the thirty six alphabets, there are eight vowels (Udaume): A E I Į O Ọ U Ụ; Nineteen consonants (Mgbochiume): B D F G H J K L M N Ň P R S T V W Y Z; and nine blends (Udamkpi): GB GH KP SH CH GW KW NW NY.

The Onwu Orthography is in existence since 1962. The Roman script form of Igbo alphabets was existing side by side with the "Nsibidi". The "Nsibidi", were pictograms in Ekpe society and Okonko fraternity before 1500. They were less popular, and gradually and finally gave way for Roman script. Today, they are only limited to secrete societies as a secrete form of communication. As a result of many dialects, an agreed standardized Igbo language became very difficult. The Dr. Ida C. Ward proposal of adopting the Ezinihitte dialect in central Owerri province in 1939 as the central Igbo, which was recognized by missionaries, writers and publishers across the region, was later in 1972 viewed by "the society for promoting Igbo language and culture" (SPILC) as imperialistic. Instead, this society constituted a body known as "Standardization Committee" whose aim was to found an embracing and encompassing type of central Igbo, which takes into consideration the importance of all the Igbo dialects, especially, those that are outside the central areas. This committee was more inclusive. Despite the efforts of the standardization committee to incorporate all the dialects in forming a comprehensive central Igbo, there arose still the need to borrow some words from other foreign languages. This was necessary since in Igbo language there exist no original names to some foreign terminologies. What the committee could do was to igbonize the terminologies where it is possible, and in other cases just to re-write them unadulterated. Nevertheless, Igbo language is rich in its grammar and constructions. In outlining this richness, let us call to mind what Patricia L. Carrell says in terms of Igbo typology, descriptive adjectives, prepositions, comparisons, adverbs, passives, personal pronouns, gender differentiation, and so on. According to her:

> With regard to the basic order typology, the relative order of subject, verb and object in simple declarative sentences with nominal subject and object is SVO [...] There is a great deficiency of descriptive adjectives in Igbo, and relative clauses are used to translate both

---

3. Mid Level.
No monosyllabic word of any kind exists in the language with an essential mid – tone (with the exception of m, ge, ya, ha (pro. or poss. adj.). But a mid – tone occurs:
(a) as part of the necessary pattern of a number of nouns and adjectives of two or more syllables (actually there do not appear to be a large number of these):
agu (-_) leopard, ego (-_) money, mma (-_) beauty, good, nkita (-_) dog
(b) in certain closely related groups of words; e.g.
isi ya (-- _) his head, Elu isi (--- _) top of the head, ime ya (-- _) to do it." (Ida C. Ward, An Introduction to the Ibo Language, Cambridge 1936, 10 and 12).

95

relative clauses and adjectives from other languages [...] Igbo is a prepositional rather than a postpositional language [...] Comparatives and superlatives are translated by the verb 'ka' [...] Various bound forms and clause constructions are used to express adverbial notions ... Passives are indicated by the use of the indefinite personal pronoun 'A' and / or the use of emphatic sentence type [...] Igbo personal pronouns have three categories of person and two categories of number [...] Igbo has no grammatical gender distinguishing masculine, feminine and neuter, or male, female and common. [173]

A big challenge to Igbo language at present is threat to extinguishing. The main factor responsible for this development is inferiority complex. It is often said that he who plays the piper dictates the tune. The superiority of the "first world" countries or the developed countries has serious undermining effects on the development of the so-called third world countries, or better still, the under-developed countries. The Igbo country as a third world country is equally not spared. According to G.E.Igwe and M.M.Green:

> There seems to be a lack of appreciation among Igbo speakers of the richness and subtlety of their language, with its finely balanced verbal structure and its wealth, for instance, of suffixes. And part of its interest resides in its tonal structure, which gives it a distinctive character com- pared with languages such as English and French, and is thus of such significance to linguistics. [174]

Today the Igbo child is happier when he can speak any foreign language very fluently even if he cannot make a correct statement in Igbo language. Most of the Igbo parents are more proud of their children and lavish gifts on them as an appreciation that they can now speak foreign languages better than their mother tongue. I am not in any way against any foreign language, but the mother tongue should not be sacrificed at the altar of foreign languages. The Igbo language is very rich in its structures, synthesis and analysis. It is a language that is complex but very interesting to study. In the practice of Igbo traditional religion, therefore, to what extent does the Igbo language perform? Below are some details.

3.6 The concept of Performative word in Igbo traditional religion

In chapter one of this work, we have defined performative word as a language act in which to say something is to do something or in saying something is to do something or by saying something is to do something.[175] The situation before the utterance is no longer the same after the utterance. In performatives, one does not consider whether a sentence is true or false, but whether it is happy or unhappy. In performative word, sign and symbol are expressed in order to realize an effect. Sign is determined right at

---

173 Carrell, Patricia, A Transformational Grammar of Igbo, Cambridge 1970, 2–5.
174 Igwe, Georgewill and Green, Margaret, Igbo Language Course, Igbo Language Study, Ibadan 1967, 9.
175 Cf. Austin, How To Do Things With Words, 12.

first instance, but symbol is dominant in the entire sentence. In a performative utterance: "I promise to buy a car", both sign and symbol interplay. In this performative utterance, an information is given about "promise of buying a car". Information as we have already noted belongs to "sign". This "promise of buying a car" is at the same time a communication made to someone. In this case, it is symbolic, and because the communication strongly runs through the utterance, one concludes that symbol is a dominant factor in every performative utterance. While performatives have to do with information and communication, they are considered to be made up of signs and symbols, and symbols are dominant. Igbo language is a language where performative words play vital roles, and not excluding the very aspect of religious rites and rituals. The performative utterance: "E kwere m gi nkwa izuru gi Ugboala" is translated into: "I promise that I will buy you a car". There is both "sign" (information) and "symbol" (communication) in this same performative utterance. In performatives, therefore, sign and symbol are likened to the two legs of a word. Performative word needs the two legs to be balanced, and when one is not there to support the other, the whole system becomes incomplete. Names that explain that Igbo word is performative include: Ekwueme–word performs, Okwudire–word is active, Okwuka–word is supreme, Okwudike–word is powerful, Okwubundu–word is life. Certain expressions give testimony to the performative character of Igbo word. These expressions include: okwu ekwuru ekwu bu obi afuru anya–word empowers action, amaghi ekwu kpatara amaghi sa–word results to action, ire oma ka ejula ji aga na ogwu–word summounts all problems, akpa akpa arahu na ute–word leads to resolutions.

According to Igbo traditional religion, performative words can be explored not only for their meanings but also for the effects they have on the lives of the participants. Performative words are recognised as powerful : prayers come true, curses become real, oaths must be kept or else dire consequences will occur. Any discussion on the performative character of Igbo word cannot, of course, be separated from the cultural values of the Igbo people, most especially, in matters relating to ritual practices and religious beliefs, and Parrinder G. would say: "The poetry of African prayer, delight in expressive words, and the subtleties of traditional aphorisms are not allowed to detract from practical purposes".[176] In Igbo rituals, therefore, spoken words present events believed to have the power to effect meaningful transformations. Some of the acts, gestures, enactments, generally construed are performative in the sense that the essence or identity that they otherwise express are sustained through pre-decided signs and words and a mutual understanding of the participants about the ritual meaning.

Performative power of Igbo words is again exemplified in such expressions as "Igbo Kwenu!". Here two words are involved : Igbo and Kwenu . The term Igbo refers to the Igbo people-men and women of all ages of tradition and modernism. Kwenu refers to agreement, endorsement, solidarity, unity, bondedness, strenghth and collective will. When Igbos say in a gathering "Igbo Kwenu!", they answer in a chorus "Yaa", thereby referring to the common spirit of "Gidigidi bu Ugwu Eze" (action

---

176 Parrinder, Geoffrey, Religion in Africa, London 1969, 67.

is might), in which they are as a group synonymously pushed into action. So "Igbo Kwenu" is clearly understood as performative expression. In gathering of all sorts, namely marriage, rituals, celebrations, age grade meetings, war, wrestling, hunting and village political affairs, Igbos assert their emotions and psychology together through calls to order of solidarity such as invoking the "Igbo Kwenu". Traditionally, when a person among the gathered group intends to speak and has masterly and skilfully summoned attention with "Igbo Kwenu", he is authomatically granted audience. That means, as a performative expression "Igbo Kwenu" is a supreme call to attention to speak in a culturally appropriate way. Once "Igbo Kwenu" is announced and responded to, all ears will listen.

A central way to explain the symbolism of "Igbo Kwenu" is to refer to a local proverb which says: Ukwu diri otu, a kuo ulo gbam – gbam, ma Ukwu adighi otu, a kuo ulo akirika (if we are united, the house will be roofed with raffia palm). One can boldly state that the phrase "Igbo Kwenu" corresponds with a reached Igbo mind or spirit for action in a given circumstance. Igbo Kwenu is a cultural tick – tack of agreeing to move on. Equally, it can be said to be a wooden gong in words for preparedness in line with any mutual community voice and action. Igbo Kwenu initiates the voices, due process or rule, custom or law and action for the community of people involved. The meaning and the interpretation of the performative words in Igbo religion should, of course, be based on the understanding that "every religion is best defined in its socio-cultural context"[177], and not to be understood in the sense of self – suggestion or auto-suggestion or better still positive mental attitude. This is the situation whereby one presumes the transforming power of a spoken word in a religious event. This is mostly experienced in foreign religions, especially in the healing ministry of most adherents of the christian religion. Narrating such a session between mother Gacambi and Archbishop Emmanuel Milingo, Austin Echema writes:

> He just told me to sit on the armchair and he stood beside me and said something to this effect: 'Lord, when you were on earth the human bodies were subject to you, make this body be subject to me.' And then he put his hand on my head saying: 'Mama go to sleep'. I literally went to sleep. Peacfully, calmly and completely relaxed [...] that kind of sleep whereby one is half conscious and half asleep [...] I continued to hear the Archbishop ordering the various parts of the body ; Heart, in the Name of Jesus pump the blood to all parts of the body [...] thanks be to God.Deo gratias', [...] He went on to call the bones of the pelvis to go back to their place [...] calling on the Name of Jesus involving the saints and the Blessed Virgin Mary [...] I came to full consciousness when I heard the Archbishop say 'Mama wake up' and with his hands on mine lifted me from the chair [...] I realized the session had taken almost two hours. [178]

This type of encounter as narrated above makes the participant believe every word of the minister as performative. The performative power of a word, however, does not depend on the number of times it is repeated or presumed. In the traditional Igbo religion, where there is no special session for healing ministry as witnessed in other

---

177 Oborji, Francis, Towards a christian theology of African religion: issues of interpretation and mission, Nairobi 2005, 29.
178 Echema, Anointing of the Sick, 20–21.

religions, such presumptions about the performative word do not exist. Rather, the culture of the Igbo people helps to build a favourable ground on which the performative power of the words are genuinely experienced in rituals and religious acts. In the hey–day of traditional religion in Igboland, the word of mouth was considered much more sacred than the written word is now. A hundred years ago, there was no way in which the verbal last statement of a dying person would be substracted from, added to or disputed. Only one person may have heard it, yet it would be honoured. This made Fabian J. to conclude that performatives: "Need authors and audiences, positions to be made from and situations to be addressed to".[179] It was certain that no person would put into the mouth of the dying person what he had not said. Igbo traditional religion does not tamper with the spoken word. Ceremonies of vital importance such as Naming ceremony, enthronement of a chief priest, marriage rites, oath taking, covenant making, initiation of a youth into secret society, commissioning of a warrior, are all performed with rituals and words; nothing is written down. To break a verbal oath is one of the greatest felonies in Igboland. Now, how do we explain the Igbo word in the light of explicit and implicit forms of performative word?

3.7 Forms of performative word in Igbo traditional religion

The J.L.Austin's two forms of performative word: explicit performative word and implicit performative word can both be associated with Igbo traditional religion.

3.7.1 Explicit performative word

Explicit performative words are in themselves distinct and definite by presenting themselves as behavitives in making explicit utterances relating to human behaviour "I criticize that ..., I apologize that ..." or expositives "I admit that ..., I predict that ..." or verdictives relating to judgements given in a certain situation "I rule that ..., I declare that ...". Because the utterances have qualifications, one does not need to seek for further clarifications.[180] Explicit performatives are normally positioned in the first person present tense. The utterance "I declare that he will succeed " is an explicit utterance because it has a qualification "I declare that ...", and therefore, the meaning it conveys is clear.

Similarly, there are evidences of explicit performative words in Igbo traditional religion. In the administration of an oath in the Igbo traditional rite or in the rite of the Igbo traditional covenant-making, the parties involved make declarative statements

---

179 Fabian, Johannes., Power and Performance, ethnographic exploration through proverbial wisdom and theater in Shaba, Zaire, London 1990, 263.
180 Cf. Austin, How To Do Things With Words, 73.

such as: "I, MR/S ... HEREBY DECLARE THAT I STAND BY THE EVIDENCES I HAVE GIVEN AS TRUE, AND SHOULD IT NOT BE TRUE LET THIS ORACLE TAKE MY LIFE". Because this utterance has qualification "I declare that ...", it is explicit, and therefore, conveys a meaning that is clear. It is equally positioned in the first person present tense. When we consider too certain statements made by certain institutionalized authorities in Igbo society such as the Chief Priest or the Family Head, especially when they offer prayers, we discover also some evidences of explicit performative words, and Shorter Aylward would say: "prayers in their own right, but, as frequently happens in Africa, are accompanied by gestures and postures which render their meaning more explicit".[181] Again, when there is a violation of the traditional societal norm such as theft, and the culprit is not known, because the land must be cleansed at the expense of the offender, the chief priest may go about this by making such a pronouncement: "I PRONOUNCE CURSE ON WHOEVER HAS COMMITTED THIS CRIME AGAINST OUR LAND THAT HE OR SHE SHALL PROCURE AN INCURABLE SICKNESS WITHIN THE NEXT EIGHT MARKET DAYS". So, his utterance is clearly a pronouncement, and therefore, explicit. As a matter of fact, verdictive form of explicit performatives dorminate in Igbo traditional religion.

3.7.2 Implicit performative word

Implicit performatives lack qualifications. Because they lack qualifications, the utterances are not clear and the meanings they convey are doubtful.[182] This situation calls for the need to ask for clarifications by asking such questions like: "what does the speaker mean by that ?" And "what type of utterance is that ?" The answers from the above questions will determine if the utterances are , for example, declarations, apologies or prophecies. The utterance "I shall swim" is unclear if it is a promise or not, and therefore needs to be qualified. There are situations where there are evidences of implicit performative words in Igbo traditional religion. Igbo proverbs are examples where implicit performatives are manifested. Because Igbo proverbs are highly sophisticated and need deep reflections to be understood, the meanings they convey may seem to be complicated. Therefore, one may ask: "what does the speaker mean by that utterance?" Or "what type of utterance is that?" The answers one gets from such questions may then help him to qualify the utterance. Likewise, riddles and the speech genre in Igbo traditional songs make them to be implicit in their performance such that in listening to the songs, one may ask: "what type of song is that?" Or "what does the singer mean by this song?" In order to be clear on how to regard an Igbo utterance as performative, it is necessary to study the criteria under which it can qualify as performative.

---

181 Shorter, Aylward, Prayer in the religious traditions of Africa, Nairobi 1975, 22.
182 Cf. Austin, How To Do Things With Words, 72.

3.8 Criteria for performative word in Igbo traditional religion

J.L.Austin himself summed the criteria regulating performative word into three main groups:
i. There must be a conventional procedure.
ii. The procedure must be executed by all participants both correctly and completely.
iii. The same emotion regulating the feelings and thoughts of the audience must guide the speaker.

These criteria, therefore, regulate both the speaker, the audience and the word itself.[183] The violation of the criteria (i) and (ii) makes the act purported, and therefore, void. This may be either because the speaker is not in position to perform the act or the words and the circumstance are not appropriate. Such violation is referred to as "Misfire". This means, the act is purported but has no effects.[184] There are three interpretations associated with "Misfire": "Misinvocation", when either there is no such procedure or that it cannot be applied in the given circumstance,[185] and "Misapplication" in which the procedure although it exists but is not possible to be implemented as purported.[186] We have equally "Misexecution", when the purported act is applied but full of inconsistencies.[187] Violation of criterion (iii) is known as "Abuse". In this case, the act is achieved but insincerely.[188]

Again, the same criteria regulate performative words in Igbo traditional religion. In our later discussion, we shall come across certain agents of performative word in Igbo traditional religion which would include the Chief Priest, the Family Head, the Downtrodden, among others. These are considered to be the official speakers of performative words in Igbo traditional religion. They do not just talk from nowhere. Certain circumstances must necessitate their utterances, and they must take into consideration the feelings and thoughts of the audience in order to arrive at the desired affect. For example, the traditional Igbo people understand sickness as punishment from gods for whatever evil they might have committed, and therefore, seek for solutions and cure from gods. In this case, no other speaker is most appropriate than the Chief priest. His words must be proper to the situation. The people are in urgent need of solutions and cure, and when this same thought and feeling guide his utterances, these utterances in effect control the actions of the people who would not hesitate in acting in accordance with these utterances. In this case, the words perform because the required criteria are observed. There are also cases of "Misfire" in the way performative words are handled in Igbo traditional religion. For example, one

---

183 Cf. Austin, Philosophical Papers, 224–226.
184 Cf. Austin, How To Do Things With Words, 16.
185 Cf. Austin, How To Do Things With Words, 17.
186 Cf. Austin, How To Do Things With Words, 17.
187 Cf. Austin, How To Do Things With Words, 17.
188 Cf. Austin, How To Do Things With Words, 39.

hears stories of how a chief priest is struck dead by his oracle because he has been bribed to issue inconsistent and false utterances, and sometimes create a procedure that is not comprehensible and inadquate. In this case, the chief priest has purported an act and what he says is void. Under this fallacy of "Misfire" there is "Misinvocation" because the chief priest is no longer observing the conventional procedure; there is as well "Misapplication" because he has invented a situation of deceit; there is also "Misexecution" because his actions are marred with flaws. We cannot, however, deny the situation where the chief priest successfully deceives a client in the name of the oracle just for his selfish interest. This is what is referred to as "Abuse". As an old religion, Igbo traditional religion has a lot of values when closely studied in the light of performative word. Let us examine its different aspects of endeavours where performative word can be reflected.

3.9 References to performative word in Igbo traditional religion

I consider that performative identities, performative symbols, performative theater and performative magic are associated with Igbo traditional religion. Below are discussions on these four references to performative word in the light of Igbo traditional religion.

3.9.1 performative identities

One's identity is considered to be performative. In other words, a person's identity hinges on how words define who he is and what he is. Two things are necessary for words to define an individual. Firstly, the value must be inherent in the individual, and secondly, it must be recognized by others. This means, both the individual and others join together to bring about performative identity. Performative identity, therefore, is a team work.[189] For instance, a person is known as "Michael". Whenever he hears this name mentioned, he is attracted to react spontaneously even without knowing whether it is referring to him or not. In this way, both the bearer and the caller fulfil their roles to make the name "Michael" perform. So, when considered in the light of J.L.Austin's performative word, the identity "Michael" performs in the bearer through the saying of "Michael" or in the saying of "Michael" or by the saying of "Michael". If one should ask about the qualification of performative identity, I would say that it is a confirmation: "I confirm the name Micheal ...". Likewise, in Igbo traditional religion, performative words establish a person's identity, and as it were, this identity is equally based on a team work in which the individual himself and other people have important roles to

---
189 Cf. Austin, How To Do Things With Words, 117.

play. Take the case of title-taking in traditional Igbo society. When somebody is known with the tilte "Ezeudo"–peace maker, and this title is suddenly mentioned to his hearing, the immediate reaction may be a spontaneous answer even without knowing whether he is being referred to or not. In this way, we may say that his identity as "Eze udo" has performed.

3.9.2 performative symbols

Performative symbol establishes the fact that symbolic languages initiate actions, and "symbolic action, however, may become even more elaborate, involving a whole complex of actions, a cast of actors or officiants and a combination of material object, gestures and words both spoken and sung".[190] Symbolic language is appreciated in the sense of "talking to someone" and not "talking about someone". When considered according to J.L.Austin's teaching on performative word, we understand the talking to someone to mean saying something or in saying something or by saying something in order to arrive at an action. It can, therefore, be interpreted as the bedrock of human language in which convention plays a very important role as a uniting force which makes a people live together in understanding and in agreement concerning their societal system. This implies that symbolic language should not be understood in isolation but its relevance depends on the interpretation it gets through convention.

In Igbo traditional religion, there are evidences of performative symbols. In a typical Igbo gathering, it is common or normal to hear someone announce "Igbo Kwenu!", and the assembly responds "Yaa!". This is a performative linguistic symbol that calls to actions, for example, call to solidarity or call to attention. If one should ask about the type of utterance it is, we may say it is an appeal: "I appeal that we listen … I appeal that we pay attention …".

3.9.3 Performative theater

Utterances by actors in theater are considered to be performative. It is true that what is presented in theater is acted and can be fictious or non-fictious, nevertheless, the performance of the word is expected to be the same as it would be when used outside theater. In an Igbo drama, the utterance "Igbo kwenu!" is used to call for attention just as it would be used to serve the same purpose outside drama. That it serves this purpose of calling the attention of people means that this phrase performs regardless that it is in a drama. This means that the actions of performative words are not limited to normal situations only, but perform even when they are acted.

---

190 Austin, How To Do Things With Words, 117.

3.9.4 Performative magic

Performative magic refers to the actions of the word in performing magic. Words used in performing magic may be strange to the audience. What is important in this circumstance is not whether the people understand the words, but whether the words perform. This is on the understanding that: "The magician's playing on the people's intelligence and his devising entertainment strategy are paramount importance to the art [...] The basic principle is: The more you look, the less you see".[191]

In performative magic, both the actor and the audience have important role to play. It is a team work in which the actor has the role of uttering the words to make a thing assume a certain presumed reality, and the audience plays the role of acknowledging this presumed reality. When words succeed to achieve this goal, it is known as performative magic. Performative magic is not strange to Igbo cultural society in particular and to Africa in general. On this note, Nwaoru O.E. further says: "Africans had their original notion and usage of magic before they came in contact with western missionaries and colonialists."[192] Different names that have the same meaning are used to refer to magic in many African societies, viz: "ndi amansi (Igbo), pidanpidan (Yoruba), mai dabo/mai sihiri (Hausa), egbeneke (Urhobo). These words literally mean those who perform magic".[193] Performative magic is experienced in the "Abrakadabra" (incantations) that is associated with the Igbo traditional priest, and presumed to be the performative language of the spirits. The traditional Igbo priest intones these incantations which are known only to him in order to effect some reactions in his client because "the art of manipulation is the bedrock of all forms of magic in Africa".[194] He may succeed in putting some fears in his adherent but does the fact that the adherent acts in fear make these "Abrakadabra" to be performative? Should J.L.Austin not be interpreted to mean that the performative word itself must first of all be a human language in order to be performative? Since the incantations have no base in human language, and since neither the chief priest nor the adherent may claim to understand what is being uttered, my critique remains that the performative power of word in magic remains presumed. Let us now consider a few of the individuals whose words, according to the Igbo belief system, are most performative.

---

191 Nwaoru, Emmanuel, Another look at magic in the African culture, article in Chakana, vol.3, edited by missionswissenschaftliches Institut Missio e.V (MWI), Frankfurt am Main 2005, 39.
192 Nwaoru, Another look at magic, 37.
193 Nwaoru, Another look at magic, 38.
194 Nwaoru, Another look at magic, 40.

3.10 Agents of Performative Word in Igbo traditional religion

In Igbo world, there are certain people whose words carry a lot of influences and implications, and are therefore taken seriously. This may be as a result of the position they occupy by divine allocation, or as a result of the nature of their duty, or more still, as a result of the various predicaments they find themselves. We now consider a few of such people.

3.10.1 Chief Priest

A chief priest occupies a very prominent and important position in the religious belief of Igbo people. He is easily qualified with the gods whose mouthpiece and messenger he is. Awolalu J.O puts it better: "In time of calamity, war or pestilence it is their business to declare what ought to be done to make the divinities propitious [...] They are, therefore, the mouthpieces of the divinity".[195] And so, between him and the gods there is only a very thin line of difference in the eyes of an ordinary man. In issues concerning a community in general or an individual in particular, the chief priest's utterances are final since it is the gods speaking through him. Likewise, the judgement he delivers is divine and cannot be reversed because: "The priests are trusted to be faithful, never to lie and always upright in their dealings with men and women".[196] This merits him such names as "Onu Mmuo"– spokesman of gods; "Okara Mmuo okara Mmadu"–half divine half man. On this platform, no word of the chief priest is taken lightly because it is heavy, and carries a lot of consequences. By the power of his words, the chief priest spells out doom when the people attract god's anger upon themselves. This evil comes to fulfilment accordingly. For example, an oral tradition tells story of a woman who by desecrating the shrine of a kindred was cursed by the chief priest, and as a punishment, the chief priest made the following pronouncement upon her, saying: "I GAGHI ATU; I GAGHI AMU NKE A GA ANU AKWA NWA NA ULO GI"- you will neither conceive nor nurse a baby. This pronouncement remained as it was said, and her lineage was deprived of future generation. The mouth of the chief priest, however, is not only restricted to curses, it can also be a channel of blessings. When the divine favour is around a particular people or individual, the chief priest often times in his unusual visits declares these blessings to the conscious awareness of the recipients.

---

195 Awolalu, Yoruba Beliefs and Sacrificial Rites, 109.
196 Ogbalu, Igbo Institutions and Customs, 57.

3.10.2 Family Head

Family head performs functions similar to chief priests but in an unofficial and very limited circumstance. He is seen as the mouthpiece of the lineage members, and as such his words commands loyalty from the family members.[197] In the words of Lieber J.W: "Decisions taken by a council of elders, each representing a family, is binding on all members".[198] So, when a family head speaks, the members see their family gods and their ancestors speaking through him. This is out of the conviction that old age means nearness to antiquity. Narrating how powerful the words of the family head are, Awolalu J.O writes:

> It is the head of the family who sits at the ancestral shrine and prays that it may be well with the woman in her husband's home. When there is a funeral ceremony, the family head gives necessary guidance. If a member of the family breaks a taboo, it is the family head who presides and gives where applicable, the necessary offerings to the ancestors [...] and he also decides what punishment to give to the culprits.[199]

The above clarification explains the reason why the words of a family head are very powerful, and highly effective. His words can mean blessing as well as curse. This explains also why in most cases, members who receive blessings from their family head are progressive. These blessings are ignited verbally when a family head prays for his members. Such words of blessings are associated with a family head: "O GA ADIRI GI MMA NWAM "- it shall be well with you; "CHUKWU GOZIE GI "- may gods bless you; "NWA GI GA EMERE GI OTU A "- your own offspring will look after you well, and so on. They are short prayers that are brought to fulfilment the way they came out from the mouths of a family head. On the other hand, disobedient members receive from their family head such words as: "O GAGHI ADIRI GI MMA "- it shall not be well with you; "I GAGHI AFU IHEOMA N' UWA GI "- you will never know any favour throughout your life, and so on. They are also short prayers that must also come to pass. A family head can, however, retrieve these evils back when situation occasions that, such as, when the dissident member shows some remorse and is repentant. In this case, the family head performs what is known as "IBUCHA ONU"- recalling back the evil that was pronounced. Sometimes, these blessings or curses procured by the members from their family head become hereditary. That means, they do not stop with a generation, but are inherited by generations upon generations. In the case where it is a blessing, it is always desirable and admirable. On the contrary, when it is a curse, it becomes unfortunate, and innocent generations may continue to suffer it until some remedy is reached. This is the power of the words of a family head.

---

197 Cf. Anyanwu, The rites of initiation, 31.
198 Lieber, Ibo village communities, 65.
199 Awolalu, Yoruba Beliefs and Sacrificial Rites, 109.

3.10.3 The Downtrodden.

This refers to the people who in the society are unjustly deprived of their rights as a result of various misfortunes that befall them either out of natural or unnatural causes. The people in this group are not limited to a particular age or gender and extend to various affiliations, and various societies in Igboland.

Sometimes, it is evident that in some traditional Igbo society, widowhood is made to be an ugly experience that no Igbo woman would like to have.[200] To start with, Igbos hardly accept death as a natural tragedy. When a man dies, the cause of his death is always attributed either to the gods or to fellow human being. In most cases, a woman who loses her husband becomes the first to be accused of the death. She needs to prove her innocence before she is vindicated. She does this by going through rigorous processes, and subjected to humiliating situations which she is expected to bear without complaint. She is mobbed, insulted and disgraced, thereby, inflicting double pains in her: the pain of the loss of a dear husband, and the pain of the false accusation. It may happen that in trying to prove her innocence, she may pronounce "Nemesis" upon the perpertrators of her predicament. An example of such pronouncement is: "ONODU M NO NA YA BIAKWARA UNU "- may you all be victims of the situation of mine. Sooner or later, especially in the case of an innocent widow, the perpertrators in such inhuman act begin to find themselves in a similar situation.

Barrenness is a taboo in Igbo society, and leads to serious troubles.[201] When a woman marries and has no children, or is childless because she lost her children to death, she is treated as a witch. Automatically, it is understood that she has anger of gods upon her, and she is regarded as evil, and treated exactly so. Her rightful place is denied her, she is isolated and always kept miserable by her neighbours who constantly remind her of her situation. At the heat of this situation, when the condition becomes unbearable, she could be moved by her emotions to voice out her wish of the same predicament to whoever mocks her. It happens, then, that in no distant time, such people who mock her fall victim of the same situation of barrenness.

---

200 Basden George narrated some of his findings concerning the excruciating process an Igbo widow has to undergo and the pains associated with it: "After the initial outburst, which may last for several hours, she cries loudly for about half an hour for four or five days, beginning each day just before daybreak. At the end of this period, she moves from her deceased husband's house to a small hut in another part of the compound. While dwelling in this hut, she wears no clothes unless perhaps a rag; she must sit on a block of wood (ugbo-ukpa) and nowhere else; instead of a sleeping-mat, a banana-leaf must suffice. No man is allowed to see or to speak to her for three native weeks. She may not pass in or out of the main entrance to the compound; a specially made opening through the wall is made for her. Should she go out through this prepared opening, it is taboo for her to be seen; should this happen, it will be necessary to offer sacrifice to make amends. For seven native weeks she neither works nor cooks; her sole occupation is to sit in the hut, mourning for her dead. She is prohibited from washing her body or combing her hair" (Basden,George, Niger Ibos, London 1966, 278–279).
201 Cf. Basden, Niger Ibos, 226.

Orphans are another group of the downtrodden whose utterances are very powerful. A motherless and fatherless child who utters a revengeful words on another child for abusing his less priviledged situation, most often, have these utterances accomplished. There are many other groups of individuals who are in this category of the downtrodden. We gave the above few examples in order to demonstrate how words can perform through these agents. Let us now examine how word performs in the celebration of the various Igbo rites.

3.11 Performative word and the celebration of rites in Igbo traditional Religion

In making use of what we have earlier learnt in this chapter about the Igbo Beliefs and practices, let us briefly see how the performance of the Igbo word is reflected in the celebration of various Igbo rites.

3.11.1 The rite of initiation

Initiation in Igbo worldview means an introduction into a cult, and symbolizes ritual cleansing. It is a central bridge in the life of an Igbo man. It brings together one's youth and adulthood. It is a period of ignorance and that of knowledge, separating a person from one's life, and also joins him to another by dispersing the early state of passive life, and then, integrating it into a production state, and knitting him with the community. The process of initiation has much to do with performative words, most especially where it involves the ritual languages used, the names and titles given, and so on. In whichever case, these ritual languages or names or titles provoke actions. Circumcision is the first among the initiations that one has to undergo in life. This is not only practised in Igboland but in many parts of Africa, and is highly treasured in traditional life. Writing on this rite J.S.Mbiti has this to say:

> This circumcision blood is like making a covenant, or a solemn agreement, between the individual and his people. Until the individual has gone through the operation he is still an outsider. Once he has shed his blood, he joins the streams of his people, he becomes truly one with them.[202]

Child naming ceremony is another form of initiation. Child naming is regarded as very important and always marked by a ceremony otherwise known as child naming ceremony. As for when a naming ceremony can take place after child bearing, Ogbalu F.C writes: "The actual naming ceremony takes place on the Izu nato (three traditional weeks) ceremony when the child is presented before the family idols and okpesis in

---

202 Mbiti, John, Introduction to African Religion, London 1975, 94.

the presence of the members of the family".²⁰³ At the naming ceremony, water, cola nut, alligator pepper and a special type of leaf are involved. An elder takes the child and taking water with this leaf, purifies the child. He chews the cola nut with the alligator pepper and puts small portion of this mixture in the tiny mouth of the baby and still carrying him or her announces his or her name to the great applause of the people who gathered. Then the mother carries the child from the elder and everyone present starting from the mother and the father has now the honour of giving a name to the child. Later in life, the child as an adult can give himself or herself a name depending on chances or changes of his or her life. These names are understood as outward signs to explain what the givers of the names intends inwardly. The name given is not randomly selected or done through some guess work or through some research work carried out on names. These names are complete expression, which are not only meaningful but reflect on certain experiences and circumstances that occurred during childbirth, human sojourn on earth, and also on social expectations. Igbo names also reflect joy, sorrow, death, prospects, potentials and so on. They are great performers for when a person's name is mentioned the individual bearer reacts accordingly.

Another form of rite of initiation is the prestigious title – taking. While some say that Igbo tradition is gradually disappearing in some areas or aspects of Igbo culture, it is still thriving in several others especially in the taking of and bearing of titles. These titles are highly performative. When an Igboman is addressed by his title, he goes to any length to acknowledge it, as well as, to prove it. Acting under the influence of the title with which he is addressed proves the performative power of Igbo titles. The traditional elements in the initiation ritual in title taking include red cap, feathers, hand beads (iga), working stick (mkpo), metal staff (oji), fan (akupe), elephant tusks (odu). Women receive thick arm bracelets carved out of elephant tusks. These are symbolic, and pass performative messages traditionally.

3.11.2 The rite of purification

In Igbo traditional religion there is the belief in pollution and purification rite. Igbo beliefs about pollution are closely bound up with cosmic order. The world-view describes the model shared by Igbo communities found mainly in the northern and western parts of Igboland which are under the ritual authority of Eze Nri (King of Nri), whose authority rests solely on his ability to institute, abrogate, and cleanse pollutions. The total world of Igbo experience consists of two closely linked sections – uwa (visible world) and ani mmuo (spirit – world). The visible world is a manifestation ,and as it were, of a carbon copy of the invisible world. Chukwu is the creator of the world. He is transcendent and relates with man through different manifestations. Any act against the cosmic order, God or neighbour is taken serious. It is pollution in the land, and according to Professor Metuh:

---
203   Ogbalu , Igbo Institutions and Customs, 71.

There are major pollutions which the Igbo would call abominations, because they threaten the community as a whole, e.g. pollutions arising from murder, incest, birth of twins, bestiality, e.t.c. There are also minor pollutions which may effect only the offender and his immediate kindred e.g., adultery or sex with a menstruating woman. [204]

The purification rites of both major and minor pollutions are called "ikpu aru" (dragging pollution). The character of purification rites vary according to the gravity of the crime and the nature of the offence. The Igbo term "aru" (pollution) in its verbal form may mean "to defile", and it also means "to desecrate". The Eze mmuo (priest-king of Nri) claims for himself the status equivalent to that of the spirits. He has the ritual powers to establish, cleanse, and abrogate prohibitions connected with their cult. As symbols of this authority, he receives the ofo (ritual staff) and the oji (ritual spear) used for the rites of establishing and washing "aru" (pollutions). The Ofo-carrying Nri priests still settle among different Igbo communities to provide pollution-cleansing services. There are three different types of rituals for dealing with evil, and the Igbo have different names for them: "Ichu aja" (sacrifices to drive away evil spirits); "imeria mmuo" (sacrifices of propitiation); and "ikpu aru" (sacrifices of purification).

The purificatory rites properly so called centres around the defiled worshipper, or the human surroundings not the deity. The pollution resulting from the sins of the community is so much that a substitutionary offering of a scape goat kind is made. An animal victim is substituted for the community. The offering is dragged through the polluted places in the community to ritually sweep clean or absorb the dirt (aru). While dragging the animal victim along, the officiating priest utters such words as: "KA ANUMANU A BUGHARA ARU OBODO METARA, KA O BUGHARA YA MA MEE KA OBODO NWERE ONWE YA NA EBE IKPE OMUMA DI; NA NA EBE MBIBI DI; NA NA EBE OKE ONWU; AJO ORIA; UBIAM NA NA EBE IHE OJOO DI ICHE ICHE DI-ISEE" (may this sacrificial victim carry to himself the pollutions, and so avert for the community the wrath of destructions, deadly sicknesses, hardships, and evils of all sorts-Amen). The animal victim thus loaded with dirt is thrown away, and by the power of the above utterances, the community is once more cleansed. So, such utterances of cleansing may be categorized as an intercession. In making the implicit character of the above performative utterances to be more explicit, we may as well put it this way: "the chief priest intercedes that …".

3.11.3 The rite of healing

An Igbo man is aware of human predicament. He is aware of the hazards of life. The most disturbing element in Igbo life is the fear of bad magic, socery and witchcraft. These are some of the greatest enemies of Igbo society. The Igbos fear diseases, sickness, illness, accidents, barrenness, misfortunes, suffering, attacks by insects and

---

204 Metuh, Emefiena Ikenga, African Religions in Western Conceptual Schemes: The problem of interpretation, (Studies in Igbo Religion), Jos 1985, 78.

animals, troubles from spirits, and above all death. Indeed death is the most devastating enemy, which comes at the end when other enemies have done their worst. The Igbos of Nigeria believes in life after death. J.S. Mbiti has this to say:

> In Nigeria some people (Igbo) believe that the dead appear before God to receive their judgement depending on what they have done with their lives. They are then sent to a good place where they join their relatives who departed before them, or bad place where they remain in misery for a long time until eventually God takes pity on them.[205]

The good spirits are in communion with the people. Ancestor reverence is very prominent in Igbo religion. The member of the community who lives a bad life is never remembered. Death is always believed to be caused by something or somebody. So care must be taken for the sick and dying. The sick person is prepared for life after death. The influence of the medicine man in matters relating to healing is prominent. He is a physician psychotherapist and spirit healer. There is medicine to cure the physical conditions of illness, as well as the mental and religious causes of illness and all sicknesses of every kind. The medicine man is not only expected to cure the sickness, but also to announce who is responsible for it. A great emphasis is attached not only on the concoctions to be taken by the patient according to the prescription of the medicine man, but more on the incantations the patient has to pronounce before taking the medicine. Before the patient takes the medicine, he says such words as: "ORIA ISI NA MMUO ISI NA MMADU KA OGWUA WETA OGWUGWO, KA UCHU GBAA HA, KA AKA NA ABO JUO HA OYI" (Whether this illness is from the gods or man, may this medicine bring back the good health, and so put the ailment to flight). The sick Igbo man believes that the efficacy of the medicine depends on this incantation. This incantation can be interpreted as a prayer. Thus, in the light of our discussion on J.L.Austin's teaching on performative word, we may make the above incantation assume an explicit form by saying: "the patient prays that ...".

In Igbo traditional religion, everything possible is done to prevent the sick person's death. The relatives of the sick man do all they can to bring about healing by consulting the best medicine man they can afford. Ogbalu F.C points out an important precautions that must be taken in this regard: "Even when a person is sick and a doctor has to be found, the afa man must be consulted in order to find out which doctor can cure him".[206] Where health fails, he is prepared for life after death.

3.11.4 The rite of the Igbo traditional Priesthood

In Igbo traditional religion, the priest is called "Isi-mmuo"-head of spirit cult. Priests, diviners, and medicine men occupy different positions and play different roles in Igbo societies. They represent three different professions which however could be combined by one person. Most priests may also be diviners and herbalists, yet, the

---
205 Mbiti, Introduction to African Religion, 117.
206 Ogbalu, Igbo Institutions and Customs, 58.

converse does not necessarily hold. A priest holds a culturally recognized status and role in society as the official minister of a particular deity which has a shrine and an organized cult. In summary there are four categories of priests in Igboland:
(i) The Okpara-the family heads who are priests of ancestral shrines.
(ii) The Isi-Mmuo-the heads of spirit-cults who take charge of the village spirit shrines.
(iii) The Ezeani-the chief priest of the Earth-goddess in-charge of the shrine of Ala of each village group.
(iv) The Eze Nri-the priest king of Nri town, accorded with the title of High priest.

In discussing priesthood in Igbo traditional religion, a controversy arises as to whether it is a "call" or a "vocation" or simply by hereditary. It must be mentioned that Cardinal Francis Arinze, the then Archbishop of Onitsha, in his book, Sacrifice in Ibo Religion, affirmed that priesthood in Igbo religion is hereditary and never by election. It is hereditary; a person is a priest of a certain spirit because his father was the priest of that spirit. When the Archbishop treated the priest of the spirit Onirhe of Asaba, whose priesthood was vocational, he said:

> This is not the normal way of being called to the priesthood. The normal thing is hereditary succession according to age. No one dares take up the office of the priesthood when he is not the next rightful successor in the priestly family or specially selected as in the rare cases just mentioned. The future priest is known in advance. [207]

By "rare cases" Arinze means the vocational way. Materials and evidences available to us do not support the view of the Archbishop. Suffice it here to mention Chinua Achebe's Arrow of God as an example. It was to Umuachala village that the priesthood of Ulu was conferred at the installation of the Ulu deity and it was to Ezeulu's family that the priest was to come. Yet it was the sole prerogative of Ulu, according to Igbo belief, to choose from among the sons of Ezeulu who would be his successor. The lot fell on Nwafor:

> Although he was still only a child, it looked as though the deity had already marked him out as his future Chief priest. Even before he had learnt to speak more than a few words he had been strongly drawn to the god's ritual. It could almost be said that he already knew more about it than even the eldest Nevertheless no one would be so rash as to say openly that Ulu would do this or do that. When the time came that Ezeulu was no longer found in his place Ulu might choose the least likely of his sons to succeed him. It happened before.[208]

From the above passage, it would be wrong then to hold that the future priest is known in advance. Though this does not rule out entirely that from disposition, people could guess correctly who the future priest could be. The priest designate is expected to show from childhood some right dispositions and these include moroseness, love of solitude, psychic qualities-high intellectual work and retentive memory. He would be gradually

---

207 Arinze, Sacrifice in Igbo Religion, 68.
208 Achebe, Chinua, Arrow of God, London 1975, 28.

introduced into the cult of the deity and so when he is eventually installed, he would also be ritually and officially initiated into the cult and be proclaimed the priest. His authority must be based on those of past priests, and from whom he received the priestly spirit and character. This is why in the case of Ulu, their skulls must be hung round the rafter of the shrine of the deity to look on him, to watch and guide him, and to kill him if he deviates from the path they have trodden and set him to continue and maintain. Being a priest in Igbo traditional religion, therefore, means to carry a deity. To carry a deity is synonymous with being a priest. By implication, he becomes the mouth-piece of the deity. His words are deified because he speaks on behalf of his deity. He has access to the supernatural realities because he communes with the deity and in return pronounces the divine messages that begin to perform in reality before the people.

The symbolic elements that are involved in the rite of the installation of a traditional Igbo priest are in themselves very performative. These symbolic elements include Nzu (cohise chalk), Uhie (camwood), priestly gab, anklet (ola muo), tutelary ring and sacred pot or basket. The rubbing of one part of the priest initiate with Nzu, and the other with Uhie–cohise chalk and camwood respectively, is the rite of purification. It is this purification rite that makes him a go–between man and the deity. It makes him to be a man with dual nature–half man and half spirit. The Nzu symbolizes that he is alive as one who still lives in this world, and the Uhie presents him as dead–his access to the spirit world. This explains why in Igboland, Nzu is robbed on a new born child as a symbol of life, while Uhie is part of the mortuary preparation of a corpse before burial. The wearing of the priestly garment shows a concrete participation in the world of the deity. Wearing of the anklet (ola muo) establishes a special union between him and the deity that lasts till death. In some areas in Igboland, the priest initiate in addition wears the tutelary ring in his ear. The carrying of the sacred symbol of the deity in the sacred pot or basket of the deity to the deity's market is what is called "ipu ahia muo". It is a public appearance of a new priest, and through it, he is openly declared and acclaimed the priest of a particular deity. In some Igbo villages, after the priest has gone to the market, he will end-up going to the most revered shrine sometimes called–Ihu Chineke, to pay homage. In a similar account, J.C.U Aguwa recounts that the rites of initiation into a cult of deity as priest diviner begins on the evening of Eke market day and ends the next day which is Orie. According to him:

> The candidate dresses in loin cloths. His hair is completely shaven and his body distinguished with coatings of pastes of white chalk, yellow chalk and red clay. He is brought to lie Supine at the shrine with the wooden and clay statues of agwu lined up on his head side. Assistants who are dibia hold him in position while spicy medicine is poured into his eyes. He must not show feelings of pain. The dog and the fowl are slaughtered and the blood spilled over him and into his eyes, mouth and ears. The officiating dibia articulates the intentions of the rite in a prayer addressed to agwu. As he does this he holds the ofo with the right hand.
>
> > Agwu, nwa gi a emejuputala ihe a na atu anya n' aka ya.
> > O nyele gi nkita, nye gi okuko.
> > O nyele gi oji, nye gi mmanya.
> > O tuola gi, O kpobatala gi ulo.
> > Ugbua o rule gi aka:

Nye ya umu; nye ya Oganihu
Buru ya agwu udo, agwu aku n' uba.
Ikpo ya igwo ogwu, gosi ya ezi mgborogwu
Ma ehihie ma uchichi

Ikpo ya Igba afa, too nti n' ala ma o kpoo gi
Gi na ya, onye ga – igho ibe ya aghugho
Ofo gbuo kwa ya – ihaa
Ofo gbuo kwa ya – ihaa
Ofo gbuo kwa ya – ihaa

(Agwu, this child of yours has fulfilled all expected of him.
He has given you dog, given you the fowl.
He has given you kola, given you wine.
He has made images of you, and made a home with you.
Now it is your turn:

Give him children; give him progress.
Be to him the agwu of peace, the agwu of wealth.
If you call him to be healer, -
Show him the right herbal roots.
Both in the day and in the night.
If you call him to be diviner, -
Listen to him when he invokes you.
You and he, whoever deceives or cheats the other –
May the Ofo kill him – ihaa
May the Ofo kill him – ihaa
May the Ofo kill him – ihaa)

The prayer ends with the enunciation of the conditions of coexistence between agwu and the dibia. At every mention of the word ihaa (may it be so), the officiating dibia taps the Ofo gently on the ground. A pact is thus made.[209]

This prayer is a request partly for favours and partly for doom. As performative utterances, the above prayers may be made more explicit in this way: "the officiating dibia requests that the priest-candidate be blessed with … and be doomed if …". So, we qualify the prayers as requests.

The installation processes declare clearly the functions of a priest. A priest is the man who leads the community in religious matters, and through rituals, sacrifices and prayers protects the community and removes obstacles for it in its dealings with spirit world. In trying to relate the role Agwu[210] plays in the choice and the installation of a priest, Jude C.U Aguwa portrays priesthood in Igbo religion as a divine call. Still on the functions of a priest, Dawson writes:

---

209 Aguwa, Jude, The Agwu Deity in Igbo Religion, A Study of the Patron Spirit of Divination and Medicine in an African Society, Enugu 1995, 84–85.
210 Agwu is sometimes described as the patron god of the medicine men. Every medicine man has his own personal Agwu which he carries along wherever he goes. He is bound to offer him kolanut or any gift first before he himself is allowed to partake of them. It is designed in human form, carved from ogirisi tree.

The institution of priesthood has a two-fold origin. On the one hand, the priest is servant of the god, the minister of the temple and the diviner who ascertains the divine will and decree. On the other hand, he is the master of the sacrifice without whose power and knowledge the sacred rites cannot be performed. He is the bridge builder and the guardian of the threshold between the world of men and the world of gods. It is in his powers to open and close the channels by which divine blessings are conferred on the community so that he himself comes to share in some measure in the power and prestige of the gods.[211]

So the very important function of a priest as we have seen from the above citation is that he goes ahead of his people, daily removing the obstacles on their way to life, leading the community in religious matters, and through rituals, sacrifices and prayers protects the community and removes obstacles for it in its dealings with spirit world.

3.11.5 The rite of the Igbo Traditional Marriage

The Igbos say – otu onye anaghi anu nwanyi, that means, marriage is a family affair. In support of the above statement Ogbalu F.C writes: "The expression 'otu onye adighi alu nwanyi' (not only one person marries a woman) sums up the people's attitude. The choice of a wife is not just the concern of the man, it is that of the whole family whose approval must be obtained".[212] The process of marriage among Igbos is a long and protracted one, sometimes taking years to complete. Igbos regard marriage as the centre of life and therefore take great pains to effect it. Socially and culturally, Igbo is patrilinially organised on the basis of Umunna[213] (kindred); children of the same father which is made of posterity in the male lineage of ancestors. The posterity ranges from nuclear to minor and major sublineages and could find abode anywhere both far and wide with blood relationships as the bond. This is strongly behind the reason why marriage inquiries are very important so as to certify that the two people preparing for marriage have no blood relationship. Despite the facts that Igbos have Igbo as their common language, marriage ceremony differs from place to place. Marriage is commonly regarded as the normal sequel to the rites of adolescence, whose purpose was to prepare for this stage. Igbos just like other Africans believe that marriage is the highest point of any relationship, and indeed, the focus of existence. All the dimensions of time meet here, and the whole drama of history is repeated, renewed and revitalised. Marriage is a drama in which all are involved,

---

211 Dawson, Christopher, Religion And Culture, London 1949, 91.
212 Ogbalu, Igbo Institutions and Customs, 13.
213 Umunna (kindred) includes all the children of the same father. Father in this sense refers to ancestor. Because of this ancestral root, the children are prohibited from inter-marrying. Umunna connotes the ties of extended families as distinct from the western notion of family as nuclear. It is the basic socio-political unit in any Igbo traditional society. It comprises the descendants in the male line of the founder ancestor whose name the lineage is sometimes called. The Umunna is organized on three levels of ascending hierarchy viz: the family, the Ebo, and the village.

otherwise, he who does not participate in it is a curse to the community, and he or she is a rebel and a law–breaker. It means that the person concerned has rejected society and society rejects him in return.

In the choice of a wife, Igbos give prefence to a girl with long thin limbs which are regarded as signs of fast growth and hugeness later on in married life. As a general rule, fat young girls with stout brawny joined limbs are not ranked among the beautiful according to Igbo standards. This is because such usually scarcely ever added an inch to their low stature later in married life. Whereas ideas of female beauty vary from people to people, the horror of disease or of physical deformity can be said to be universal. A huge woman (not necessarily a fat one) is the choice of most people. This has many obvious advantages, for not only that she commands respect and is the pride of her husband, also she will be able to do farm work and in childbearing, she would generate her kind. Furthermore, it has an added social advantage. Such a woman because of her size is easily recognisable in the assembly of women. Given the average skill and intelligence she usually becomes the leader of her dance-group or the president of the women's council.

Since Igbos are patriarchal people, marriage is deemed an indispensable factor for the continuation of the family line of descent. Children occupy central point in Igbo marriage. The first and foremost consideration is the fertility of the couple. Parents long for this and the father of the family requests this every morning in his kolanut prayer. The mother begs for it while giving cult to her Chi during annual festival. So if you ask ordinary Igbo man or woman why he or she desires to marry, the spontaneous response is in order to beget children, to get a family. This love for having one's own children gives rise to such native names as: Nwabugwu–a child is prestigious; Nwakego–a child out–values all money; Nwadiaguu–a child is desirable, a man is literally famished with the hunger for children. This idea is still present in the Igbo society today. A childless marriage, therefore, is recognised as Chi ojoo–a bad omen, a source of serious disappointment and sooner or later leads to serious trouble between man and wife. Until she begets a child, the position of the woman remains shaky and unpredictable. She becomes really secure after the birth of a male child. It is at this stage that she is welcomed as a responsible house wife in her husband's extended family. In fact, the birth of the child gives her the title of wife, before this time she may be a wife only in anticipation.[214] Traditionally, Igbo marriage rites basically comprise the following five stages:

*Iku aka-Knocking at the door
*Iju ese-Stage of inquiry
*Inete ani-Probation
*Ime ego-Paying of bride price
*Igba nkwu-Wine carrying

---

214 It is to be noted with particular emphasis that for the traditional Igbo community, marriage must be fruitful. Its fruits are children. Therefore, marriage and procreation in Igbo community are a unity. Without children, for the Igbo, marriage is incomplete. To die without children, in Igbo traditional society, is to be completely cut off from the human society, to be disconnected and to lose all link with mankind.

Three types of marriage arrangements are evident in traditional Igbo society. In the olden days, and up to 1956 when it was abolished by law, child marriages were common: On one side, such arrangement begins when the child was still in the womb, and when it was born must uphold the marriage arrangement that had been already planned by the parents: On the other side, such marriage arrangement begins when the child had been born but was not yet of the age to make decisions. In such marriages, the consent of the child was not sought. It was taken for granted if the parents or guardians had given their consent. The following reasons may be behind such arrangements:

i. To cement family to family friendship
ii. To associate with some cherished values which are found in a particular family
iii. To be associated with the popularity and achievements of the other family

The current type of marriage arrangement which is the third type of marriage arrangement is by the individual himself. It is born out of courtship.[215] In this case, the youngman makes a personal decision on whom to marry. Thanks to the era in which we live. In this personal decision, however, parents' or guardians' approval are sought before the individual can proceed forward. Certain signs are visible when a grown-up is ripe to marry. Such signs are summed up under the following considerations:

i. Risky adventures–climbing tall palm trees, severe hunting, intensive farming
ii. Unnecessary quarrels–with domestic shores, at least provocation
iii. Choice of Association–found comfortable companionship with his father and reputable elders
iv. Assuming an elder–exempting himself from juvenile practices.

When an individual exhibits the above mentioned signs, the next thing that follows suit is complaint about ordeal in cooking his meals after the fatigue of his daily work. Such complaints support the already mentioned signs in saying that the individual is now ripe to marry. To this effect the Igbos say–okokporo tamuba gbasara isi nri, I mara na inu nwanyi agubana ya, that is, when a bachelor begins to complain about cooking his food, it indicates his desire to get married. As a result, his father or guardian would in turn ask him basic questions concerning marriage. The next crucial question is whether the individual has found somebody to marry. If the answer is in the affirmative, the ceremony would begin with the first stage which is Iku aka na uzo-knocking at the door.

Iku aka n'uzo–knocking at the door is the stage of the initial declaration of the intention by the bridegroom–to–be of his intention to marry the desired bride–to–be. This process is not done in isolation. Both the families are involved. The youngman in question has to confide in his parents or guardian of his intention to marry a particular

---

215 Courtship in Igbo traditional society is considered as betrothal. Unlike the ancient Igbo tradition where a girl is betrothed to a boy while still in the womb or as an infant or teenager, the modern betrothal or courtship is a free choice of the young couple born out of a certain period of friendship in which they have come to understand each other and are convinced that they can share the rest of their lives together as husband and wife.

girl that appeals to him. It is left to the parents or guardian of the youngman, after duly discussing with their son, to send message across to the family of the girl about their intending visit. In our time, the purpose of a visit of this nature is considered an open secrete, since sometimes such visits are arranged by both parties who already know the intention of their children. This stage has to do with the official declaration of intention on the part of the youngman, and official confirmation of consent on the part of the girl. The visiting party are mainly made up of few individuals, especially the father of the intending bridegroom or his guardian and a few other people. Usually it is a visit that is accompanied with wine. The visiting party is well received by the hosting party and presented with cola nut. It is after this gesture that the visitors through their spokesman who in most cases is the father or the guardian of the youngman, by presenting the accompanying wine, introduces the purpose of their visit. This may be done in this or other similar words:

a. We are pursuing a precious animal and it ran into your compound, and we have come to catch it.
b. We saw a riped fruit in your compound, and we have come to pluck it.

In some exceptional cases where the father or the guardian of the girl is not willing to give out his daughter, he answers politely in the negative. He gives such excuses as:

a. She is still schooling and should be allowed to finish.
b. She is still too young to marry.

In any case, this does not prevent the parties from drinking the wine that has been presented. In a different situation, after the declaration of the intention by the visiting party, the hosting party by the acceptance of the wine, relies on their daughter to determine what next to say. In this case, the girl is called in and informed of the wish of the visiting party. In the case where the girl gives his consent, there is relief on the part of the guest, and this is followed by clapping, joy often expressed through shaking of hands, warmth embrace and singing. The success of this first stage marks the beginning of the ogo (In–lawship) that will be later cemented and officially declared. From this stage, the both parties do no longer remain strange to themselves but recognise themselves as parties who have some tie that relates them, a bond that unifies them. This means, the youngman can freely visit the girl's family as part of the family without fear of either harassment or embarrassment from the father of the girl or her mother. Likewise, the girl can freely visit her home-to-be and be accepted as part of the family. She merits special names from her mother in–law–to–be if she is still alive. Sometimes, these names are lavished upon the girl partly out of admiration, and partly out of making the assurance double sure that she does not change her mind tomorrow. In this case, she is always giving the best treatment whenever she comes visiting. Her visits, however depends on how near she lives to the boy's parents.[216] Sometimes, the knocking at the door is done by a neutral person called

---

216 Cf. Anyanwu, The rite of initiation, 252; see also Okonkwo, Emmanuel, Marriage in the Christian and Igbo traditional context: towards an inculturation, Frankfurt am Main 2003, 77.

intermediary. The move is initiated by the groom's family and carried out through the intermediary. This is because it is considered that tradition forbids the suitor and his family from approaching the girl's family directly. The intermediary, therefore, serves as a mediator, brings the message to the bride's family and sends the feed-back to the family of the groom. This stage is normally very brief. Where a favourable response is obtained, the second stage would commence.

The second stage, Iju Ese–Inquiry, or "ihe ajuju" [217] is very important in marriage and very vital to the rest of the marriage process. After the groom has declared his intention to marry the bride, inquiries begin by both families. Lieber J.W puts it this way: "When the families are informed of the young couple's intention to marry, they at once begin to investigate each other's lineage and consult diviners to determine whether the marriage will succeed".[218] The inquiries are very thorough and remote. Apart from the information obtained from various individuals, gods are consulted through the diviners to know if the marriage would be a success or a failure. The results of the inquiries will determine if the marriage will go on or not. Certain areas of interest are necessary in marriage inquiries: "Vigorous scrutiny of the background and history of the families of both parties to ascertain both past and present behavioural traits, and types of illnesses and deaths existing in any of the families engaging in the marriage contract".[219] Again, one inquires to know if the families are related or have any trace of consanguinity. This means knowing well who the parents are, their origin, whether they are free-borns or aliens to the town where they are living, or mixed. This aspect of the inquiry is meticulously carried out. Secondly, there is an inquiry as to whether any member of the family in the past has committed what the Igbos call Aru-taboo in the locality. Such taboos include igbu ochu (murder), ikwu udo (suicide), and so on. Thirdly, it is also necessary to obtain death records in the family. By this is meant the frequency by which one dies in the family either by natural cause or by accident or strange causes. Fourthly, certifying the state of health of the individual members of the family is very important. This helps to trace if there is a record of serious or incurable diseases or sicknesses in the family. Fifthly, it is necessary too to obtain information about the kind of gods the family worships. This helps to know if the family is involved in witches and witchcraft to the detriment of the family deity. Sixthly, a trace of infertility or sterility is very vital. Parents have to know if there is record of childlessness in the other family. This is because child bearing is seriously valued in Igbo tradition and is considered a sign that the marriage is successful. Therefore, no parents would like to support their daughter or their son to marry from a family where childlessness or lack of male offsprings is observed. Seventhly, high rate of divorce in any family is very detrimental and scares intending in-laws away. It is a sign that the family cannot manage it's internal crisis, that a groom cannot manage crisis in marriage. It is a sign that family peace and understanding are lacking. No parents would like to allow their son or their daughter to be

---

217 Anyanwu, The rite of initiation, 251.
218 Lieber, Ibo village communities, 66.
219 Okonkwo, Marriage in the Christian and Igbo, 45.

married into such a family. Eighthly, no family would like to marry from a family that is considered poor, and therefore, socially irrelevant. Although this is not mostly emphasized, however, a well behaved and wealthy husband is always preferred to a pauper. A family can be considered wealthy not only by the money they have but also by the fame they acquire in hunting, wrestling or other sporting events. When the inquiries are completed and both families are assured that it will be a good marriage, they become more friendly towards each other as part of the courtship, and gifts are exchanged between them. This gives way to the third stage, Ije Nnete Uno-Probation. Good manners constitute beauty. It is therefore very pertinent to test the characters of the future partners. Thus, probation is for both the groom and the bride. The bride would have to visit the family of the groom. Within this period, the groom and his family would check to know whether she possesses those qualities that make for a good wife. She is expected to be social, clean, hardworking, respectful towards her elders, obedient and even-tempered. During this time, the bride is also expected to take part in the domestic duties, such as, cooking, cleaning of house and washing clothes. Depending on her age and ability, she may take part in farming and marketing. Where the mother-in-law is alive and active, the probation is more rigorous for the bride. In former times, virginity was insisted upon, but nowadays due to the change of circumstances, it is only a recommendation instead of an obligation. The way she went about her duties will recommend her as a suitable and capable house wife. Her family background and the character of her mother have a lot to add or to subtract as the case may be. It is the duty of the parents especially the mother to train their daughters as future wives. For the groom, it is a probation to see if he is able to take care, to protect and provide for the bride. This is a test of the validity of what is concluded when inquiries were made on him. Based on high moral standard of the Igbo people, culture forbids that the intending wife should relate with her intending husband in any way that suggests consummation of yet to be marriage. For this reason, the bride is expected to be passing nights with either her mother in-law or the sisters of the groom. At the end of probation stage which lasts for days or weeks, the bride is offered some gifts both for herself and for her mother. She is accompanied home with pots of palm wine and some cola nuts. When this stage is satisfactory, the fourth stage, Ime Ego-Payment of Bride Price, commences. Explaining what Bride Price means Onwuejeogwu M.A writes: "Bride-price, marriage-payments, bride-purchase etc., are all phrases which have been adopted at one time or another by observers to describe services and/or goods given by a groom to his bride's family before a union is socially recognized".[220]

A date is fixed when the family of the groom returns to the family of the bride to pay the bride price. In the payment of the bride-price, the following observations of Hannelore Forster is very important:

> Die Geschenke für den "Brautpreis" wurden nicht mehr in Naturlien entrichtet, sondern in Form von Bargeld. Bei der Eheschließung der Tochter eines "Chief" oder eines Mädchens

---

220 Onwuejeogwu, Angulu,The Social Anthropology of Africa: An Introduction, London 1975, 85.

aus einer höher gestellten Lineage wurden größeren Beträge entrichtet als bei Eheschließung zwischen Ehepartnern mit niedrigerem Status.[221]

The payment is done by the father of the groom or his legitimate representative if he is incapacitated either by death or sickness. This is usually preceded by bargaining on both sides, although the customary bridewealth is known. When agreement is reached, the parties shake hands and substantial portion of the bridewealth is paid. Commenting on this gesture Kpiebaya G.E writes: "Payment of the bridewealth makes the marriage agreement legal thus giving uxorial and genetical rights to the husband and his lineage over the girl".[222] It is only when the bridewealth has been paid that the man can take the woman as his wife. Before then, she was only betrothed to her. It is the father of the bride or his representative as the case may be who receives the price on behalf of the bride's family. However, emphasis is made that the bride is not being sold. This is the reason why the money is not much, and regarded as a token to the bride's parents for training her.

According to Igbo custom, when the bridewealth has been agreed upon, the father of the girl gives her a cup containing palm wine. She is expected to sip it and give it to her new spouse to do likewise. In so doing she introduces him as her husband to the people who have assembled to witness the occasion. This gesture is symbolic and highly performative. The audience then shouts its approval and the bridewealth is then officially accepted by the bride's family. With the paying and collection of the dowry the man is officially described as having married and she joins her husband immediately to found a new home. A sumptuous banquet and merry-making follow, disturbed only by the weeping occasioned by the separation of the bride from her family. Those who weep are consoled by the elderly women who remind them that the bride has not died but has only embarked on a journey. Today, however, it is not enough traditionally to declare a man and a woman as husband and wife without completing what in our time is referred to as traditional marriage expressed through the ceremony called Igba Nkwu–Wine Carrying.[223] This is the public and official declaration of a woman and a man as husband and wife. It is the apex of traditional

---

221 Forster, Heirat und Ehe bei den Akan in Ghana, ein Vergleich traditioneller und städtischer Gesellschaftsformen, sozialwissenschaftliche Studien zu internationalen Probleme/social science studies on international Problems, Band 83, Breitenbach D. (ed.), Saarbrücken 1983, 34.
222 Kpiebaya, George, Dagaaba Traditional Marriage and Family Life, London 1992, 10.
223 "The young man in the company of his parents and some selected relatives will then come to the family of the young woman he intends to marry. The parents of the young woman will cook food in preparation for the visit. They also invite some of their kindred members and friends to be around. At this coming together, the okpala of the young woman's kindred will take his drinking cup and take a sip of the palm wine brought by the in-law. He then calls the young woman and gives her the cup filled with wine. She takes a sip from it and hands over the remaining to the young man who is to marry her. This attracts cheers from all sides. Then the day's business is accomplished. People chat with each other as the eating and drinking characterized the remaining part of the day's visit" (Anyanwu, The rites of initiation in Christian liturgy and in Igbo traditional society: towards the inculturation of Christian liturgy in Igboland, 252).

marriage, and respected by customary law. The term Igba Nkwu–Wine Carrying is self explanatory by the plentiful wine and sumptuous meals that are lavishly served. While the first four stages are hitherto limited to nuclear and extended family on both sides, Igba Nkwu offers opportunity for external relations and friends to participate. This is the reason why it involves much expenses. The groom has it as an opportunity to impress everybody as a worthy son–in–law. For wealthy grooms, it is an exhibition of affluence starting from the costly dresses won by the couple, their immediate assistants, distinguished groups, gifts both in cash and kind, surplus food and drinks, the music, spraying of money at the bridal dance.

The family of the bride is not saved from the expenses as they should by the ceremony of Idu uno performed within the Igba Nkwu equip their daughter with all the necessary items she would need in her husband's home. The invitation is unlimited and it is an occasion free for all. All are expected to dress traditionally. The religious dimension in this occasion is not left out. Spontaneous prayers known as "Igo ofo" expressing the good wishes for the new couple are said by the parents. In explaining the traditional elements that are involved in wine carrying, it becomes pertinent to refer to how the programme of events look like:

i. The bridegroom arrives in the company of relatives and friends and led gloriously into the compound of the bride by a fitting music. All get seated.
ii. Introductory ceremony is performed
iii. Rituals over the cola nut is performed, served and eaten with Ose Oji or alligator pepper
iv. Ushering in of the bride by the bridal train amid some background traditional music
v. Reception of wine of marriage bond. The bride receives from her father a cup full of palm wine, in the midst of the crowd, seeks out her husband, sips the wine, with one knee on the ground before the husband, offers him the cup of wine. Nathaniel I.Ndiokwere sees this particular action as the highlight of the celebration, and in his words:

> The highlight of the traditional wedding rite is the final consent made publicly by the girl by way of handing over a cup of palm wine to the prospective husband. The girl collects the cup of wine from her father or eldest uncle or another representative of the family and searches for the prospective husband in the midst of other young men at the scene. Having identified the husband she hands the cup of wine to him and the man drinks. As from that moment they would be free to sit together in the assembly. After few admonitions from some selected elders, presentation of gifts from the girl's family and other friends, merriments begin. The marriage contract is sealed.[224]

The husband while accepting the wine from her, lifts her up, drinks the wine amidst cheers and clapping of hands from the crowd. This action is very remarkable. It marks the exchange of consent sealed by sharing one cup of wine from the same cup.

vi. Together, both the groom and the bride return the cup to the father of the bride and kneeling before him, the father offers prayers known as Igo Ofo for such wishes

---

224 Ndiokwere, Nathaniel, The African Church Today and Tomorrow, vol. II, Ibadan 1986, 145.

as: family peace ,love, understanding, tolerance, fruits of the womb, progress and protection. The prayer of the father of the bride is an evidence of the performance of word in Igbo rituals. This prayer is highly efficacious because the resultant effects of it are evident in the new family that has begun,viz: fruits of the womb, family peace, family protection, and so on. This prayer is very important and can be interpreted as a plea. In the light of what we have discussed about J.L.Austin's performative word we may explicitly qualify this prayer in the following way: "He pleads that they have family peace ...". In this journey through the marriage rites, one personally observes how words perform, and how actions confirm the reality of what is being celebrated. The bride for example, does not need to make verbal statements in order to contract her marriage with the would – be life partner. Her action of handing over a cup filled with palm wine, and the drinking together from the same cup, is performative symbol of the marriage contract.

3.11.6 The rite of kolanut (Iwa Oji) / Sacrifice (Ichu Aja)

Kola nut plays a significant role in Igbo society. In fact, the Igbos celebrate kola nut. Kola nut or Oji is another aspect of the performatives that is symbolic. It symbolizes life and for this reason, many profound and mysterious interpretations and formalities are accorded it. Kola is a symbol which hold the Igbos together. "Oji ", therefore, is interpreted to mean: "O" – Omenala (custom), "J"–Jikotara (that unites), "I "–Igbo (Igbo people). Igbos gather with such attentiveness, dedicated interest, respect and carefulness at the celebration of kola nut. Despite the present day modernizations, the place of Kolanut-Oji in Igbo world–view remains unchallenged. Kolanut rituals are intergral part of the Igbo identity among Africans, and its significant role cannot be denied. No official, as well as unofficial gathering in Igboland may meaningfully hold without the Kolanut rituals. Indeed kolanut, it is often said that among the various tribes in Nigeria, the Yorubas[225] produce the kolanut most, the Hausas[226] consume it most but the Igbos ritualize it most. It is so among Igbos because of their belief on what kolanut symbolizes, and according to Edwyn Bevan: "Symbols purport to give information about the things they symbolize, to convey knowledge of their nature, which those who see or hear the symbols have not had before or have not otherwise".[227] The Igbo, therefore, believes that kolanut is a symbol of life. Thus, one hears among

---

225 Yoruba is one of the three major tribes in Nigeria, and indeed one of the largest ethnic groups in West Africa. It lies in the western region of Nigeria. The language of the Yoruba is Yoruba and constitute 21 percent of Nigeria population. Outside Nigeria, some sizeable number of Yoruba form minority groups in Republic of Benin, Ghana and Togo.
226 Hausa is also one of the major tribes in Nigeria. The language of the Hausa people is Hausa, and the Hausa ethnic group is located in the northern region of Nigeria. Approximately Hausa, which has the Fulanis joined to it, constitute 29 percent of Nigeria population. It is highly influenced by Islamic culture. Sizeable number of Hausas are also found in Sudan, Cameroun, Ghana, Ivory Coast, Chad and Niger Republic.
227 Bevan, Edwin, Symbolism and Belief: The Gifford Lectures, 1933–4, London 1962, 10.

Igbos: "onye wetara oji wetara ndu"- he who brings kolanut brings life. Kolanut is also a symbol of welcome to a visitor, as well as goodwishes. According to Rems Nna Umeasiegbu: "Hospitality may take different forms, but by far the most important of all their outward manifestations of good neighbourliness and camaderie is the sharing of Kolanuts (cola acummata). It precedes all other forms of hospitality".[228] This explains the reason why every Igbo man first of all presents his visitor with kolanut. Ogbalu F.C expresses this in the following words:

> It is the very first thing which is presented to a visitor familiar or unfamiliar, relative or non relative before any other thing or discussion on any subject. In the same way, it is the first thing to be presented to an idol or god before any other offering or request is made.[229]

In Igbo society, certain ceremonies cannot hold without the presence of kolanut. In the words of Nzeako J.U.T: "o nwere otutu ihe o ga-abu ma ahughi oji, ndi mmadu agaghi eme ha. Ihe ndia bu igbu ehi wee chie echichi, ikwasa ihe n' arusi, ita oji ala, ikpe ikpe ala na idozi okwu, ilu nwunye na ichi echichi",[230]-there are many functions which without kolanut may not be carried on with. These functions include slaughtering a cow for title taking, settling disputes, marriage contract and title taking. Kolanut is also used for offering sacrifices, and in the performance of other rituals, such as, in burying the dead, in naming ceremonies and in various traditions. Although kolanut may be analysed as the seed of a kola tree with bitter caffeine that is chewed as a condiment and stimulant, and by its physical appearance is compared with chestnut, but by its function it is more valuable than a mere chestnut among the Igbo people. It is always carried with respect, neither with one hand nor with left hand but with both hands. The Igbo kolanut defines friendship and partaking of it ratifies the bond of this friendship. However, before the partaking in the Oji, there are some earlier ritual stages: Iche oji (presentation of kolanut), Igo oji (consecration of kolanut), Iwa oji (breaking of kolanut), and Ike oji (distribution of kolanut).

"Iche Oji"-presentation of Kolanut introduces the Kolanut rituals. As a sign of not being evil-minded, the host publicly touches the Kolanut with his lips before handing it over to the guests. In the case of the host who is married, it is the duty of the wife to fetch the Kolanut for the husband. Taking the kolanut from his wife, and after touching it with his lips, he hands over the kolanut to his guests by declaring: "Ibe anyinu Oji abiala o"-dear guests here is kolanut. He can also do this declaration through other words. In some ceremonies like marriage and likewise, the host does not present the kolanut directly but does so through the head of the kindred or the authorized individual among the group as the case may be. The eldest among the guests accepts the kolanut on behalf of the group while the youngest among them takes over the kolanut and shows it round to the acknowledgment of the guests. Sometimes this process may take a different dimension. For example, names, especially of the eldest among the guests, may be mentioned as the kolanut is being handed over such as: "Nna anyi Okolo oji abiala"-Chief Okolo here is kolanut. Then, chief Okolo accepts the kolanut

---

228 Umeasiegbu, Rems, Words are Sweet, Igbo stories and storytelling, Stuttgart 1982, 5.
229 Ogbalu, Igbo Institutions and Customs, 71.
230 Nzeako, Tagbo, Omenala Ndi Igbo, Ibadan 1986, 3.

and responds: "Dalu oji"-thanks for the kolanut. Instead of the youngest showing the kolanut round, Chief Okolo may also choose to pass it on to the next person to him, so it rotates until all the guests have a look at it. While handing over the kolanut to one's neighbour, it is accompanied by the mentioning of the neighbour's name, and may be, his title and little introduction about him. By so doing, the people present find out who comes from where. It is often said: "Oji agawala njem itu agbulu"-by the ritual of presentation of kolanut, it embarks on a journey of establishing lineage. By the "relay race" of the kolanut, an introduction of the guests is at the same time not avoidable. One is able to discover, for instance, sons of women born in the kindred, sons-in-law. Such people are given some priority over the other guests. Care is taken to avoid mistakes in the "relay race" of the kolanut since such mistake will attract penalty. Our people do say: "Ebute oji ebutue okwu na uka"-when a kolanut is presented sometimes problems are inevitable. When the kolanut has finished going round, it is returned to the host with the words: "oji eze di eze n' aka"-the king's kolanut is in his hands. This means according the host the honour due to him. He may then, before praying over the kolanut, hand some to certain individuals according to what they represent as "oji rue uno, okwue ebe osiri puta"-when kolanut reaches home, it will say from where it comes.[231] It is the duty of the host to consecrate the kolanut for the Igbo say "mmadu anaghi abu nwa n' anu o gburu"-honour is given to whom honour is due. If the gathering is such that the kindred or clan or community is involved, the eldest does the consecration. He takes up the kolanut, clears his throat, for the Igbo say: "okenye kwacha akpiri, ndi mmuo egee nti"-when an elder clears his throat, the spirits listen. He raises up the kolanut and begins to consecrate. There are not already-made formular. He prays spontaneously and for various intentions including for long life, good health, wealth, progress, fruits of the womb, against wicked people and bad spirits. The words of the consecration is very powerful and performative in invoking a mood that makes the presence of the ancestors and the deities present and very much felt. Here is a typical prayer for consecrating a kolanut:

> Chukwu Abiama bia taa oji
> Nna anyi ha bianu taa oji
> Umu mmuo na-ejere anyi ozi bianu taa oji
> Onye biri ka ibe ya biri
> Nwoke di ka nwanyi di
> Okenye ga-ebi nwata ga-ebi
> Ndu nwoke ndu nwanyi

---

231 The tradition of handing over kolanut to various individuals among the guests is from the understanding that they are like messengers sent by the people they are representing as their mouth-piece in the gathering. These representatives have the duty to narrate to the people they represent what they have experienced in their mission. The kolanut they take home is a sign that they were well received. It is a sign of benevolence on the part of the host for the people they are representing. The take-home kolanut must not be consecrated before hand, otherwise, if one gives his guest a consecrated kolanut, what is he to tell his ancestors and deities at home? No ancestor or deity would accept a kolanut already dedicated to another ancestor or deity. So the host gives the kolanut to his guests for home-taking before consecrating, splitting and sharing the rest.

Ndu okenye ndu nwata
Anyi choro ndu na ihe e ji enyere ndu aka
Anyi choro ihe anyi ga-eri ma hapu ihe ga-eri anyi
Anyi choro ogonogo ndu, ahu isiike, omumu na oganihu[232]

There are many other intentions that may be added, and the participants respond at intervals : "isee !"-so shall it be. At the end of the consecration, the type of aura that one feels is understood in the following words: "okenye goo ofo o dika o were nye ndi mmuo n'aka"- when an elder consecrates, he gives directly to the spirits. The participants may add such utterances as : "ka igolu ka olelu"–as you have prayed so shall it be done.

"Iwa oji"-breaking of kolanut follows. In Igboland, this ritual differs from one place to another. In certain areas like Awka, Onitsha, Nnewi, Njikoka and some Riverrine, it is the official duty of the eldest to break the kolanut after he has consecrated it. In a situation where the kolanuts are many, he breaks the one he has used to pray while other people present help him to break the rest. In other places like Enugu, Ngwo, Nsukka, Owerri, Orlu, Abakaliki, Umuahia, Ngwa, it is the official duty of the youngest among the group to break the kolanut. Title holders, when around, take up the breaking of kolanut in places like Ohaji-Egbema and Oguta. But in their absence, the eldest in the group takes up the duty. Although women traditionally have no place in the kolanut rituals, in Asaba, Issele Ukwu, Ubulu Ukwu area, titled women are allowed to break kolanut. When the kolanut is broken, it is normally served by the youngest. He begins the service from the eldest, and then down to the youngest. In a mixed gathering, men are served first before women. However, in a tradition that recognizes titled women, they are served before the untitled men. Children, when present, are not permitted to eat kolanut, exception can only be in the naming ceremony of a newly born baby. Because kolanut is accompanied by introduction of the guests and because it leads to prayers, we may conclude that the performative verbs-to introduce and to request, are highly associated with the rite of Kolanut: "I introduce myself as ... the elder by praying over the Kolanut requests that ...".

Sacrifice is another important rite in Igbo traditional religion, and is called "aja". Sacrifice usually involves the slaughtering of animals before a shrine or any selected spot associated with the cult of deity. The blood and parts of the flesh of the victim are offered to the deity while the remaining meat is consumed by the worshippers. In some cases the victim is not killed but offered and allowed to live around the shrine as a property of the deity. There are different sacrifices in Igbo traditional religion, such as: "ilo mmuo or imeria mmuo"- propitiatory sacrifice, "ikpu aru"–purificatory sacrifice, "ichu aja"-exorcist sacrifice, and "igo mmuo"-consecratory sacrifice. There are also other sacrifices as petitive and thanksgiving sacrifice. For sacrifices to be efficacious and to achieve their purpose, the Igbo believe that they must be offered

---

232 God the All-Knowing come and eat Kolanut. Our ancestors come and eat Kolanut. Our benevolent spirits come and eat Kolanut. Let everyone live. Let man live and let woman live. Let the elder live and let the child live. Long life for men and long life for women. Long life for the elder and long life for the child. We want what to eat and not what will eat us. We want long life, good health, children and prosperity.

at particular spots, by particular persons and at a particular time of the day, week or year as the case may be. Sacrifices could be offered to the deities, to the alusi, to ancestors, and to chukwu-God. The sacrifice to chukwu-God is different from all the others, and is referred to as "Aja Eze Enu"-sacrifice to God, king of heaven. This "aja eze enu" is very widely diffused in Igboland. This sacrifice is mainly carried out during the rainy season. Objects required for the sacrifice include: a white chicken, eggs, yams, an eagle's feather and a long pole (ofolo ngwo). The minister, usually a dibia (medicine man), ties the chicken, the yams and the feather to the end of the pole with a white cloth, which he then plants in the ground, with the fowl (alive) and the objects suspended in the air. He then offers another chicken and egg at the foot of the pole while pronouncing the following words: "Eze Enu receive these our gifts for the preservation of our families, our relatives, our friends. Increase our children and our crops, so that by this time next year we may have something to give thee."[233] When we analyse this prayer in the light of J.L.Austin's performative word, we qualify it as a request: "the chief priest resquests that …". After sacrifice there follows the sacrificial meal and the congregation departs.

3.11.7 The rite of Oath Taking – Inu Iyi

It is a well-known fact that Africans in general, and Igbos in particular dread traditional oath taking, often referred to as Inu Iyi. In Igboland, Oath-Taking is the surest means of ascertaining the truth in matters shrouded in doubts. It equally serves as a deterrent against false claims and false evidence. The efficacy of traditional oaths may depend largely on the belief prevalent in the traditional cultural milieu that supernatural consequences and sanctions are attached to false oaths. The belief is that the gods will instantly or eventually punish any person who swears falsely. There are countless instances even in the contemporary era of persons being smitten by evil after taking false oaths. Ogbalu F.C writes in affirmation:

> This is the final court of appeal. If a person agrees to swear an idol as to his innocence or veracity of his statement, the actual swearing ends the matter. If one year elapses after the swearing and the person does not die, he is deemed to be innocent.[234]

The belief in the supernatural is so strong in Igboland, and the belief still to a large extent regulates the lives of many. Even the Elites routinely consult traditional diviners and look for traditional solutions to problems confronting them. Modern courts should recognize that customary law arbitrations determined by Juju Oaths are in a class of their own. Once oaths are resorted to, the matter is submitted to the gods, it is no longer open to human discretion, neither can the courts reopen the matter again nor can the parties resile from the process at that stage. The courts should not

---

233 Metu, African Religion in Western Conceptual Schemes, 52.
234 Ogbalu, Igbo Institutions and Customs, 73.

interfere with customary law arbitrations decided by Juju. The theology of oath in the Igbo traditional religion is based on the following elements:

(i) An immediate mystical sanction
(ii) Eventual community sanction
(iii) The use of an explicit and powerful symbolism which appeal to people's experience.[235]

From all these then, we can be sure that the Igbo traditional religion, like other religions, favours oath-taking. Oath in Igbo traditional religion could be said to be theocentric. Essentially, the oath in the Igbo traditional religion is community centred. It is a social affair and a means of enforcing discipline in the society. No person, of course, who is qualified to take an oath, is exempt. Whoever that tries, under any pretence, to evade the communal oath is seriously suspected and enforced to take it. Where he persists, he is subjected to some sanctions, some serious penalties like expulsion from the community in principle and in interaction. Not only that the individual is excluded from the community, his rights are denied him and more still, it is believed that the ancestral spirits would continue to avenge for such an effort to bring the society to ruin. Another distinguishing feature about the Igbo traditional oath is its variety. The Igbo traditional religion has many different forms of oath-taking. Just as they identify spirits and gods in many objects surrounding them, so also do they take recourse to or reflect all these objects in their oath-taking.

Our chief objective is furthering our inquiry into how words play important role in the administration of these Oaths. To achieve this purpose, the important roles Oracle, Ofo- symbol of authority and justice, and other essential valuables play must be considered. In Igboland Oracles are one of the most powerful ways of administering Oath. Asked why people seek for the divine intervention through Oracles, the answer is not far-fetched from the prevailing injustices of the time, moreso with the rich against the poor; the elite against the illiterate; and the vocal against the downtrodden. Emphasizing more on this point George O. Ehusani writes:

> The real problem today is the conspiracy of a greedy elite to further impoverish the poor, through the selfish appropriation and reckless plunder of the mineral and agricultural resources of our fatherland. This tiny class of Nigerian elite, are represented in the north as well as in the south. They could be found among muslims as well as christians; and among the serving and retired army generals as well as civilians.[236]

Hence, a common Igboman is left with the option of seeking and obtaining this justice from the oppressor by finding refuge in Oracles. Indeed, how does he achieve this? How does the operating wave-length of the Oracles look like? In giving answer to this questions permit me to limit myself to Okija shrine in Anambra state of south- eastern Nigeria. This shrine is also referred to as Ogwugwu-Akpu Okija. It is located in a very thick bush that cannot be described easily, and far removed from living area. Normally the agents to this great Oracle summon the accused to the shrine in the early days by sending one of them to deliver the message, but today by sending a letter demanding that

---

235 Cf. Shorter , African Culture, 117.
236 Ehusani, George, A Prophetic Church, second edition, Ibadan 2003, 73.

he reports within a specified date. If after the settlement of a case and the culprit finally dies, it is reported to the chief priest who allows the corpse to be brought and thrown into the shrine forest, buried or left just like that by the relations of the dead person. The deities have no guns and no knives. It is guilty conscience that kills any offender.

In addition, when Arusi kills the offender, his people inform the chief priest who in turn will demand from the people money, cow, goat, reasonable amount of cash running into thousands so that he will call the Arusi back and resolve the issue for them. Also to be brought is the entire property of the deceased including cars, household items and wearing apparels. Another priest of a higher statues had the sole responsibility of executing this strange will with the assistance of other priests. Interestingly, the measure by which the Oath is administered in the shrine defines the importance of word in the ritual-process. The culprit is made to stand or kneel before the Oracle. At times a coffin-a reminder of the awaiting death should the culprit fall victim-is placed before him, and over which he is to give his testimony. This testimony he has to say aloud to the hearing of the assembly by repeating carefully the wordings as are dictated by the administering minister. Sometimes these wordings read as follows: "I, MR/S (Name mentioned) HEREBY TESTIFY THAT I FIRMLY HOLD CLAIM TO THE POSITION I HAVE TAKEN IN THE ISSUE AT HAND AS THE TRUE POSITION, AND SHOULD IT NOT BE TRUE LET THE ORACLE TAKE MY LIFE". We interpret these wordings to be highly performative and indeed very explicit. When considered from the qualification, there is no doubt that this utterance is a testimony: "I hereby testify …". Then, the culprit jumps over the coffin as a sign of ratification for the Oath he has taken. Often times, the culprit reads from an already prepared tablet, or can speak freely and spontaneously, but the words he says must correspond to the demands of the situation. When these conditions are satisfactorily fulfilled, and the Oath successfully completed, all the parties wait for the result within the specified period, either the death of the culprit or his vindication. It is important to mention that the revered "Ofo" (the traditional insignia of authority) plays a vital role in the administration of oath in Igbo traditional society. Attesting to this fact Kalu O.U writes: "The Ofo stick could be used to swear an oath with deadly consequences for the offender. Ofo was like a double-edged sword. It restrained the judge from a wilful miscarriage of justice, and the defendants from perjury themselves".[237] In the situation whereby the aggrieved member reports his case to the elder, a date is fixed in which both the accuser and the accused are summoned for settlement. At the extreme case where the case cannot be handled amicably, the last resort is the administration of Oath by the use of Ofo. This revered piece of wood is brought out with all the reverence and handed over to each of the parties in-turns, who reading out or repeating aloud the wordings of the Oath- administration while holding the Ofo in upward position, is fully aware of the consequences. Very important to note is the weight of the wordings in the Oath administrarion. The individual rounds up the oath – taking with such words as: "O BURU NA IHE M KWURU ABUGHI EZIOKWU

---

[237] Kalu, Under the Eyes of the Gods, 45; see also Anyanwu , The rites of initiation in Christian liturgy and in Igbo traditional society: towards the inculturation of Christian liturgy in Igboland, 31.

KA OFO A GBUO M"-if what I said is not the truth let this Ofo kill me. Then, the elder takes the Ofo back from his clients, raps up the process in his authoritative pronouncements, and may knock the Ofo three times on the floor or on the head of each client as a sign of ratification. The Ofo is then sent on a mission, and within a specified period, it either kills or vindicates the culprit. Again, we consider these words of the client to be performative and we can interprete it to mean a pronouncement of innocence by the accused. In order to justify the above utterance in the light of J.L.Austin's performative word, and to make it more explicit, we may put it in the mouth of the client this way: "I pronounce my innocence by praying that the Ofo kills me if I am guilty …".

There are as well certain valuable objects used in the administration of Oath in Igboland. These objects can be animate or inanimate, and they form part of performative symbols. Inanimate objects include Kolanut, the traditional Palm Wine, cherished possessions like house, land, car, and so on. In the case of Kolanut, it is used in form of prayer in which whoever administers the Oath prays that it serves as a channel for blessings or curses upon whoever is vindicated or guilty, as the case may be. This Kolanut ritual is often referred to as "Ikpu Oji"-mouth-lifting of Kolanut, where it is performed in a shrine of earth-goddess. In this case, the Kolanut is placed on a ground before the great goddess, and the culprit is made to stoop low and with his mouth is expected to lift up the Kola from the ground. Similarly, all wait for the divine judgement to be delivered within specified period. Where other inanimate objects are used, the culprit stands the risk of losing these objects should he be found guilty. The terms of the Oath that is to be carefully read out by the culprit himself make this clear. Animate objects can also be used in oath-taking. In Igboland, we often see and hear people swearing by their heads, by their families, by their children, by their parents, by their generations, and so on. Whatever they say in this ritual-process remains binding.

3.11.8 The rite of Covenant making – Igba Ndu

In every community in Igboland, in every family, in every kindred, in every association or in gathering of two or more people, there are bound to be misunderstandings, mistrust and suspicions in so far as there are individual differences, varied opinions, selfish attitudes and approaches to issues that concern common good. To further restore this trust where it is lost, to create again understanding where there is misunderstanding, and to make common interest prevail over selfishness, Igbos turn to covenant making, traditionally known as "Igba Ndu". Covenant making, as it were, is an ancient concept that is not limited to Igbos alone. It is equally scriptural so much that "in the form ,testament' it has provided the title for the book".[238]

Through "Igba Ndu"one's life is entrusted to the care of the accused, and the accuser goes on living in reassurance of his safety, and vice versa. The method of executing the "Igba Ndu" ritual differs from one Igbo community to another. This notwithstanding,

---

238 McCarthy,Dennis, Growing points in Theology: Old Testament Covenant; a survey of current opinions,

the importance of words in the ritual-process, however, remains unique. Depending on the community, kindred, family or individuals, such material objects like Kolanut and traditional palm wine are used.[239] The individuals come forward before the assembly and in turns make a declaration of this or similar nature: "I (name), HEREBY DECLARE THAT I HAVE NOT HAD THE INTENTION, AND WILL NEVER HAVE THE INTENTION OF DOING HARM TO (name of the accuser) ; AND THAT I WILL NOT IN THE PRESENT OR IN FUTURE BE PART OF ANY COUNSEL NEITHER IN THOUGHT, WORDS NOR ACTION AGAINST HIM; SHOULD I GO AGAINST THIS SOLEMN DECLARATION OF MINE LET THE DIVINE JUSTICE BE UPON ME". The performative verb "to declare" involved in this process is very explicit: "I declare that ...". In addition, the above ritual process carries along with it a pronouncement of curse should the client lie. So, to be explicit, we may put it in the mouth of the client in this way: "I pronounce curse upon myself shold my declaration be false ...". So, the qualifications: "I declare that ... I pronounce ..." have exposed the explicit nature of the performative word in the above utterances of the covenant-maker. This covenant is sealed by both parties eating and drinking from each others Kolanuts and Palm wine. Also, a ceremonial feasting with provision of assorted foods and drinks from both parties may follow. There are still three major areas in the Igbo cultural milieu where the J.L.Austin's performative word is highly vital. Let us now consider how performative word is applied in these areas.

3.12 Additional References

Namely, Folktales (Akuko ifo), Traditional songs (Abu) and Proverb (Inu) are the three special areas in Igbo traditional milieu where we can still experience the application of the J.L.Austin's performative word.

3.12.1 Performative word in Igbo Folktales

The term Folktale "Akuko Ifo" is a word made up of two parts: Tale (Akuko) and Folk (Ifo). In the words of Helen Chukwuma, Folktale is: "A fairytale, a tale of fantasy, an equivalent of German Märchen. It is entirely an imaginative enactment very earthbound with man in

---

239 Oxford 1972, 1. Pedersen offers a multiplicity of forms of covenant making in Israel to include: "an exchange of gifts, the shaking of hands, the eating of something together, oath, and a host of other things, could be used to form covenantal relationships. Apparently even ceremonies with oil could produce a covenant, an alliance between nations. There is even another kind of covenant which is designated by the material apparently used in making it, the salt covenant [...] now it is suggested that the salt refers to the curse element; certainly conquered rebels faced having their cities destroyed and strewed with salt" (McCarthy, Growing points in Theology: Old Testament Covenant; a survey of current opinions, 41–42).

its centre."[240] Folktales are partitioned into three main components: The animal tale, the human tale and the mixed tale. In animal tale, animals become the chief actor and perform vital roles in the narrative. In the human tale, man occupies the central place in the narrative as the protagonist. He acts in a quasi type of world. This world is often referred to as "Iduu". It is quasi because on the one hand, the Iduuland is really located within Benin kingdom, and on the other hand, the narrative is unrealistic because it is full of fantasies and imaginations. Mixed tales are combinations of the animal tale and the human tale. Here, the two characters of animal and man are meant to interplay in a narrative, sometimes to show a peaceful co-existence, and other times, to show just the opposite. Every Folktale has the function of making the listener to experience at the moment the situation and the circumstance inherent in what is being narrated or conveyed. For non Igbos, Folktales play a vital role of making him or her, using the data provided by the tales, to be introduced into the culture of the Igbo people, although he may not have neither personally lived among the Igbo people nor have read any document provided by anthropologists or professionals about Igbo culture. Thus, by listening to the words of the storyteller, he is invariably informed of the people's culture. According to Rems Nna Umeasiegbu:

> Information is about the life cycle, the importance attached to material wealth and the criteria for assessing a person's affluence, the type of food eaten by the people and their methods of earning a living. Also, one can picture the religious affiliations of the people by piecing together folkloristic data. Title-taking, crimes and the punishment of criminals, building, relaxation habits are also dealt with.[241]

Traditionally, Folktales are not produced with titles or themes. The story-teller simply goes ahead with his story, and it is left for the audience, at the end of the story, to discover the appropriate title that should be designated to the story. Oftentimes, these titles come from the lessons that the stories intend to impact. In Folktales, the story-teller achieves three important objectives: he introduces a story, he allows his audience to wander in phantacy as to the direction the story goes, then, he impacts the proper enlightenment on the audience. This means, a Folktale has three principal parts: introduction, body and conclusion. By introduction, we mean, the Folktale may begin with the following phrases:

Storyteller: Chakpi-ii-ii-ii
Audience: W-o-ooo (noisy response from the audience,
accompanied by a shuffling of feet).
Storyteller: Chakpi-ii-ii-ii
Audience: Wo-o-oo (a drawn-out response).
Storyteller: (smiling) when a dog hangs a bag around his neck?
Audience: (a few members of the audience beckoning on one
Another as if to say, "Did I not tell you?") : The
Faeces in the bush will be devoured.
Storyteller: (after a long pause): I have a story for you.
Audience: (General excitement): Please tell us [242]

---

240 Chukwuma , Igbo Oral Literature, 32.
241 Umeasiegbu , Words are sweet, 13.
242 Umeasiegbu, Words are sweet, 11.

There are also some other ways of introducing Folktales such as: "once upon a time", "Mbe dee-de-gbai-gbai-asirikasi-asiri egbunam-umuakwukwo nyara akpa akara agwu n' ukwu Mango" (these are onomatopaic introduction that has no immediate translation). The body of the Folktales tests the ability of the audience to follow the direction of the story. It is a test on their intelligence. The conclusion is the climax of any Folktale. The success of any Folktale lies on how humorous the story is, and on how the story is successfully ended. Folktale is meant for relaxation periods in Igboland. This explains the reason why it is always told at that time of the night when children have taken their supper and are free from house-hold works. Story-telling improves the social life of the society members and thereby establishing healthy interactions and contacts. Not everyone is a good story-teller. Story-telling, therefore, is viewed as an art and the mannerism by which the story-teller goes about this art is considered as a divine gift. Everybody enjoys story-telling, and children can abandon their meals in search of Folktales. I remember as a child, we would go to the extent of fetching water or providing fire wood for one of the story-tellers in my village, and in reciprocity, he would satisfy us with series of Folktales. His ability to endear us to him through his Folktales is not separated from his ability to dramatize the stories he was narrating. So, story-tellers share common features with dramatists. Just like the actor in a theater cannot perform without the audience, likewise a story-teller cannot perform without the audience. This is because Folktale is a social event. The success of any Folktale, therefore, depends on the audience. The reaction of the audience determines if the story-teller has made any impact on them or not. Good performers measure their success from the ovations from the audience. This is interpreted to mean that the words of the story are properly used to bring about an effect (ovations) from the audience. This audience may not always be made up of the indegenes of the village. Sometimes they may be mixed-up with their neighbours who come from nearby villages. Just as I have said earlier, Folktales are best done at night, although there is no rule prohibiting them to be told during the day. The only reason is that night is the best relaxation period after the day's work. And so, Folktale at night is considered as reward for a day well spent in farms. On the contrary, Folktales during the day is considered as act of laziness, and therefore, not in the nature of the Igbo people.

Sometimes, the audience has right to tell the story-teller the type of story they would like him to tell. These stories oftentimes revolve around some animal tricksters. According to Helen Chukwuma:

> However there are archetypes as for example the trickster. In animal trickster tales the tortoise usually but not always fills the trickster slot. Nwaebunoako, the child-ram also takes the trickster role and so does Nza, the little sun-bird. Thus even in a common category of stories actors are variable but actions are constant.[243]

Although most often, animals are at the center of Folktales, there are also other situations where animals and human beings are presented as co-actors in a certain stage. Story-telling is an act enjoyed by children and adult, young and old, especially, under

---

243 Chukwuma, Igbo Oral Literature, 121.

moonlight, either infront or behind the family house. Only death of an important person in the community could momentarily prevent Folktales. The place of Folktale in Igbo society is so highly elevated that even in primary and secondary schools, opportunities are offered where pupils would continue to exercise this art, and to perfect its effect in their fellow pupils. In order that these Folktales survive for posterity, many prominent Igbo scholars invested their energy and expertise in collecting, editing and studying these Folktales:

> In 1954, Cyprain Ekwensi had a collection of tales in translation published in London. F.C. Ogbalu wrote Ilu Igbo (1965), Mbediogu and Nza na Obu. R. Umeasiegbu devoted the second part of his The Way We Lived to narratives. In 1971, Uche Okeke brought out a collection of Folktales Tales of Life and Death, R.Egudu's A Calabash of Wisdom and other Igbo Stories, 1973; and Chinua Achebe and John Iroaganachi adapted a traditional tale in The Leopard's Claw, Eluigwe's collection of Beside the Fire, 1974 is also one of the recent Folktale collections same as Omalinze 1977, a collection of stories written in Igbo by Ugochukwu, Meniru and Oguine and edited by Nolue Emenanjo. R.N. Umeasiegbu's Words are Sweet: Igbo Stories and Storytelling came out in 1982.[244]

And in the words of Fabian J: "Efforts made by Africans to collect and preserve ancestral customs, stories, songs and dances exist and are attested to since the very beginning of urbanization and the spread of literacy".[245] We must accept the fact that before fifties and sixties, these Folktales were not separate entities from Anthropology or Religion. This means that before then, Folktales had no independent status of existence. They were seen as an avenue through which a people's culture and belief were expressed. Although Folktales are narrated by certain individuals who have the art, they are however communally owned and communally transmitted. This means, nobody, not even the story-teller has claim of ownership of the very stories he narrates. He can only claim ownership of the mannerism with which he narrates. Considering the society as very much oracular, even in the face of writing culture, and taking Folktale as an Igbo traditional form of literary expression, it could be that the story-teller narrates a story that has been in existence generations before his great grand father, may be, in a new dimension. That he adds few things to make the narration suit the taste of the time does not make him to be the originator of the story he tells. Sometimes, the audience are trickled by a Folktale not because they have not heard of that narration before, but moreso, because of the new dimension in which it has appeared. Folktale is appreciated not because of its imaginative value but for its ability to make its words produce effect in the minds and hearts of the audience. Helen Chukwuma concludes:

> It combines the fullest expression of language and perception, fusing the imagined and the real to provide entertaining knowledge for the people. Attention is drawn primarily to the verbal medium, a poetic language which invokes strange settings and figures, analogies possible and present but not known, and produces formations of rhymes and contractions appealing to the ear and the intellect. The articulation of an oral form, (performance) its realization is the intrinsic feature of its literariness.[246]

---

244 Chukwuma., Igbo Oral Literature, 7–8.
245 Fabian, Power and Performance, 271.
246 Chukwuma, Igbo Oral Literature, 21.

With the above remark, Helen summarizes the usefulness of Folktale to the subject matter of our investigation which is the performativeness of the words of Igbo Folktales in the audience. And so, when one listens to those Folktales, one is not only concerned with the artistic compositions but also their ability to deliver, their ability to perform. Because the Igbo Folktale lacks theme but allows the listeners themselves to search out the theme proper to the folktale being narrated, and because the listeners do this by carefully analizing the story, we may rightly relate this process to what J.L.Austin meant by implicit performative word.[247] Thus, the listeners arrive at the theme of the Folktale by asking: what does the story-teller mean by his story? Or, what type of story is that? From these questions, it may be discovered that the story may hinge on gratitude, or apology or pronouncement or declaration, and so on. So, we may conclude that performative verbs operate in Folktales implicitly.

3.12.2 Performative word in Igbo traditional songs

Songs are another aspect through which words are meant to arouse actions in the audience. These actions determine the tone and the nature of the songs. That means, the nature of the actions determines the categories of the songs. Igbo songs are sometimes accompanied by local instruments such as ubo-local guitter, ogene-metal gong, udu-resonating pot, ekwe-wooden gong, ichaka-rattles, and naturally by human clapping of hand. These instruments give a befitting rhythm to the words of the songs and in most occasions push the audience into dancing. There are about eight categories of traditional songs distinguished by their themes and the occasions of their use. Among these categories are: Birth Song-Abu Nwa, Children's Song-Abu Umuaka, Work Song-Abu Olu, Praise Song-Itu Afa, Ritual Song-Abu Echichi, War Song-Abu Agha, Festival Song-Abu Emume, Funeral Song-Abu Onwu.

Birth song is a song that expresses joy and thanksgiving that a new baby is brought into the world, and that the mother has delivered safely. Such songs take place at the visit to a mother who is delivered of a new baby, and are naturally sung by the visiting women. Another occasion for birth song is at the naming ceremony of the newly born baby. An example of such birth song reads:

> Erimeri na aso uso erimeri erimerie
> Onwu egbuna nwanyi na afo ime
> Ka o mutara anyi nwa
> Ka anyi taa Okporoko
> Nuo mmanya ngwo [248]

The above song conveys the goodwishes of the singers to the mother and her child. It expresses their joy that a child is brought into the world, and that the mother has

---

247 Cf. Austin, How To Do Things With Words, 72.
248 Entertainment is good. May an expectant mother never die while delivering; so that she delivers a new born baby; so that we gather to eat and to drink.

delivered safely. It is also a form of prayer for greater tomorrow for the mother that she remains fruitful so that they gather to celebrate, to eat and to drink. To appreciate that the child is recognized as the chief host and is responsible for all the food and drinks that they are presented with, the guests may roar into such a song as:

> Obughi ma nwa
> Onye ga enye m?
> Nri utala ji
> Onye ga enye m?
> Nri osikapa
> Onye ga enye m?
> Mmanya ngwo
> Onye ga enye m?[249]

The people do not just seat down and sing. The words of these songs bring about the emotion of joy and the atmosphere of celebration. The result is that the gathered community of friends and relations are moved by this euphoria to rise up from their seats and begin to dance.

We have children's song and it is naturally meant to cuddle a child and draw away his attention from the present predicament. This type of song is called lullaby. It has the capacity of luring a child into sleep, as a means of making him not to feel the pinch of the circumstance that confronts him, for example, the absence of his mother. By persistant repetition of such a song, the baby-seater who can be a sister or brother or somebody employed to do the work, gradually succeeds to put the child to sleep. Below is an example of an Igbo lullaby:

> Onye mere nwa na ebe akwa?
> Egbe mere nwa na ebe akwa
> Weta uziza weta ose
> Ka umu nnunu rachaa ya
> Ka otu okpukpu kpochaa ya
> Egbe e egbe nu.[250]

This song is monotonous and is supported by the singer tapping his or her foot on the floor, or gently tapping the crying baby on the back. By continuous singing, the tempo by which the child cries eventually reduces, and step by step, the child doses off into sleep. And when this happens, the suiting words of the lullaby have achieved the goal they are meant to achieve. Sometimes, the aim of the words may not be to lead to sleep, but just to quieting the crying child. In this case, the singer manipulates the child's psychology by applying words of praises for the child in the songs-telling the child how he has been a good child, how he has been friendly, how he has been strong, how he has been loved by everybody. By these words gradually assimilating in the mind of the child, he is tricked to stop crying in acknowledgement of the

---

249   If it is not because of a child, who will give me? Pounded yam, who will give me? Rice, who will give me? Palm wine, who will give me?
250   Who has caused the child to cry? A kite has caused the child to cry. Bring pepper so that the Kite can partake of it, so that it receives its punishment. Be warned dear Kite.

praises heaped upon him. It happens that a child is beaten or punished because of an offence, such as telling lies, and while he cries, the parents may cuddle him to stop crying not by telling him that they are sorry for punishing him and making him to cry but by telling him the virtues he should cultivate in order to escape such punishment in future. E.B Idowu puts it in the following song:

Be truthful, do good;
Be truthful, do good;
It is the truthful
that the divinities support.[251]

The words of this song becomes a teacher and aims to inculcate into the child, the necessary qualities he should posses as a child that should lead him all through his life. The song sets a guiding principle for the child, which is, that God rewards an honest life.

There is work-song and its wordings are meant to motivate an individual or a group of people and compel or challenge them to a task that confronts them. This type of song is conditioned by the nature of the task to be carried out. I remember as a youth in my village, we undertook a long journey normally on foot in the company of our village masquerade, and at a point we came across a hill and none of us had enough energy to climb this hill. All of a sudden, a member entoned this song:

Ugwu ndi mmuo
Ugwu ndi mmuo
Ugwu onye amughi oria Ugwu ndi mmuo .[252]

By singing this song with all enthusiasm, and accompanying it with clapping and all the liveliness it required, we were challenged to overpower the hill, and before we knew it the hill was far behind us. There are often situations where a group is meant to do an uphill-task. By this I mean a challenging work, such as clearing a very large hectar of land for agricultural purposes. Naturally, such a work is by manual and very much challanging. Usually, the group resort to such motivating songs as:

Anyi gwara onye?
Anyi gwara onye na
anyi ama aru
Anyi gwara onye? [253]

By the application of such and similar songs, the group is energized and each member works competitively, and the work is finished with ease, happily and very smoothly. There lies the African 'Ujamaa',[254] and indeed the Igbo spirit of commu-

---

251 Opoku, Kofi Asare, West African Traditional Religion, USA 1978, 159.
252 A hill of the spirits. A hill climbed without practice. A hill of the spirits.
253 Whom did we tell? Whom did we tell we shall not finish the work; whom did we tell?
254 "Ujamaa is an African word with Arabic roots. It is a Swahili word. It is important to emphasize that Julius Nyerere did not construct, or invent, the word ujamaa, nor did he use it simply to project his personal, novel ideology or utopia. It is not an ideological word in the sense of a new word invented by the ideologue to convey a novel a novel concept, project, or system. The word existed before Nyerere used it. We are saying that it is not his word. But he used it in a

nalism. Just as I have said above, work song is not only applicable to group work, an individual who undertakes a particular work is energized by the wordings of the songs he sings to himself while he works. Sometimes, the themes of his songs are selected ramdonly and may not have to do with the work he is doing. What is important is that these songs energize him and leads him to successfully finish the task that confronts him.

Next is praise song and it is very prominent in Igbo society. Three outstanding entities are subjects of praise song: God, man and community. In a traditional Igbo society, an Igbo man begins to talk to God, for example, when the head of the family prays before his ancestral shrine or at the breaking of Kolanut, by first of all according praises upon the name of God– Chukwu. Patrick C. Chibuko writes:

> By invoking God first in the prayer, one declares the supreme and pre-eminent position of God in the hierarchy of Igbo pantheon. He is the Great God-Chukwu, the king who lives in the sky: Eze bi na Igwe, observer of all things both open and secrete: I na ahu na ihe na ahukwa na nzizo etc. Then after Him, are the other deities and ancestors.[255]

Sometimes the participants throw their support as the elder pronounces these praises by chorusing after each praise: "otu a"-so is it. There are other praise names with which the Igbo venerate God, among them are: Onye bi na elu ogodo ya na

---

definite context to project a specific concept [...]Ujamaa, in the African family as we know it, therefore needs not be re-translated, in its content and concept, into the African context from a foreign language, since a translator i soften a traitor, because its meaning, the idea and ideals it brings along; the concepts it encodes, the attitude it conditions and helps people develop, for public and private life and behaviour, are authentically African and Christian" (Onwubiko, Oliver, The church as the family of God(Ujamaa):In the light of Ecclesia in Africa, Nsukka 1999, 11). "In trying to bring back this traditional 'work-spirit', Julius Nyerere has proposed the philosophy of Ujamaa. Ujamaa, in the literal sense means 'togetherness', 'familyhood'. Family here does not depend on consanguinity. It depicts a ‚community spirit' of togetherness which considers all people as ‚brothers.' In Africa brotherhood is real and concretely based on family-hood, that is, it is situated in the family where the welfare of each individual becomes the direct concern of the members of the 'clan vital'. Applied to team work or and agriculture, Ujamaa means ‚bloc-farm system.' In the philosophy of Ujamaa, Nyerere's idea is that African traditions should serve as the basis for all future African development. He goes to apply this by the founding of Morogaro Agricultural College in 1965. An interesting practical dimension of the agricultural training at the college is the contact students make with the people of the surrounding districts. This is aimed at organising 'Ujamaa villages'. Generally speaking, the goodwill and brotherly atmosphere, normally inspired and sustained during the work period, by music, justifies its usage. But what is more important is the solidarity it fosters. Solidarity is such a vital value that individuals cannot but work and identify themselves with it. The rights and duties of individuals appear as elements of corporate rights and duties so that the solidarity of the unit is stressed but not at the expense of the individual's private interests or loyalties that ultimately do not disrupt the community[...]. The dynamism and relevance of the African Sense of community in today's Africa is daily being justified" (Onwubiko, Oliver, The christian mission and culture in Africa,vlo.1:African Thought, Religion and Culture, Enugu 1991, 17–18).

255 Chibuko, Patrick, Igbo Christian Rite of Marriage, A Proposed Rite for Study and Celebration, Frankfurt am Main 1999, 112.

akpu na ala-The heavenly dweller whose garment stretches to touch the earth below; Ama ama amasi amasi-the incomprehensible; Nwoke obodobo anya-omniscience. These praise names according to Parrinder G are "the attributes of God expressed in praise names which are repeated and savoured like salutations to a great chief [...] Anyone who has listened to African prayers must have been impressed by the sonorous rehearsals of divine qualities".[256] The recitation of these divine praises permeates the hearts and minds of both the speaker and the participants and arouse their confidence in God. If the speaker has the ability, he may sing the whole of the praises or part of them.

Man is also a subject of praise songs. He may formulate his own praise songs but not in the sense of self centeredness but because it is the individual who really knows himself well and can identify his positive values that others can then appraise. There are situations where other people seek and find out some admirable values in a person and fashion praise songs for him based on those values. These values may be from what he has achieved in life or his position in the society. For example, somebody who as a result of his efforts becomes rich may be accorded with the title "Ogbuefi"-Killer of cows. By cows, the Igbo do not mean life-cows but what they represent which is wealth. If one is considered brave, he may be accorded with the title "Ogbuagu"-Killer of Leopards. He may not have killed any leopard but because he is considered courageous such praise is showered upon him. The title "Ogbuebunu"-Killer of Rams goes to someone who performs spiritual duties in the society. He is killer of rams because rams are meant for sacrifices and he is the one that performs this ritual. In his comments on praise song-itu afa, Ogbalu F.C expresses a similar view:

> Aha otutu (praise song) does not replace the person's infant name in documents. It is merely greeting name and it usually depicts the special talent of a person, his quality, belief in life or achievement. A person who performed a special feat e.g killing a leopard, stag, elephant, cow or horse takes a new name from the act e.g ogbuagu (leopard killer), ogbu-enyi (elephant killer), ogbuanyinya (horse killer), ogbu ehi (cow killer), et.c [257]

Sometimes, an individual receives praise songs indirectly. By this I mean, he may not be the person who directly merits such praises but has inherited such praises from his family lineage. In indirect praise songs, the role of "nwa"-son becomes very prominent. The "nwa"-son is attached to the praise songs as a reference. For example, nwa ogbuagu-the son of the killer of leopards, indicates that the bearer of this title only enjoys the honour conveyed on him by the merit of his father or forefather. This runs through the family lineage and remains an indelible honour to the family and her members. Community can also have praise songs associated with it. I mention here certain towns and villages and their praise songs in order to illustrate clearer the point I am trying to make:

---

256 Parrinder, Religion in Africa, 67.
257 Ogbalu, Igbo Institutions and Customs, 71.

Name	Status	Praise Song
Ozubulu	Town	Ozubulu Alakpu
Ebenator	Town	Ebenator Ozulogu
Mputu	village	Mputu ike di na ji/ego
Amihe	village	Amihe di asaa rie otu ebe[258]

The goal of praise songs is always to give honour and to compliment the good values of the praised. Praise songs make use of idioms, proverbs, images and symbols in driving their messages home.

We have ritual song which is an important aspect of any initiation in Igbo tradition, be it the prestigious ozo title taking, making of kingship, initiation into masquerade group or age grade, or initiation into cult of any deity as chief priest-eze mmuo or dibia, and so on. In each circumstance, the content of the song articulates the ritual process, and praises the qualities inherent in the individual that undergoes the ritual process in particular. There is no standardized form of these songs. Each geographical zone in Igboland has its perculiar way of rehearsing the songs and not losing the substantial elements by which they are recognized anywhere in Igboland. Jude C.U Aguwa gives us an excerpt from such ritual songs:

                Chorus: Owe Owe Owe
                Ewu new egbere owe

Aga m atu ya anya	I will open your eyes- chorus
Anya e ji eri ji	Eyes to eat yam with
Anya e ji akpa aku	Eyes to make wealth with
Anya e ji ahu uzo	Eyes to see with
Aga m atu ya anya	I will open your eyes
Umudibia abiala	The dibia have come
Umudibia abialanu	The dibia have really come
Anyi tewe egwu	Let us dance
O rule mgbe o labu	It is at such a time
Madu ama ebe ya	One knows oneself
Orule mgbe o labu	It is at such a time
Nwanyi amara di ya	The woman respects the husband
Enyimma	My good friend

---

258 Ozubulu Alakpu, Ozubulu the land of cassava; Ebenator Ozulogu, Ebenator the land of the warriors; Mputu ike di na ji/ Mputu ike di na ego, Mputu the land of yam produce/ Mputu the land of wealth; Amihe di asaa rie otu ebe, Amihe the land of brotherly love.

> Umudibia abiala   The dibia have come
> Enyimma ...   My good friend ...[259]

The above verse is rehearsed at the "Itu anya"-opening of the eyes ceremony, one of the aspects in the process of initiation as "dibia" into the Agwu deity in Igboland, and Jude C.U Aguwa further writes: "The rite of opening the eyes sums up the whole exercise of initiation. It enables the dibia to possess the prophetic spirit and to foresee the future, to see the messages embodied in the fall of the afa and to interpret them".[260] To facilitate this, the eyes of the initiate is severally washed with "ogwu"- medicine in certain locations like the shrine itself, market place, evil forest and roof top. The medicine with which the eyes are washed is mainly a concoction mixed with the blood of a slaughtered animal and are poured in his eyes and in the marks made on his chest, and this ritual is accompanied with some incantations. The initiate is overpowered by this ritual and falls into a deep slumber and all the participants await his awakening with anxiety. It is often the case that the initiate is prevented from waking up by the malicious acts of some evil-minded dibias, and that would lead to the death of the initiate. This is the reason why his coming back to life is celebrated with joy.

There is war-song. War in Igboland, whether inter village war or inter clan war or the like, arises as a result of vengeance on the part of the offended against the offender. Such offences may include killing of a village or community member, land dispute, and so on. Commenting on the weapons used in fighting war in Igbo traditional society E.N Akwaranwa writes:

> Weapons of war included, bows and arrow, sharp knife (akparaja or akpara isi ngu), "agara", (sharp hooked Spear with wooden handle), dane gun and club. Trenches (nkoro) were dug into which defence line escaped direct enemy missiles and bullets. Wizards and charms were also used to harm enemies.[261]

Similarly, Ogbalu F.C expands the list of the Igbo traditional weapons of war in the following words of his:

> Instruments of warfare are okpiri (clubs), mma (matchets and swords), guns (egbe), opi or ube (spears), shield (ekpeke or okoloto), strings (ebe), and stones (okute), traps (obu) and trenches (ekpe) were also made round some towns as a defence.[262]

War songs are divided into three categories: pre-war song, war song and post-war song. Pre- war song is a kind of prayer offered to the deities for the protection of the warriors. The warriors at the threshold of war are assembled before the shrine of their deity and the chief priest in the presence of the elders performs the ritual of "Igbuchi ahu"-strenghtning of the body against the attacks of the enemies. He invokes divine protection and guidance over them and commissions them to confront the enemies courageously. So, pre-war has to do with the spiritual preparations before

---

259   Aguwa, The Agwu Deity, 96.
260   Aguwa, The Agwu Deity, 95.
261   Akwaranwa, Emmanuel, A Politico – Cultural History of Ngwa and Ukwa people of Imo State of Nigeria from Pre-Colonial Times to 1984, Owerri 1988, 91.
262   Ogbalu, Igbo Institutions and Customs, 44.

the actual war. Then the warriors, fully spiritually charged and bodily energized, march into the battle ground eager to devour whichever enemy that come their way. They are accompanied on their way by such songs: "Onye adokwana agu aka na odu ma odi ndu ma onwuru anwu".[263] Such songs are chorused repeatedly and they are means through which warriors express their emotions, and the means through which their bodies and their minds are motivated to fight even to the last drop of their blood. There are post-war songs. These are songs that accompany warriors back home. They can be happy songs or unhappy songs. They are happy songs when the desired victory is achieved. In this case, the warriors chant the songs happily towards home, taking along with them what they have looted including the captives and some of their valuables. At times, the heads of the dead enemies, especially, their leaders are brought along. The songs are unhappy when the warriors suffer defeat and loss of their members. In this case, the entire community is put into mourning mood and expiatory sacrifices are carried out in the community shrine.

We have festival-songs. Festivals are very vital in Igbo society. They are opportunities of celebrating events associated with the life of the society. These festivals do not just take place, rather they are celebrated according to their times and seasons, and are stipulated in the society's calendar of events. In discussing about festivals in Igboland, one must take note of the following:

> There are no festivals that are national in the sense of involving the entire Ibo speaking people everywhere. Each town has its 'national' festivals and each village its own local ones. In most cases however, they have the same pattern everywhere and in a number of localities the same names.[264]

Some festivals measure the cultural richness of the society and have more of religious orientation while some other festivals are more concerned with the social aspect of the societal life. Thus, festivals provide links between man and his fellow citizens on the social level, as well as, links between the living, the dead and gods on the religious level. The festivals which have religious motivations are generally referred to as feasts and have observances and worships associated with them. Festivals which are purely social only participate in the nature of the festivals that are purely religious, and serve as the socializing aspects of those religious festivals. In Igboland, therefore, the social festivals are expressions of the religious festivals. An example of the Igbo festival is "Iwa ji"-New yam Festival. It is a religious festival and is associated with "Ani"-the earth goddess, who among other things, is responsible for agriculture and its produce. She receives from the society at this celebration worship in form of libations and prayers for various intentions. This new yam celebration, although religious in nature, offers at the same time, opportunities for social festivals such as "Igba mgba"-wrestling matches, "Igba egwu"-dancing contest, "Iti mmanwu"- masquerading. One can, therefore say, that those festivals that emphasize social aspects derive their existence and their interpretations from the religious festivals. This implies, no community or a group can just embark on a social festival unless a religious festival

---

263 Let no one pull the tail of the leopard, whether he (the leopard) is alive or dead.
264 Ogbalu, Igbo Institutions and Customs, 63.

is being celebrated, and Ogbalu F.C would say: "There seemed to be no festival that was not connected with worship of idols and gods".[265] Sacred songs and dances are part of the festival celebrations and are not allowed outside the context of the festival. According to O.A Onwubiko:

> During the Isu Achara, celebrated by the people of Ubowala in Emekuku in Igboland, in honour of their deity Uramuru (which is also the goddess of their river), there is a sacred song which the priest of Uramuru Ukwa intones to declare open the period of peace which must be observed before the "Isu Achara". This is regarded so sacred that singing it outside this period is a taboo; and since it declares open a festive period, it is the prerogative of only the Uramuru Ukwa priest to intone it, therefore no one can sing it unless after the priest had intoned it officially with his flute. This he does on a sacred tree found in front of Uramuru Ukwa shrine. The intensity of the festival is expressed in the wordings of the sacred song itself.[266]

While celebrating Mmanwu in some parts of Igboland, the wordings of the songs describe each situation and energize the initiates into actions and the atmosphere assumes an entertaining euphoria. I give an example of such songs:

Otirigo nje na ekwuru
Ajo mmuo na eti aba
O si ngaa tiri aba
Otirigo nje na ekwuru [267]

As soon as the initiates begin this song, the mood of the celebration is hightened with more of expectations. Both the initiates and the participants anxiously await an action from the masquerade. Following the rhythm of the song, the masquerade suddenly begins to knock its head on the ground to the excitement of all. This it does so long this motivating song lasts. This is the highest point of the excitement and is brought about by this song that is full of motivating words. Festivals in Igboland have strong influence on the Igbo worldview, and are most widely celebrated in the period between the end of the farming season and the beginning of the new farming season. This period is the period of plenty and relaxation. It is the period of plenty because a harvest has been made and the community has a lot to feast on. It is the period of relaxation because no farming activities take place in this period. So it is the best time to celebrate. It is a taboo to fight or quarrel within this period, instead, it is a period to settle old scores and to heal old wounds. It is a period of peace. No burial ceremonies arc allowed in this period, anyone who dies in this period has died at the wrong time and his corpse is ignored.

Again, we have funeral-songs. Funeral songs are essential parts of funeral ceremonies in Igbo society. They are meant to arouse emotion and to provoke anger and sorrow. There are no stereotyped funeral songs but each sector of Igboland has its own perculiar way of singing funeral songs. These songs are partitioned into three

---

265 Ogbalu, Igbo Institutions and Customs, 63.
266 Onwubiko, Alozie Oliver, African Thought, Religion and Culture, Christian Mission and Culture in Africa, vol. 1, Enugu 1991, 49.
267 It knocks its head on the ground. A masquerade that knocks its head. It begins the knocking here and there. It knocks its head on the ground.

different groups: Funeral songs before the burial, during the burial and after the burial. Funeral songs announce the commencement of the burial ceremonies. This is expressed in the form of "Ibesu ozu"-wailing. Very early in the morning of the burial day, "Enenke", the traditional pipe, is blown and this is followed by wailing in the family of the deceased. Describing this episode, Peter Ositadinma Akogu writes:

> Okorobia, kräftige, junge Menschen, ziehen mit grüne Zweigen in ihren Händen in der Ortschaft des Toten umher und singen Trauergesänge [...] während weibliche Verwandte des Toten in Haus beweinen. Wird ein Toter nicht in dieser Form beweint, nennen die Igbo ihn unglücklich.[268]

The above explanation by P.O Akogu depicts the scenerio before the actual commencement of the ceremonies. What is said in the wailing songs conveys the wailers anger, sorrow and depression over the death, and even provokes tears in whoever listens to them. In today's modern Igbo society, this ritual is not thrown away but is briefly observed to give room for the same ritual through playing of already recorded melodies that convey the same messages. Funeral songs play a great role at the burial rite proper. At the moment when the deceased is being lowered to the mother earth, it is all about wailing, pouring of grieves and a matter of hopelessness. In this situation funeral songs come to aid in order to relieve. This funeral song comes to my mind:

> Bedebe nwannem ebezina
> Igwe nile jije na uzu
> Mmadu nile jije be Chukwu
> Bedebe nwannem ebezina. [269]

The rhythm and meaning of the words of this song offer consolation to those who grieve and strengthen their courage, and replace their hopelessness with hopefulness. This is an important function that funeral songs perform. After the burial, if the deceased was a youth, the youths do what is called "Ngaghari iwe"-wailing procession, in which a family member leads the procession carrying the enlarged picture of the deceased. The entire group goes around the vicinity chanting funeral songs in honour of the deceased. Their songs lead to the actions they subsequently perform "the wailing procession". Below is an example of such songs:

> Chom chom chom
> Anyi na acho ya anyi afughi ya
> Cho ya be nna ya
> Anyi na acho ya anyi afughi ya
> Cho ya na nzuko
> Anyi na acho ya anyi afughi ya. [270]

---

268 Akogu, Peter, Leben und Tod Im Glauben und Kult der Igbo, München 1984, 118.
269 Cry no more my dear. Every metal goes back to the metal smith. But every human being goes back to God. Cry no more my dear.
270 Searching for him (the deceased). We search for him but in vain. Search for him in his father's house. We search for him but in vain. Search for him in our gathering. We search for him but in vain.

In the case of a deceased who was a married woman, the "Umuada" or "Umuokpu"- the married daughters of the extended family perform the funeral dirge instead of the youth. In any case, the purposes of such songs remain the same. These songs are often accompanied by much clappings and are equally being danced. In some cases, local instruments are used, and the songs bring into light the qualities and the achievements of the deceased.

Just like Folktales, traditional songs when considered in the light of J.L.Austin's performative word, are implicit in their performance. Whether it is birth-song or ritual-song or festival-song, and so on, the fact remains that the listener needs to ask: what does the singer mean by this song? Or what type of song is this? The answer depends on the disvovery of the key performative verb in operation. Funeral-song, for example, may have consolation as its focus; war-song may have warning as its keyword; birth-song may have congratulation as its message, and so on. Because these keywords are not explicit in the songs, it will not be wrong to say that performative verbs operate in traditional songs implicitly.

3.12.3 Performative word in Igbo proverbs

Proverb is defined as "A token of well-established ideology, realized in a certain form and according to the rules of a communicative rhetorical praxis".[271] Proverbs are identified with wisdom and their origins are attributed to the forefathers. This is the reason why sometimes people begin proverb by saying: "according to our forefathers …". Proverbs, therefore, are associated with tradition and are accorded their due respect. As words of wisdom, proverbs originated as a result of accumulated experiences that are founded on truth. With proverbs alone, one can express all that one literally intends to say but this demands only a deep reflection to understand. A deep reflection is necessary because proverbs are in themselves sophisticated form of speech meant only for the wise to understand. Igbo express this in the following proverbs:

> Atulu inu ka ogbaa ofeke gharii
> Ofeke amaghi mgbe ekele nku ukwa
> Omalu asu osuo na ikwe omaghi
> asu osuo na ala . [272]

Proverb is traditional in nature, very sophisticated in application but full of meaning in conception. Fabian J. identifies three essential criteria for proverb in the following words:

> There must exist a communicative rhetorical practice which encourages or even requires the use of proverbs; there must be a tradition, or more exactly, a repertoire of statements that can

---

271 Fabian , Power and Performance, 29.
272 A proverb is used in order to fool the unwise. The unwise does not recognize the sayings of wisdom. The wise understands proverbs but the unwise fails to understand.

be quoted as proverbs when the occasion arises; and there must be properties which make a statement recognizable as a proverb.[273]

Proverb is a qualitative form of speech art that is transmitted orally from one generation to another.[274] Although some proverbs are newly introduced and some old proverbs are intentionally or unintentionally lost, one associates them with antiquity and one is mainly interested not in its origin or how they are formulated but in their usage. Proverbs are structured according to their units. We have monopartite proverbs (one unit), Bipartite proverbs (two units), and compound proverbs (three to six units).

i) Monopartite proverbs (one unit)
These are the examples: "Onye ara na uche ya wi; Ochi abu uto".[275]
These two proverbs have no partitions that will form units. They are one unit of subject, verb and complement.

ii) Bipartite proverbs (two units)
These are the examples: "Onye ruo/ ya rie; Onye ju ogwugwu/ onuru udo".[276]
Each of the proverbs is made up of two phrases: a phrase that has noun and a phrase that has verb. Each of the phrases compliments the other. The noun phrase is seen as the causality while the verb phrase is considered the effect.

iii) Tripartite proverbs (three units)
Examples are: "Mbe si/ onye ekotaghi/ ogodo ya ekotara ya; Ka abia/ ka abia/ mere na awo epughi odu".[277] These proverbs have three partitions and are therefore referred to as three units proverbs. The first proverb begins by identifying the speaker while the second begins by repetition of the first statement.

iv) Quadripartite proverbs (four units)
Here are some examples: "Egbe bere/ ugo bere/ nke si ibe ya ebena/ nku kwaa ya; Agwa nti/ ma nti anughi/ ebere isi/ nti anu".[278] Again, the proverbs are partitioned into four units indicating four intervals of break. Four units form of proverbs are seen as doubling of the two units proverbs although each has its own perculiar features and with independent existence.

---

273 Fabian, Power and Performance, 27.
274 "The boys are normally more privileged than the girls in acquiring idiomatic (proverb) expressions. This is the case because, at the meeting of the elders or titled men, only the boys are allowed to accompany the men carrying their seats and bags. The boys in this way are introduced into what happens at the gathering of the elders or titled men" (Anyanwu , The rites of initiation in Christian liturgy and in Igbo traditional society: towards the inculturation of Christian liturgy in Igboland, 49).
275 The madman has his intelligence as his companion. Salutation is not love.
276 He who works should enjoy the fruits of his labour. He who refuses to swear by Ogwugwu (a male deity) should prepare to swear by Udo (a female deity).
277 The tortoise says when one directly avoids any blame may be he may indirectly merit it. Procrastination is a lazy man's apology.
278 Let Kite live let Eagle live and whichever that refuses the other to live let him have his wings broken. When the ear refuses to take advice, it ends up following the head to the grave.

v) Sixpartite proverbs (six units)
For example: "Okwa gwara umu ya/na odi okemkpa/haririji/hariri mgborogwu/ Ka o ga abu mbosi onye new ji gwuuru ji ya/ka ha ribmgborogwu".[279] The six units double the features of the three units but retain their separate existence and features. They are six units because the partitions are of six units. The Igbo proverbs, when used, push one into the act of reasoning, reflecting, thinking in order to understand the meaning of what is being said, and when they are understood, they prompt one into responding positively to what is being expressed in those proverbs. This highlights our objective that by uttering a proverb an action is effected, and this is expressed in the proverb: "Uka akpara akpa bu isi ka eji ekwe ya" – once a proverb is uttered an action follows. As we have said before, proverbs are sophisticated and one needs a deep reflection to understand them. In relation to J.L.Austin's performative word, one, therefore, needs to ask: what does the speaker mean by this proverb? What type of utterance is this? It may sometimes be that the proverb serves as a warning (Cf. the quardripartite above) or an advice (Cf. monopartite and sixpartite above) or an encouragement (Cf. bipartite above), and so on. Since these performative verbs are not explicit in Igbo proverbs, we may rightly say that they operate implicitly in Igbo proverbs.

An essential aspect of Igbo proverb is Igbo riddle. Igbo riddle is a speech art that is grouped under proverb, and sometimes referred to as metaphor.[280] It is literally translated as "Gwam Gwam Gwam"- tell me. It is a question type of statement that demands immediate answer. Riddle and proverb are often considered as being similar that sometimes the former is only viewed as an aspect of the later. The Igbo phrase "Gwam Gwam Gwam" also serves as an introduction to the riddle itself. Everyone who wishes to present a riddle declares his wish to the audience by saying: "Gwam Gwam Gwam". By hearing this introductory phrase, the attention of the audience is drawn to the riddle that is being presented in order to strike at the answer. Riddle, therefore, is a question type of speech art composed of:

i) Introduction (Gwam Gwam Gwam)
ii) Body (Riddle)
iii) Conclusion (Answer)

Riddle tests one's intelligence of arriving at the desired answer through analogy. It is complete when the correct answer is given, otherwise, it remains incomplete. The speaker presents a question and the audience is expected to supply the correct answer by discovering the compatible in reality. For example:

Question: Gwam Gwam Gwam Gwam okolo oji gba aka ari oji?
Answer: Ahuhu oji

---

279 The mother bird told his children to taste the roots as well as the yam so that when the owner of the yam harvests the yam, the roots will be left for them to feed on.
280 Anyanwu, The rites of initiation, 300.

Question: Gwam Gwam Gwam Gwam ihe ruru na ututu nwee
Ukwu ano, ruo na ehihie nwee ukwu abuo, ruo na Mgbede nwee ukwu ato?
Answer: Mmadu.[281]

By uttering a riddle, the audience is led into the act of thinking or reflecting in order to unravel the mystery and draw the analogy with an existential fact. Credit is given to whoever discovers the answer first. This means that riddle is not only a test of intelligence but also of the ability to reason very fast and accurately. Riddle has a lot of features in common with proverb in terms of their short structural forms and figurative contents, and are meant to train one in intelligence. There are, however, some minor areas of differences. While proverb can go a bit further outside itself in order to realize its full meaning and interpretation, riddle only draws likeness from the question it presents and does not go further than that. Again, proverb is logical but riddle is pragmatic. Proverb nourishes a word and makes it palatable at its presentation while riddle is satisfied with testing one's intelligence alone. In relation to Austin J.L's performative word, the listener needs to figure-out what the speaker intends by his idiom, and what the idiom actually means. It may be that the idiom may serve as a confirmation, or as a pronouncement or as an assessment, and so on. This means that in idiom, performative verbs equally operate implicitly because in idiomatic utterances we observe that they are not explicitly applied.

3.13 Conclusion

In this chapter, we have tried to analyse J.L.Austin's concept of performative word within the context of Igbo traditional society. It was to enable us arrive to this point that it became necessary, first of all, to understand who the Igbo people are. To establish the Igbo identity, this chapter finds it very important to begin by discussing the historicity of the origin of the Igbos. Unfortunately, the ethnologists have advanced the view that the Igbo people have no common traditional origin but are migrants from Bini, Igala, Nri and Ibibio. Yet there is the tradition that strongly advocates that the Igbo people are not migrants but original inhabitants of Igboland. The word Igbo refers both to the territory and the domestic speakers of the language, as well as, the language spoken by the people. This language is a tonal language and its alphabets are written in roman script. We have come to understand from this chapter that the performance of Igbo word is closely related to the Igbo worldview.[282] The Igbo

---

281 Tell me a black man that climbs an iroko tree with bare hand? A soldier ant. Tell me what in the morning has four legs, in the afternoon has two legs and in the evening has three legs? A human being: A human being as an infant crawls with the two hands and the two legs (total 4); as an adult he walks with his two legs; as an old man he supports his two legs with a walking stick (total 3).
282 The Igbo worldview consists in defining the world as being just one, which, in spite of its complexity tries to explain the being of things in the world and their specific infra-structural and religious order. This world is occupied by both visible and super sensible beings which

worldview, of course, cannot be separated from its religion which is tied to various rites and rituals. In Igbo rites and rituals, spoken words present events believed to have the power to effect meaningful transformations. In Igbo traditional religion, spoken words, therefore, are considered more sacred than the written words. Hence, the ritual ceremonies such as initiation, purification, healing, installation of a priest, marriage, oath-taking, covenant making, breaking of kolanut and sacrifice, are all performed with ritual words. To act contrary to a verbal word is one of the greatest felonies in Igboland because the verbal word is performative and sacred. To enrich us more about the concept of performative word in Igbo traditional religion, our present chapter confirms that the two essential forms of J.L.Austin's performative word, explicit and implicit forms, are associated with Igbo traditional religion. The excerpts at oath-taking or covenant making are examples of explicit performative word, while Igbo Folktales, Igbo traditional songs, Igbo proverbs and idioms serve as examples of implicit performative word. Again, this chapter upholds the J.L.Austin's criteria for performative word as being the same guiding principles regulating how the Igbo words perform in ritual ceremonies. This chapter refers also to performative identity, performative symbol, performative theater and performative magic as being evident in Igbo traditional religion. It proposes chief priest, family head and the downtrodden, among others, as the agents of performative word in Igbo traditional society. This chapter has guided us through the whole process of discussing the efficacy of Igbo words at the celebration of traditional Igbo rites and rituals and in relation to our key concept: the J.L.Austin's performative word.

Earlier on, we have carried out the same discussion in relation to sacramental theology. We may now be in the better position to know if the J.L.Austin's concept of performative word is totally related to Igbo traditional religion the same way it is related to sacramental theology, or are there differnces? This is the question our next chapter, chapter four, will be responding to as it focuses on comparing sacramental theology and Igbo traditional religion with regard to their conception of J.L.Austin's concept of performative word.

---

interact with one another and are mutually interdependent. Visible beings refer to created things whether animate or inanimate. Super sensible beings refer to Creator-God, deities, spirits and ancestors. Igbo worldview also seeks to asses man's behaviour with reference to God, divinities and the ancestors.

4 Performative word in sacramental theology and in igbo traditional religion: towards a comparative analysis.

4.1 Introduction

The key concept: performative word, and how this concept is perceived in sacramental theology and in Igbo traditional religion are already discussed in the various chapters we have seen. What we are setting out to achieve in this chapter is a comparative analysis in the way our key concept "performative word" performs in both religions. I intend to undertake this comparative analysis by exposing the basic areas of similarities and dissimilarities in the way performative word is perceived in both religions. This is necessary in the process of making the authentic Igbo word serve the need of the proper incarnation of the gospel message in the Igbo cultural milieu.

4.2 Similarities

Our discussions on performative word in both sacramental theology and Igbo traditional religion have some similarities in terms of the way the concept of performative word itself is understood, and the same similarities extend to the way explicit performative word, the criteria regulating performative word, performative identities, performative symbols and performative theater are perceived in both religions. Below are some details about these areas of similarities.

4.2.1 The concept: Performative word

The concept of performative word is already established in chapter one of this work and which has run through our discussion up to this point as a speech act in which to say something is to do something or in saying something we are doing something or by saying something we are doing something.[283] It concerns itself in proving the various ways in which people through the use of words bring about actions in accordance to the appropriate criteria. By so doing, the relationship between words and actions is established.[284]

---

283 Cf. Austin, How To Do Things with Words, 8.
284 "In the cultural Igbo society as well as in the world of the christian Liturgy, the intrinsic connection of word to rite stands out significantly. The working together of word and rite in a community ritual context inaugurates already a celebration. It belongs fundamentally to the nature of word to be graduated into action. And only the word that remains faithful to the natural

In catholic theology, the relationship between word and sacrament is that of performative unity which is "irreversible and dynamic".[285] By divine word, God determines the growth and destiny of his people in dynamic ways. Word is so important to sacrament that it cannot be separated from it, and together the both entities form a strong bond, a unique and unified medium of communion between God and man. In order to understand how important word is to sacrament, we have to go beyond the metaphysical notion of the word and rediscover its performative power as an instrument of the divine will. The power of the word was recognised, with joy or with dread, throughout the Old Testament period. The New Testament itself bears testimony to the performative power of God's word, beginning with the words of Jesus himself and transmitted by the apostles, who formulated in various but similar ways the redemptive meaning not only of his words but of his actions. The power of Jesus' words becomes literally visible with the healing miracles (Cf. Mt 8,16; Lk 4,36; Mk 4,41). His words affirm his ultimate authority to forgive sins (Cf. Mk 2,7).

The word comes to its fullest expression within a sacramental context. Whether the word is proclaimed through Scripture reading and preaching, or sung in the form of antiphons and hymns at the solemn sacramental celebrations, it is primarily performative. As in the experience of the disciples at Emmaus, the gathered community only perceives the full revelation, it only opens its eyes to a true understanding and acceptance of the divine economy through a personal and intimate acceptance of the word. It is in the liturgy of the word that the sacraments derive their fulfilment and the word is transformed from a message about Jesus into a true participation in his divine life. Thus, within the church's celebration the word assumes sacramental value. The sacramental rite itself is the framework in which the word comes most powerfully to expression. For example, in the celebration of the eucharist, the words of consecration brings about transsubstantiuation; in the sacrament of reconciliation, the words of absolution[286] perfects the act of divine forgiveness; in the sacrament of holy orders,

---

regulation of being action oriented holds also in an effective way the capacity to be religious word. In the beginning the word is only a way to an action. It longs for actualization in action. For the human person, it is in a certain sense the original action. It is the action through which the human person asserts himself as such. Whoever speaks intervenes with his personal existence in the natural course of the thing spoken about" (Anyanwu, The rites of initiation in Christian liturgy and in Igbo traditional society: towards the inculturation of Christian liturgy in Igboland, 299).

285 Uzondu, Celestine Chibueze, The hypostatic union as the principle of the eucharist, a systematic-theological investigation, Rome 2000, 55.

286 "Die priesterliche Absolution erschien als besondere Amtsvollmacht [...] Insofern die Sündenvergebung durch die contrio, also durch die Reue mit votum sacramenti, von der kirchlich-sacramentalen Absolution mitbestimmt ist, kann gesagt werden, dass im Sakrament die Vergebung mittels der Absolution bewirkt wirkt, ohne dass die sündentilgende Kraft der inneren Reue in Frage gestellt wird [...] Das 6. Kapitel (DH 1684–1685) behandelt die Absolution als Form des Sakramentes. Nur Priester und Bischöfe können in Vollmacht die Schlüsselgewalt der Kirche ausüben (Cf. Cyprian, laps.29; Ambrosius, paen. 1,2,7; Leo 1., ep. 108,2: DH 323; dort wird schon die Praxis eines geheimen Bekenntnisses vor dem Priester erwähnt). Auch die Priester im Stande der Todsünde können durch die Kraft des Hl. Geistes, die ihnen in der Weihe mitgeteilt ist, als Diener Christi die Nachlassung der Sünden ausüben; ihnen kommt

the prayers of the ordaining prelate and the imposition of hands ordain a candidate; likewise, in all the sacraments, through the use of the appropriate words and under the appropriate criteria, actions particular to each sacrament are realized.

The concept of performative word in Igbo traditional religion is equally understood in the same frame-work in which the act of saying something or by saying something or in saying something an action is realized. Igbo answer such names as "okwuka"-word is supreme. A closer look at a hermeneutical interpretation of the aforementioned name discloses how highly the Igbo appreciate word. That word is supreme means that it occupies a central position in Igbo worldview. This is because, the Igbo believe that word is the engine that ignites all to action. Based on this fact, the Igbo say: "Ekweghi ekwu mere onu, anughi anu mere nti; Okwu na ebute osisaword provokes action".[287] These phrases, among others, emphasize the fact that in Igbo cosmology, just like in sacramental theology, words can be performative in their value and function. The Igbo in their philosophy of language uphold that mouth is the special instrument through which utterances are made, and when the spoken word of the mouth is brought forth, it achieves its aim by effecting actions in the minds and hearts of the hearer, and when this action is not achieved it may be that the necessary conditions are not fulfilled. This is the meaning of the first phrase above, "when the mouth does not speak, the ear does not hear". Secondly, that action comes by speaking is the meaning of the second phrase above. The way a word is uttered determines the way it would be responded to. In this way, the Igbo try to prove that word provokes action.

4.2.2 The form: Explicit performative word

Explicit performative word is discussed in chapter one of our work and re-echoed in chapters two and three as an utterance that is definite and is determined by whether it is behabitives (I apologise that), Expositives (I testify that) or verdictives (I declare that)[288]: For example, "I apologise that I came late" is a definite utterance which distinguishes itself as an "apology".

In sacramental theology, the sacramental words are explicit because they are definite utterances and do not put anybody in doubt about the type of utterances made: "Take this and it eat ... Take this and drink from it ..."[289] are the words of the Eucharistic con-

---

dieser Dienst nicht Kraft persönlicher Heiligkeit zu. Die Lossprechung erschöpft sich nicht im Dienst der Verkündigung des Evangeliums oder in der bloßen Deklaration eines (auserhalb des Sakramentes) geschehenen Sündennachlasses" (Müller Gehard Ludwig, Katholische Dogmatik für Studium und Praxis der Theologie, Freiburg 2005, 719,720, 724).

287 When the mouth does not speak, the ear does not hear; Word provokes action.
288 Cf. Austin , How To Do Things With Words, 69.
289 Some exegetes differentiate between the actual words of consecration and the words of the administration of the consecrated bread and wine to the disciples. They insist that the actual words of consecration are not yet known, and that "This is my body ... This is my blood ...", were not words of consecration spoken immediately after Jesus had blessed the bread and the

secration which do not put anybody in doubt that it is a command. In Igbo traditional religion, there are also evidences of explicit performative words. In accordance with what we have already said earlier in chapter three about the traditional oath taking in Igbo traditional religion, and excerpt reads: "I, MR/S ... HEREBY DECLARE THAT I STAND BY THE EVIDENCES I HAVE GIVEN AS TRUE, AND SHOULD IT NOT BE TRUE LET THIS ORACLE TAKE MY LIFE". This utterance made by the parties in the administration of the Igbo traditional oath-taking puts nobody in doubt about the type of utterance because of its qualification "I declare that ...", and therefore, explicit.

4.2.3 The criteria for performative word

Once more, we remind ourselves of the criteria that regulate performative word, and which we have already stated in chapter one of this work, and has been repeated in chapters two and three: That there must exist a conventional procedure; that the procedure must be executed by all participants both correctly and completely; that the same emotion regulating the feelings and thoughts of the audience must guide the speaker in order to achieve the desired effect.[290] This means, three important precautions are necessary: conventional procedure, execution of the procedure and the emotional operation. Both sacramental theology and Igbo traditional religion adopt the above criteria laid down by J.L.Austin. For example, in order that the words of consecration bring about transsubstantiation in sacramental theology, the speaker must be a validly ordained minister who, in communion with the church, has the mandate to fulfil this obligation by using the approved words within the context of Eucharistic celebration in which the appropriate devotion of the minister unites with those of the participants. Likewise, in Igbo traditional religion, the person who stands as the mouth-piece of the deity must be the priest of the deity, and he must speak exactly what the deity has said to him, and by identifying with the sorrows and joys of the adherents, he serves as a true go-between.

4.2.4 The reference: Performative identities

Again in chapters one, two and three of this work performative identities is discussed as a process through which, by use of words, one is defined with regard to what one is. J.L.Austin explains this point by giving an example with a ship named Queen Elizabeth in which he says "I name this ship the Queen Elizabeth has the effect of naming

---

wine, but that they were words of administration spoken by Jesus as he was delivering to the disciples the fragments of the broken bread and cup.' Again, the Gospel of Mark (14:23,24), equally implies that the words "This is my blood ..., by no mean followed immediately the blessing of the cup. (Cf. Oulton J.E.C., Holy Communion and Holy Spirit, a study in doctrinal relationship, London, 1954, 26).
290 Cf. Austin , How To Do Things With Words, 14–15.

or christening the ship".[291] Because the words do the active function of identifying, they are called performative identities. Performative identity is a two-way process in which the identified and the identifier play their specific roles in order to arrive at an action.

In sacramental theology, the application of performative identities is not in doubt.[292] Take for instance the explicit performative formular: "I baptize you ...", I am named "Alexander". It is then the case that the uttering of this baptismal name by anyone performs in me. What do I mean by this? Assuming that I am in a given situation where there are many other people or walking along a street and someone from a near distance shouts the name "Alexander", it follows that I automatically react by answering or looking at the direction from where this name is mentioned without knowing yet whether it is my own "Alexander" or not. In this way, my identity as "Alexander" performs in me whenever it is uttered. In Igbo traditional religion also, performative words establish a person's identity, and as it were, both the individual himself and other people have roles to play in order to establish this identity. The Igbo carry-out naming ceremony as well as title giving. These names and titles, as we have already discussed in chapter three, have their influences on the bearer whenever they are mentioned. For instance, if the bearer of the Igbo name "Obinna" works along the street and suddenly the name is mentioned to his hearing, he responds in one way or the other even before he recollects whether it is his own "Obinna" or another's. So, the Igbo name "Obinna" has performed. In this case, Igbo names and titles prove to be performative identities.

4.2.5 The reference: Performative symbols

In chapter one of this work, and indeed in all the subsequent chapters, we came to the conclusion that symbolic language can be performative. We were able to arrive at this conclusion by citing the two examples of symbolic languages used by J.L.Austin himself viz: Hurrah and Damn: "Suppose, for example, somebody says 'Hurrah.' Well, not true or false; he is performing the act of cheering [...] Or suppose he says 'Damn'; he is performing the act of swearing, and it is not true or false".[293]

Well, J.L.Austin himself acknowledges the difficulties in recognizing symbolic languages as performative partly because it does not follow the explicit performative formular. In this case, it does not correspond to say, for example, "I damn that ... or I hurrah that ...". But, on the other hand, he recognizes the fact that these symbolic

---

291 Austin, How To Do Things With Words, 117.
292 Performative identity was very much associated with the early christian communities. These christian communities which were more of eucharistic in character were recognized as informal professions of discipleship. Acceptance of Jesus Christ as God's son and saviour was the Hallmark that united the faithful together. Thus, these communities of the faithful were identified as "Jesus People", an identity they differentiated them from non-believers, and which at same time merited them much trials and deaths. (Cf. Cooke, Bernard, Sacraments and Sacramentality, Mystic, Connecticut 1987, 97).
293 Austin, Philosophical Papers, 233.

languages perform various action like cheering and swearing which, as it were, make them to be performative.

We are to refer to what we have already said in the earlier chapters of this work that performative word judges its action based on whether it is "happy" or "unhappy" and not whether it is "true" or "false". When we consider the fact that the actions of "Hurrah" or "Damn" which are "cheering" and "swearing" respectively cannot be said to be "true or false", then they are taken to qualify as "happy" and "unhappy", and in which case they are taken to be performative words.

Again, for a word to be performative, it must not necessarily follow the explicit performative formular because certain performative words, as we have already known, are as well implicit. Implicit utterance needs to be defined, and this definition comes in form of questions, viz: what does the speaker mean by such an utterance? Is the utterance a curse or wish? To attend to these questions with regard to the symbolic languages: Hurrah and Damn, we can say that by uttering these words the speaker intends to make the person(s) addressed to be motivated and to be dismayed respectively, and to answer the second question concerning the qualification of the utterance, we can say that they are goodwishes and curses respectively.

There are as well numerous examples of symbolic languages that come to mind. The utterance "Hi" in America or "Gruß Gott" in Bavaria are symbolic languages. Because one cannot say, for example: I Hi that … or I Gruß Gott that …, invariably implies that these symbolic languages do not follow the explicit performative formular. By applying the questions: what does the speaker mean by these utterances? And are the utterances a threat or a curse? We come to the answers: The speaker by uttering these words intends to be cordial. Secondly, these words are greetings. Other symbolic words like "Mama mia" uttered by an Italian, "Wao" by an American, "Houlala" by a French and "Wahnsinnig" by a German are all symbolic utterances with which the speaker expresses surprises. They do not follow the explicit performative formular but are implicit in the performance of their actions.

It is pertinent to know that the problem associated with the linguistic symbolism is not only continental but global. Human languages are always deep with meanings and stand not in isolation but in the light of conventional meanings. To understand the linguistic symbolism of a people, one must be deep-rooted in the people's worldview. Symbols concretize people's belief system and are emblems of people's political, cultural, religious and social values. They are associated with the people's worldview, and to ignore them is to put this world-view into crisis. They express ideas and transmit them from generation to generation, thereby, preserving through specific actions, the cumulative experience, belief and thought pattern.

Symbols are both multi-referent and uni-referent. They are multi-referent when their interpretations are dynamic, that is, made to be understood in the light of new developments, and continue to give conventional meanings they are supposed to do. Symbols are considered successful multi-referent when they abandon the old interpretations and embrace new ones according to the needs of the time without doing any harm in the process. Otherwise, they can be multi-referent in the sense that they can simultaneously represent variety of meanings that are accepted as authentic within a given context.

We are not only living in a symbolic world but the symbolic world lives in us. In this sense, symbolic language performs in a fascinating way more than we can imagine. Symbolic language is action-oriented right from time, and as Gerd Heinz-Mohr would say: "In der antiken Welt spielte das Symbol, im Wortsinn des Zusammenfügens, eine praktische Rolle".[294] When we posit the question: what type of performative utterance a symbolic language is, Gerd Heinz-Mohr answers in the following way: "Es dient als Mittel zur Erkenntnis, zum Bekenntnis und zur Beschwörung".[295] But we are not limited to these options alone because symbolic language as we have noted above can as well be a command, a promise, a decree, a threat, and so on.

In sacramental theology, symbolic language serves as "ein Wort, das den gleichen Sinn wie 'Glaubensbekenntnis' hatte: der Versuch, das Sagbare und das Unsagbare über Jesus Christus, den wahrhaftigen Gott und wahrhaftigen Menschen, verbindend und verbindlich zu bezeugen".[296] To highlight on the importance of symbolic language to the celebration of the sacraments Klaus Schilling says: "Dennoch ist unbestreitbar, dass Symbole für Religion und Glaube eine zentrale Bedeutung haben, dass religiöse Erfahrungen, Leben aus dem Glauben ohne Symbolsprache nicht zu denken sind".[297] Of course, the word of God that we listen to at the sacramental celebrations are full of symbolic languages, and Klaus Schillings would suggest: "Greifen wir beispielsweise Jesu Gleichnisse und seine Wunderhandlungen heraus, so wird deutlich, wie der Kern biblischer Botschaft in Symbolen spricht. Sollen die jungen Menschen die Inhalte des Glaubens im Sinne der biblischen Botschaft hören und für ihr Leben bedeutsam werden lassen, müssen sie in der Lage sein, die Sprache der Symbole zu verstehen".[298] Apart from the symbolic languages we witness in the biblical parables and wonder-workings of Jesus Christ, read in the liturgy of the word, symbolic languages are equally witnessed in some other ways. In the celebration of the Holy Eucharist, for example, we chant "Alleluia" before the reading of the Gospel, and by the reception of the Holy Communion we say "Amen" before the minister proceeds to hand over the Holy Communion to us the recipients. How do we interprete these two words, Alleluia and Amen? There is of course no other name suitable than to say that they are symbolic utterances. The important questions now come: How do they perform? And what type of performative utterances are they? To the question: how do they perform? We may say that they perform implicitly because they do not follow the explicit performative formular. With regard to the type of utterance, we may say that they are proclamation and declaration respectively. How do we explain this? We can say that the chanting of 'Alleluia' is a proclamation of the joyous expectation of the announcing of the Gospel to be done shortly by the deacon or the priest. Secondly, that we say 'Amen', and the Holy Com-

---

294 Heinz-Mohr, Gerd, Lexikon der Symbole: Bilder und Zeichen der christlichen Kunst, Köln 1983, 9.
295 Heinz-Mohr, Lexicon der Symbole, 9.
296 Heinz-Mohr, Lexicon der Symbole, 11.
297 Schilling, Klaus, Symbole erleben: Glauben erfahren mit Hand, Kopf und Herz, Stuttgart 1991, 22.
298 Schilling, Symbole erleben, 27.

munion is offered to us is a declaration of our worthiness or preparedness to receive the Holy Communion.

Symbolic language also performs in Igbo traditional religion. Certain Igbo words are symbolic and they are uttered to bring about certain actions. Let us consider these words: Tufia, Chaa, Ise and Ihaa. These Igbo words are symbolic and action-oriented. What do these words mean? They can be grouped into two: Chaa and Tufia perform the action of warning. When a goat approaches where it should not go, entering a living room, for example, the owner warns it to go away by simply shouting "chaa!". Ise and Ihaa are affirmations. They are choroused, for example at the end of prayer in any traditional Igbo society. By implication, Tufia, chaa, ise and ihaa are implicit in nature since they do not follow the explicit performative formular. There are equally Igbo phrases that are symbolic and performative. When in a neighbourhood someone or some people suddenly begins or begin to shout: "onye ekwena uzo ga", what does he or what do they intend to achieve? And what type of utterance is that? Such an Igbo phrase is issued when someone has stolen and is on the run to escape capture. The victim whose property is stolen calls for help from neighbours to blockade every route and join in search of the thief. So we can say that this phrase is an appeal. Again, another Igbo phrase: "Ebewu ebenebe gburu" is symbolic and performative. What does the speaker mean by this phrase? What type of utterance is that? It can be explained with what happens in a traditional Igbo society when someone dies. The village-crier goes around at dusk shouting "Ebewu ebenebe gburu". This phrase serves as an introduction before he gives out his message which is announcing the death. So we can say that this phrase is an appeal for audience.

Igbo idiomatic expressions, proverbs, riddles and songs are full of symbolic languages and are performative. For instance, when an Igbo elder says in proverb: "Ukpana Okpoko buru nti chiri ya", he means that a grasshopper overpowered by a noisy animal has himself to blame because the noise of the animal-enemy is enough signal for him to scamper for safety. When we ask for the type of utterance this might be, the answer is that it can be taken to be a warning to whoever the elder might be addressing. During the Nigerian-Biafran war of the late sixties, the Igbo soldiers used to sing: "Nzogbu enyimba enyi zogbuo nwoke enyimba enyi zugbuo nwanyi enyimba enyi". This song is not to be taken literally because it is symbolic. What did the singers mean by this song? And what type of utterance was that? Well, we may say that by singing this song the soldiers wanted to prepare their minds for the battle ahead. The song, without any doubt, is a warning for the enemy about what the soldier-singers could do.

4.2.6 The reference: Performative theater

In chapters one, two and three of this work, we discussed that languages used in theater are performative, and performative thinkers have argued that languages used in theater are performative because in theater words create imaginary situations, and because these words themselves have power over imaginations, they can go further to make these imaginations assume certain presumed realities. This means, performative words do direct our imaginations, and play writers are conscious of this fact and do employ appropriate words in writing plays. Actors apply these words to make them perform in the audience. Performative words, therefore, help to shape the way we imagine situations, bringing these situations into being. This means that the actions of performative words are not limited to normal situations only, but perform even when they are acted. When in a drama the chief actor tells a co-actor "come here ... or go away", what does he mean by those utterances? We may say that they are orders. So, we may as well put it this way: "I order that you come here ... I order that you go away ...". The same actions these orders perform in a normal situation are the same actions expected of them when uttered in a theater.

In Igbo traditional religion, the issue of play writing or acting, talkless of theater, was totally absent. Part of the reason is because the Igbo traditional religion has no literary genre because the religion itself is not a religion of the book.[299] But today, however, the introduction of drama within the traditional life of the Igbo society cannot be denied. It has even been tremendously improved to suit the taste of the modern time. The most commendable thing, however, is that the words used in Igbo drama are as well performative because they perform the same actions expected of them in a normal situation. When a chief priest in an Igbo drama tells his client "I see doom hovering over your head ...", and we ask: What does the chief priest mean by this utterance? We may say that it is a prophecy. So, we can as well put it this way: "I prophesy a doom hovering over your head ...". The same action this prophecy should have in a normal situation is expected of it even as it is uttered in this drama.

Likewise, in sacramental theology performative theater can properly be applied because the sacramental actions are often described as a 'holy drama' in which: the world is the theater, God is the play writer, the ordained minister is the actor, Jesus Christ is the performative word, the people of God gathered in worship are the audience, the altar is the stage and conversion and sanctification are the effects of the performative word. So the same action associated with any performative word in a normal situation is expected of it even when it is acted. For example, the essence of acting the institution narrative is to evangelize through theater, and most of the people who might not have read the actual text in the Bible have been influenced by acting this event, likewise the audience who have watched the drama. So, the words perform similar to the way they should have performed had one read the event directly from the Bible.

4.3 Dissimilarities

In order to give a comprehensive appraisal to the task we have set out to achieve, a careful study is to be made on the areas where our discussions on performative word are dissimilar in both sacramental theology and in Igbo traditional religion. These

---

299 Cf. Metu, African Religions in western conceptual schemes, 23.

areas of dissimilarities include the analysis of the concept of performative word which includes discussions on the sacredness of performative word, the scriptural orientation of performative word, its sacrament-orientation, its theology-orientation and "ex opere operato"; other areas of dissimilarities include also discussions on implicit performative word and performative magic. Below are the details on these dissimilarities.

4.3.1 The conceptual analysis

Although the concept of performative word is the same in both sacramental theology and in Igbo traditional religion, there exist some differences in the way this concept is interpreted in both religions. Below is an examination of these differences.

4.3.1.1 Performative word as a sacred word

In sacramental theology, every performative word is sacred. This is on the ground that celebration of sacrament is a sacred act, and therefore, demands a sacred language. This means that performative word within the context of Sacramental theology is a sacred word. This, however, does not in any way imply that all sacred words are performative words. In sacramental theology, performative word by implication is not to be compared with any other words that are mundane, but because it is sacred, it is divine, and as it were: "the Holy Spirit, through whom the living voice of the Gospel rings out in the church- and through her in the world- leads believers to the full truth, and makes the Word of Christ dwell in them in all its richness".[300] So, in sacramental theology, performative word is sacred and because it is action-oriented, it is performative. In its performance, it establishes interaction between God and man, as well as the consequences of such relationship. Sacramental theology, therefore, does not consider performative word as an abstract language. On the contrary, it is a performative language that is sacred. As an action language that is at the same time sacred, its words arouse faith in the hearers, and motivate them to live in accordance to what they have heard for the sole purpose of sanctification and salvation. Again, because the performative language is sacred, it causes the manifestation of the divine reality among the community of the faithful. For instance, the words of the epiclesis (invocation of the Holy Spirit at the Liturgy of the Eucharist), leads to transubstantiation in which God is present in the sacred species. The words of the exchange of consent at the celebration of the Holy Matrimony bind the couple into husband and wife. So, the sacred character of the performative word empowers it to effect actions as it is being uttered in liturgical celebrations. Thus, the word we utter in sacramental celebrations becomes an utterance of faith in action.

---

300 D V, no. 8.

The acceptance that the words of sacramental theology is sacred is based on the fact that they are recognized as divine, and because they are divine they are considered as inspired, substantially because they are biblical. We support this view with the following texts: "Great indeed, we confess, is the mystery of our religion: He was manifested in the flesh, vindicated in the spirit, seen by angels, preached among nations, believed on in the world, taken up in glory" (1Tim 3,16–17). St Peter in one of his epistles writes: "First of all you must understand this, that no prophecy ever came by the impulse of man, but men moved by the Holy Spirit spoke from God" (2Pt1,20–21). So, inspiration offers the basis or the fundamental explanation for which the word is considered sacred and for which it performs in the hearts and minds of the hearers.

The cultural, social and religious life of the Igbo people in their traditional society are undivided. Within the social and cultural life of the Igbo people is the religious life celebrated. It is therefore difficult to distinguish one from the other. This means that to regard performative word in Igbo traditional religion as a sacred word alone is unacceptable. There is no doubt that performative word in Igbo traditional religion is sacred but not limited to it. This means that not all the Igbo performative words are sacred because of the mixture of the circumstances of the celebration. We have earlier discussed war songs in chapter three, and more so, within the context of symbolic language in this chapter. It is crystal clear that the performance of the wordings of war song cannot to be categorized as sacred words. This does not mean that "ise" chorused at the end of any ritual act in Igbo traditional religion is not sacred. So, while every performative word in sacramental theology is sacred, moreso because the priest acts in the person of Christ "in persona Christi", not every performative word in Igbo traditional religion is sacred just for the same reason that the priest of the Igbo traditional religion does not act in the person of his deity but only as a mouth-piece.

4.3.1.2 Performative word as scripture-oriented

It is not conceivable to discuss performative word in sacramental theology independent of the scriptures. This is because the Holy Bible is one of the important sources upon which the teachings and practice of sacramental theology are based.[301] In Old Testament and New Testament, therefore, one experiences actions of the word as they are being recorded under the divine inspiration.

It was by the power of the word that the whole universe and its content came to be. In the story of creation, when God says "Let there be light ...", we observe the performative use of word. We can similarly understand the utterance to mean "I command that

---

301 The relationship between the Scripture and the sacraments is more vivid in the New Testament, namely, the gospels and epistles. The story and the account of how Christ instituted each of the seven sacraments is revealed in the New Testament. This relationship suggests that the sacraments should be studied not within abstract treatments of supernatural grace but within the concrete context of salvation history and the redemption wrought by Christ's death and resurrection. In so doing, we acquire the implicit understanding of what we are celebrating expressed in the prayers and physical gestures that accompany our sacramental worship.

there be light". In this way, the type of utterance is clear that it is a command. When the Lord God told the childless Abram that his children would be uncountable as the stars of heaven are uncountable (Cf.Gen 15: 5), what type of utterance is that ? It can as well be arranged to be written: I promise you that your sons will be uncountable as the stars of heaven. By this utterance, therefore, God performs the act of promise. When Elijah told Ahab that there would neither be dew nor rain in the land that year (1Kgs 17,1), what type of performative utterance would have been made? It would be a prediction when we take it to mean "I predict that there would be neither dew nor rain in the land". When king Nebuchadnezzar sent out his word that all within his kingdom should at the sound of pipe, horn and trumpet bow down and worship the golden image, what type of performative utterance shall we ascribe to it? We call it a decree: "I decree that when you hear the sound of pipe, horn and trumpet you should bow down and worship the golden image". Again, when the prophet Elisha told Naaman the army commander to go to river Jordan and bath for seven-times to cure his leprosy (2Kgs 5,10), what type of performative utterance is that? We may say that this is a recommendation or advice: "I recommend that you bath seven times in river Jordan or I advice that you bath seven times in river Jordan ...". The New Testament is also full of the narrations about the performative power of word through numerous miracles of Jesus Christ and his apostles. The word of Jesus has immense power. The performative power of his words in performing miracles can be categorized as "command". Here is an example of the healing power of his word: "The official said to him, 'Sir, come down before my child dies'. Jesus said to him, 'Go; your son will live'. The man believed the word that Jesus spoke to him and went his way. As he was going down, his servants met him and told him that his son was living . So he asked them the hour when he began to mend, and they said to him, 'Yesterday at the seventh hour the fever left him'. The father knew that was the hour when Jesus had said to him, 'Your son will live'". (Jn 4,49–53). All Jesus did to heal this man's son was to speak, even though Jesus was not in the same place as where the child was lying. So, he commanded and the child was healed.

By the power of his word, Jesus raised the dead back to life. In fact, in the gospels there are several accounts of persons Jesus raised. For example, a twelve year old girl died in her bed but Jesus came, took her by the hand and told her "child arise" (Lk 8,54), and she got up. Jesus, as well commanded, and the child arose from the dead. The performative power of Jesus word as a command was more explicit at the raising of Lazarus from the dead: "Lazarus, I command you come out" (Jn 11, 43).

Jesus goes further to show how sins can be forgiven by the power of his word: "And when Jesus saw their faith, he said to the paralytic, , My son, your sins are forgiven'"(Mk 2,5). For those who reflect on what took place, the miraculous cure is seen as the confirmation of the truth proclaimed by Jesus and perceived and opposed by the scribes, that he (Jesus) has power on earth to forgive sins. Again, when we ask: What type of performative utterance is this? We might say that it is a pronouncement: "I pronounce that you are forgiven ...".

After the death of Jesus, the apostles carried on their master's ministry, and their words were also confirmed by the miracles that followed. Peter for example cured a paralytic in front of the Temple. By the power of the words, many who listened to what they were saying were moved to conversion: "So faith comes from what is heard, and what is heard comes by the preaching of Christ" (Rm 10,17).

Igbo traditional religion is no religion of the book. It has no literature and it has no formal record, and neither has it any archive. So it is difficult to relate its teachings to a common source. So, making references to a common source is unfortunately not possible. Our proposition on performative word in Igbo traditional religion, therefore, is based on our attempt at gathering together the different evidences we are able to assemble in the study of Igbo traditional religion itself, and arranging these findings in order to build-up a formidable teaching on the performance of word in Igbo traditional religion.

4.3.1.3 Performative word as sacrament-oriented

Sacramental theology teaches how important word is to sacrament, and although the two are separate concepts, they relate very closely. Writing on the two concepts, word and sacrament, Louis-Marie Chauvet concludes that "the word happens in the sacrament",[302] and that "it is the word which constitutes the sacrament".[303] The word constitutes the sacrament through its performance within the context of the sacramental celebrations. By implication, the action of performative word in sacramental theology is directed towards the realization of sacraments. In a similar understanding Theodor Schneider writes: "Sakramentales Wort ist 'forma sacramenti', ist performativ, d.h. wirklichkeitssetzende Rede, deren volle Bedeutung allerdings nur im Gesamt der liturgischen Feier erkannt werden kann".[304]

Theodor Schneider explains how word performs in the celebration of the sacraments by saying: "Ich spreche Dich los [...], ich nehme Dich zum Ehemann [...], ich taufe Dich, solche Sätze vollziehen, was sie ausdrücken, bewirken, was sie sagen".[305] St Augustine had earlier in his Easter homily propounded the teaching that the word acts on the elements and brings about the sacraments. This means that the sacraments are the manifestations of the actions of the word (verbum visibile). So, Theodor Schneider supports the notion that in sacramental theology, performative word is sacrament-oriented, and to state this point clearly, he writes: "Wenn dort von der performativen Rede gesprochen wird, ist genau das gemeint, was sich auch im sakramentalen Wort vollzieht: Performative Rede meint wirklichkeitssetzende Rede, Worte, die bewirken, was sie ausdrücken".[306] Being sacrament-oriented, performative word according to sacramental theology, therefore, has the duty to nourish, strengthen and express the faith of the recipient through

---

302 Chauvet, The sacraments, The word, 97.
303 Chauvet, The sacraments, The word, 97.
304 Schneider, Theodor, Zeichen der Nähe Gottes: Grundriß der Sakramententheologie, Mainz 2005, 44.
305 Schneider, Zeichen der Nähe Gottes, 44.
306 Schneider, Zeichen der Nähe Gottes, 43.

the reception of the sacrament which it offers.[307] Igbo traditional religion cannot be associated with sacraments. This means that performative word in Igbo traditional religion is not sacrament-oriented. It cannot be said that the word performs in Igbo traditional religion in order to bring about sacraments. This, however, does not imply that there are no sacramental realities in the various rites and rituals in Igbo traditional religion. Of course, we have already studied these realities in chapter three of our work.

4.3.1.4 Performative word as theology-oriented

The church's sacraments have a formidable theology that establishes and sustains it all through the ages. This theology is at the very base of the church's teachings about her sacraments. It is as well the force that directs those principles of the church's doctrine on sacraments which is accepted as the article of faith, and which should be jealously guarded against any changes and chances, and upheld as unshakeable dogma that should be defended everywhere and at everytime. Any discussion on the theology of the sacraments, therefore, should not be done in isolation from the discussion on the theology of the word because the theology of the word compliments the theology of the sacrament. It is in the theology of the word that the theology of the sacrament is born. So, when we are discussing performative word in sacramental theology, we are not discussing it in a profane manner, and we are not discussing it as an informal or unorganized concept. On the contrary, the study of the concept of performative word in sacramental theology is considered as a systematic venture, organized in a way that it is directed towards a certain belief with its body of principles, in other words, its theology towards which it is channelled. In attempt to provide a strong theology to the sacramental word, certain doctrines like incarnation and inspiration have been propounded. This we have also discussed in chapter two of this work. Many theologians across centuries and ages have contributed to the development of this theology (confer equally chapter two of our work). Various councils and popes have in different times reiterated this teaching and encouraged its acceptance and spread.

To associate theology with the rites and rituals of Igbo traditional religion may not yet be appropriate because concise and organized teachings on the beliefs and practices of this great religion are not yet reached. It logically follows that the word which performs in its religious rites and rituals cannot be said to be theology-oriented since the religion itself has not yet got a commonly defined and standardized theology of its own. It does not mean that this goal cannot be reached in future, but until then, to identify performative word in Igbo traditional religion as theology-oriented would be premature. Because Igbo traditional religion lacks a standard theology of its own, it cannot equally be said to have standard theologians because all is on the making. So, although the word which performs in Igbo traditional

---

307 S C, No. 59.

religion may be interpreted to be religious in its connotation and application, it does not mean that its religiosity is synonymous with it being theological.

4.3.1.5 Performative word as incarnate word

In chapter two of our work, the Old Testament explains performative word as God's own creative intervention. This creative intervention has transformative power in various forms and ramifications, namely: it shapes our concepts and ideas, and directs our thoughts and visions. It is by the performative power of the word that the world and its content, including man, were created. This means that God's word is an expression of his divine will. God willed that light be, and this divine will became materialized by its expression through the divine utterance. This was the same for every created thing; and this was the same for every directed thoughts and visions, and for every concepts and ideas. The New Testament conception of the divine word does not vary from the Old Testament. The ability of the divine word to create and to transform is experienced in both Old and New Testaments (Gen 1,1–25; 1Kgs18,30–39; Ps 29,4–9; 33,6–9; Jn 4,49–53; Lk 8,54; Mk 2,5; Rm 10,17).

However, the New Testament adds that this creative word of God, that this transforming word of God in time became flesh (Jn 1,14). I must, however, caution that the doctrine on ‚Logos' is a separate theology that is not directly related to our thesis. The church in her liturgy of the word, therefore, does not celebrate the word of a book but rather a person-the second person of the Blessed Trinity, Jesus Christ, who took flesh and dwells among us. This Jesus Christ is the word of God, a personified word, and eternal word. Jesus Christ, the word of God, became incarnate in time and space in order to give opportunity to all humankind to hear the saving message of God who created all to know him, to love him, to serve and to live with him for ever in his eternal kingdom of light, life and love.[308] This is the reason for which Jesus Christ instituted the sacraments for us: for our sanctification and salvation. Thus, Jesus Christ is nearest to us in his sacraments. The church teaches that it is in the celebration of the sacraments that the incarnate nature of the divine word is experienced directly and most powerfully because the minister acts only "in persona Christi", in the person of Christ. This means, when the minister baptizes, it is Jesus

---

308 Incarnation is from the Latin word "incarnatio" meaning that the Word ort he Son of God assumed human nature or became man not simply in an external bodily form but completely. At this point, Jesus the second person of the Trinity became Jesus of Nazareth and identified with human nature in everything except sin. He is truly God and truly man. St Paul described the mystery of incarnation in a hymnic language: "though he was in the form of God, Jesus did not count equality with God a thing to be grasped, but emptied himself, taking the form of a servant, being born in the likeness of men" (Ph 2,6–7). Letter to the Hebrews described it in a historic language: "In many and various ways God spoke of old to our fathers by the prophets;but in these last days he has spoken to us by a son, whom he appointed the heir of all things, through whom also he created the world. He reflects the glory of God and bears the very stamp of his nature, upholding the universe by his word of power. When he had made purification for sins, he sat down at the right hand of the Majesty on high" (Heb 1,1–3).

Christ himself who took flesh in the womb of the Blessed Virgin Mary that baptizes; when the minister pronounces the words of consecrating the bread and wine at the Eucharistic celebration, it is Jesus Christ son of God and son of Virgin Mary that pronounces those sacred words; when the minister absolves sins at the confessional, it is Jesus Christ true God and true man that absolves, and so on. So, at the celebration of the sacraments, Jesus Christ is both the minister as well as the victim. We, therefore, come to the conclusion that in the celebration of the sacraments, the son of God, who took flesh to be revealed as Jesus Christ, performs as an incarnate word. Performative word in Igbo traditional religion is neither personified nor is there anything like the doctrine of incarnation in its religious belief and practices. The deity for which the priest remains the mouth-piece in history never assumed any human form and Igbo traditional religion would not pretend in future to introduce such assumption in imitation of the christian faith. So, Igbo traditional religion never considers Igbo performative word as incarnate word.

4.3.1.6 "Ex Opere Operato"

The phrase "ex opere operato" is from Latin and literally means "from the work done". By interpretation, it is employed by the church to affirm that the efficacy of the sacraments does not depend on the holiness or merits of the minister or the priest but rather depends on the action of the sacraments themselves. By implication, it means that because the priest acts in the person of Christ (in persona Christi) who is both the priest and the victim, it means that when the priest utters the sacramental words it is no longer him that utters those words but Christ utters them in him. So the efficacy of those sacramental words does not depend on the priest who is only an instrument in God's hand but on Christ Himself who speaks those words in the priest. And in order that these sacraments act on the recipient, a proper disposition is demanded: "So lehrt das Konzil zwei kernaussagen: Die Sakramente verleihen die Gnade bei entsprechender Disposition immer und allen, und: Die Sakramente verleihen die Gnade beim Vollzug des sakramenten Zeichens".[309] However, it remains a grave sin for a minister, under normal circumstance, to celebrate in a state of mortal sin, and likewise for the recipient to receive the sacrament in an unworthy state. It is to be emphasized, however, that the good disposition of the recipient is not the cause of the grace that is derived from the sacraments but Christ himself who offers it as a gift. We must add that the teaching on "ex opere operato" is met with tough resistance from the reformers, and is described by them as the worst blasphemy of the sacraments: "Hier wendete sich die reformatorischen Kritik gegen die Annahme eines Heilsautomatismus in der Praxis der Sakramentenspendung."[310]

"ex opere operato" is in sympathy with the J.L.Austin's criteria although with a careful interpretation of the three dominant words : conventional procedure, proper situation and similar emotions, feelings and intentions. Once the sacrament is cel-

---
309 Klöckner, Sakrament im Wort, 84.
310 Klöckner, Sakrament im Wort, 84.

ebrated by a validly ordained minister who is still in communion with the church, and once he celebrates in accordance with the church's guidelines and in accordance with the proper intention, the actions of the sacramental words become completed. In the same line of thought with J.L.Austin's concept of performative word, therefore, the teaching on "ex opere operato" upholds that the efficacy of the sacramental words does not depend on the merits of the minister who utters them, rather on the actions of the sacraments themselves, once the criteria are fulfilled.

Although Igbo traditional religion accepts all the J.L.Austin's criteria, the priesthood in Igbo traditional religion is not based on the conception of "ex opere operato", instead it associates the effectiveness of any celebrated Igbo traditional ritual and rite to the merits of the priest celebrant. Igbo traditional religion teaches that on account of gross misconducts such as taking bribe from clients and overturning the truth, and thereby obstructing the cause of justice, which as it were, hinge on lack of adequate feelings, thoughts and intentions on the part of the chief priest, his utterances are rendered ineffective. This ineffectiveness does not depend on whether the client is aware of the insincerity of the chief priest or not. And when his words are no longer considered effective, he risks the chance of rejection not only from the people but also from the very deity he represents. There is another side to this. The deity itself is liable to possible destruction by its adherents. This is what Oliver A. Onwubiko calls "killing the spirit". He goes further to explain how this is done:

> The "killing" of a spirit in this way is only by destroying its shrines and thereby chase it out of the community and it enters into the realm of "unlocalised", "unknown", and "unworshipped" spirits, and thus claim no specific rights from any community.[311]

The killing of spirit is brought about when the adherents feel that their deity has either turned against them to inflict much miseries and sufferings on them or has grown too powerless and incapable of protecting them. In this case, the people resort to destroying it, not by themselves but by employing the services of a stronger cult like the Chukwu cult of Arochukwu whose fee was very exorbitant. The destruction of a deity, therefore, means termination of the services of its priest, and making his words ineffective. The installation of the priest is rendered invalid, and he ceases from being a mouth-piece of god. His words are no longer those of god's, and therefore, they lack performative effect.

4.3.2 The form: Implicit performative word

In the previous chapters of this work, we have discussed the meaning of implicit performative word as an utterance that is unclear, and therefore, conveys meaning that is doubted,[312] thereby leading to the following questions: What does the speaker mean by that? What type of utterance is that?

---

311 Onwubiko, African Thought, Religion and Culture, 86.
312 Cf. Austin, How To Do Things with Words, 32.

Evidences of implicit performative word are found in Igbo traditional religion. Igbo proverbs, already discussed in chapter three of this work, are full of implicit performative words. By this I mean, Igbo proverbs lack explicit performative verbs, and are sophisticated and need proper reflections in order to be understood. Because the meanings they convey are complicated, there is need for verifications by asking: What does the speaker mean by that? What type of utterance is that? Igbo riddles and traditional songs, also discussed in chapter three of this work, lack explicit performative verbs as well and are rich in sophisticated speech genre, and because one needs to posit the above-mentioned questions in order to understand them, they are implicit. Although implicit performative word is not popular with sacramental theology, it does not mean that it is totally absent in sacramental celebrations.

4.3.3 The reference: Performative magic

Performative magic is a process of using words to make something assume a presumed or seeming reality. It is a team work in which the actor has the role of uttering the words to make a thing assume a certain presumed reality, and the audience plays the role of acknowledging this presumed reality. When words succeed to achieve this goal, it is known as performative magic. In sacramental theology, performative magic is totally unacceptable. What the church celebrates in her sacraments is an unadulterated truth that sanctifies and saves, and according to Gehard Ludwig Müller:

> Die Sakramentalität als theologische Kategorie kennzeichnet die innere Einheit von göttlicher Selbstmitteilung in der inkarnatorischen Gestalt der Gnade und in der durch sie ermöglichten menschlichen Gottesverehrung im ganzen Lebensvollzug, in Glaube und Nachfolge Christi.[313]

So, celebration of sacraments is celebration of eternal truth and the sacramental words cannot be associated with magic. On the contrary, performative magic is experienced in the "Abrakadabra" (incantations) that is associated with the Igbo traditional priest, and presumed to be the performative language of the spirits. The traditional Igbo priest entones these incantations which are known only to him in order to effect some reactions in his client. He may succeed in putting some fears in his adherent but does the fact that the adherent acts in fear make these "Abrakadabra" to be performative? Should Austin J.L not be interpreted to mean that the performative word itself must first of all be a human language in order to be performative? Since the incantations have no base in human language, and since neither the chief priest nor the adherent may claim to understand what is being uttered, my critique remains that performative magic remains on the level of "presumed performative word".

---

313 Müller, Katholische Dogmatik, 628.

4.4 Conclusion

From our investigation in this chapter, it emerged that the application of J.L.Austin's concept of performative word in sacramental theology and in Igbo traditional religion has some similarities as well as some dissimilarities. Our study reveals that our key concept relates similarly to both sacramental theology and to Igbo traditional religion on the way it is defined. The three senses in J.L.Austin's concept of performative word are duly reflected in the way performative word is as well conceived in sacramental theology and in Igbo traditional religion, namely: to say something is to do something or in saying something we are doing something and by saying something we are doing something. The sacramental rite itself is the framework in which the word comes most powerfully to expression. The same can be said of the action of word within the framework of Igbo religious rites and rituals. Our chapter goes on to highlight that both sacramental theology and Igbo traditional religion apply explicit form[314] of performative word in their ritual ceremonies. In Eucharistic celebration, for example, the words of consecration of bread and wine are explicitly expressed as a command: "Take this and eat it ... Take this and drink from it ...". The same explicit form of performative word is identified in Igbo religious rituals, for example, in oath-taking: "I (name), hereby declare ...". This is undoubtedly a declaration. There is no difference in the criteria[315] regulating performative word in sacramental theology and in Igbo traditional religion. We have in this chapter, and indeed, in the previous chapters discussed performative identities, performative symbols and performative theater.[316] This chapter teaches that they are conceived the same way in both sacramental theology and in Igbo traditional religion.

Besides, the present chapter presents also the basic differences in the way the J.L.Austin's concept of performative word is interpreted in sacramental theology and in Igbo traditional religion. For example, in sacramental theology, every performative word is sacred because it is uttered within the context of ritual ceremonies. The Igbo cosmology does not totally agree to this because of its inseparability of cultural, social and religious life of the people from one another. It may, therefore, not totally

---

314 Explicit performative word clarifies the force of the utterance by defining the action that is being performed. J.L.Austin classified explicit form verbs into behabitives, I apologise that ...; expositives, I testify that ...; verdictives, I pronounce that ...; commisives, I undertake to ...; exercitives, I appoint ... . Implicit performative word is unclear because it does not define the action that is being performed, and therefore, its meaning is doubted.
315 These criteria are summed up in the following way:
  i. There must be a conventional procedure.
  ii. The procedure must be executed by all participants both correctly and completely.
  iii. The same emotion regulating the feelings and thoughts of the audience must guide the speaker in order to achieve the desired effect.
316 Performative identities explain how words define who we are. Performative symbols do not stand in isolation but beed convention in order to have a uniform interpretation and in order to perform. Performative theater explains how words perform in the audience. It helps the actor to represent already pre-existing reality, as well as, to create a reality that has not existed before.

be correct to say that all the performative words within the context of Igbo traditional rituals are sacred. Again, the teachings of sacramental theology implies that performative word is scripture-oriented, sacrament-oriented and theology-oriented. Bible, of course, is the major source upon which the teachings and practice of sacramental theology is based. Likewise, the word constitutes the sacrament through its performance within the context of sacramental celebrations. The actions of the word is geared towards realization of sacraments. Again, in sacramental theology, performative word has a defined theology that sustains it, which, as it were, may be referred to as the theology of the word. It is this theology of the word that compliments the theology of the sacrament. On the contrary, Igbo traditional religion is not a religion of the book, and therefore, there is no association of performative word to any written source within Igbo traditional religion. Although there are some sacramental realities in Igbo religious rites and rituals, it will be totally wrong to say that performative word in Igbo traditional religion is sacrament-oriented. It may not be logically accepted that performative word in Igbo traditional religion is theology-oriented. This is because Igbo traditional religion itself has not yet got a commonly defined and standardized theology of its own. Sacramental theology in its doctrine of incarnation, personifies performative word to be Jesus Christ, whereas, there is no such personification in Igbo traditional religion. Furthermore, our present chapter shows that the teaching of sacramental theology on "ex opere operato" is in sympathy with J.L.Austin's concept of performative word, whereas, the "ex opere operato" has no place in Igbo traditional religion. Whereas sacramental theology operates within the framework of the explicit form of performative word, Igbo traditional religion associates itself as well to the implicit form, for example, in its proverbs and idioms. Performative magic is totally unacceptable in sacramental theology, whereas, in Igbo traditional religion, poreformative magic is encountered in the ritual incantations.

Now that we have discussed and compared our key concept "performative word" in both religions, how can we translate the knowledge we have got in a more practical terms and in the way it will be of a great help in the work of evangelization in Igboland? Our discussions, of course, will not be beneficial if we fail to apply them in concrete terms. Within the frame-work of the goal we have set out to achieve which hinges on the impact of performative word in the use of Igbo language for effective evangelization in Igboland, we need to show the relevance of all we have discussed about J.L.Austin's performative word to pastoral theology. Indeed, this is what the next chapter will be focusing on.

5 Performative word versus use of igbo language for effective evangelization in igboland

5.1 Introduction

This final chapter gives pastoral relevance to our key concept. It is an attempt to highlight on how J.L.Austin's performative word can be interpreted in the light of pastoral theology. In other words, it sets out to show how performative word can be pastorally applied in order to make the gospel message act among the Igbo people within their cultural milieu and thereby achieve authentic conversion which is the goal of evangelization. One may ask: How is J.L.Austin's performative word related to pastoral theology? Pastoral theology, as we know, is interested in applying the gospel message within a particular people's culture. Likewise, J.L.Austin's performative word does not act in the air but in order to perform, needs a people's language which is the bane of their culture. So, culture is the contact-point, or as it were, the meeting-point where J.L.Austin's performative word and pastoral theology relate to show how by use of particular language of a particular culture, a particular action can be achieved.

Another important question might be: In what ways can we interpret J.L.Austin's performative word in the pastoral work among the Igbo people and within the context of Igbo language? In order to attempt this question and to offer an adequate answer, we must refer to the J.L.Austin's definition of performative word, the infelicities, and the explicit performative form. Furthermore, we shall make our explanations more concrete by describing how word performs in the missionary efforts among the present day Igbo, viz: prayer ministry, crusade, family ministration, parish retreat, parish weekly adoration, charismatic prayer group, homily, catechism classes, school apostolate and counselling. This chapter, therefore, proposes evangelization as a means through which the J.L.Austin's concept of performative word can be appreciated and be interpreted in the light of making authentic Igbo christians. Our discussions on evangelization would include salient issues beginning with the scriptural background to evangelization, the meaning of evangelization, the goal of evangelization, the methods of evangelization, the evangelizer and the evangelized, attempt by the early missionaries to evangelize Igboland, what evangelization means in the new vision of the church, and the place of the local language of the people in evangelization. Furthermore, we shall be considering the two concrete steps in attempt to evangelize the Igbo natives, namely: inculturation and dialogue. We shall then round up the chapter by recommending various areas where the use of authentic Igbo language is vital for proper conversion and formation of authentic Igbo christians, and thereby making our discussions on performative word to be pastorally relevant.

5.2 Performative word versus Igbo word

J.L.Austin defined performative word in three senses whereby to say something is to do something; or in saying something we are doing something; or by saying something we are doing something.[317] This means, performative word is an action word because the verb 'perform' is associated with noun-action.[318] Thus, performative utterance is understood in terms of 'doing something' and not 'saying something.' So, there is a strong relationship between utterance and action. Performative word, therefore, shows how people use language to do things.

Igbo people's understanding of spoken word is the same with the J.L.Austin's definition of performative word. Igbo word is action-oriented. In Igbo traditional society, spoken words are very much valued because of their performance. Therefore, to break a verbal oath is one of the greatest felonies in Igboland. According to Igbo belief, words of prayers are believed to come true, curses become real and violation of oath has disastrous consequences.

That the Igbo people interpret the action of Igbo word in the context of J.L.Austin's performative word has a lot of pastoral advantages which the evangelizer should utilize. The goal of evangelization is conversion. Since Igbo word leads to action, invariably it would lead to a definite action when uttered under a definite intention, viz: when the Igbo chorus 'ise' at the end of a traditional prayer, they express their consent to the prayer just offered; when they say 'Igbo kweenu!', they call for attention. Giving consent and attention are the various actions arising from the Igbo words 'ise' and 'Igbo kweenu!' respectively. It would not be out of place for a missionary to implement these words while ministering to the Igbo. The phrase 'praise be to Jesus' is often applied in place of 'Igbo kweenu' and 'Amen' in place of 'ise'. The use of 'ise' and 'Igbo Kweenu!' will make the corresponding actions original to our people.

5.3 Infelicities

J.L.Austin's performative word has a set of criteria that regulates them.[319] Violations of these criteria are what we refer to as infelicities.[320] These infelicities include misinvocation, misapplication, misexecution and abuse.[321] How do these infelicities make J.L.Austin's concept of performative word to be pastorally relevant in Igboland?

---

317 Cf. Austin, How To Do Things With Words, 12.
318 Cf. Austin, How To Do Things With Words, 6.
319 Cf. Austin, How To Do Things With Words, 14–15.
320 Cf. Austin, How To Do Things With Words, 14.
321 Cf. Austin, How To Do Things With Words, 18.

5.3.1 Misinvocation

Misinvocation occurs when a certain procedure which does not exist is applied. In this case, J.L.Austin would say that the act is purported but not achieved.[322] It would also be said that there are evidences of misinvocation in traditional Igbo society. For instance, according to Igbo religious belief-system, only males are legible for the office of the traditional priesthood and the installation rites and rituals are designed based on this understanding. Should a situation arise where a woman is installed a traditional priest, according to Igbo customs and tradition, such installation is not recognized because the norms of the traditional society do not approve of it and there is no provisions for the rites and rituals of such installation.

That the Igbo people accepted the infelicity of misinvocation in their traditional society is a pastoral advantage for the christian evangelizer who would in turn find it easier to transmit certain church's teaching, such as, regulations regarding sacramental and liturgical rites and rituals. For example, the church teaches that only males are legible to receive sacred ordination (Cf.c.1024CIC). Therefore, J.L.Austin's misinvocation which is also found in Igbo traditional belief-system would make it easier for the church to pastorally foster its teaching on invalidity of women ordination. What J.L.Austin and Igbo traditional religion in their discussion about misinvocation call "purported but not achieved" is the same with what the church considers as "attempted but invalid".

5.3.2 Misapplication

According to J.L.Austin, misapplication refers to the infelicity whereby a statement is considered purported but not achieved because the procedure involved is not correctly applied.[323] In Igboland, when any rite in a ritual ceremony is not properly applied, the Igbo people would consider the process as "omenenu". The term "omenenu" is synonymous with the concept of misapplication in J.L.Austin's performative word. For example, in Igbo traditional society, the priest-elect must posses certain essential qualities such as, moroseness, love of solitude, psychic qualities-high intellectual work and retentive memory.[324] To install somebody who fails to acquire the above qualities as a priest in Igbo traditional society is unacceptable and such an act would be "omenenu" which is the Igbo man's understanding of misapplication. Therefore, Igbo people would judge such an act as purported but not achieved. This concept of "omenenu" (misapplication) among the traditional Igbo people again offers a favourable atmosphere for the Igbo to accept and appreciate what the christian pastor teaches about requirements for the admission of people to sacraments, and in this case, to the

---

322 Cf. Austin, How To Do Things With Words, 17.
323 Cf. Austin, How To Do Things With Words, 17.
324 Cf. Onwubiko, African Thought, Religion and Culture, 76.

sacrament of Holy Orders (cf.cc.1041,1042CIC). The church's language of invalidity applies to anyone who receives the sacrament of Holy Orders without fulfilling the demands of canon law in this regard. By invalidity, the church teaches that the reception is purported and therefore not achieved. In other words, the reception is "omenenu" or misapplication.

5.3.3 Misexecution

A procedure is declared misexecution when the act is vitiated by a flaw.[325] In this case, the statement is considered as purported but not achieved. There are evidences of misexecution in Igbo traditional society in which case a ritual ceremony is repeated because the earlier conducted ritual is declared null and void, and the reason may be that the ritual performer had not observed the essential aspects of the ritual ceremony. We take the example of "ọzọ Onitsha" (traditional title taking of the Onitsha) in Igboland. Because of the tradition of paying of homage to the cult of "ani" (the earth goddess) which the Onitsha traditionalists consider the most essential aspect of the title taking, and invariably performed at the shrine of "ani" at night, there has been a tension between christianity and Onitsha traditionalists. Christians of Onitsha who wish to participate in their "ọzọ" tradition had attempted to perform the "ọzọ" traditional title taking without going to the cult of "ani" to perform any ritual. But the Onitsha tradition has always failed to recognize such "ọzọ" title because it considers the ritual processes as marred with flaws and views such attempt as purported but not achieved.

There are also evidences of misexecution according to the teachings of the church. We give an example with a recipient of the sacrament of penance. In a situation where someone confesses his or her sins insincerely without any contrition and firm purpose of amendment, the act of confession he or she has done would be judged by the church as being marred with flaws because the essential processes are not observed ,and therefore, no forgiveness is achieved. Pastorally, because J.L.Austin's misexecution is inherent in Igbo traditional society, a christian missionary would find it easier to teach and convince the Igbo christians about the importance of good sacramental confessions and the dangers of bad sacramental confessions.

5.3.4 Abuse

Abuse is an infelicity whereby the procedure is marred with insincerity or infractions or breaches but the act is achieved.[326] This type of infelicity exists also in Igbo traditional society. For example, prayer over kolanut is a function carried out by a male

---

325 Cf. Austin, How To Do Things With Words, 17
326 Cf. Austin, How To Do Things With Words, 39.

participant in any gathering. In a situation where the group is made up of females and a kolanut is presented these women sort the service of even the youngest male-child available. Even if the male-child is too tender to know how to pray over the kolanut, he is made to touch the kolanut with his hand and that suffices for the prayer. The male-child might not understand the ritual he is performing but his act is achieved. In this sense, we could see the link between J.L.Austin's "abuse" and the situation we have just described.

The church's teaching on "ex opera operato"[327] is similar to J.L.Austin's "abuse". That the Igbo people has been practicing what is entailed in J.L.Austin's "abuse" would offer the missionary a favourable atmosphere to teach the Igbo natives what the church means by "ex opera operato", and sure, his explanation would be expected to have acceptance because such attitude is already in existence within the Igbo traditional society.

5.4 Explicit performative form versus Igbo word

Explicit form of performative word makes a statement clear by qualifying the type of utterance that is made.[328] Explicit performative words are also employed when Igbo people perform certain rituals, especially, in oath-taking: "I declare that …"; when the chief priest places a curse: "I pronounce a curse upon …"; when the family head settles a family dispute: "I judge that …".

Explicit form of performative word is most pronounce in the celebration of the church's sacraments. At the celebration of the eucharist, the church declares that at transubstantiation the bread becomes the Body of Jesus Christ and the wine His Blood: "This is my body … This is my blood". The church absolves the penitent from his sins at the sacrament of penance: "I absolve you from your sins …". Because the explicit role words perform is already witnessed in Igbo traditional society, the pastoral effort in communicating to the Igbo natives on how explicit the sacramental words are, would be easier and most welcomed to the utmost conviction of the Igbo people.

What I have been trying to achieve so far in this chapter is to show the link between J.L.Austin's performative word and pastoral theology. In other words, to give pastoral relevance to our key concept. Interpretation of J.L.Austin's teaching on performative word would be a valuable tool at the disposal of the church in no small way, especially, as it would offer the missionary the necessary assistance required to accomplish his

---

327 "ex opere operato" is a teaching employed by the church to affirm that the efficacy of the sacraments does not depend on the holiness or merits of the minister but rather depends on the action of the sacraments themselves. This is because the priest is only an instrument. The sacramental actions he performs are not his own but those of Christ himself who performs them through him. That is why the priest at the celebration of any sacrament acts "in persona Christi" (in the person of Christ).
328 Cf. Austin, How To Do Things With Words, 69.

evangelizing mission. Let us further consider, in more concrete realities, where and how word performs in the pastoral work of the present day Igbo church.

5.5 How does the word perform in today's Igbo church?

We have been considering the performance of word in general sense, so to say, but we need to point out concrete situations where word performs, most especially, in the pastoral work of the present day Igbo church. This session, therefore, presents these concrete situations to include prayer ministry, crusade, family ministration, parish retreat, parish weekly adoration, charismatic renewal prayer group, homily, catechism classes, school apostolate and counselling.

5.5.1 Prayer ministry

Prayer ministry as part and parcel of the church's ministry has a lot of pastoral contributions to make with regard to performance of word in the evangelizing mission of the church. It has been part of the mandate of Christ to the church, and as it were, an old tradition which the church inherited from its founder. Jesus went about his mission of preaching and healing the sick and his fame spread throughout Galilee and beyond. Those who were suffering from diseases and painful complaints of one kind or the other were brought to him and he cured them (Mt 4,23–24; Mk 1,39; Lk 4,14–15). Large crowds followed him, coming from Galilee, the Decapolis, Jerusalem, Judea and Transjordan. The people were astonished by the way Jesus carried out his mission that they began to say that he taught not like the Scribes and the Pharisees but like one who has authority, that even the evil spirits obey his words. Even John the Baptist who was his forerunner had to send his own disciples to find out whether he was the awaited Messiah or not. Jesus answer to John was simple: "Go and tell John what you have heard and seen; the blind recover their sight, the cripples walk, lepers are cleansed, the deaf hear, the dead raised to life and the poor has the gospel preached to them" (Mt 11,2–6). There were no limits to the healing power of Jesus Christ. His healing was holistic. Jesus healed people spiritually, emotionally, mentally and physically. He healed people in their relationship with God and with one another. His healings confirm that the power of the kingdom of God had come and demonstrated Christ's victory over evil. Jesus has great love for humanity and his deep compassion on those who were sick led him to the great mission of healing.[329] So his healing ministry was out of love and compassion. Jesus earthly life was a complete and total mission of reconciliation and healing. As there are different kinds of sickness, so there are different dimensions of healing that Jesus wrought when he

---

329 Cf. Lambourne R.A., Community, Church and Healing: A study of some of the corporate aspects of the church's ministry to the sick, London 1963, 126.

was on earth. He rescued men and women who were declared social outcasts by the Jewish society by healing them of their sicknesses that were the root of the high solid boundaries separating them from their brothers and sisters. Jesus did not stop his healing ministry or his healing works with his own time. He saw the need to extend the ministry to other ages and to other nations of the world. Jesus transmitted the gift of healing to the church, to equip her to be effective instrument of the witnesses of the kingdom. Hence the commissioning of the twelve who were his immediate and close followers to carry the gospel mission of preaching and healing the sick to the ends of the world. So the healing ministry was an endowment of the commissioned witness (Mk 16,17–18). This power given to the church had been used by the church and is still available and being used by the church in various forms. Christ categorically stated that healing power would be associated with believers who in his name will cast out demons and cure the sick. Throughout the history of the church, this ministry has never ceased. Organic diseases or even functional disorders have been healed without resorting to the skills of experts in medicine. What is new today is probably the proportion and dimension this healing ministry has assumed, especially, in Igboland. The church in Igboland understands well that the Igbo is naturally religious and very eager to get to the Supernatural, and therefore, he is easily attracted to whatever seems to be providing a response to this quest of his. The Igbo love sensational participation and celebration in worship that can animate the spirit in him. This need is today satisfied in the various existing prayer ministries which were not in the lime-light in the church in Igboland before the 10th of May 1973.[330] The prayer ministry seem to be offering solutions to these certain basic needs. Thus, the prayer minister occupies a central position as a healer, a wonder worker and an agent of Christ who came to liberate oppressed humanity from their various predicaments. So, the Igbo flock to these prayer houses in search of solutions to their various problems which could be spiritual, psychological, emotional and economical. Since these factors are not limited to a particular class of people, these explains why even the learned in the Igbo society, as well as the unlearned do not hesitate to be part of the adherents of these prayer ministries. They attend prayer sessions with variety of problems ranging from diseases, psychosomatic illnesses, barrenness, protection from enemies and fulfilment of their ambitions and hopes. Of course, as we have already seen in chapter three of this work, Igbo believe that all forms of misfortunes including poverty, sickness, barrenness, death, mental disorder, family problems, indeed, all kinds of misfortunes, are caused by the activities of evil spirits, angry gods, angry ancestors, evil men who operate as witches and witchcraft. It would not be an exaggeration to say that Africa in general is a continent that is characterized by much misery, a continent full of bad news.

Igboland as part of this great Africa knows much poverty, hunger, illiteracy, sickness and other man-made problems. Our people are caught in a web of poverty, misery, disease and ignorance. There is a total collapse of social and economic infrastructure, decadence of educational system, erosion of moral values, enduring state

---

[330] Ikeobi, Godwin, "What I think God is doing in and through me", Enugu 1992, 23.

of political instability, general insecurity of lives and property, unemployment, low wages and income, delayed payment of salaries, poor health care delivery, high mortality rate, and so on. The list of misery is indeed endless. In this state of hopelessness, the immediate option available to our people is turning to God of miracles who they believe are most especially available in various prayer ministries, and who is ready to salvage them from their predicaments. So, to the question: Why do our people flock to prayer ministries? One might in summary answer that the reality of abject poverty which is closely related to illiteracy and ignorance is responsible for this. Even in this modern time, many Igbo people, even among the class of elite, believe that certain illnesses are not cured by modern medicine, and they attribute such illnesses to evil spirits, and therefore, bring such patients to prayer houses for cure. Fr Godwin Ikeobi gives us an insight on how these problems are handled at the prayer ministry:

> At the Prayer of the Faithful, we all kneel, and one person belonging to the group called out leads all of us in the particular supplication: Pregnant women, Barren women, sick people, people in more than ordinary hardship, e.g. no employment, no progress in trade, promotion overdue, etc., young men and women who want marriage but can't get married for obvious difficulties, the ordained ministers and those who are aspiring to religious life, our members who for one reason or another could not attend the day's prayer session [...] Finally, our members who have died [...] When exams start-end-of-school year exam, W.A.S.C. exams. Etc.,- we make it also an intention.[331]

What method does the prayer minister use in ministering to the people? This question touches really on the theme of this research. The outstanding method used in prayer ministries is "the power of the word". Many prayer ministers claim that they are following the example of Jesus Christ who healed principally through the power of his word (Mk 5,41–42; Lk 4,35–36). This section will attempt to describe what exactly takes place between the prayer minister and his clients both during individual healing session and in a group healing service. A healing session for an individual patient begins by what is referred to as "consultation". It is expected that a prayer minister should have an office hour in which the client is given the opportunity of person-to-person interacting hour with the prayer minister. The client enters into such consultative session already with the assumption that the prayer minister has the solutions to his problems. This type of assumption has already prepared the mind of this client to accepting whatever the prayer minister utters. Fr Godwin Ikeobi confirms this by saying:

> There is yet no one factor that places the priest at a greater pastoral advantage than a prayer session well conducted. The people, most of them for the first time, are disposed to really LISTEN to God and are prepared to give Him a chance in their lives. There is no more willing audience than the group gathered for healing prayers described above.[332]

---

331 Ikeobi, Godwin, Catholic Response to the Challenge of 'Prayer Houses'-Origin of the ‚Tuesday Prayer' in Onitsha, in: Nwosu, Vincent, The Catholic Church in Onitsha, Peoples, Places and Events (1885–1985), Onitsha 1985, 272.
332 Ikeobi, Catholic Response, 273.

Of course, prayer is an essential element in this consultation and it disposes the client all the more to accepting whatever the prayer minister says. Such prayer can sometimes be very intensive, leaving the prayer minister exhausted. The content of the prayer combines a direct calling on the name of God repeatedly in relation to what is being prayed for. Sometimes, there are cases of hypnotism under the disguise of praying for a client and in which case the client is ordered to close his eyes and naturally he or she would obey. Then, the prayer minister would pray pacing around the client and in a loud voice. At the end of this personal encounter with the prayer minister, the client is fully prepared to accept and do exactly what the prayer minister would say. Since most clients have cases of barrenness and sicknesses, this session ends up pointing accusing finger at who is responsible and offering a remedy. As a remedy, the client is given some prayers (inye ekpere) which he or she is expected to say for a specified number of times. Usually, these prayers are made up of psalms and other biblical texts and including recitation of chaplets, said at different hours of the day not excluding midnight. Very interestingly, these prayers end at each time with a key word such as "Holy Ghost-Fire!", and which should be repeated over and over again with fisted and swinging arms, and directed to whoever the client is told that is responsible for his or her predicament. Before the client gets up from his or prayer position, he or she covers himself or herself with the "Blood of Jesus". By the recitation of the prayers, and especially, the shouting of "Holy Ghost-Fire! Blood of Jesus", the client feels both protected and liberated from his predicament.

A typical public healing session takes place within the Holy Mass. A preliminary preparations are also needed before this session. Such preparations include consultations, confessions, counselling, reconciling of warring groups. While these preparations go on, the atmosphere is invoked through singing of soul-inspiring songs accompanied by clapping and dancing. Songs play an important role at public healing session. Only in few cases are the public healing session held inside church buildings or halls. Nowadays, such public healing sessions are held at prayer grounds secured by prayer ministries. At the healing Mass proper, the prayer minister exhibits all the charisma he possesses, most especially, at sermon. It is at this point that the performance of the word is mostly witnessed. A certain tone of voice is adopted by this minister-preacher. His voice at this moment can be described as being sometimes cajoling, and some other time, commanding and threatening. Depending on the extend he manages his voice adequately and how befitting the message he tries to communicate to the audience he is ministering would determine, for example, the number of people that would fall down on the ground or the number that would come forward at the end of homily to give testimonies or to be delivered. During the testimonies, people give account of what God has done for them in the past. Sometimes, people would even testify to how the word of God touched them (performed) while the minister was preaching. Another area where the influence of the word of God heard during the homily is witnessed is at the offertory. Those who have received favours or deliverance or specially influenced by the word they have heard are expected to show appreciation and donate generously. There are certain cases where such appreciations could turn into a mini launching, presentation of gifts and donations of large sums of money.

Prayer ministry contributes positively to evangelization in Igboland, such as, strengthening of the people's faith and confidence in God. Many Catholics, for example, who left the church are coming back with the emergence of prayer ministries. People who use charms and other types of magical powers, as a result of their encounter with the word of God at these prayer sessions, reject them for a true faith and trust in Christ Jesus. Of course, we recall that the first catholic prayer ministry in Igboland by Fr. Godwin Ikeobi was initiated as a means of controlling Catholics who were drifting away to the independent churches and traditionalists. Fr Godwin Ikeobi narrates how it all began:

> One day a middle-aged woman came to my office saying that the catechist told her to report herself to me for frequenting Ufuma Prayer House for five years. She said she went there because for twelve years after her church wedding, she hadn't had a child. What came to my mind was that I said to her: "Tell the catechist I've seen you and that I ask him to allow you go to confession. On Wednesday next week you come with your bible, we pray for a child, you will get one." [...] That day too a boy came asking to be prayed for and blessed. He said he was a student of Boys' Secondary School, Emene, and was suffering from epilepsy. He too was asked to report for prayers the following Wednesday. During the sermon at the intervening Sunday, I dwelt on the place of suffering and pain in our salvation history. Concluding the sermon I said that our God lives and still works those consoling deeds he showed through His son Jesus Christ, if only we can train ourselves to take Him at His words, that there would be a prayer session on Wednesday the following week for healing chiefly. Those interested were free to attend.[333]

Since then, prayer ministry has continued to strengthen the faith of the christians who frequent it. The idea of christians visiting the traditional oracles and shrines under the cover of darkness in search of security and health has been minimised and replaced with visits to healing and prayer centers. Jesus Christ came to free humanity from all forms of bondage and to give life in abundance. He casted out evil spirits from those they possess, healed the sick and raised the dead. The prayers of deliverance and healing of the church's rituals show that there are powers of the devil that should be attacked and subdued, but only in the name of Jesus Christ. There is no known factor that places our people nearer to God and to the church than healing or prayer ministry that is well organised. Hence, most of the people who attend organised prayer sessions behave well and practise their faith well. Fr Godwin Ikeobi again makes this point clearer by saying:

> The consequent growth in their faith is strikingly shown in the way they behave both during prayers and in their homes and places of work as testified to by people. Action usually follows knowledge. They now know more better, and so they relate better in life. One person's problem is the problem of all; the joy of one is that of all. The terms "Brother" and "Sister" come to them spontaneously for that is what they are to themselves and to others.[334]

---

333 Ikeobi, Catholic Response, 269–270.
334 Ikeobi, Catholic Response, 274.

Prayer ministry contributes also positively towards authentic inculturation of the gospel message in Igboland. A detailed discussion about inculturation will later in our work be discussed. However, what is imminent now is discussing various ways through which prayer ministry inculturates. Culture, of course, is a mirror through which a living human society sees its experiences from different spheres of life. The most important element being the invisible, underlying system of values, meanings and view of the world. The vehicles of this invisible element in a culture are manifold: symbols, rituals, art, literature, philosophy and all that is comprised under the rubric of oral culture, for example, proverbs, riddles, songs, stories, myths, epic, poems and ballad. All these are shared with a group so that culture is essentially communitarian. Igbo culture as we have earlier seen in this work is the pivotal of the people's life and it is in a dynamic process of growth. This is because of its contact with other cultures. Because of the resilient nature of Igbo culture, it is kept growing and alive. Prayer ministry is no doubt an important player in making the Igbo culture relevant within the context of christian liturgy. The major contribution of the prayer ministry in this regard is in the format of the celebration of Holy Mass for the sick and the needy or what we may call "Healing Mass". Prayer ministry has fine-tuned "Healing Mass" and has made it suitable to the religious quest of the Igbo. Uzukwu Eugene writes in affirmation:

> Despite the room for adaptation of the Roman Liturgy to local situations, (SC 37–38), very little has been done apart from translating Latin liturgical texts and permitting dancing during the offertory procession. Among the predominantly Roman Catholic Igbo, the liturgical texts have not been completely translated, gestural behaviours such as clapping or dancing are unknown in the Eucharistic liturgy except during special fund raising masses such as harvest festivals and bazaars. However popular Charismatic movements and healing ministries are gradually introducing into the Roman Catholic Church symbolic objects and gestures that characterise the spiritual churches.[335]

Today's eucharistic celebrations in Igboland is marked with pomp and ceremony associated with prayer ministry. In all the Igbo parishes, Mass is sung in the local language of the people from beginning to the end accompanied by locally made musical instruments. Hymns are locally composed expressing the people's faith and sentiments. This attracts a lot of people to the church, especially, the youth. A lot of people who ordinarily would not have come to the church do attend nowadays to participate in the liveliness of the celebration. They not only enjoy the heart-warming music locally composed to suit the religious longings of our people but also join in accompanying the melody through clapping and dancing. Offertory period offers opportunity for this expression. By offertory procession, people visit the Altar premises up to two or three times clapping and singing praises to God. Certain practices associated with offertory at prayer ministry, such as sprinkling of Holy Water at offertory procession is fully incorporated in every parish eucharistic celebration. Today, while people dance to the Altar bringing along with them their offerings, they are sprinkled with

---

335 Uzukwu, Eugene, Inculturation and Liturgy (Eucharist), in: Gibellini, R. (ed.), Paths of African Theology, London 1992, 95.

the Holy Water. Average Igbo catholic like to be bathed with Holy Water no matter how expensive the clothes he or she is putting on. He or she is said to believe that the Holy Water poured on him or her takes control of all his or her problems and drives away all evil spirits from him or her. In Igbo traditional culture, of course, it is believed that rain or water brings good tidings. The Igbo believes that any journey preceded or interrupted by rain is a successful one. Rain is also said to bring fertility to the earth. One will, therefore, not be surprised why the Igbo christian gets home satisfied that his or her dress is soaked in Holy Water at the eucharistic celebration. So here is one important area where prayer ministry has very much helped in bringing the ministry of Jesus Christ home to the Igbo people. Also, prayer ministry has taught people how to pray better and from the heart. This praying method, linked to prayer ministry, has reshaped the way the Prayer of the Faithful is being conducted in today's eucharistic celebrations in Igbo parishes. During the Prayer of the Faithful, the faithful render beautiful spontaneous and inspiring prayers garnished with beautiful proverbs and idiomatic expression. One hears the intercessor at the Prayer of the Faithful expressing his or her attribute of God with the following words "Nwoke obodobo nti", this means, one with a big ear. This inwardly assures the praying community that this God of theirs is there to listen to all their petitions. There are other expressions which the intercessor frequently use that play a great role at the psychic of the faithful, for example, "onye ana akpo otu oku oza ugboro iri" (one who is called once but answers many times). These types of expressions keep on assuring the praying community that their God is a God who is quick in responding to their needs. Prayer of the Faithful is so much influenced by the present day prayer ministry, so much so that, depending on how the intercessor is able to lead by applying all the necessary rubrics of the prayer ministry, one could see some participants yielding to certain spontaneous emotions. A good organised prayer ministry has been known to instruct the faithful on the importance of prayers and how to say the prayers well and by themselves. One really sees a good number of the faithful taken up in the prayers.

5.5.2 Crusade

"Crusade! Crusade!! Crusade!!! There will be a Fire-pact and Spirit-giving all-night encounter with the Lord from 28th to 31st December at the central school field Amanagu. The lame will work, the blind will see, the dumb will speak and the people with all kinds of illnesses will be cured. The barren will conceive, the spinster will get husband and the bachelor will get wife. Come and be part of this great event. Guest speakers are special anointed men of God, namely, apostle NwaChineke, senior evangelist Ofunammuo, pastor Nwaatuluocha and Rev Obungwongwo. The chief host is most spiritual OtimkpuJesus. Come one! come all!! God will bless you as you come". Our people are used to such radio and television announcements all through the year, and especially, at special celebrations like Christmas and Easter. Nowadays, the organizers have extended their network of coverage to include certain social celebrations such as local festivals

(Afia olu), mass-return, new yam festivals, and so on. Today most of the radio and television houses in our land are able to pay their workers and do routine-maintenances and keep broadcasting as a result of the money accruing from such announcements. As if to say that such announcements are not enough, the organizers of these crusades go as far as printing and distributing posters, caps, stickers, and so on. Lamenting on the cost of organizing crusade Peter Nlemadim DomNwachukwu writes:

> Banners bearing "Jesus Christ the same Yesterday, Today and Forever" are common sights in almost every community in Igboland. These banners indicate Crusade arrangements by churches and other christian groups. Crusades have become the major avenue for outreach programs. Those who conduct crusades spend large amounts of money and many hours preparing for crusades. They spend money for radio and/ or television announcements, and for the printing of handbills and posters. In some cases, crusade organizers hire musical groups and dramatic players and pay them much money. Other items which attract significant amounts of money spending include: transportation, housing and feeding. [336]

In what way does crusade bring the theme of our work to concrete terms? To answer this question, we must understand that all the guest-ministers are invited to come and minister to the people through the proclamation of the word to convert those souls for Christ. Peter Nlemadim DomNwachukwu again stresses this point by saying:

> Crusade planners spend weeks, months and in some cases years planning for crusades. The sole goal of these efforts is the salvation of the individual sinner [...] The Deeper Life Bible Church is truly aggressive in their attempt to reach many souls for Christ [...] The Assemblies of God, the Baptists, the Evangelical Churches of West Africa and also Anglicans, Presbyterians, Methodists and Catholics organize some kind of crusades to reach souls for Christ. Almost every christian group in Igboland uses crusades for conversion of souls. [337]

Faith, of course, comes through hearing. It is, therefore, desired that through the preaching and the proclamation of God's word at crusade, certain hearts might be touched and these souls arrested for Christ. It sometimes happens that some luke-warm christians or people who do not attend church and who merely attend crusade just out of curiosity or leisure or come with evil intentions end up being touched by the word as it is being proclaimed by the preacher, and end up converted and giving their lives totally to Christ. This is an instance of how word performs at Crusade. This is not all. Word performs at crusade when heart-uplifting music is sung and hard-hearted individuals are caught-up within the powerful spiritual waves that proceed from such melody upon such hearts leading to personal decisions of abandoning their old life to a more meaningful life in Jesus Christ. Word performs at crusade when fellow participants give certain heart-touching testimonies and the other is motivated and encouraged by such verbal testimonies because "listening to the testimonies of other sufferers has a therapeutic value: through listening to the sufferings of others, they create enough courage to help them endure their own problems".[338] Again word performs at crusade

---

336 DomNwachukwu, Peter Nlemadim, Authentic African Christianity: An Inculturation for the Igbo, New York 2000, 166.
337 DomNwachukwu, Authentic African Christianity, 166–167.
338 Mbaefo, Luke, Priests and Healing Ministry in the Nigerian Church: A Theological Reflection, Enugu 1992, 2.

during ministration and when the minister orally empowers the participant to carry out an assignment. By this verbal empowerment, the participants would not hesitate once ordered to carry out such command as clearing of "bad bush" (ajaofia), attacking the traditional places of worship of our fore-fathers, fighting the masquerade, defiling traditional places of worship and objects, flouting taboos, exposing traditional secrets and mysteries, condemning local titles, and indeed fighting against everything that has something to do with the "modus Vivendi" of the people. This again likens today's crusade to the earlier times when crusade assumed only violent form and was a means of spreading the christian faith:

> By 1240 several linkages between crusade and conversion were on record. At one extreme, the enforced christianization of Saracens was openly presented, for instance, by the French knights at Constantinople in 1147, as a central aim of the crusade. More moderately, Jacques of Vitry hoped at one point that the arrival of the crusader army would permit conversion-minded Saracens to overcome their fears and accept baptism. Oliver of Cologne justified the crusade as an act of legitimate defense, made inevitable by the Saracen prohibition of christian preaching. Gregory IX, by granting the crusader indulgence to the Mendicant missionaries of the Holy Land, accorded the same importance to crusade and mission, without spelling out his view on the relationship between the two.[339]

Radicalizing crusade, however, constitutes one of the major abuses of crusade in our land. I still remember vividly what happened in 2002 as I was the parish priest of one of the parishes in my diocese. It was Easter season and one of the Pentecostal churches within the same town had organized crusade. It was four days crusade and the fourth day was supposed to be the climax. On this fateful day, the so called most powerful guest-speaker had empowered the participants, those of them who perhaps were of catholic faith and had their rosaries and sacramentals with them to bring them forward to be collected and burnt. This order was promptly and willingly obeyed. These sacramentals were burnt and which later caused outrage within the catholic fold when the news was heard. Another instance where empowerment had been abused is not far-fetched. It happened in one of the towns in Idemili where an itinerant preacher had ordered the participant at crusade to go out in the middle of the night and attack and dismantle all the local shrines of our traditionalists thereby carting away and destroying all their cherished religious objects and places of worship. This order was carried out and what followed was outrage. Consequently, Peter Nlemadim DomNwachukwu remarks:

> While we are aware of the positive feelings of many evangelists and pastors world-wide for crusades, we recognize some tension between crusades and dialogical evangelism in Igboland. It appears that crusades suggest a militant method of gospel communication. If this is true, the crusade, as a method of gospel communication to Igbo audiences, is a misfit. Crusades run contrary to the dialogical method of communication. Therefore its use in any Igbo community is irrelevant and non-productive. Therefore, it should be dropped.[340]

---

339 Kedar, Benjamin, Crusade and Mission: European approaches toward the muslims, New Jersey 1984, 159.
340 DomNwachukwu, Authentic African Christianity, 168.

Outlandish testimonies and self advertisement of the preachers are other abuses associated with crusades. Giving of testimonies have been part and parcel of the mode of operation of crusade. Giving of open testimonies to God during crusade by those who received one favour or the other is encouraged as a sign of gratitude to God and to encourage the people's faith and belief in the healing work of Jesus Christ. There is nothing wrong in giving thanks to God and acknowledging the wonders he has wrought in one's life but the problem is that sometimes these testimonies are exaggerated. Unlike Christ himself who never encouraged those he healed to go about advertising him, some healing ministers utilize testimonies at various crusades to sound their own personal trumpet and to give outlandish testimonies on miraculous activities attributed to themselves whether genuine or not and thereby seeking for fame and honour and canvassing for larger crowds of clients. Jesus Christ never advertised his own healing works and even hid away from the people who wanted to make him a king or make him popular. He even warned his disciples not to rejoice that the devils obey them. They should instead be happy that their names are written in heaven.

Another grave danger to crusade is commercialization. We are aware of the level of poverty that ravages our people. Everybody wants to get rich and to get it quickly and come out of this excruciating situation. Everybody wants to get rich over-night even when it involves divine deceit. For such people, the end justifies the means and that is why they can deceive in God's name just to achieve their aim. Selfless and non-profit venture are gone. Religion is utilized as the opium of the people. Most of the crusades have been turned to "the more you look the less you see". Some organizers of today's crusades invest so much money into their preparations with the hope to get hundredfold of what they have invested in return. They operate on the platform of "nothing goes for nothing". What a commercialization! We never read that Jesus Christ or any of the apostles collected money from those they prayed for. Elisha the prophet found it unnecessary to accept Gold and Silver from Naaman whom he cured of his leprosy (Cf. 2Kgs 5,15–19). Inordinate accumulation of money or wealth has a way of confusing or distracting even the virtuous.

5.5.3 Family ministration "olu ezi na ulo"

This is a phenomena that originates as a result of various consultations conducted at prayer houses. We have earlier discussed that prayer ministry has two-folds, viz: individual healing session and group healing session. The individual healing session is characterized by consultations and it is these consultations that sometimes lead to "Family ministration" (olu ezi na ulo). In most cases, the minister-healer tells his client during consultations that his or her problems have roots in his or her family and can only be dismantled by a visit to the family for an intense prayer-session. Family ministration (olu ezi na ulo), therefore, derives its name from the fact that the ministration is carried out in the client's family. It is based on the biblical assumption that punishment for certain evils are allowed to befall a family from generation to generation: "And the word of the Lord came to Elijah the Tishbite, saying, 'Have you seen how Ahab has humbled himself before me, I will not bring the evil in his days; but in his son's days I will bring the evil upon his house' " (1Kgs 21, 28). This evil in the case of the Igbo-client come in form of barrenness, lack of progress in business, sickness, lack of unemployment, frequent deaths, lack of family peace and similar misfortunes. In order to combat the evil, the minister-healer finds it necessary to go to the family concerned to minister on the understanding that these various misfortunes are inherited from previous generations, and therefore, the primary cause which is the family-root must be addressed. Hence, in family ministration (olu ezi naulo), one hears such expressions as "healing from family root".

The mode of operation "modus operandi" at family ministration is of an interest to our key concept. Because the healer-minister is already believed to be a great seer and a great prophet, the family in question is already disposed to believe and act in accordance of whatever he would say. Before his arrival at the family, his "prayer warriors" (his special prayer group most often made up of illiterate and unemployed young girls and boys) would be busy conducting prayer sessions among the family members aimed at preparing the minds and hearts of the family members and providing the befitting atmosphere. Such preparations, most often, is done all through the night. The healer-minister usually arrives at dawn to conclude the all-night prayer session by making certain pronouncements which the family members are already disposed to accept and to act in accordance. If, for example, the complaint is that the family suffers from premature deaths, the healer-seer might tell them that their dead grandfather was a witch and is responsible for all the deaths. The family members would immediately accept this prophecy and would do anything that the healer-minister would say in order to bring solution to the problem. Like in the previous cases we have examined, family ministration is equally not free from certain abuses. Of course, in order to make himself and his prophecy worthy of acceptance, the healer-minister would have to mystify certain rituals and practices, such as, burying crucifixes at the four corners of the compound to ward off the entrance of demons or evil spirits, burying of bags of salt and live animals in the family compound: "shall the devil not be more afraid to see a hanging crucifix than the one buried and gradually destroyed by the sand?"[341]; performance of nocturnal rituals at the family grave yards in order to ward off the spirit of the dead ancestor and the celebration of what they call black mass in the family compound. These practices appear superstitious and are rather in conformity with Igbo Traditional Religion. The dangers such practices pose to the christian faith cannot simply be ignored. In short, this is dangerously stepping towards the destruction of the much cherished christian rubrics on the celebration of the sacramentals in our area. According to K.Chigbo:

> Our people have old ways peculiar to them through which, they believed demons were exorcised or expelled and through which sickness were cured. They offered sacrifices to spirits believed to be responsible for cases of ailments, infliction and misfortunes. The role of traditional medicine men, herbalists and priests was to offer the appeasement and expiatory sacrifices [...] Today for some christians, crucifixes, candles, portraits, relics and holy water have become charms and amulets.[342]

---
341 Onoyima, Thaddeo, Attention Please, Enugu, 1996, 14.
342 Chigbo, Kingsley, Catholic Healing Ministry on Fire, Abakaliki 1997, 42.

There are other uses of sacramentals that call for review and catechesis such as the issue of hanging bottles of holy water in farmlands or on trees to act as charm or watchmen. It has also been observed that some use candles in a manner not different from Igbo Traditional Religion. Today, it is not only the traditional religionist that asks his client to carry out his sacrifice at a four-junction pathway. The christian healer-minister makes the same demand by asking the family members to position seven or more lighted candles at seven pathways as a way of warding off the calamity that befalls the family.[343] There are also situations where the healer-minister prescribes that his client prays with lighted candles in form of a cross and the client lying to sleep within such a cross. According to the findings of K. Chigbo:

> The patient is forced to lie flat with a cross drawn on the floor according to his/her height. The patient does not rise from that position, even to ease himself, until one set of candles burns out. The candles are placed at the 12 corners of the cross. The victim often lies there on a bare floor without clothes, except pants or wrappers at the waist: gross indecency and torture.[344]

The healer-minister who prescribes for his client to lie in between the burning candles should first of all consider the torture and the danger involved which are obviously great. A reasonable person should consider the danger of the fire from the candle burning the client or even setting the whole house on fire while the client is immersed in meditative prayer or slumber. Again, asking the client to go to prayers naked and on bare cemented floor is both indecent and unhealthy.

5.5.4 Parish annual retreat

In accordance to the church's law "At certain times, according to the regulations of the diocesan Bishop, parish priests are to arrange for sermons in the form of retreats and missions, as they are called, or in other forms adapted to requirements" (c.770 CIC). Pope John Paul II goes further to explain the aim of organizing such a spiritual activity for Christ's faithful within a parish as gearing towards:

> Developing understanding of the mystery of Christ in the light of God's word, so that the whole of a person's humanity is impregnated by that word. Changed by the working of grace into a new creature, the Christian thus sets himself to follow Christ and learns more and more within the church to think like him, to judge like him, to act in conformity with his commandments, and to hope as he invites us to.[345]

Igbo parishes respond generously to this demand and every parish priest endeavours to organize annual retreat for his parish which sometimes holds more than once or twice a year, preferably Easter period, Christmas period and at long vacation (between June and September). Retreat period, as it were, should be:

---

343 Onoyima, Attention Please, 13.
344 Chigbo, Healing Ministry on Fire, 81.
345 Pope John Paul II, Catechesi tradendae, no. 20.

The period in which the Christian, having accepted by faith the person of Jesus Christ as the one Lord and having given him complete adherence by sincere conversion of heart, endeavours to know better this Jesus to whom he has entrusted himself: to know his "mystery", the kingdom of God proclaimed by him, the requirements and promises contained in his Gospel message, and the paths that he has laid down for any one who wishes to follow him.[346]

These spiritual intentions for organizing annual retreat would indeed be of a great benefit for the church in Igboland where neo-paganism still thrives despite church's tremendous success in evangelization. There is yet another dimension to today's parish retreats in our Igbo parishes which is of an interest to our research work. It is true that the aim of retreat is authentic conversion but retreat is also the avenue through which the Igbo christian shows that the conversion is achieved mostly through proclamations and which implies, through hearing. I now explain what I mean. Again it happened at the time I was a parish priest in one of the parishes in my diocese and had the task of organizing annual retreats for my parishioners. I had finished announcing the parish annual retreat that was fast approaching, and thereafter, a middle aged woman approached me in the sacristy and the question she asked was quite interesting: "Fada kpotakwalu anyi Fada kara aka" (Father please we want a powerful priest as the retreat moderator). What did this woman mean by "Fada kara aka" (powerful priest)? How does one recognize "Fada kara aka?" How do people quantify these powerful priests? From that day I came to realize that the slogan "Fada kara aka" was not peculiar to this woman alone but generally used by the faithful in identifying priests who are associated with a lot of signs and wonders when they preach, sing and pray. Because most of such priests are engaged with prayer ministries, the retreats they moderate are usually characterized by speeches that participants consider as "fire-pact", talks that are interpreted as being "healing", utterances that are understood as "prophetic". People are already disposed when such priests moderate retreat for them and are at the disposal of the influence of any word he utters the way he desires it. It is said that some of such priests, by private counselling during the retreat, tell their sick client that he or she has now received instant cure and does not need to take medicine any more. I do not intend to go into denouncing such practices because we all know that this is an atrocity. The response of the sick client is very interesting. The client comes out from the counselling and throws away all his or her medicines and goes about parading himself or herself as having been cured just because the "powerful priest" has said so. I do not need to say that some of such victims end up dying pre-maturely.

5.5.5 Parish weekly adoration

The centrality of the eucharist should be apparent not only in the worthy celebration of the sacrifice but also in the proper adoration of the sacrament. Therefore, the church

---

346 Pope John Paul II, Catechesi tradendae, no. 20.

has advised that such worship can be carried out in different churches and religious institutions in the form of eucharistic adoration. The law of the church stipulates:

> It is recommended that in these churches or oratories, there is to be each year a solemn exposition of the blessed Sacrament for an appropriate, even if not for a continuous time, so that the local community may more attentively meditate on and adore the Eucharistic mystery. This exposition is to take place only if a fitting attendance of the faithful is foreseen, and the prescribed norms are observed.[347]

Today in all the churches in Igboland eucharistic adoration has become part of the parish life and is attended in a great number. Because of the religious nature of our people and their willingness to spend most of their time in God's house, it became necessary that this eucharistic adoration should not be limited to once a year but at least once in a week. Each parish and each individual priest prepares a programme for the eucharistic adoration that best serves the pastoral situation of the flock to which he is the shepherd. The eucharistic adoration offers Christ's faithful the opportunity to demonstrate their worship to Jesus who is truly present in the most holy sacrament of the eucharist.[348] Vatican II goes further to say:

> The piety, therefore, which moves the faithful to adore the blessed Sacrament inspires them also to participate more fully in the paschal mystery and to respond with grateful heart to Christ's gift of himself, who through his humanity is ever bestowing divine life on the members of his mystical body. Remaining closely united to Christ, they enjoy intimate familiarity with him and offer heart-felt prayer to him for themselves, for all those who are dear to them, for peace and for the salvation of the world, offering their entire lives with Christ to the Father in the Holy Spirit.[349]

So the essential elements of eucharistic adoration in our parishes and religious institution are worship and prayers. Accordingly, the pattern of events are so much designed to accommodate much singing. There are readings from the scriptures sometimes derived from the Mass of the day. This is followed by reflections. Thereafter, various prayers are conducted for various intentions and the concerned individuals to be prayed for assemble before the altar and the officiating minister prays over them using powerfully selected words of his choice (if the minister is eloquent in the words of his prayers then his prayers would all the more be considered as being more efficacious). The power of this prayer is most often judged based on how the prayer-minister is able to command and order the devil to flee from his clients and allow them to be freed from their problems, viz: "I command you to ... in Jesus Name!; I order you to ... in Jesus Name!!!", and how he is able to forcefully invoke divine favours upon them, viz: "Pregnant woman deliver like the Hebrew women in Jesus Name!; Barren women you shall conceive in Jesus Name!; You suffering from various sicknesses receive your healing in Jesus Name!; You being pursued by your enemies who want to destroy you I pronounce life upon you and not death you shall live in Jesus Name!" At this moment the people being prayed for claim the fulfilment of the words of this prayer

---

347 C. 942 CIC
348 E S, no. 3.
349 E S, no. 80.

by shouting "amen". Then the various objects of worship brought along by people are blessed as sacramentals and the holy water is sprinkled upon them and upon the people. The eucharistic adoration is concluded with benediction. The people go home convinced in faith that the words of the prayer-minister are already fulfilled in their various situations.

It is said that this usual parish eucharistic adoration sometimes gives birth to the popular prayer ministry. As the number of the attendants grow and the testimonies of divine favours spread, what was once a simple parish eucharistic adoration might graduate into a full-blown prayer ministry, such that we have already discussed earlier.

5.5.6 Charismatic renewal prayer group

Charismatic movement is an offspring of Pentecostalism,[350] and Pentecostalism is a phenomenon that began in the USA in 1901 and was transported to Nigeria (Igboland) in 1970s. The church, as it were, was caught up within this wave and as a response, charismatic renewal sprang up in the same USA in 1974 to respond to the needs of those Catholics who, otherwise, would have been attracted to Pentecostal churches that were seriously gaining momentum. Gradually, charismatic renewal spread to different continents and countries. In Nigeria, charismatic renewal was able to arrive in Igboland through the instrumentality of the Dominican Fathers working in Nigeria and who after the visit of one of their members, Francis MacNutt,OP,[351] were dedicated to establishing this movement to every corner and cranny of Nigeria.[352] But DomNwachukwu argues that there has been indigenous charismatic movement even before the arrival of Francis MacNutt,OP:

> The Nigerian Charismatic movement does not share the same roots with its Western counterpart. While the root of the Western charismatic movement is the 1906 Azuza Street revival in Los Angeles, USA, the Nigerian expression has an indigenous origin.[353]

---

350 Cf. DomNwachukwu, Authentic African Christianity, 84.
351 Father MacNutt is a priest of the Order of Preachers, the Domincan Fathers, and very much renowned in America for his active involvement in healing ministry.
352 Cf. Umoren, Anthony, Jesus and Miracle Healing Today, Ibadan 2000, 33.
353 DomNwachukwu, Authentic African Christianity, 84; Earlier on, Pastor Dr. R.J. Burdette of the Temple Baptist Church in Los Angeles had on Sunday morning, September 23, 1906, had castigated these emerging Pentecostals who were then holding Fellowships at the Azusa Street Mission in that city and had regarded them being a composition of African Voodoo superstition combined with some sort of madness associated with New Age which would no sooner or later be part of the past as those who attempted such acts before them. The dawn of the 21st century, however, defied this Movement as having rapid progress through wide-range acceptance in the wider-world (cf. Robeck, Cecil, The Holy Spirit and the Unity of the Church: The Challenge of Pentecostal, Charismatic, and Independent Movements, in: Donnelly, Doris (ed.), The Holy Spirit, The Church And Christian Unity: Proceedings of the consultation held at the monastery of Bose, Italy (14–20 October 2002), Leuven 2005, 355).

The arrival of charismatic renewal became for some Catholics a sign of relief from what they would consider as the tyranny and control of the hierarchy. Charismatism is characterized by a growing faith experience judged by docility to the Spirit. It highlights the Holy Spirit and teaches that every christian worth the name must be liberated from the bond of law but instead lives according to the freedom of the children of God guaranteed in the Holy Spirit.[354] The word "charism" though found only in the New Testament comes from the Greek word "charisma" meaning "gift". The term does not occur in the Old Testament but the concept of charism can be related to powerful effect of the divinely given spirit of the Lord as manifested in some powerful kings and in some selected individuals like Samson, Samuel and Gideon (Judg 14,6; 1Sam 11,6; Judg 3,39). Pope John Paul II goes further to explain: "The charisms are graces of the Holy Spirit that have directly or indirectly a usefulness for the ecclesial community, ordered as they are to the building up of the church to the well-being of humanity and to the needs of the world".[355] St Paul made the most extensive and comprehensive discussion about charisma, namely: "Now there are varieties of gifts, but the same spirit, and there are varieties of service but the same Lord, and there are varieties of working but it is the same God who inspires them all in everyone. To each is given the manifestation of the spirit for the common good. To one is given through the spirit the utterance of wisdom and to another the utterance of knowledge according to the same spirit, to another faith by the same spirit, to another gifts of healing by the one spirit, to another the working of miracles, to another the ability to distinguish between spirits, to another various kinds of tongues. All these are inspired by one and the same spirit, who apportions to each one individually as he wills" (1Cor 12,4–11). Again, St Paul's response to the concerns of the Corinthian church brought to his attention the rich manifestation of the Spirit within the church such that he said: "You are not lacking in any spiritual gift" (1Cor 1,7). However, there arose problems in the Corinthian church regarding the proper exercise and evaluation of these various gifts of the Holy Spirit. There was the problem of some members of the church claiming monopoly of the gifts of the Holy Spirit. They consider themselves more charismatic than the others. But the whole church is charismatic in its members. Using the analogy of the human body, St Paul explains that each member of the body has its function to perform, and the exercise of the gifts of the Holy Spirit cannot lead to divisions in the body but that parts should have the same concern for one another (Cf.1Cor 12,25). Donald Gelpi would, therefore say: "These gifts, it will be recalled were named "gratuitous graces" by medieval theologians. As such they were distinguished from sanctifying graces (gratia gratum faciens); for, it was argued, they are ordered, not to the sanctification of the one who possesses them, but to the edification of the christian community".[356] The charisms should, therefore, be received in gratitude both by the individual and by the church for they are source of vitality in the evangelizing mission of the church as well as source of holiness for

---

354 Cf. Robeck, The Holy Spirit and the unity of the church, 361.
355 John Paul II, Christi Fidelis Laici, 30 December 1998, 59.
356 Gelpi, Donald, Charism and Sacrament: A theology of christian conversion, London 1976, 63.

Christ's faithful provided that the gifts are properly exercised in accordance with the will of the Holy Spirit and under the guidance of the church.

Today in Igbo church the exercise of these charisma most of the times leads to chaos and confusion. Many adherents want to have uncontrollable independence of their actions all in the name of possession of the gift of the Holy Spirit. Most of these adherents appear stubborn and disloyal in the exercise of their religious belief as if to say that the Holy Spirit is a spirit of confrontation and disobedience. Many of them find it hard to accept the leadership of their priests, especially when the priest is considered by them as not being charismatic. Robeck Cecil expresses the motive behind this attitude, and he writes: "they reacted against institutionalization and the routinization of various charismata. Sometimes their challenges were theologically driven-they accuse the church of doctrinal confusion, of compromise, even of faithlessness because ecclesial leaders no longer possessed or acted upon the truth".[357] The Bishops' Conference of Nigeria weighed into the matter and on 22 February 1986 issued a document signed by the then chairman of the Conference and the secretary Bishops G.G.Ganaka and E.S.Obot respectively. In this document, the Bishops outlined some directives on how the Charismatic movement must be operated within the catholic church in Nigeria. It has eleven point-agenda and the first point states that no Charismatic Renewal group should operate in Nigeria without a chaplain appointed by the Bishop of the Diocese. The Bishops' Conference again in 1991 published Guidelines to this effect. Explaining the dangers of acting in disobedience to the ecclesiastical authorities, Taddeo Onoyima says:

> We are not those leading the Spirit which the Authorities also have [...] There must be always somebody to moderate what is happening around us. When anybody refuses this, the person may be thinking of his or her own church. This is how many churches sprang up in the name of ministries. Disobedience and pride are behind it.[358]

The validity and the use of charisms in the church have been totally misconceived and misinterpreted by most of the Igbo charismatics including "charismatic priests" who are said to possess some of the charisms. This resulted to a group of catholic charismatic movements in the Owerri Diocese in Igboland becoming a separate entity under a new name "Catholic Watchman" and has no ecclesiastical or organizational ties with the mainline catholic church. Any charismatic should guide against pride, disobedience and the like. Uzukwu Eugene observes:

> In Port Harcourt, Onitsha, Enugu, Orlu, Aba dioceses to name a few, our Bishops find it difficult at times to exercise their supervisory ministry over the powerful "priest healers". The charismatic priests appear to be very conscious of their power which is often times maintained through the exploitation of the superstitious and the irrational, of which distressed faithful are easy victims. The orderly exercise of charisms for the benefit of the community appears not to be uppermost in the minds of some healers.[359]

---

357 Robeck, The Holy Spirit and the unity of the church, 353.
358 Onoyima, Attention Please, 29.
359 Uzukwu, Eugene, A listening Church: Autonomy and Communion in African Churches, New York 1996, 123.

We are interested in discussing charismatic renewal in Igboland because of its contributions in showing how by the use of words certain actions are performed. We may highlight this point by discussing the unnecessary emphasis, by most of the Igbo charistmatics, on the influence of demons. They have certain false illusions that African continent is dominated by battalions of the agents of darkness and of evil, and therefore, is in urgent need of deliverance. There is also this illusion that everything including food and drinks in this continent is infested by demonic powers and needs exorcism at each second of the day. Human beings are not excluded from this possession. Most of the charismatic songs, therefore, are fashioned as protective weapons against demonic powers which they believe at times are in the form of certain individuals they possess. Most of the songs either accuse the devil or evil spirits of one problem or the other or tell the devil that he has no power over the children of God. Some chant songs of war or defeat over the strength of the wicked and evil spirits as if life is all an attack of the demons and evil spirits. These songs include: "zogbue Ekwensu n'ukwu zogbuo ya na ekpere Ekwensu na-agaghari Ikechukwu emerigo" (march the Devil to death); "Ekwensu odighi ihe ipuru ime m aka Chukwu ojidesigo m ike aka Chukwu" (Devil you can do me nothing I am under the protective hand of God); "Ekwensu ka ihere mee gi n'uwa ka ihere mee gi ma gi ma ndi otu gi ka ihere mee gi" (Devil shame unto you). These songs are sung at any place and at any occasion and at any time. While singing such songs, the singer or singers feel(s) protected and powerful over the devil and its agents. Indeed, these and similar songs strengthen and energize the singers into daring the devil and its agents in whatever form they operate. The songs liberate the singer or singers from any form of cowardice and inflame them with the burning zeal to testify for their faith at any cost, and they do believe that: "a word or deed performed in faith is an event which reveals the power and anointing of the Spirit in the one who performs it".[360]

Another trend in charismatic renewal that exposes it to our key concept is "speaking in tongues" which is the expression of the biblical Pentecost experience: "When the day of Pentecost had come, they were all together in one place. And suddenly a sound came from heaven like the rush of a mighty wind, and it filled all the house where they were sitting. And there appeared to them tongues as of fire, distributed and resting on each one of them. And they were filled with the Holy Spirit and began to speak in other tongues, as the Spirit gave them utterance" (Acts 2,1–4). This biblical "speaking in tongues" brought with it certain actions, viz: "the multitude came together, and they were bewildered, because each one heard them speaking in his own language" (Acts 2,6); "Now when they heard this they were cut to the heart" (Acts 2,37); "So those who received his word were baptized" (Acts 2,41). The hearers being able to understand the apostles in their own different languages; being cut to the heart; and being baptized, are the evidences of how "speaking in tongues" performed during the Pentecost. The same similarities can be derived from the today's "speaking in tongues" by our charismatics. When charismatics pray, especially during their various prayer meetings, there is a special period for "open prayer". I describe it as

---

360   Gelpi, Charism and Sacrament, 107.

"open prayer" because at this point, the leader at prayer orders that all should be vocal as all pray and according to the method and mode one chooses. There are some who would choose to sing heart-touching melodies for divine forgiveness or mercy, and so on. There are some others who would begin to invoke blessings upon themselves and their beloved ones. There are still others who would choose to begin to cast and to bind some evil spirits that they say are hovering around. But no matter which direction one chooses, be it singing, invocation or casting and binding, there are always some atoms of strange and incomprehensible utterances that are involved and which among charismatics are interpreted as "speaking in tongues". This charismatic form of "speaking in tongues" is usually accompanied by certain actions, namely: emotional changes (for example, some will begin to cry and even fall on the ground while the "speaking in tongues" is being directed towards them), public confessions, deliverance and conversions.

No one in his correct senses contests the existence of demons and evil spirits but giving an undue attention to them is unacceptable, and attributing to devil all forms of sicknesses and misfortunes will be over-exaggerations. Some members of charismatic renewal in Igbo church do a lot of funny things in the name of casting and binding devil. When most of these charistmatics pray, their prayers are mostly long, flamboyant and full of shoutings and commands at God to get rid of the evil spirits as if everybody in the gathering is possessed and needs exorcism. Sometimes one begins to wonder if the prayer warrior himself or herself is not possessed by the evil spirits. In short, certain abuses associated with charismatic renewal stems from the presumption that evil spirit has dominated everywhere and everything and need to be cast out at every given moment and occasion, and they do this by creating their own ritual for casting and binding of devil. For the people to see evil spirits in everything in life is not healthy. Seeing demons where there are none, blaming them for all troubles, having obsessive fear of them and making them the central teaching of the church are unchristian and far from what the magisterium of the church teaches about devil and evil spirits. Instead, such beliefs are in alliance with Igbo traditional religion. Commenting on this trend to cast and bind the devil found among most of our charistmatics, Christopher Ejizu writes:

> They do not for a moment deny the presence of spirits to be cast out, Witchcraft spells to be housed, but faced with them they assert the power of God to free and to restore. In practice there seems to be a wide range of response at one end clearly controlled by a Christian sense of God and Christ; at the other it is still rather deeply embedded in the religious metaphysics underlying traditional treatment.[361]

Casting of evil spirits is an integral part of the mission of Jesus Christ, a mission which he entrusted to his church. Jesus Christ himself who did not allow the devil to destroy his beloved ones did not exaggerate the devil's existence and power but casted him out not by being flamboyant with words and not by shouting but by simple and short speeches ordered them to leave the individuals they possessed. Jesus gave the

---

361 Ejizu, Christopher, Cosmological Perspective on Exorcism and Prayer-Healing in Contemporary Nigeria, Enugu 1992, 16.

same power to his disciples, and indeed, to his followers, and he expects that they cast out evil spirits by the same choice of words as he did. A prudent charismatic should not jump into casting and binding of devil as if to say it is a hobby.

5.5.7 Homily

Homily could be considered as the oldest method through which the gospel message is made to perform among the Igbo hearers. According to DomNwachukwu:

> Sermon delivery is the most popular form of communicating the gospel to Igbo hearers. The foreign missionaries used this method at the beginning of christian work in Igboland. They used this method everywhere they went, in people's homes, at village squares, in the schools and in the houses of worship. The format of the delivery was monological. People listened and responded to the preacher's invitation to either join the church or get baptized.[362]

DomNwachukwu reminds us that homily is not limited to a particular situation or venue. Homily should be delivered everywhere and at any time provided there are people who are available to hear the divine message being proclaimed. Andreas Wollbold suggests that sacramental celebrations provide the best occasion for great attendance, whereby people willingly converge to hear the word of God as it is being proclaimed at the reading of the gospel and at homily:

> Nirgendwo sonst kommen so viele Christen regelmäßig zusammen und hören das Verkündigungswort. Nirgendwo sonst können sie sich so sehr darauf konzentrieren, das Evangelium zu hören und zu verstehen. Zudem ist die Predigt meist in die Feier eines Sakramentes eingegliedert. Nirgendwo sonst sind Handeln Gottes und Sprechen von ihm so eng miteinander verbunden. Auch entscheidet sich heute zunehmend für Menschen die Qualität eines Gottesdienstes an der Predigt.[363]

What Andreas Wollbold describes above can perfectly be applied in the case of the Igbo. The Igbo, as it were, could be described as the busiest people who at one time or the other are preoccupied with their daily shores. They are found either busy buying and selling or in their various farms or in places from where they obtain their means of livelihood. In these busy moments the language the Igbo could be disposed to hear is the language of money. The Igbo might not be disposed to give much attention to the preacher in these moments because he believes that there is time for everything and that every second at business time means money. So, he prefers to give the gospel message all the attention it deserves when he attends liturgical celebrations. This is the reason why most of the liturgical celebrations in Igboland last so long. The celebration of the Holy Mass, for example, can last up to two and half hours and out of which homily takes over an hour. The homily takes such time because the preacher knows that it is the only opportunity to put the word of God across to the people.

---

362 DomNwachukwu, Authentic African Christianity, 163.
363 Wollbold, Andreas, Handbuch der Gemeindepastoral, Regensburg 2004, 186.

DomNwachukwu observes that homily motivates people to join the church or get baptized, in other words, homily initiates certain actions in the hearers. This is the point that really borders on the theme of our research work. DomNwachukwu has mentioned only an aspect where homily performs (conversion and baptism). This is not peculiar to Igbo church alone. We saw this also in the case of St Augustine who got converted by listening to the homily of Bishop St Ambrose the Great. Homily has also been used in various ways in Igbo church to initiate actions in people, for example, at fund-raising. Igbo church depends largely on the benevolence and generosity of the people for its financial sustenance, and the church's annual Harvest and Bazaar is one of the numerous sources through which the church raises fund for its minor and major projects throughout the year. For this event, every parish priest and his parish council do their home-work well by searching out a prominent preacher for the eucharistic celebration that marks the occasion. The reason is very simple. Our people are easily motivated to undergo a task provided the motivator strikes the right key by using suiting words in gingering the people. A congregation that could raise a little amount when preacher "A" appeals could as well raise triple times more than the amount when preacher "B" appeals. The difference lies on the method and the choice of words adopted.

5.5.8 Catechism classes

The relevance of catechism classes to our theme cannot be over-emphasized. In his speech about Catechism, Pope John Paul II himself in 1985, during the extraordinary Synod of Bishops, said:

> This catechism aims at presenting an organic synthesis of the essential and fundamental contents of the catholic doctrine, as regards both faith and morals, in the light of the Second Vatican Council and the whole of the church's tradition. It's principal sources are the sacred scriptures, the fathers of the church, the liturgy and the church's Magisterium. It is intended to serve as a point of reference for the Catechisms or Compendia that are composed in the various countries.[364]

Catechism deepens our knowledge of the unfathomable riches of salvation (Cf.Eph 3,8). It strenghtens our hope to accept and portrays the truth in christian teaching which brings the community of christians together. It strengthens also the bonds of unity in the same apostolic faith. No one, therefore, should disregard the importance of catechism in understanding and deepening the christian faith. Throughout the church's history, catechism has always played the preparatory role in producing formidable christians, and according to Peter Phan: "Rooted in the ancient practice of linking catechesis with the profession of faith in baptism and with the sacrament of penance, modern catechisms took to their origins in the Reformers' efforts to remedy

---

364 Pope John Paul II, On Extraordinary Synod of Bishops 1985, Final report 11 B, 4.

the state of alarming religious ignorance among the laity".[365] In our time, the pastoral nature of catechism can be demonstrated at several points. First and formost, we need the force of catechism in our time to dilute effects of modernism with christian morality. Catechism provides a guiding light in building up of our christian faith. Solid catechism helps us to be formed into ardent christians and truthful members of God's people.

Catechism encourages and assists the spread of the christian faith "taking into account various situations and cultures, while carefully preserving the unity of faith and fidelity to catholic doctrine".[366] That Igboland is today regarded as a christian land is largely due to catechism as an effective method of evangelization. These catechism classes are not only for children but for adults as well. They are not limited to the people preparing for sacraments (Baptism, First Holy Communion, Confirmation, Martrimony) but for everybody (both the practicing catholics and those who have fallen in faith but want to return to sacrament). Catechism classes are mostly offered in Igbo churches four times in the week, namely, Sundays, Mondays, Wednesdays and Fridays. There are opportunities for intensive classes, especially, when the time for the administration of the sacrament approaches. This intensive teaching of catechism has provided the opportunity for inculcating the authentic christian theology in the Igbo right from the time he first enrolled into a catechism class either as a catechumen or a candidate for First Holy Communion. The reason for this is because of the teaching materials "Katekism nke Nzuko", an Igbo version of the universal catechism book, which makes the doctrines understandable and digestible to the Igbo; Igbo versions of the catholic Bible and prayer books. Through these native materials "what is specifically christian will emerge when the core of the christian faith can be articulated in such a way that people see themselves brought face to face with the fundamental alternatives of their lives and inserted within the liberating remembrance of God in the history of God's dealings with mankind".[367] This is the case in Igboland. Even the high theologies learnt in higher institutions of learning are to some great extend no longer new to an authentic Igbo christian because he had encountered these teachings in one way or the other in the various catechism classes. Another reason why catechism have contributed to an effective evangelization is its method of teaching the faith, namely, questions and answers, use of plays and folklores, which of course are embedded in Igbo background, in explaining the biblical messages. I remember one of such plays titled "ima na Jesus na asu Igbo?" (Do you know that Jesus speaks Igbo?). It is an attempt to illustrate the passion and death of Jesus Christ within an Igbo context. Many Igbo have been influenced by what they saw in such biblical play which at the same time is truly Igbo due to the Igbo background it assumes.

---

365 Phan, Peter, Mission and Catechesis: Alexandre de Rhodes and Inculturation in seventeenth-century Vietnam, New York 1998, 107.
366 Pope John Paul II, Fidei Depositum, October 11, 1992, no.4.
367 Metz, Johann-Baptist, Schillebeeckx, Edward (ed.), World Catechism or Inculturation?, Edinburgh 1989, 59.

5.5.9 School apostolate

School apostolate is another viable means through which the gospel message is meant to permeate the hearts of the Igbo. Almost every parish in Igboland has its own school or schools which sometimes may comprise kindergarten (nursery school), primary school and even secondary school. This is in line with the spirit of Second Vatican Council which states:

> The catholic school pursues cultural goals and the natural development of youth to the same degree as any other school. What makes the catholic school distinctive is its attempt to generate a community climate in the school that is permeated by the gospel spirit of freedom and love. It tries to guide the adolescents in such a way that personality development goes hand in hand with the development of the new creature that each one has become through baptism. It tries to relate all human culture to the goodnews of salvation so that the light of faith will illumine everything that the student will gradually come to learn about the world, about life, and about the human person.[368]

These catholic schools set out to plant the gospel message in the hearts of the Igbo children and youth, and to nurture it to maturity. This objective is meant to be achieved through integrating the catholic values, beliefs and practices in the schools' curricula with the understanding that a God-centered academic programme builds character and integrity in students and leads them to a successful life. In these schools, our children and youth begin early enough to avail themselves the frequent opportunities of encountering God in his word and sacrament, namely:

* The school term begins and ends with Holy Mass
* Each morning the school day begins with the morning assembly in which morning prayers are said with students leading in turns.
* There are periods for weekly religious and moral instructions.
* There are opportunities for catechetical instructions and admission to the sacraments of Baptism, Holy Eucharist and Confirmation.
* Retreats are organised periodically for students.
* Religious rallies, workshops and conferences are periodically organised, most especially for secondary school children, both on the diocesan and inter-diocesan levels.

These programmes are arranged to assist one in the proper formation of his or her conscience and to establish christian values that will promote christian living. They educate one on the tenets of the catholic faith thereby exposing him or her, right from onset, to the essential knowledge of the catholic faith. They are meant to introduce the student to an authentic love for God expressed through interior conversion and readiness to live in the spirit of ever deepening friendship with Jesus Christ.

---

368   Pope Paul VI, Gravissimum Educationis, October 28, 1965, no.8.

5.5.10 Counselling

The Igbo say "Mmadu bu chi ibe ya" (man is a god to man). This Igbo expression emphasizes the importance of counselling in Igbo society, and which of course, relates to the theme of our research work. Man being god to fellow man is considered, in this case, from how man by use of words, alleviates his fellow man from the shackles of deplorable conditions or decisive moments. Similarly, Emmanuel Yartekwei Lartey considers counselling as:

> A helping activity undertaking by people who recognize a spiritual or religious dimension to life, which by the use of verbal or non-verbal, direct or indirect, literal or symbolic modes of communication, aims at preventing or relieving the anxieties of persons and fostering their growth as fully functioning human beings and the development of a society in which all persons can live a human life.[369]

In Igbo society one is counselled in various situations of joys and sorrows, namely, when someone is bereaved, in sickness, in agony due to misfortunes, when someone is about to make a difficult decision, in celebrating successes, and so on. Counselling earns various names depending on the type of situation in which it is offered. When it is a situation pertaining to sorrow it is called "okwu nkasi obi" (words of consolation). When it is a joyful situation it is known as "okwu ndumodu" (words of advice). Whether it is in sorrowful situations or joyful situations, counselling performs a definite action, and that is, making the individual to whom the counselling is offered to feel better: counselling offers consolation to the bereaved; encouragement to the wearied, hope to the oppressed, wisdom to the ignorant, fulfilment to the insatiable, and so on. Counselling is very much effective in the pastoral situation in our land. Our people believe so much in their priests and look unto them as people from who they can receive the best encouragement when in despair, the best consolation when in agony, the best advice when in the moment of making a vital decision, and so on. Our people are very much disposed to the counselling from their priest. When a priest makes a home visitation of the sick it is usually not only for praying and anointing but he takes out time to interact with or to counsel the sick parishioner and offers him the encouragement that he or she will get well soonest. Interestingly, in most cases, the sick begins to respond positively and quickly to the treatment he or she receives in the assurance that the priest has told him or her that he or she will be well soon. Most of the people who are depressed because someone they love so much is dead have been made to come out of depression because the priest has taken out time to counsel them, to talk to them in a way that they came to realize that the death of their dear ones is for them an easy access to heaven.[370] Through the priestly counselling, most of our people, especially the youth, have discovered meaning in their lives and

---

369 Lartey, Emmanuel Yartekwei, Pastoral Counselling in inter-cultural perspective: A study of some African (Ghanaian) and Anglo-American views on human existence and counselling, Frankfurt am Main 1987, 115.
370 Cf. Bryant-Jefferies, Richard, Counselling for death and dying: Person-centred dialogues, Oxon 2006, 73–86.

have achieved a better future. Our people are known for visiting office hours of their various parish priests mainly to receive counselling from their priests. They submit their worries to the priest from whom they receive suiting advices and guide. These people come out better and feel relieved because the preist has talked to them about their problems. We can go on enumerating various situations where counselling is an essential tool in the pastoral care of the souls. It is not at the disposal of the priest alone, many of our lay faithful do successfully apply counselling while fulfiling their christian obligations, and as it were, "the life and ministry of Jesus as recorded in the four gospels provide christians with a framework in which to develop their own counselling skills".[371]

Through the above examples, we have been trying to expose how particular use of words initiate particular actions under particular events. In other words, we have been trying to give concrete examples of where and how words perform in the evangelizing mission of the church in our land. These concrete phenomena have in no small measure helped the today Igbo towards finding the word of God active and heart-warming. They proffer a big help to the church's work of evangelization among our people. We may, therefore, find it necessary to understand what evangelization really means in order to appreciate the role it has to play within the context of our discussion.

5.6 Scriptural Background to Evangelization

We must admit the fact that the term "evangelization" is a biblical term. In Old Testament, it is written in Hebrew *Basar*, and in New Testament in Greek *eu-angelos*. In Old Testament, *Basar* is taken to mean the public announcement of something wrought by God.[372] That which is publicly announced must be of special significance to a group or to a people. Thus, this portrays a concept of evangelization in Old Testament. Israel is called to be God's witness before the nations as "a light to all peoples" (Is 42,6). For the light shining in darkness draws people to it while at the same time it goes outward crossing all boundaries to other lands. It is against this background, and the background of Israel's notion of God as One Superior to all other deities (Dt 32,8; Is 24,21; Jer 46,25) and the messianic promise of salvation, that the Old Testament notion of evangelization is to be understood. In Ps 87,4–5, it is clear that while God's primary concern was Israel, he did not exclude other peoples: "I will count Egypt and Babylon among my friends, Philistine, Tyrian and Nubia shall be there, and Zion shall be called a mother in whom men of every race are born". In Old Testament, evangelization acquires a messianic meaning, announcing of the victory of Yahweh and of a new age (Is 51,16; 52,7; 60,6; 61,1; 56,6–7). Despite these evidences of the Old Testa-

---

371 Smith, Linda, Effective counselling: A groupwork manual on interpersonal skills for pastoral teams, England 1995, 28.
372 King James version of the Bible translates it as "to bring or publish good tidings", while the Revised Standard version translates it as "herald of good tidings" (Cf. Is 40,9; 52,7; 61,1).

ment account of evangelization, we must establish the fact that Old Testament gives no explicit divine mandate to evangelize the nations.

In New Testament, the notion of evangelization is deeply rooted in Jesus Christ. The divine mandate to evangelize is derived from (Lk 4,18).[373] Again, in Mk 1,14–15 Jesus announces "the time has come; the Kingdom of God is upon you; repent and believe the Gospel". In the gospel of Luke and in Acts of the apostle, evangelization seems to mean "to announce something new to the people who know nothing" (Cf. Lk 4,18; 2,10; Acts 8,35; 17,18). In New Testament, the mandate to evangelize is not explicitly given to the Jews, even though Jesus' ministry has global-mission significance. Some New Testament texts support the global mission of Jesus Christ from which the New Testament mandate to evangelize all nations takes its bearing, viz: In Mt 5,13–14, Jesus says: "You are the salt to the world [...] you are the light of the world." In Mt 8,11; Lk.7,10, Jesus says : "Many [...] will come from east and west to feast with Abraham, Isaac and Jacob in the Kingdom of Heaven". Even though his ministry was confined to Jewish territory, the universal character of his mission is not lacking. This is confirmed further by the following gospel accounts: His journey to Jerusalem (Lk 9,51); the story of the good Samaritan (Lk 10,29–37); the parable of the lost sheep (Lk 15,4–7).

5.7 What is evangelization?

The term evangelization has been introduced into Roman Catholic theological vocabulary since the Second Vatican Council as a way of understanding itself and its mission. Etymologically, the term evangelization is derived from the Greek *euangelos*, which means goodnews. Evangelization according to Bernard Häring could be understood as "the explicit proclamation of the mystery of Christ and a direct invitation to adhere to his gospel".[374] It is the mission of every Christian to be an evangelizer. To be an evangelizer, therefore, is to be a proclaimer of the goodnews of our Lord Jesus Christ.

Proclamation is the announcing of this Goodnews of Jesus Christ, of these mysteries of the God made man, so that people may have a chance to hear his Gospel, to accept it, to believe it, to be renewed and elevated by it, and to reach new and otherwise unattainable levels of communication with God. This proclamation aims at the restoration of all things, and especially of every man and woman, in Christ. Its purpose is the salvation of everyone. St Paul saw himself as a servant of the mysteries of Christ and as their proclaimer (Cf. Eph 3,1–13). Fidelity to the mission of proclamation demands that those who preach the Gospel should be faithful to the

---

373 Mendes, Angela, Heil für die Welt: Kriterien eines gegenwärtigen Missionsverständnisses, entwickelt aus den Diskussionen der Bischofssynode von 1974 über die Evangelisierung: Diplomarbeit zur Erlangung des Diploms in katholischer Theologie an der Katholisch-Theologischen Fakultät der Ludwig-Maximilians-Universität München 2005, 10.
374 Häring, Bernard, Evangelization Today, England 1974, 43.

whole Gospel. Proclamation should be complete and authentic. This means, proclamation should not be subjected to the desires of the world. It should confess at every time and in everywhere the faith that Jesus Christ is the one and only saviour of all humanity. Proclamation in union with: conversion, witness to life, celebration and transformation, form a formidable elements of evangelization. The word evangelization challenges us to break out of the stagnation or complacency into which we all can easily fall as disciples of the Lord. In effect, evangelization connotes movement or dynamism. We must remember Pope Paul VI's challenging understanding of evangelization as the transformation of humanity and the whole world from within. We who are the church must not allow ourselves to be paralyzed by a kind of spiritual narcissism. The evangelizer must not give in to compromise, lack of interest, hopelessness and disenchantment, which are real obstacles to evangelization. To evangelize is to become instrumental in facilitating and continuing God's self-revelation to our world. In evangelization, we proclaim the Word of God, Jesus Christ, to the world.[375] To evangelize is to help another person pay attention to, celebrate, and live in terms of the living God, revealed fully by Jesus, and present in our human experiences.

5.7.1 The goal of evangelization

Conversion is the goal of evangelization. The church evangelizes because it seeks to convert, solely through the divine power of the message it proclaims. So, in the church's mission to evangelize, conversion occupies the central place. Conversion itself must operate within the limits of common sense.

A Catholic biblical theology of conversion recognizes that there is no single understanding of conversion normative for all of Scripture. Rather, there are many understandings operative, some complementary and others that seem to compete. The contemporary biblical theology of conversion has been most richly nourished in the christian scriptures.[376] The conversion preached by John the Baptist was a reminiscence of the prophetic demand for purity of heart. By his baptism in Jordan, Jesus affirmed the rightness of John's message, but he thereby also enacted prophetically Israel's repentance and acceptance of salvation, in other words, its conversion.

The call for conversion by Jesus himself took the form of proclamation of God's reign and an invitation to be part of this kingdom. Jesus adopted different methods to achieve this conversion in the hearts of the people, viz: through his words and deeds, through his parables, by life of witness, and so on. Jesus himself is the object of proc-

---

375 Mendes, Heil für die Welt, 10.
376 The Jewish Scriptures contain classic prophetic notions of conversion that reflect an evolving personal sense of sin, together with a progressive interiorization of the idea of return to covenant fidelity. Also present in the Jewish Scriptures are the Deuteronomic writings whose theology of conversion stresses more the repetitive cycle of grace-apostasy-punishment-repentance, as well as later, more legalistic notions of conversion as obedience to the Torah or the performance of cultic ritual.

lamation. In the experience of the post-resurrection apostolic community, conversion assumes meanings. The Matthean community was concerned with church order and was more interested in its universality perspective than the Lucan community. The theology of conversion in Pauline and Johannine communities followed different perspective. The different understanding of conversion even within New Testament resulted in different pastoral approaches and different methods of evangelization.

The church's liturgy offers us also a peculiar version of the theology of conversion. Liturgy has been looked upon from the earliest times as the primary embodiment of the faith of the church. Thus, the rites of baptism and penance are the church's two major rituals of conversion. The Catholic liturgical theology of conversion teaches that conversion can be understood as an establishment of a covenant; as Christ-centered; as church-centered; as sacrament-centered; as a spiritual journey; as a rebirth. Conversion is a process and not just an event. It is a lifelong process and not something that ends with formal membership in the church. It is all about falling in love with God and God's people. That means that as part of conversion, one begins to speak the language of love, of prayer and of holiness.

5.7.2 The methods of evangelization

There is no one style of Catholic evangelization. There are varieties of methods just as there are many evangelizers, viz: proclamation, christian witness, catechetics, mass media, person to person encounter, popular piety, sacraments and liturgy, charity works, school apostolate, and so on. Diversity in method is very important because the communities to be evangelized, we must know, are also diversified. That means, a method that works in a particular community may not be applicable in another community. He who wills the end wills the means. If Christ tells us to evangelize, he will enlighten and strengthen us to do it. With the power of the Holy Spirit, we can find the more effective methods to evangelize the people to whom we are sent.

Catholic evangelizers, for the most part, are to some reasonable extent well educated and somewhat sophisticated, yet, they must know that often they are dealing with unsophisticated and less well educated people. Therefore, for a Catholic evangelizer to be effective in his method, he must design and use very popular, quite simple, and at times fairly emotional approaches to share the Gospel. In designing such approaches, the community to be served must be kept in mind, most especially in terms of their language and cultural affiliations. There will be no true evangelization if the language of the evangelized is neglected. Any method of evangelization, no matter how popular or simple or emotion it may seem to be, that is not deeply rooted in the local language of the people, and not in the language of the colonial masters, is like building on a sand and will be shallow. This is why I always strongly propose the effective use of Igbo language so that the Gospel message be deeply rooted in Igboland.[377] Evangelizers should consider themselves as "marketers of the Gospel" or as "advertisers of the today's Catholic church". Their work is to convert those to whom they are sent not by the use of strange language, which will make the Gospel message more sophisticated for these unsophisticated people, but by adopting the language of the people in order to make the message comprehensible to the people. This is the primary method of all the other methods.

5.7.3 The evangelizer and the evangelized

Evangelizers are all those engaged in spreading, defending and consolidating the gospel. The first and foremost evangelizer is Jesus Christ himself, who came so that all men, irrespective of race and nationalities, may have life and have it abundantly (Cf.Jn 10,10). By virtue of being Jesus' followers, the apostle inherited this mission with every mandate. It was precisely for this purpose that Jesus chose them and set them apart from the rest of men. Then, there are others who through the apostles became evangelizers. They are often referred to as disciples,[378] and they were meant to qualify to be evangelizers under the conditions that they should have sound knowledge of Christ's doctrine, that the transparency of their lives should not be doubted and that they should be full of apostolic zeal (Cf.Acts 1,21–22). Until today, many adherents of the faith are called to be evangelizers by the virtue of being christians

---

377 The early missionaries' method of evangelization in Igboland can be classified into direct and indirect methods. Direct method designates those ventures that bear directly on the main missionary aims. They involve the direct way of reaching those to be evangelized. They deal with missionary evangelization as already discussed. Direct method includes explicit proclamation, Christian witness, catechetics, popular piety, sacraments and liturgy. Indirect method deals with the services offered and institutions provided to dispose the potential converts for the reception of the Gospel message. Indirect method includes physical presence, charity works, Christian villages, school method.

378 The term "Disciple" occurs about 260 times in the gospels and Acts, and used in various ways: a) to mean an adherent of almost any great leader or movement. There is then, disciples of Moses (Jn 9,28), Of the Pharisees (Mt 22,16; Mk 2,18), and perhaps Paul (Acts 9,25). Jesus own followers are usually called not "the" but "his" disciples as though to distinguish them from other similar groups. b) It designates believers in Christ. In this context, it occurs 20 times in Acts. John uses it in an inclusive sense. From the beginning, therefore, Jesus had many disciples in Judea (Jn 1,35–50, 73; 8,30–31;9,27–28;11,54). These include some of his followers, and were to be found particularly among the Jewish leaders. c) It refers specifically to one or more of the twelve. It occurs about two dozen, e.g., Lk 9,54; Jn 6:8; 12,4), more than half of which are in Matthew which is the only NT book to speak of "twelve disciples" (Mt 10,1; 11,1; 20,17). The author of Mark never limited the term in this way but seems occasionally to think of a small group who appear in a boat (Mk 6,45; 8,10) or "in the house" (Mk 7,17; 10,10) or talking with Jesus privately (Mk 4,34; 9–28). When used in the singular it refers only to the nature of discipleship. This is found only in Matthew and Luke where it appears only on Jesus' lip. We adopt here the second meaning which is also the common meaning for the early Christians.

for St Paul writes "How could anyone spread the goodnews without a commission to do so?" (Rm 10,15). Consequently, every evangelizer is a delegate of Christ. The evangelized are all nations and peoples everywhere. The church, as we know, is a sign of this universality. It has no limitation of time or place. The Goodnews of our Lord Jesus Christ is meant to reach individuals or communities in their religious, cultural and social circumstances. The New Testament demonstrates this universality in the scope of evangelization by the parables of the lost sheep, the lost coin and the prodigal son. These parables highlight both the individual and communal aspects of beneficiaries of mission.

5.8 Early evangelization among the Igbo natives

To begin, it is necessary to recall that the sowing of the catholic faith in Igboland can be compared with the biblical parable of the mustard seed. It all began on December 5, Saturday, 1885 with just a very few number of missionaries: "Father Joseph Lutz was the pioneer French missionary, who, with Father Horne and Brother Jean Gotto and Hermas laid the foundation for the Catholic faith flourishing today among the peoples of Eastern Nigeria".[379]

Although at this time, it would mean a great sacrifice to be in mission in this part of the world, but that these great men of God would volunteer to come was because: "Divine Providence wanted the Eastern Nigerians to see the salvation of God and so sent the missionaries to lead them to the knowledge of the truth – CHRIST!"[380] Of course, these missionaries suffered some difficulties and set-backs such as initial hostility from the natives, language problem, malaria attack and deaths. Unperturbed by these eventualities and determined to accomplish their mission of making christians out of the Igbo people, they grew from strength to strength in their endeavour, thanks to their successful missionary methods, especially, the school method.

Why did the early christian missionaries come at the time they did? We may simply say that it was divine providence. God desired it to be at that time, and God's choice is incontestable. Out of obedience to the vicar of Christ, and at that time it was the great Pope St Leo XIII, the Holy Ghost missionaries came to seek for the spiritual welfare of the Igbo people.[381] We respect their great courage because despite other challenges, Igboland, and indeed the entire black continent was regarded as "white man's grave" due to malaria from mosquito bites. At the time of their arrival, we should recollect that colonization had been in place, so, there was already a prominent European presence. The colonial era was marked with exploitation and dehumanization of Africans, especially the Igbos in different forms such as human trafficking otherwise

---

379 Nwosu, Vincent, (ed.), The Catholic Church in Onitsha: People, Places and Events (1885–1985), Onitsha 1985, 125.
380 Obi, Celestine, A Hundred Years of the Catholic Church in Eastern Nigeria (1885–1985), Onitsha 1985, 2.
381 Nwosu, The Catholic Church in Onitsha, 22.

called slave trade. Also, the malicious activities of the British Royal Niger Company (R.N.C) and the inhuman treatment they often inflicted on the natives could not allow the natives at the initial stage to note the difference between the white missionaries and the white colonial masters. Judging from this background, one would say that Igbo people first came in contact with the church's missionary effort to evangelize in the context of colonization and a dehumanizing phenomenon. We should equally remember that with God nothing comes by sudden nor by coincidence. Soon, the natives themselves began to notice the good-will of these servants of God towards them: schools were opened to educate as much number of the natives as possible, dispensaries were opened to care for the sick, centres were opened for religious instructions, other forms of charity such as distribution of clothes and other materials was also extended towards the natives. This made it easier for these missionaries to win over the admirations of the natives and made conversion easier.

As we mentioned earlier, the civil administration of the Igboland had been in the hand of the British colonial masters through their agents, the Royal Niger Company (R.N.C), many years before the coming of the early catholic missionaries. It is important to emphasize the word "catholic" because the British, as it were, advanced their colonial imperialism by coming along with them, the English religion, otherwise called "Anglicanism". The Igbo natives, of course, were not fooled. They soon discovered that Anglican missionaries were merely tools in the hand of the British administrators, who used them only to advance their imperialism in Igboland. This led to low record of conversions of the Igbo natives by the Anglican missionaries. On the other hand, the early catholic missionaries, though they were late comers in comparison with their Anglican counter-part, distinguished themselves with their high level of dedication to God's work and their goodwill towards the natives, and these won for them more number of converts and a lot of progress. Naturally, one would expect reactions from both the Anglican missionaries and the Royal Niger Company. The Anglican missionaries felt their position threatened by the rapid changes and the relatively numerous converts being made by the Catholic mission. The Royal Niger Company did not get on with the Catholic missionaries either. Because the catholic missionaries did not fear to correct or reprimand many foreign workers of the Royal Niger Company for their scandalous living which tended to nullify the efforts of the missionaries to inculcate the christian virtues into the natives, relationship became more strained. Also, the catholic missionaries at this time were mainly of French nationality, and this made the British administration through the Royal Niger Company to suspect these French missionaries of being agents of the French government and French commercial companies.[382] By and large, the success of the early catholic missionaries in Igboland can be attributed to their missionary methods. Although the methods applied at these given time depended largely on the convinctions of the apostolic prefect at the time, the intention had always been towards a successful work of evangelization among the Igbo people. The pioneer missionary, Fr Lutz, for instance, resorted to building "christian village" as a missionary method of

---

382 Nwosu, The Catholic Church in Onitsha, 1.

evangelization where he was housing the slaves he redeemed, quite separated from the rest of the villagers, in order to offer them protection and a sound christian faith. Life in the "christian village", however, was so severe and regulated, and therefore became detestable by some inmates who could not cope up.[383] A different method of evangelization was later introduced by Fr Leon-Alexander Lejeune, one of the successors of Fr Joseph Lutz. Fr Lejeune was dissatisfied at cost of running "christian village". Besides, "christian village" succeeded in securing a very small number of the natives in comparison with the total population of villagers. Instead, Fr Lejeune declared education as his main method of evangelization. The success of this method merited him support, even from the colonial administrators.[384] Evangelization through formal education seemed to be more fruitful that after Fr Lejeune, his successor Fr Joseph Shanaham continued this method, and saw education and evangelization as part and parcel of christian mandate to teach all nations (Mt 28,19). In his zeal to spread the christian faith through formal education, and in his desire to give the Igbo natives the full benefits of christianity, Fr Shanaham embarked on "Bush Schools", meant to establish schools right in the hinterland. His strategy was not to educate just a few but to educate everybody as far as his resources could permit. One can, therefore, rightly say that the European missionaries laid the foundation for formal education in Igboland. Indeed, an account of the development of formal education in Igboland which does not give credit to the early catholic missionaries should be considered as misleading. The advantages of school method in particular was responsible for the church's tremendous achievement in the conversion of the Igbo natives.

Today, it is incontestable that the church in Igboland has continued to witness this grown in the number of her adherents and in her structures. Hardly, in this modern time, does one come across a person who is not baptized. On Sundays and at various liturgical celebrations, churches are filled to the brim with large number of the faithful both young and old, children and adults, men and women to the extent that many who cannot find accommodation inside have to stay outside. Despite this seeming success story, instances of luke-warm christians, half-baked christians and fallen christians are on the increase. One may then ask: To what extent has the christian message spoken to the Igbo man? This situation, of course suggests that today there is yet need for the church to introduce a new vision in the work of evangelization.

5.9 Evangelization in the new vision of the church

The new vision of the church in its evangelizing mission is nothing but the church's change of attitude to other cultures which would lead to the church's better appreciation of other cultures. This, too, would, for example, initiate a new vision towards African religions and cultures by today's christian missionaries, and would give birth to what I may regard as transcultural evangelization. Transcultural evangelization

---

383 Nwosu, The Catholic Church in Onitsha, 22.
384 Nwosu, The Catholic Church in Onitsha, 130.

is an essential element in the new vision in evangelization. It is interested in being in contact with other cultures, and bringing the Gospel message to today's culture centers.[385] In this way, the church would be interested in the mission *ad extra*, and to be supported by an ecclesiology of *ecclesia ad extra*.[386] This is in contrast to the notion of the church as imperialistic. The Roman Empire had for a long time taught that the church in Rome, and as it were, the whole Catholic world inherited symbols and systems that helped to give the impression that the ecclesial destiny of Rome depended on its imperial and secular destiny. But it was time to change this wrong positions and directions. It was time for the sacred vocation of the ecclesial Rome to open her mission to the entire world and cultures, not under the expression of, nor with the symbols of "an emperor". The resilience of the church has depended, in part, on this. Pope Paul VI had previously noted the difference between the Rome of the emperors and the Rome of the apostles. From this emerged the new image of Rome as the Rome of the Catholic faith, the Rome of the episcopacy, and the Rome of the papacy. Indeed, a new image of the church appeared. This is a new image of the church with a new vision in her mission of evangelization. Pope Paul VI realized this and insisted on it. He was, by this insistence, initiating a new era in which the Rome of the apostles would look less like the Rome of the emperors in regalia, in the use and vision of authority. We should remember that Pope Paul VI was the last Pope to be crowned, and we must remember that the three-in-one crown "tiara", was once believed to symbolize the royal authority and power of the Pope in heaven, on earth and over the gates of the hell .[387] In this way, the unique nature of the new vision of the church is established. The church is no longer to be considered as the church for Europe, and outside Europe, an imperial mission. No, instead, the new vision of the church today teaches that the universal mission of evangelization must permit religious freedom so that the christian message can be proposed to the people and not imposed on the people.

Based on this understanding, the church has come to recognize the importance of the cultural values of the people in evangelization. The 1990 *Lineamenta* on the Special Synod of Bishops for Africa, has recognised that, for effective evangelization in Africa, the church must have recourse, without hesitation, to the philosophy and wisdom of the people, which, of course borders on the people's language and worldview. It is on record that the early christian missionaries came to Africa with biased

---

385 Cf. AG, no. 37.

386 This is the theology of the existence of the church and of ecclesial realities which are moving towards catholic unity. Therefore, one can see that it was not difficult for "Lumen gentium" to relate the not yet evangelized with the evangelizer and the evangelized, and at the same time assert that even the non christian have the possibility of attaining salvation depending on their circumstance.

387 Pope Paul VI disposed the "Tiara" and it eventually arrived at Washington DC, the capital of the very democratic North Americ. When one hears of the final destination of "Tiara", one begins to wonder whether by this gesture, an era of a democratic mission has been initiated, or was it better to secure this symbol outside Europe lest it finds its way back into papacy? Together, with "Tiara", imperial appendages were also abolished.

minds about the people, their culture, custom and language. They might have been influenced by the understanding that Africans belonged to the continent described as "dark continent ", and therefore, has nothing good to offer. Hence, they developed the attitude of understanding the people's culture and custom as devilish, even their language. This negligence on the people's language as an important vehicle in evangelization made practically all the white missionaries not to have interest in learning the native language of the people they intended to evangelize, instead, they would prefer to use interpreters. Researching on this matter, Celestine A. Obi confirms: "None of the people interviewed could recollect having heard any of the early missionaries preached fluently in Igbo. There was always an interpreter".[388] In order to prove the extent of the negligence of the people and the condemnation of their culture, the early missionaries preferred to formulate a prayer "for the conversion of the Africans", a prayer in which Africans were described as a people without orientation in life, a people with a worthless culture and language. Therefore, these early European missionaries intended to christianize the people's culture, custom and language, and this is where they got it wrong. Instead, they could have embarked on incarnating the Gospel message in the people's culture in which they would have relied on the people's language as a vehicle to achieve this. Peter Nlemadim Domnwachukwu remarks:

> The Igbo language is the vernacular to Igbo people. We believe that the use of Igbo as the primary language of teaching the Bible to Igbo people will be the best thing to do and will also lead to a better and deeper understanding of the Bible and its teaching. To the contrary, many of those who teach Igbo audiences use the English language and, in some cases, teach through interpreters.[389]

It is a good gesture that the church later realized this mistake, and today it is the great advocate of inculturation. For the work of evangelization today to be effective, the people's language must play a vital role. We must not forget the opening address of Pope Paul VI to the second session of Vatican II in which he made reference to ecclesial reform which includes a more diligent study and a more intensive proclamation of the word of God.[390] In the process of this proclamation, every race and nation should be considered as the new people of God, or we may call it God's people in Christ (Populus ille messianicus habet pro capite Christus).[391] This shows an effort to achieve a new vision of evangelization, and the need to make into the messianic community all nations, races and cultures of the world. The people of God in Christ are not to be characterized by a particular economic, political, social or cultural distinction. Rather, the new vision is open to universal access, and open to personal and individual participation.

The new vision of the church in evangelization is not without some challenges. There is the danger of regarding the church's effort at interreligious dialogue as a

---

388 Obi, A Hundred Years of the Catholic Church, 82.
389 Domnwachukwu, Authentic African Christianity, 171.
390 Cf. Pope Paul VI, Address At The Opening Of The Second Session Of The Second Vatican Council, September 1963.
391 Cf. L G, no.9.

replacement for its mission of evangelization. Again, the church's support for religious freedom tends to be misunderstood as Vatican II's attempt to discredit evangelization. The recognition of the fact that salvation is possible outside the church is misunderstood by some elements to mean the Vatican II's attack on the mission of the church to evangelize.[392] This is a dangerous precedence which tends to question the very existence of the church. But the existence of the church and its mission to evangelize is vividly contained in the Vatican II document.[393] This mission is continued through the Holy Spirit as a mission to evangelize in obedience to Christ himself: "The time is fulfilled, and the kingdom of God is at hand, repent and believe in the Gospel; [...] The spirit of the Lord is upon me, because he has anointed me to preach good news to the poor. He has sent me to proclaim release to the captives and recovering of sight to the blind, to set at liberty those who are oppressed, to proclaim the acceptable year of the Lord" (Mk 1,15;Lk 4,18). In *Redemptoris mission*, Pope John Paul II addressed the question: why mission?[394] He came up with the answer that mission is consequence of faith. There is mission because there is faith, and the love of Christ compels us to obedience to this divine mission (Eph 2,14; 2Cor 5,14).

The issues at stake in ecclesiology today involve balancing the canonical mission of a theologian and his commitment to defending and protecting the orthodoxy of Catholic theology, implied in the theology of mission based on the missionary mandate. It was Pope Paul VI who, in 1957, as Cardinal Montini, set up an essential link between orthodoxy and mandate, and in which "orthodoxy concerns the content of the message to be handed on; the mandate concerns the capacity to hand that content on".[395]

The same Pope Paul VI could be regarded as to have introduced the new vision for the church in the quest to evangelize the people of our time. Prior to Pope Paul VI, Pope John XXIII by convoking the Second Vatican Council opened the windows of the church to the whole world, and by continuing it in the way he did, Pope Paul VI opened the doors of the world for the church to enter for its mission of evangelizing the world. His Holiness Pope John Paul II's avowed determination to move the church along the lines of Vatican II is testified in the policies that have marked his pontificate. He himself participated in the Second Vatican Council in various capacities as a well known theologian and an auxiliary Bishop and attended the first session of the council in that capacity. It was during the course of the council that he became an archbishop, a position that brought him nearer to the altar built on St Peter's tomb. He collaborated in the drafting of many of the council's documents, especially, *The church in the modern world*. His numerous encyclicals and other documents bear eloquent testimony of his dedication to this new vision of evangelization.

---

392   Cf. John Paul II, Redemptoris Missio, no.4.
393   Cf. L G, no.1
394   Cf. John Paul, Redemptoris Missio, no.11.
395   Hebblethwaite, Paul, Paul VI : The First Modern Pope, New York 1993, 272.

5.10 Evangelization by means of implementing the language of the people

The depth of success in planting the Gospel message on a particular soil is measured not by external signs, even on sacramental level, but by the use of the language that reflects the thought of the people. George De Napolis made this point clear by saying:

> At least in ideal, it is commonplace now for missionaries to try to learn the language of the people to whom they are sent and to immerse themselves in the local culture. But what this means in the concrete is not simply an adaptation to food, dress, liturgical posture and the daily rituals of social existence. If, as we have maintained, culture is the common meanings and values of a community, then to communicate adequately the message of Christ, those common meanings and values have to be thoroughly understood by the communicator.[396]

The use of native language can help to create an indigenous atmosphere and bring out the transparency of liturgical celebrations, and in doing so, this language permeates the hearts of the local faithful and leads them to the authentic conversion which is the goal of evangelization. Majority of the Igbo is still uneducated and there is no doubt about this fact. Therefore, being dogmatic about use of foreign language, for example "Latin", in celebrating the liturgy is not helpful. Most often one may think that illiteracy is limited within rural areas of the Igboland. This is a false assumption. The reality is that most of our rural areas have been deserted and the cities are over-crowded due to quest for better life. The over-crowded parishes in our cities are merely maded up of parishioners who could no longer stay back in their villages but who rushed to the cities not to enrol themselves in schools but to struggle for survival through whatever business they could do. These people hardly understand any other language except Igbo. Therefore, to insist on "Latin Mass" or the singing of "O Salutaris" and "Tantum Ergo" every Sunday evening at the Benediction of the Blessed Sacrament, does not allow for interior conversion for these people who in actual fact do not understand what they recite or sing but merely do that as a routine. As long as the church prays and speaks in a foreign language whose pattern of thought and mode of expression is alien to the people, all efforts at evangelization remain superficial. This means that the church has not penetrated the realm of the spirit nor fully appreciated the native genius of the people. Language is an authentic manifestation of the way people form ideas and interiorly react to objective reality. Language communicates the soul and spirit of the people and betrays their most secret sentiments.

Anywhere the word of God is powerfully proclaimed in the local language of the people and in its proper idiomatic expressions, poetic forms, proverbs and wisdom titbits, with good liturgical and cultural music to help to design the word, the situation is quite different. The same should be applied to the Igbo society. Such ceremonies are usually full and the christian life and culture boom. Then in response, the people take up responsibilities to solve social problems, because they are now fully armed with

---

396 De Napolis, George, Inculturation as communication, in: De La Cruz Aymes, Maria, (ed.), Effective inculturation and ethnic identity, Roma 1991, 77–78.

Christ, and all these of course lead to reverence to the word of God and the sacrament being celebrated. There is absolute need to wake extra effort now to proclaim the word of God with dignity, and make the crucified Christ central in all things.

5.11 The call to evangelize is a call to inculturate

Most Nigerians regard the majority of the Igbo as christians. Almost everyone in Igboland claims to be a christian. Christianity is popular in Igboland but we are concerned that christianity in Igboland does not adequately meet the people's socio-cultural and spiritual needs. This situation is detrimental to the healthy growth of christianity in Igboland. The consensus among most Igbo is that Igbo christianity lacks cultural identity. This condition makes it difficult for the average Igbo to understand the true essence of christianity and what it means for him or her existentially. Unfortunately, christian religion with foreign cultural models were planted in Igboland. Igbo culture, customs, traditions and institutions were treated as inferior to their western counterparts by most missionaries and the Igbo christian converts were subjected to the agony of going through the very difficult process of becoming Western in an Igbo society in the name of religion. On the surface, most Igbo christians think, talk, sing, preach and behave like Westerners because this is what christianity has required. This tradition has carried on from the mid-nineteenth century to the present day. This is traumatic for persons to practice their faith in an atmosphere of pretence and chameleon-like life-style. This has resulted to producing Igbo christians most of whom are not convinced in their christian faith. Some of those people regard the church as a social status and come to church merely to show that they belong to this status. They consider the church as providing avenues for fellowship and social interaction. Some others also go to church to seek solutions for their problems only, while some others go purely for economic reasons. This understanding stems from their initial orientation to the christian faith whereby the christian faith disregarded the Igbo cultural worldview, part of which emphasizes the ideology of "uwa ezuoke" (no man is Mr. have all). Instead, the missionaries knowingly or unknowingly operated on the platform of "uwa zuruoke" (Mr. have all) by promising all the good things of life in the name of making conversions. This played out well among the Igbo people ravaged by hunger and poverty and who would readily position themselves at the receiving end in order to answer "Mr have all." So the Igbo cultural heritage became at logger-heads with the new faith and the church built on this anti-Igbo cultural ideology and has made the Igbo church even till this present day as a "receiving church". Proper evangelization in the present day circumstance cannot be achieved when the gospel message is not incarnated in the people's culture. This incarnation of the gospel message in a culture can be described as "Gospel and Culture Encounter". In the modern term, this encounter is what is referred to as "Inculturation". Although the word "inculturation" has generated so much controversy and has so many varied concepts or definitions, the church's attitude to it should not be avoidance, rather, the church's efforts to evangelize should be geared towards an authentic incarnation of Christ's message of salvation within the cultural context of the evangelized. Already the tone of the mandate to proclaim the Gospel to all peoples (Mt 28,19) reveals Christ's awareness of the enormity of the reality of cultural diversity which not only must be tolerated but must serve as an indispensable means of rendering the Gospel meaningful. By carrying the Gospel to all the sectors of human society, the christian strives to humanize and to christianize social life in all its ramifications. This is done through the improvement of customs and institutions. The church has to use the cultural treasures of various peoples if it is to effectively proclaim the Gospel, especially, as many nations are becoming aware of their own cultural identity. The culture itself, however, must undergo some relative purification because we cannot totally exonerate the culture from falling short in some aspects of the Gospel message.[397] We may then ask: how can the church's call to evangelize at the same time imply call to inculturate? We attempt this question by recognizing the fact that there is no race without its own culture, and that basically, culture of a people is the sole of that people. Anything that touches on a people's culture touches on their life as a people. Therefore, in order to influence a people, their culture must not be left out, otherwise, the impact of such influence remains at the superficial level. The Igbo in their cultural circumstance have their peculiar way of expressing their devotions and worship within their religious rituals which provokes in them a certain kind of deep religious awareness and inner connection to the divine. Among the various cultural sentiments within the Igbo religious rituals is "mbem" (exclamations). The "mbem" could be described as a native dirge which, as it were, successfully introduces the people into the mood of any ritual celebration. The words of "mbem" are carefully chosen to express the content of the celebration, and indeed, stimulant. People are carried along whenever "mbem" is sung and this is manifested in the way it influences the hearers who either dance to the tune in acknowledgement of the words of the singer or express other forms of actions. "Mbem" creates atmosphere of happiness or sorrow depending on the choice of words and the nature of what is being celebrated. Evangelization is proclamation of goodnews of our Lord Jesus Christ. This is celebration of the joy of the mystery of our salvation. Placing "mbem" in its proper place in this celebration will make the celebration to be truly Igbo. For example, in the celebration of the eucharist, "mbem" can either be introduced in place of "Alleluia" or sung immediately after consecration. Failure to identify inculturation as an essential partner in the church's evangelizing mission amounts to making only external alterations or even paternalistic concessions behind which lies some conscious or unconscious assumption that christianity is something ready-made, finished and only to be adapted to new situations. Moreover, it would give the impression that expatriate missionaries proclaim the Gospel in terms of their own culture and that

---

397 Every culture contains desirable as well as undesirable elements. Desirable elements act as seeds to the word while undesirable elements could be against the Gospel. In purifying a culture, the desirable elements are retained while the undesirable elements are corrected and elevated to the level of the Gospel. The purified elements, thus, become best suited as tools of evangelization.

the local church must adapt this message to local conditions. The church should not allow such wrong conception to spread. Therefore, the marriage between Gospel and Culture is necessary. This marriage is recognized in the modern term as "inculturation", and what do we mean by "inculturation"?

5.11.1 Inculturation

Inculturation is no longer a new terminology in theology. Before we start-off with discussing how inculturation would be an essential step towards the authentic use of Igbo word in the work of evangelization, it is necessary to have a background knowledge of the word inculturation itself.

5.11.1.1 The Historical Background

Inculturation has an old history that is very much associated with the mission of the apostles received directly from Christ himself: "Go therefore and make disciples of all nations" (Mt 28,19; Mk 16,15). By this mandate, the apostles were commissioned to carry the Gospel message to various peoples of the earth, who as it were, have different cultures and practices. St Paul preaching in Athens can be considered as the first missionary experience of church-culture conflict:

> Thus, even though his basic message was to a large extent drawn from the OT and from the life, death and resurrection of Christ, Paul found it necessary to use non-christian ideas in order to reach his Greek audience [...] Thus Paul's speech at the Areopagus is a good example of early Christian preaching adapted to a Hellenistic Gentile audience. In speaking of Gentiles Paul took a different point of departure than the OT, and the speech of Acts 17 can be seen to incorporate several common Pauline themes, including the typical apocalyptic elements of resurrection and coming judgement associated with Jesus [...] This is an example of inculturation.[398]

Again, the issue of circumcision was another cultural problem that challenged the mission of the apostles and led to the first council of Jerusalem (Cf.Acts15,1–33). The resolutions from this council could be seen as the first attempt at inculturation, and according to Oliver A. Onwubiko: "Seen from this angle the council had formulated the principles of intercommunion which make it possible for Jews and Gentiles to live in one community and worship together in harmony".[399] It could be rightly said that tension between christianity and culture is a major issue right from this early period, across different empires, and up till this present day. Certain attempts have

---

[398] Osei-Bonsu, Joseph, The inculturation of christianity in Africa, Frankfurt am Main 2005, 30 and 34. See also: Scherer, James, Bevans, Stephan (ed.), New directions in mission and evangelization: Faith and Culture, New York 1999, 139.
[399] Onwubiko, Alozie Oliver, The Church as the family of God (Ujamaa): In the light of Ecclesia in Africa, Nsukka 1999, 174; see also Osei-Bonsu, The inculturation of christianity in Africa, 27–30.

been made by missionaries as well as theologians at different ages to bring solutions to this tension, and to give a new face to church-culture relationship, which in today's concept may be understood as inculturation. In order to give our contributions to this old-age problem, and in order to continue to promote the work of establishing a better relationship between church and culture by means of inculturation, it is necessary to begin by understanding the meaning of inculturation.

5.11.1.2 The Meaning of Inculturation

By implication, inculturation could be viewed as an effort to prove that marriage between church and culture is possible. This does not mean replacement of the authentic christian gospel with another gospel. On the contrary, it means making native the message of the gospel that is proclaimed.

In most African countries, Igboland not an exception, colonization created an opportunity for missionary work of evangelization. As a result, there arose in some minds of the natives the wrong interpretation of mission as a tool for colonial expansion. The attitudes of some missionaries and their missionary methods did not help matters. In some cases, the missionaries misunderstood the culture of the natives and failed to appreciate some of the good cultural values. The consequence is that up till today, despite much progress in terms of the tremendous increment of the number of the faithful, the christian message is yet to have root in Africa, and indeed in Igboland. How do we make the christian gospel to be rooted in Africa? Mbiti J.S makes the following suggestion: "Analog dazu muss Afrika die Form von Christentum entwickeln, die im afrikanischen Boden echte Wurzeln hat".[400] Mbiti calls for a development of a form of african christianity. This does not mean a different form of christianity, but the same christianity that allows an african to be a christian as an authentic african. It does not mean compromising christianity with the values that oppose the christian faith. Instead, it calls on an african to live in full the teachings of the gospel as a true african. It is a call on an african to practice the authentic christian teaching in an authentic african way. The process to achieving this goal is called inculturation. How can we define inculturation? According to Ayward Shorter, inculturation is: "The on-going dialogue between faith and culture or cultures. More fully, it is the creative and dynamic relationship between the Christian message and a culture or cultures".[401] Peter C. Phan defines it as "The process of introducing the christian faith into a local culture".[402] According to Francis Anekwe Oborji: "Inculturation means allowing the word proclaimed to grow and mature, using the soil nutrients of the place where it is being planted".[403] Prior to Vatican II Council, the concept of inculturation had always

---

400 Onwubiko, The Church as the family of God (Ujamaa), 74.
401 Shorter, Alyward, Towards a Theology of Inculturation, New York 1988, 11.
402 Phan, Peter, In our own tongues: perspectives from Asia on mission and inculturation, New York 2003, 4.
403 Oborji, Francis, Concepts of Mission: the evolution of contemporary missiology, New York 2006, 110

existed and had been suggested by the Bishops from mission lands such as Africa and Asia. How then did the term 'inculturation' come to be used? According to Aylward Shorter:

> The introduction and popularization of the term 'inculturation' seems to be very largely due to members of the Society of Jesus. The very first recorded use of the word in a theological sense seems to be by Fr Joseph Masson SJ, professor at the Gregorian university in Rome, shortly before the opening of the Second Vatican Council in 1962.[404]

Subsequently, seminars and debates were held concerning this term ‚inculturation' and at the end: "The 32nd Congregation of the Society of Jesus which took place from December 1974 to April 1975 used the actual word 'inculturation' fairly frequently in its texts, and included a decree on inculturation".[405] The seminars and debates gained a recorded success, and "the word 'inculturation' also appeared in a papal document in 1979".[406] Inculturation has been a current phenomenon that has caught the attention of various popes and the official documents of the church. To this effect Peter C. Phan writes:

> It has been treated repeatedly and in various ways, by papal documents, from Paul VI's Africae terrarium (1967) and Evangelium nuntiandi (1975) to John Paul II's Catechesi tradendae (1979), Slavorum apostoli (1985), Redemptoris mission (1993), and Fides et ratio (1998); by official church declarations, such as…the Congregation for the Clergy's General Directory for Catechesis (1979), the Post-synodal apostolic exhortations following the special assemblies of the Synod of Bishops for Africa (1994) [407]

Despite the momentum that inculturation has gathered, and despite the success achieved so far, there is this argument that what is actually meant by inculturation has not got a general consensus among theologians and missiologists, even in the official church documents. This is because similar terms tend to portray the same meaning attributed to inculturation, and which had existed and in use long before Vatican II Council. Peter C. Phan has the list of these terms: "translation, accommodation, adaptation, localization, indigenization, contextualization, incarnation, acculturation, and so on".[408] Responding to these terms Oliver A. Onwubiko writes: "Each of these terms has its use in inculturation and none of them, as such, can be substituted for inculturation".[409] Explaining further, Oliver writes:

> But adaptation gives the impression of an extrinsic activity, accommodation gives the impression of a syncretic practice, contextualization gives the impression of the Gospel preached and moderated within and by a given context. Indigenization is often associated

---

404 Shorter, Alyward, African culture and the Christian church, an introduction to social and pastoral anthropology, Dublin 1973, 10.
405 Shorter, African culture and the Christian church, an introduction to social and pastoral anthropology, 10.
406 Shorter, African culture and the Christian church, 10.
407 Phan , In our own tongues, 4.
408 Phan, In our own tongues, 4.
409 Onwubiko, Alozie Oliver, Missionary Ecclesiology: An Introduction, Enugu 1999, 48.

with nativism and the process of the domestication of the Gospel [...] Acculturation correctly gives the impression of the replacement of foreign cultural elements with native ones. [410]

The theory and practice of inculturation must be a two-way process in which there is a give and take on the part of both christianity and the indigeneous culture. Chinua Achebe expresses this well in his 'Arrow of God': "I want one of my sons to join this people and be my eye there. If there is nothing in it you will come back but if there is something there you will bring home my share".[411] That Ezeulu, the chief priest, would send his son Oduche to be part of the church shows the willingness of the Igbo traditional society to accept christianity. Also, that Oduche received a special mandate to bring home the good values of christianity, as well as, to offer christianity the good values of Umuaro community is a pointer towards the two-way process of inculturation. So, conversion leads to the two-way process of give and take which is the goal of inculturation. This is the reality the early Igbo missionaries failed to acknowledge, and their missionary method of building ‚christian village' became a failure.[412] Now let us consider the principles on which inculturation should be based.

5.11.1.3 Principles of Inculturation

There are two principles of inculturation: God's universal salvific will and incarnation. We clarify below what we mean by these two principles. The first principle, God's universal salvific will teaches that God wills the salvation of the human race, and thereby, making the created world arena of revelation and salvation. Of course, Jesus commis-

---

410 Onwubiko, Missionary Ecclesiology, 48.
411 Achebe, Arrow of God, 45–46.
412 "The buying back of slaves led to the opening of the Christian village [...] where the inmates lived a very strictly regulated life with definite hours for prayers, play and work. The missionaries considered it a most favourable circumstance where the catholic doctrine could be imparted to the catechumens away from the neutralizing influences of non-Christian neighbours, Protestants and some merchants/civil servants who, he said, lived in total disregard of all moral laws. It was a community where the freed slaves practised a kind of quasi-monastic spirituality" (Obi, A Hundred Fears of the Catholic Church in Eastern Nigeria 1885–1985, 35–36). "The constructors of the Christian village had their mind set in Europe, so much so that the Christian village which, in Africa, would be the outcome of the evangelization of a natural African village had to come ready-made and had to exist side by side with the natural village and with new European cultural emphasis. Shanahan knew early enough that the Christianity of the Christian village was not adapted to the community, and that it could not be inculturated, and therefore, would not produce converts who would practice their faith in their ordinary life convincingly [...] Shanahan did not toe the line of many missionaries who believed that those to be converted must forsake father and mother. Rather he saw the children as tiny apostles who would go home and evangelize their parents. Therefore, he did not break the child-parent relationship. Through the Holy Communion which they received, these tiny apostles would carry Christ to their parents and to their pagan environments. The school apostolate became popular and replaced the Christian village apostolate in Africa" (Onwubiko, Christian Mission and Culture in Africa, Vol. II, Theory and Practice of Inculturation, An African Perspective, 44–45).

sioned his apostles by saying: "Go therefore and make disciples of all nations [...] " (Mt 28,19). The phrase *of all nations* manifests clearly this God's universal salvific will. The disciples must go to all nations and not to some nations. Since every nation and people have their particular and independent culture, it implies that the Gospel message is meant to encounter these various cultures of the world in the process of making God's salvation reach the ends of the earth.[413] The second principle of inculturation is incarnation. Incarnation which is Christ's assumption of human nature signals the concept that presents God as coming to meet humanity in history. The incarnation, therefore, forms the test for effective inculturation. Christ's incarnation proves that the universal import of God's son does not mean the universal validity of Jewish cultural and religious traditions and practices. Paul made this point clear in the Council of Jerusalem (Acts 15). This shows that it is possible for culture to uphold its full identity and still embody the christian mystery without split and without confusion. To argue further on how incarnation is a principle of inculturation, it is clearly to be understood that no one culture was needed for incarnation to take place, instead, a cultural wrapping, irrespective of which culture, was essential. It was a matter of opportunity that it was through and in the ancient Jewish culture that God's word first came to humanity. An inculturated christian faith should follow the same process. That means, evangelization should be based on the principle of incarnating the christian faith in the people's culture. In other words, Christ should not be presented as a stranger to any culture but rather as being born into the culture of the evangelized.

5.11.1.4 Inculturation as a means of evangelization

Inculturation is an interesting means of teaching the goodnews in our time. As a method of evangelization, inculturation strives to incarnate christian values and open the gospel message to human cultures. Without exception, evangelization is directed to individuals and to all cultures. It is also important to know that inculturation does not limit itself to a particular culture. This is because some people assume that evangelization is only for the foreign cultures or missions. Inculturation is for every culture and this means that every culture needs evangelization which must be Christ-centered. In support of the truth that evangelization must be Christ-centred, Andreas Wollbold in discussing *Verwirklichungen von Kirche als Wahlheimat* is totally correct to say that "Evangelisierung kann so die Spuren an Heimat im Blick auf Christus bekräftigen und ihre Richtung feststellen, und dies auch gerade da, wo sie unter den Gesetzen der Welt zu

---

413 Right from creation, God willst hat all men should come to the knowledge of truth and be saved (1Tim 2,4). As a result, God has not abandoned humanity since after having created man. He keeps on intervening in human history in order to direct humanity to a salvific end (Acts 10,34–35; Heb 1,1–2). Hence, the Council fathers emphatically state: "God has manifested himself since the dawn of creation to our first [...] watching over the human race in ongoing fashion" (DV 3). This is God's manifestation of his redemptive love for humanity.

verwehen drohen".[414] Pope John Paul II made a tremendous contribution to this point in his *Redemptoris Missio* that in today's world, from the viewpoint of evangelization, we can distinguish three situations that need to be addressed differently. The first is the situation of the mission *ad gentes* in the proper sense of the term. Bringing the gospel to peoples, groups and socio-cultural contexts in which Christ and his gospel are not known.[415]

Secondly, there are mature christian communities that are fervent in their faith, and have a sense of the universal mission, and in which the church carries out her activities and pastoral care. Here the pope seems to describe a situation that requires pastoral care and not evangelization. The third situation is what the pope calls an intermediate situation. Within countries there are entire groups of the baptized who have lost a living sense of the faith, or no longer consider themselves members of the church. In this situation "what is needed is a new evangelization or a re-evangelization".[416] In this third situation people needed their faith to be renewed and enlivened. Others have had a little or no training in the faith and essentially need to be evangelized with the basic gospel message. This is because there are today anti-gospel proclamations that are constantly being proclaimed to christians. Christians need to be regularly inspired, encouraged and formed in their faith in order to live a christian lifestyle. This formation in faith which is the goal of evangelization should not stand in isolation from the people's culture nor be opposed to it. Instead, the people's culture should be a means through which the authentic evangelization should be achieved. This requires tolerance and acceptance of people's cultures and their languages, and implementing them as vehicles of evangelization. Suffice it to say that the call to evangelize is, therefore, a call to inculturate. The fathers of the Vatican Council II were of this opinion and further explain: "evangelization means bringing the Good News into all the strata of humanity, and through its influence transforming humanity from within and making it new".[417] The transformation from within reminds us of the goal of evangelization which is "Bekehrung mit Taufe und die Einpflanzung der Kirche als sichtbare eucharistische Ortsgemeinschaft".[418] The church has been conscious of this fact in her missionary life and work. The Vatican Council II, therefore, emphasizes the need for cross-fertilization of theological ideas in the promulgation of the documents that would shape the way for future theological work and shape the course of inculturation. Thus, Vatican Council II rejects any object that presents itself as a hindrance on the way to the goal of this evangelizing mission, and instead "Der katholische Glaube muss sozusagen die guten und wertvollen kulturellen Aspekte aufnehmen und integrieren".[419] It distances itself, for example, from the bad effects in the development of the "constantinism" in the mission of the church. It is on record that Cardinal Suenens at the close of the Vatican Council II admits that: "Vatican

---

414 Wollbold, Andreas, Kirche als Wahlheimat, Studien zur Theologie und Praxis der Seelsorge (32): Beitrag zu einer Antwort auf die Zeichen der Zeit, Würzburg 1998, 272.
415 Cf. Pope John Paul II, Redemptoris Missio, Dec. 7 1990, no. 34.
416 John Paul II, Redemptoris Missio, Dec. 7, 1990, no.33.
417 E N, no. 18
418 Mendes, Heil für die Welt, 56.
419 Mendes, Heil für die Welt, 121.

II marked the end of several epochs and that it brought to a close the Constantinian era, the era of Christendom in the medieval sense, the era of the Counter-Reformation and the era of Vatican I".[420] So, the end of Constantine era brought it home to the church the positive effects of the separation between church and state which is necessary for the true freedom required for the mission of the church to evangelize. In order to do a proper evangelization of people within their cultural milieu, the task of inculturation since the Vatican Council II has been to convince some theologians and particularly those christians with more of colonial than christian missionary zeal that christianity could enter into marriage with other cultures. Christianity stands out on its own but makes use of the good values of any given culture in which it finds itself. It does not impose a particular cultural current upon a particular people outside such current. Instead, it replaces a cultural current with another in the process of authentic evangelization.

We must, however, admit that some people have wrongly understood the call to replace a cultural current with other good cultural currents and elements as a call to replace the Gospel with another Gospel, or simply put, with anti-christian sentiments or neo-paganism. This unfortunate misplacement is interpreted as resurgence of belief in idols and traditional practices that are connected with idols and other fetish beliefs and practices clung unto by christians in the name of culture. These are, of course, the very negative influences in our culture that urgently need divine illumination. Certain unchristian terminologies and names viz: osu, osuagwu, nwaosu, which exercise strong sentiments within the cultural society can be transformed to exercise a similar influence or sentiment in the same cultural society but in a christian dimension. Instead of "osuagwu" we can say "osuchukwu"; instead of "nwaosu" we can say "nwachukwu".[421] There are, however, problems associated with this whole process of inculturation. Below are a list of certain problems that militate against inculturating the authentic christian message in Igboland, especially, where it affects the proper use of the authentic Igbo word to steer up faith in Igbo people.

5.11.1.5 Problems of Inculturating Igbo word

Certain factors are presented as problems militating against proper incarnation of the gospel in our culture through the use of the authentic Igbo word. This section will attempt to discover and to analyze these problems.

---

420   Suenens, Leon Joseph, Introduction in Theology of Renewal, vol.ii, edited by Shook L.K., Montreal, 1968, 7; quoted by Donovan, in: The Church As Idea and Fact, Minnesota 1990, 34.

421   Osu is a cast system where a person was said to have been consecrated to one idol or the other giving that person a social stigma that runs in his or her family. How can a person born again with water and the Holy Spirit still be regarded as belonging to an Idol? How can a catholic belonging to the same Body of Jesus Christ discriminate against another catholic who is said to be an "osu"? Beliefs and practices associated with the old way of life inherited from our ancestors who did not know Christ should be discarded definitively. To achieve this end there is need to allow the divine illumination upon such unchristian terminologies and names some of which I mentioned above. Therefore, "osuagwu" which means "dedicated to agwu" (agwu is a deity) can be christianized as "osuchukwu" which means "dedicated to Chukwu" (Chukwu is the Christian God), and so on.

5.11.1.5.1 The system in formation houses

When we talk of formation houses, we mean those institutions for the training of men and women for the great work in the church as professed religious men and women, or as ordained ministers. For the purpose of precision, I would limit myself to discussing seminary formation only.

Despite the good intentions of the early foreign missionaries who might have given out their best in forming indigeneous seminarians at their time, low success is recorded in terms of these indigenes who later were to transmit the gospel message to the cultural environment to which they belonged. Wrong method in formation is responsible for this. These early missionaries, so to say, were biased about the culture of the indigenes and could not trust it as a medium for evangelization. Thus, the seminarians were trained in isolation from their culture and cultural environment. Offering a solution to this situation, Oliver A. Onwubiko emphasizes: "This too would imply, on the part of the church, that there is a basic recognition of that interdependency which the church accepts as a healthy ecclesial practice and must be based on a healthy African independence".[422] This african independence was lacking. Instead of interdependence which should be a two-way process of give and take between the church and the local culture, those missionaries preferred to condemn everything about the people's culture in order to establish their own. Thus, local language of the seminarians was prohibited in formation houses, liturgies were celebrated in foreign languages and symbols, seminarians were equally trained to speak foreign languages to the detriment of their mother tongue, and trained to emulate foreign cultures but knew little of their own culture. This made them strangers to the environment in which they were later to work as evangelizers. Record of low success became imminent. It is discouraging that this hostile attitude to the local culture in our seminaries has not improved even in our time when the formators themselves are indigenes. In theory, inculturation began to be a current issue that has attracted the official support of the church, but in practice, seminarians in various houses of their formation are made to believe that foreign languages such as English or Latin are preferable in the celebration of the liturgy to their mother tongue. Lectures are continued to be delivered in foreign languages, and as Angelika Mendes would put it: "die Priesterausbildung entspricht weitgehend europäischen Vorbildern und nicht den lokalen Anforderungen".[423] Speaking in mother language by any seminarian on training would attract a fine or punishment. If seminarians are trained to regard foreign languages and cultures as ideal, how does one expect them to be effective in using their local language to work among their own people after their ordination? If the barometer for measuring a qualitative seminarian is based on his ability to be fluent in foreign languages and versatile in foreign cultures to the detriment of his native language and culture, how does one expect him, after his priestly ordination

---

422 Onwubiko, Alozie Oliver, Echoes from the African Synod: The future of the African Church from present and past experiences, Enugu 1994, 53.
423 Mendes, Heil für die Welt, 34.

to make the words of the gospel perform in the hearts of his people among whom he must minister in their circumstances of language and culture? This is why an integral or holistic formation of african (Igbo) seminarians in their cultural circumstance is very important for the successful work of evangelization.

As a step towards the integral or holistic formation, I would suggest what I prefer to call a situated seminary formation, or better still, an inculturated formation. In this respect, philosophical and theological education of the seminarians are the two crucial areas that need a critical review. Ironically, education in these two courses is densely to be for the most part western and so are the textbooks used for these courses. Eventually, one discovers that what is learnt in the seminary is not often being implemented by the students when they go out because it is either not tested or not field oriented. We may come to the conclusion that the formation prolongs a culture gap and alienation leading to split personality, which is already common among many priests in Igboland. This is the effect of a clash between two world-views: the western world-view which forms the basis of formation and virtually all philosophical-theological categories on one hand; and the Igbo world-view that is the victim of missionary mental prejudices, on the other hand. Africanized (Igbonized) formation should imply an adequate knowledge of the actual people to be evangelized in terms of their history, their world-view and their situation in life. So, the priestly formation in Igboland should not be based on the principle of *noli me tangere* but rather on *tangere me*.[424] The former evokes a closed seminary system and prohibits seminarians from being themselves and discovering their talent. The later evokes an open seminary system that allows seminarians freedom to express themselves, and especially in showing one's talent. In general, the whole formation and study programme are to be virtually geared toward evangelization. This means that theological and even philosophical training while it should not in any way de-emphasize academic excellence, should place accent equally on praxis. This proposal boils down to an inculturated priestly formation leading surely to a new orientation to evangelization. That means, evangelizing a people in a way relevant to their concrete situation. Above all, our discussions would help to make the priests and the religious complete Africans (Igbos) as well as complete priests and religious. Thus, it will give rise to a type of evangelization that suits the circumstance of the people being evangelized because it would be drawn from the people's cultural heritage and given a Christocentric import.

5.11.1.5.2 Western-oriented nature of church doctrines and rites

Although the church in Igboland is over hundred years old (1885), and despite the fact that majority of the Igbo people are christians, nevertheless, there is this feeling among them that the church is a stranger in their land. This is often times expressed in what they say: "uka biara abia mana omenala di adi", this means, the church is a stranger but our culture remains. This is a pointer that the gospel message has not yet fully incarnated in the culture of the Igbo. The Igbo man has still numerous evi-

---

424 Noli me tangere encourages a passive participation, and in this case, in one's cultural milieu. Tangere me on the contrary encourages an active participation in such a milieu.

dences of how the church and the culture run parallel lines till today. The church's doctrines and rites are formulated in western or constantinian style and mentality and are intended to be inculcated in the non-western Christians:

> This legacy may be described as the Constantinian system, because this presumption was seeded in the fourth century, when the Roman Emperor Constantine granted the Christian church special favours and privileges. In subsequent centuries, the Christian church shaped the religious and cultural life of all Europe.[425]

This attitude tends to persist till the present day, and as long as this situation continues, the church will continue to have difficulties in convincing the natives that the church is their own. This experience is not peculiar to Igboland alone but extends to entire Africa. Writing on such an attempt by the early missionaries to South Africa to dominate the native way of life with western culture and mentality, Stilz G. writes: "Africans began to realize that however well they adapted themselves to Christian European culture, they would never be allowed complete integration in the colonial society or economic structures".[426] Expressing the same concern, Amalorpavadass D.S writes:

> On the one hand Christianity has projected a bad image of itself in the course of its missionary enterprise and in its work of evangelization during the last five centuries. The christianization of a country, the acceptance of the Gospel and the expression of young churches in these countries should also adopt the culture of the missionaries and their sending churches. The Gospel had the trade-mark of western Christianity. Correspondingly it contributed to the elimination or disparaging of the local cultures of the people evangelized. Christianization meant westernization in terms of socio-cultural life.[427]

The church as a mother should be ready to accommodate any meaningful suggestions that will help to dewesternize the formulation of certain doctrines and rites that are not attractive and appealing to non-western christians "for the church ideally is reformata simper reformanda (reformed and always reforming)".[428] In the spirit of the common faith we share, those theologians and missiologists who make sincere effort to contribute to the on-going process of inculturation should not be looked upon with distrust and contempt. These contributions, however, should not in any way go against the gospel message, nor the process of inculturating the gospel be an avenue of creating a new gospel.

5.11.1.5.3 More Rationalization

Igbo traditional religion, as an african traditional religion, is a natural religion that is based on the worship of God through natural objects: "The greatest handicap in the

---

425 Guder, Darrell Likens, (ed.), Missional Church: A vision fort he sending of the church in North America, Michigan 1998, 6.
426 Stilz, Gehard, (ed.), Colonies-Missions-Cultures in the English-speaking world: General and Comparative Studies, Tübingen 2001, 277.
427 Amalorpavadass, D.S., Gospel and Culture: Evangelization and Inculturation, Bangalore 1978, 11.
428 Kirk, Andrew, What is Mission?: Theological Explorations, Minneapolis 2000, 11.

study of African religion is that, unlike the major world-religions like Christianity and Islam, African religion is not a religion of the Book".[429] As I have earlier mentioned, that the Igbo religion is a natural religion does not mean that the Igbo are not rational beings. To prove my point, Metu E.I. writes: "Some authors have been bewildered by the high concept of God found among some African peoples. Their wonder is how primitive African tribes could have developed such a high concept of God".[430]

The Igbo use natural objects to portray their high level of natural intelligence. In this way, they are protagonists of both natural philosophy and natural theology. That the Igbo consider christian religion as full of rationalizations that has little or nothing to do with natural objects is a major problem for the incarnation of the christian gospel in Igbo culture. In chapter three, while discussing the Igbo traditional religion, we pointed out that the western missionaries had described the Igbo religion as primitive, native, and so on. The Igbo religion got this description because of its nearness to nature. Since the opposite of natural may be rational or abstract, the contention is: Can the more rationalized form of religion have a common course with the naturalized religion such that both are incarnated in each other to make an authentic religious person? Angelika Mendes answers in affirmation and offers solution on the attitude required of the christian missionary in order to achieve this aim: "Die Predigt,die für Erwachsene oft die einzige Glaubensunterweisung darstellt,sollte in einfacher Sprache die wahre Botschaft Jesu Christi vermitteln und auf den zentralen Kern des Glaubens sowie dessen Umsetzung ins konkrete Leben Bezug nehmen".[431] Furthermore, this research work suggests that a cordial relationship between the Gospel and culture is a sure means to make this aspiration possible.

5.11.1.5.4 The indigeneous ecclesiastical hierarchy

Part of the problem of inculturation is the church's hierarchy itself. By hierarchy I mean those who by divine will are placed at the high positions in the church as chief shepherds to coordinate the affairs of the church. In this case, we are not referring to foreign expatriates, but rather, the sons of the land who despite their root have preferred to despise their culture and have little or no interest in promoting the incarnation of the gospel message in their culture. Instead, they prefer to see the african church remain in eternity as a receiving church, as an externally induced church that has nothing to offer to the universal church. This attitude of some indigenous ecclesiastical office holders gave rise to the following comment from Marie-France Perrin Jassy: "It seems that the Catholic Church, with the entire liturgy centered in the person of the priest, does not offer sufficient outlets for the religious aspirations of the laity".[432]

---

429 Metu, African Religion in Western Conceptual Schemes, 23.
430 Metu, African Religion in Western Conceptual Schemes, 37.
431 Mendes, Heil für die Welt, 59.
432 Jassy, Perrin, Basic Community in the Africa Churches, New York 1973, 84.

On the contrary, Vatican II Council has always admonished the hierarchy with the following words: "Bishops should present the doctrine of Christ in a manner suited to the needs of the times, that is, so it may be relevant to those difficulties and questions which men find especially worrying and intimidating".[433] I would, however, like to commend the effort of Archbishop Anthony Obinna, an Igbo Archbishop of Owerri Archdiocese, who in the spirit of inculturating the gospel message in our land, introduced the very important event known as "Odenigbo Lectures". This is a forum where the Igbo are gathered annually, and through lectures and seminars, held in the authentic Igbo language, unite to make the gospel message incarnate in Igbo culture. This is the type of effort that is desirable. We are waiting to see this spread to the rest of the Igbo dioceses.

5.11.1.5.5 The dependent nature of the Igbo church

The Igbo church must move from a church of David dressed in borrowed cumbersome armoury of doctrinal formulations, liturgical practice, and architectural structures, to one dressed in one's proper military outfit. It must move from a dependent church to a church that is relevant to the local culture. There will be no understanding of the gospel except from the context of the people's previous understanding of themselves. Kirk J.A. has right by saying:

> The community of faith would have no grounds for fulfilling its various callings unless it had settled views on its central beliefs. Its theology would be trivial and vacuous. Freedom to leave the Father's house is always available, but in the absence of adequate frameworks for deciding on appropriate action away from home it soon turns into riotous living.[434]

A culture can receive the christian message only on its own terms, and "we must do everything possible to make all persons aware of their right to culture and their duty to develop themselves culturally and to help their fellows".[435] The idea of proclaiming the gospel message to a totally virgin ears and minds or better put, to a non-cultural natives, completely innocent of a predisposition is not realistic. So, inculturation is never a matter of choice but the reality demands that, and the dependent nature of the Igbo church today on imported cultures pose no small obstacle to the authentic incarnation of christianity in Igboland. I am not in any way against any foreign culture but the task of incarnating the gospel into the Igbo culture cannot be achieved without the church engaging in an honest and sincere dialogue aimed at improving relations between her (the church) and the Igbo culture and aimed at not only making the Igbo culture be seen as a receiver in the evangelizing mission of the church but equally as a giver.

---

433   G S, no. 13.
434   Kirk , What is mission?, 11.
435   G S, no. 60.

5.11.2 Dialogue

As long as two persons or more are united by a common interest which can either be cultural, religious, political, economic, ideological, educational or social, there arises the need for dialogue among them. How do we define dialogue? Rosseau R.W. defines dialogue as "A conversation on a common subject between two or more persons with differing views".[436] A very essential element in the above definition is conversation. This implies that more than one person is involved since one cannot converse with oneself alone, a second party is needed. Dialogue, therefore, is not a monologue. It is an interpersonal relationship. Rosseau R.W. goes on to outline the goal dialogue has set out to achieve, and in his words: "The primary goal of dialogue is for each participant to learn from each other".[437]

In order to achieve this goal, certain predispositions are necessary. Firstly, the partners who enter into dialogue must not understand dialogue as a debate or argument in which a partner had already, prior to dialogue, made up his mind on which side he remains no matter the trend the conversation takes. Such a dogmatic position does not give room for the process of learning from each other. Secondly, dialogue should not be understood as an assembly of enemies who are ready to devour each other at any given opportunity. Such a wrong idea of dialogue leads the participants to allot blames and insults on one another instead, and thereby giving the wrong signal that dialogue is a do or die affair. Dialogue, rather, is an attempt to communicate, to explain, to enlighten, to understand. In the words of Heinrich Ott: "Dialogue can lead to consensus in the sense that earlier differences are no longer regarded as divisive".[438] Thirdly, in dialogue, there is no superior or inferior partner. Every member of the dialogue should see himself as an individual who believes that he has something new to learn from the other, in as much as he himself may have something to offer too. So, dialogue is a two-way process of give and take. In dialogue, therefore, none of the members is "Mr Know All", and there is no master-servant relationship. Openness is an essential aspect of dialogue. It is this openness that creates condition of trust. It is equally this openness that makes one to be sincere in making his contributions. It is under this condition that the genuine truth can be arrived at, and the participants will be able to benefit by learning the truth that is expressed. Heinrich Ott, therefore, says:

> Dialogue is a basic human reality because we can be truly human only with others and because in this togetherness with others we are oriented to truth and possible meaning. The question of truth and meaning permeates our common work and our concern for the survival of individuals and the species.[439]

---

436 Rosseau, Richard, (ed.), Interreligious Dialogue: Facing the next frontier, vol. one, modern theological themes: selections from the literature, New York 1981, 34.
437 Rosseau, Interreligious Dialogue, 34.
438 Ott Hans, Dialogue-Ecumenical Context, in: The Encyclopedia of Christianity, vol.1, Köln 1999, 841.
439 Ott, Dialigue-Ecumenical Context, 840.

So, in dialogue, there is no hidden agenda, instead "Der Dialog zwischen Experten setzt Liebe und Wahrheit und eine klare Darstellung der jeweiligen Lehrposition voraus".[440] The truth is laid bare as it is, and one has the choice to accept it or to reject it. That is why sometimes dialogue is considered a risk, especially interreligious dialogue, because even though the goal is not conversion, one may find himself accepting the truth from the other partner, and finally be converted to it. Even at this, dialogue serves its need, for conversion should come through conviction and not by violence.

Virtues associated with dialogue, therefore, are openness, mutual trust, patience, acceptance, humility and docility to the truth. On the contrary, the vices that militate against dialogue include monologue, doctrinal imperialism, religious violence, pride, intolerance, fanaticism, fundamentalism, dogmatism and superiority complex. The form of dialogue that we are mainly concerned with in this context is interreligious dialogue, but how can we define it?

5.11.2.1 Interreligious Dialogue

This is coming together of people of different religions, committed to their various religions, with the aim of promoting deep and sincere relationship through mutual understanding of one another's convictions and tenets. So, the praxis of interreligious dialogue comes forth as a need to love and understand other believers, so as to avoid anarchy and violence, hatred, mistrust and intolerance that is fast becoming the order of the day: "Today there is great confusion in the diversity and division in the religions of the world. In the name of religion much life, property, civilization, culture and heritage had been destroyed".[441]

Surely, not only christians but also all the religions are affected deeply without dialogue today. We need collaboration, we need to learn from one another, we need to listen to one another. In the words of Rosseau R.W: "One of our sins in the past has been to absolutize the christian religion and theology, implying that the other religions were false, or at any rate not true".[442] In the centuries past, moral and physical forces were sometimes used to induce people to accept the christian faith. Speaking from the christian point of view, it is the basic right of a christian to proclaim the gospel of Jesus Christ to the world. But this proclaiming of Jesus Christ should in no way hinder the freedom of religion of the other person: "One of the key truths in Catholic teaching, a truth that is contained in the word of God and constantly preached by the Fathers, is that man's response to God by faith ought to be free, and that therefore nobody is to be forced to embrace the faith against his will".[443] In the practice of theology, therefore, the interreligious dialogue is certainly to be acknowledged.

---

440 Mendes, Heil für die Welt, 71.
441 Samartha, Stanley Jedediah, (ed.), Dialogue between men of living faith, papers presented at a consultation held at Ajaltoun, Lebanon, March 1970, Lausanne-Switzerland 1971, 95.
442 Rosseau, Interreligious Dialogue, 34.
443 D H, no.10

In today's pastoral situation, evangelization requires closer and intense relationship with the people of other religions, hence, the need for interreligious dialogue, and as a matter of fact:

> Interreligious dialogue cannot be merely a polite meeting of participants from different traditions who engage in swapping superficial information. Rather it must be a sharing from the heart-from the depths of each tradition, solidly rooted in spiritual experiences and supported by centuries of accumulated wisdom.[444]

In the encounter of dialogue, there will arise questions about one's own religious tradition, and one will have to destroy deep-rooted prejudices over other religions, or overthrow certain narrow concepts. One can in all certainty say that by dialogue, christians and others walk together towards truth. In this walking together, the old attitude of isolationism will be avoided: "Our knowledge of other traditions has been the product of isolation. We have known that other traditions existed, but have had little actual contact with those traditions".[445]

Lochhead D. goes on to explain that this isolation is today no longer understood as a problem caused by geographical locations of various traditions. The today's globalization and urbanization has proved that people of different faith exist side by side in the same city, and yet the religious isolation cannot be avoided. Lochhead was emphatic in saying: "Religious isolation is not simply a function of geography. Communities that are not isolated geographically can still be socially isolated".[446] If we want interreligious dialogue to grow and bear fruit, certain obstacles, apart from isolationism, must be overcome. Again, Lochhead goes on to enumerate hostility and competition as other obstacles that hinder the spirit of dialogue. History of religion is full of hostilities whether in the form of the Christian crusade or the Islamic Jihad: "The theology of hostility is not simply a christian phenomenon. The rhetoric of hostility can be discerned right across the ideological and religious spectrum of the world".[447] Sometimes, these hostilities are products of political or cultural manipulations. What may be the cause of such hostilities may be based on true or false assumptions. However, the resultant effect is often anarchy and killings in the name of God. Superiority complex on its part causes unhealthy competition. It has its foundation on the selfish presumption that one's religion is the custodian of the whole truth: "The different religions seem to say different and incompatible things about the nature of ultimate reality, about the modes of divine activity, and about the nature and destiny of man".[448]

Christianity proclaims that in Jesus Christ the fullness of truth is revealed. We accept this fundamental conviction of our christian faith. That does not mean that

---

444 Smock, David, Interfaith Dialogue and Peacebuilding, Washington D.C 2002, 49.
445 Lochhead, David, The Dialogical Imperative: A christian reflection on interfaith encounter, faith meets faith series, New York 1988, 5.
446 Lochhead, The Dialogical imperative, 6.
447 Lochhead, The Dialogical imperative, 13.
448 Hick, John, (ed.), Truth and Dialogue in World Religions: Conflicting Truth-Claims, Philadelphia 1974, 140.

we command other religions to follow our guidance or principles. Rather, christians and other adherents of other religions should through dialogue search for that eternal truth, and such a common search for the truth would indeed bring closer all the religions to know that we all are pilgrims on earth, coming from the same God, and indeed returning to the same God. Through this search, the dialogue partners can come to a fuller understanding that God has revealed himself and is salvifically present everywhere, even in religions. The christian ought not to see other religions as totally strange or as having no relationship to christianity. And on the part of the other believers, this type of dialogue involves a coming to the awareness of the truth that has been revealed in Jesus Christ. How can the church achieve this authentic dialogue with other religions?

5.11.2.1.1 The Church in dialogue with other religions

Jesus Christ's encounter with his disciples, on several occasions, in a dialogue about the divine truth, gives us a biblical background to our inquiry. Of course, we recall the Johannine narrative of the sort of interreligious dialogue between Jesus and the samaritan woman who came to draw water at Jacob's well (Jn 4,7–42). Although the goal of interreligious dialogue is not to convert, this encounter is one of the instances where interreligious dialogue led to conversion due to one's appropriate disposition to grasp the divine truth whenever and wherever one finds it. Jesus had other interreligious dialogues that did not necessarily lead to conversion (Cf. Jn 3,1–21; 3, 25–36; Lk 2,46–49).

The theological basis for interreligious dialogue is provided in the teachings of the church, and more explicit in the documents of the Vatican II Council: "they (Christians) should establish relationships of respect and love with those men, they should acknowledge themselves as members of the group in which they live, and through the various undertakings and affairs of human life they should share in their social and cultural life. They should be familiar with their national and religious traditions and uncover with gladness and respect those seeds of the word which lie hidden among them".[449]

This implies that the missionary has the important duty to listen and to discern. In this way, a genuine dialogue built on a profound respect for the other religions is established. The council goes further to admonish: "the church, therefore, urges her sons to enter with prudence and charity into discussion and collaboration with members of other religions. Let Christians, while witnessing to their own faith and way of life, acknowledge, preserve and encourage the spiritual and moral truths found among non-christians, also their social life and culture".[450] Christians are, therefore, required not only to preserve but also to promote the spirit-given values of truth and goodness in other religious communities. Not undermining the efforts of the church towards dialogue down different periods of the church history, one may be right to

---
449 A G, no. 11.
450 N A, no. 2.

conclude that the Second Vatican Council is regarded as an important beginning for the Catholic Church in contacting people of other faiths and their religious traditions. It is the Second Vatican Council that has changed many of the church's traditional exclusivist attitudes towards other religions and opened for us the way to theological insights in the context of other religions and articulated its attitudes towards plurality of culture and religious traditions. The basic perspective of the council has been the unity of the people of God. It has developed a positive approach towards the world religions in its declaration "Nostra Aetate". This declaration is the first conciliar document to deal with the church's relationship with other religions. The other documents like *Lumen Gentium* and *Ad Gentes* also make important references to the place of these religions in God's plan of salvation.

The council is merely an opening and pointer towards understanding the signs of our time. It invites us to revisit the theological parameters to understand them in the light of the new awareness of the reality of religious pluralism. Hence, the church opened three important secretariats that are oriented towards dialogue: secretariat for interreligious dialogue, secretariat for dialogue with non-believers, and secretariat for ecumenism. By so doing, the council tried to remove the narrow traditional image of the church. Its great contribution was a change of position and a new attitude towards non-christians. By taking this new course, the council became popularly known as a "Reform Council". It brought out in an authentic manner, the essential image of the biblical passages on the church, and widens the church's traditional reflections, especially the patristic. The council puts the church back on its novel course of real participation with the whole inhabited earth.

The spirit of the Vatican II Council is the will to renew the church and faith. The council did not intend to create a new tradition but in view of the changed and changing situation, to actualize and enliven it. In relation to non-christian religions and universal salvation, the document *Nostra Aetate* states that there are already a presence of God and manifestation of the Spirit who works and dwell in every human being.[451] In search of a real companionship outside the visible catholic church, the Vatican II Council proposes several notions that have positively influenced the catholic understanding of the members of other religions. The council now teaches that the catholic church does not deny anything true and holy in those religions, and recognizes also the possibility of salvation outside the church.[452] It was the first council ever to recognize the presence of revelation in the non-christian religions and the possibility of salvation for their members. The council gave answer for this recognition by explaining that those non-christian religions posses some sacred religious truths in them, which are approachable roads to salvation.[453] In order to be more explicit, *Lumen Gentium* aptly states: "Those who, through no fault of their own, do not know the Gospel of Christ or his church, but who nevertheless seek God with a sincere heart, and, moved by grace, try in their actions to do his will as they know it

---

451 Cf. N A, no.1
452 Cf. N A, no.2
453 Cf. L G, nos 14–16

through the dictates of their conscience-those too may achieve eternal salvation".[454] Nevertheless, the church is confronted today with the task to fully realize the Council's teachings both in the human society and in her relationship with non-christian religions. Consequently, it is necessary to be acquainted with these religions, to be fair and objective in judging them, and to go deeply into their roots in order to find their a knot and string for the trans-mission and proclamation of the Gospel of Jesus Christ. In a positive manner, the council encourages the christian to borrow from the customs and cultures of the natives everything which will be of a great help in propagating the Gospel of Jesus Christ, and in our particular situation I emphasize the importance of the local language. Despite the efforts of the council, there still remain certain pertinent questions: How far did the council go in its recognition of the positive values in the religious traditions themselves? What significance did it assign to them in God's design for the salvation of humankind? How did it conceive the relationship of christianity to other religions: as one-sidedly contributing to the salvation outside christianity or as one in encounter with other religious traditions for a mutual interaction, enrichment and reciprocal advantage? It is urgent that adequate answers should be found so that we can go forward in mutual respect and trust, and that a lot of progress may be achieved in the church's work of evangelization. Now, let us bring our discussion on dialogue nearer home by relating it to African (Igbo) traditional religion.

5.11.2.1.2 The church in dialogue with African (Igbo) religion

Igboland as part of the great african continent is disadvantaged when positioned among the global society. This is as a result of much political, social, cultural and religious factors which contribute to continuously retarding its growth and never desist from presenting it as a society without future. I am of the conviction that the Igbo's problems, whether they are political, social or economical, will be less complicated if there are religious harmony brought about by mutual trust and respect among the religionists. This can only come about by interreligious dialogue. Otherwise, Africa in general or Igboland in particular will remain like a battle ground where different foreign religions with their expansionist ambitions, struggle among themselves to the detriment of the native culture and religion, and thereby infringing on Igboland the much problems and burdens it has to carry. Therefore, there is urgent need for the church's mediation bearing in mind that we can no longer regard the world religions simply as existing side by side, rather we must view them together in interdependence and interaction, and the Igbo traditional religion should not be exempted.

In order to give the Igbo traditional religion its rightful position and be carried along in the process of mutual relationship through interreligious dialogue, a sincere effort is to be made in correcting the much misrepresentations and prejudices with which it has been described. Even the Second Vatican Council, inspite of its good intentions in its constitution on the church, did not overcome the misrepresentation and prejudice

---

454 Cf. L G, no. 16

completely when it speaks of those: "who in shadows and images seek the unknown God".[455] That the Igbo traditional religion has no literary source does not invalidate it. After all, it has the three basic elements that make a religion: faith, morality and worship. These are the pillars upon which the church's cooperation with it should be based. That the Igbo traditional religion has no holy writings does not mean that it is not documented. Of course, we should bear in mind that documentation does not refer to preservation of material writings alone. Thus, Igbo traditional religion with its doctrine and rituals are documented and preserved in various ways, viz: in signs and symbols, in music and dances, in prayers and ejaculations, in proverbs and riddles, in customs and beliefs, in names of persons and places, in rituals and festivals, in shrines, sacred places, works of arts, and so on. In a special way, Igbo traditional religion provides themes for traditional songs, and offers vehicles in myths. It is rich in folks-lores, proverbs, sayings, and indeed, the bane of Igbo philosophy. These are means of remembering the past, and they are preserved and transmitted from generation to generation. These oral tradition can be described as the unwritten scriptures of Igbo traditional religion. In this oral tradition are contained the ethos and history of the religious awareness of the Igbo. Symbols and art work, as well, form an essential documentation of Igbo traditional religion. May I quickly add that for the Igbo, God is too holy to be represented in fabricated images. In arts, the Igbo display their ingenuity of representation of symbolism and symbolic values. Although the place of arts in this religion is very profound, it does not make a representation of God in images. Again, in Igbo traditional religion, word of mouth is considered much more sacred than the written word. Spoken words are not tampered with. That is why ceremonies of vital importance like the marriage rite, initiation rite, and so on, are all performed with rituals and words. To break a verbal oath in Igbo traditional religion, therefore, is a great felony. Even though christianity and other foreign religions have put heavy strains on this traditional religion, it has been resilient because it is part of people's culture, and so, is their way of life.

In the recent past, the world has witnessed series of interreligious dialogue among the so called world religions to the negligence of the grass-root religions like Igbo traditional religion. Part of the reason for not have included Igbo traditional religion may be bias, and some scholars have even openly questioned the necessity of dialoguing with a religion that has no archives, no literary genre and no formal protagonists. They presume that such a religion will be an easy prey to the social changes, and that it would easily be conquered, evangelized and converted to christianity. From what we have discussed above, we can see that these assertions from some scholars are erroneous, and this type of thought has created a hindrance in incarnating the Gospel in Igbo culture, and unless the church takes its dialogue with Igbo traditional religion more seriously, christianity may remain a stranger on Igbo soil. Cardinal Maurice Otunga, the Kenyan Archbishop of Nairobi had earlier articulated this issue in the 1977 Synod of Bishops in Rome, where he denounced the old missionary methods to African religions and cultural heritage in which the cherished African values are con-

---

455 L G, no. 16.

sidered as a *preparation evangelii* that could be discarded and be conquered through christian evangelization. As a way forward, the cardinal called for the appreciation and acknowledgement of the new and dynamic image of the seeds of the word already present in Africa's traditional ways of being human and religious.[456] Likewise, The Episcopal Conference for Africa and Madagascar (SECAM), in its Synod in Rome in 1974, urged for the need of promotion of the particular incarnation of christianity in each country, in accordance with the genius and talents of each culture, so that a thousand flowers may bloom in God's garden.[457] The seventy bishops that participated in this Synod declared unanimously and in unequivocal term, that christian life in Africa was insufficiently incarnated in African ways, customs and traditions. They pointed out that the christian life was very often only lived at the surface without any real link of continuity with the genuine values of traditional religions.[458] Cardinal F. Arinze of Nigeria, the former president of the pontifical council for inter-religious dialogue, observes that even if African traditional belief seemed detachable from the supernatural faith, it is the duty of theology to relate this belief to the christian message of salvation and to preserve the same world-view from the erosion of religious pluralism. Theology will be able to achieve this if its pastoral aspect is human-centred and does not practice exclusivism. I, therefore, totally agree with Andreas Wollbold who says "Je mehr sich Pastoral somit auf die menschliche Seite einläßt, um so mehr entspricht sie ihrer gottgegebenen Sendung, und umgekehrt".[459] There is the need to strengthen African communion, which gives rise to the examination and inquiry of how the Good News of salvation can penetrate into the life of Africans, especially, into the religious and cultural conditions of christians in that continent, using this element as basis prepared by the divine providence.[460] So, there is immediate need for this dialogue, and we outline below the necessity of this interreligious dialogue.

5.11.2.1.3 The necessity of interreligious dialogue

The world has known much conflicts, hatred, divisions and wars. Most often, these phenomena are caused by religious factor, and when other factors like politics and economy are responsible, there is still manipulation of religion in order to realize the selfish interest. So, religion can be a dangerous instrument in the hands of evil-minded individuals, and being that any given society is an amalgamation of individuals with different religious affiliations, any spark in this direction can result to disas-

---

456 Cf. Otunga, Martin, African Culture and Life-Centered Catechesis, art. in:AER, 20/1, 1978, 65–68.
457 Cf. Bishops of Eastern Africa, Report on the Experiences of the Church in the work of Evangelization in Africa, art. in: AER, 17/1, 1975, 43.
458 Cf. Bishops of Eastern Africa, Report on the Experiences of the Church in the work of Evangelization in Africa, art. in: AER, 56–58.
459 Wollbold, Andreas, Pastoraltheologie, Homiletik, Religionspädagogik, Paderborn 2001, 34.
460 Cf. Arinze, Francis, The Church and Nigerian Culture, Onitsha 1973, 112.

trous consequences. Nigeria is a study-case where such spark has resulted to religious conflicts mainly between Christians and Moslems. Pastor Bitrus from Jos, one of the affected cities in northern Nigeria gives his explanations:

> Die Ideologie der islamischen Fundamentalisten erreichte auch Nigeria und viele Hassprediger aus dem arabischen Ausland konnten in den Moscheen zur Gewalt aufrufen. So waren die Christen plötzlich nicht mehr Freunde und Nachbarn, sondern Ungläubige, die bekerht oder vertrieben gehörten. Und diese schrecklichen Feindbilder kriegt man nicht mehr so einfach aus den Köpfen.[461]

Besides, similar sparks in the direction of religion have got similar consequences. The prisoner of Iran/Iraq 1982 war, Nazar Hasquil from Iraq has the following experiences: "Für die Iraner war Nazar nicht nur ein verachteter Kriegsgegner. Er war auch noch ein Christ, ein Ungläubiger. Und so hatte er doppelt zu leiden".[462] Other instances are abound that show how deep and strong the religious tensions in our world have reached. To add to these instances: "Rund 30 bewaffnete Muslime haben in Mominpura Thaiki in Südostpakistan eine christliche Kirche schwer beschädigt und einige Häuser in der Nähe angezündet".[463] Although the instances above are some of the reported conflicts between christians and moslems, we should be quite aware that religious conflicts are not limited to christians and moslems alone. All the religions in the world cannot claim innocence of this fact. In Igboland which is our area of concern, we hear of "Olu Ezi na Uno", that means, family ministration. It is an attempt by some christian ministers to bring liberation to family members from sicknesses, poverty and various other problems through what they call "healing from the family root". In actual fact, this may be a violation of the fundamental principle of interreligious dialogue because these christian ministers end up rooting and carting away the cherished valuable objects of traditional religious worship found in the family, sometimes against the will of some of the family members. It happens that in some cases, an adherent of the traditional religion in the family may stand the risk of being identified as a witch simply because he does not belong to the christian folk. Christian crusades in Igboland offer opportunities for the vandalization of sacred objects of worship in various sacred shrines of the Igbo traditional religion. Having been empowered by the itinerant preacher-minister, the over-zealous christians, full of fundamentalism, are determined to destroy what they should rather preserve, and thereby making the road to interreligious dialogue very rigorous.

In the face of these religious tensions in our world of today, one does not hesitate to see the necessity of interreligious dialogue for harmony and peace in the world, as well as for proper incarnation of the Gospel in our culture, most especially by appreciating those values in the culture, particularly the language, and utilizing them for effective evangelization. So, the point I have been trying to establish is that an introduction of the authentic Igbo word into the celebration of the church's sacraments can

---

461 Hilfsaktion Märtyrerkirche (HMK), Wir müssen mit einer Stimme sprechen, in: Stimme der Märtyrer, no. 38 (2006), 11.
462 Hilfsaktion Märtyrerkirche (HMK), Wir müssen mit einer Stimme sprechen, 7.
463 Hilfsaktion Märtyrerkirche (HMK), Wir müssen mit einer Stimme sprechen, 8.

come about only through authentic inculturation which is realizable through sincere dialogue. Below are some of my personal recommendations to this effect.

5.12 Recommendations

The following recommendations are necessary for effective performance of Igbo words in the celebration of the sacraments in our Igboland. I must repeat; these recommendations of mine are ways of showing how the concept of J.L.Austin's performative word can contribute positively and pastorally to the effective use of Igbo words in the work of proper evangelization of the Igbo people. My emphasis on Igbo word is because I am writing within the context of Igbo society. These recommendations are meant to offer the average Igbo man and woman the opportunity to embrace christianity in the most authentic way and practice it as an authentic Igbo christian.

5.12.1 The right disposition of the agents of evangelization

Below are discussions on the right dispositions the indigenous priests, religious and lay faithful should acquire to be pastorally effective in their teaching apostolate among the natives.

5.12.1.1 Priests and religious

Earlier in this chapter, I have explained that in various houses of formation, vernacular is highly prohibited for seminarians and aspirants under formation. Any seminarian or aspirant caught in the act of speaking his or her mother-tongue is fined or punished. Even lectures and the entire seminary life are centered on foreign languages and culture. Holy Masses in Igbo language are only allowed once or twice in a week. The opportunity to recite the rosary commonly in Igbo language is very rare., and therefore, majority of seminarians who later became priests cannot lead the faithful confidently in the recitation of the rosary in vernacular. Such priests and religious, instead, isolate themselves from visiting marian groups, not simply out of lack of interest, but out of their inability to lead in such prayer sections. A good number of our priests and religious, today, cannot celebrate the holy liturgies, especially, the Holy Mass entirely in Igbo language with much ease. This problem is not unexpected. It is often said that practice makes perfect. Since as seminarians in formation, these priests and religious lacked the opportunities of being groomed in their language, how does one expect them to perform wonders as priests?

That the Gospel message is often times uninteresting to our people depends largely on the manner and the language it is being presented. Angelika Mendes puts it better by saying: "Manchmal wird die Verkündigung nicht gehört, weil die Welt taub ist, sondern weil die Hirten stumm oder ihre Worte kraftlos sind."[464] From current calculations, not many people attend Masses celebrated by a priest who is considered as incapable of expressing his Gospel message in the language of the people. For the people who attend such Masses, it may be because they have no alternative, and they do so out of faith.[465] There is even the danger of the people deserting the church and finding solace among our separated brethren once they can satisfy this need of listening to the gospel message in their authentic native language. So, it will be a good idea if in our seminaries and religious houses, formation is done in the native language. The academic formation, the philosophy and theology that are to be vital companions in the priest's teaching apostolate should be done in the mother-tongue for effective and fruitful apostolate. The spiritual aspect of the formation, the liturgy of the hours should be celebrated in Igbo language so that the prayers of our lips should be part and parcel of our life. In other words, priests and religious who are the primary agents of evangelization, therefore, should begin early enough , as seminarians and aspirants , to be disposed towards the Igbo language right from the formation houses. They should be disposed to love the language as their own, be dedicated in learning all the aspects of its speech genre, and be ready to apply them intelligently in the field of apostolate. On such proper application, Anyanwu C.C.U writes: "Post initiation faith drilling lessons punctuated with Igbo proverbs should be introduced [...] Folklores should be used to explain more deeply the nature of the rite of initiation-Baptism, Confirmation and First Holy Communion".[466]

5.12.1.2 Lay Faithful

Because of the hierarchical structure of the church in which at the parochial level, the priest stands as the sole authority under whom the lay faithful diligently live out their rightful christian obligations, there is , among majority of the natives, the wrong understanding of Catholicism as "Uka Fada", that means the church of the clergy.[467] This is of course, a wrong interpretation of Catholicism and a wrong interpretation of hierarchical structure of the church.

---

464 Mendes , Heil für die Welt, 59.
465 We equally recognize the fact that there are priests who by their talent would be eloquent but are incapable because of the following reasons: stammering, nervousness, fast speech, and son on. Special attention should be given to such priests so as to help them overcome their various predicaments.
466 Anyanwu , The rites of initiation, 329.
467 To the present, what we have among the Igbo is an ultra-clerical church. When most Igbo want to differentiate the catholich church from other christian denominations they call it "Uka Fada", that is, literally, the church that belongs to the Reverend Father. But it has other nuances. It means the church whose leader and chief functionary is called Fada (Reverend Father) in contradistinction from the protestants whose leaders are called pastors. It also implies the church in which everything depends on the "Fada", in which only the priest has the say, in which he is the person who really matter.

In order to correct this wrong notion, the Second Vatican Council insists: "Indeed, the Church can never be without the lay apostolate; it is something that derives from the layman's very vocation as a Christian [...] Laymen have countless opportunities for exercising the apostolate of evangelization and sanctification". [468] In the local church, therefore, efforts are made to engage the lay faithful in the liturgical and pastoral life of the church. The identification of the laity as an important partner in the mission of the church in Africa was emphasized by Bishop James Sangu from Tanzania in a paper he delivered on evangelization in Africa in the second sitting at the synod of Bishops on 28th September 1974 in Rome, and Angelika Mendes presents the stand of the Bishop in the following words: "Die Wichtigkeit einer größtmöglichen Teilnahme der Laien am kirchlichen Leben sei der Kirche in Afrika bewusst. Die Laien zeigten bereits rege Beteiligung auf allen Ebene kirchlicher Aktivitäten".[469] At the celebration of Holy Mass and other liturgies, the lay faithful are permitted to undertake the readings and participate in the prayer of the faithful. In other pastoral ministries, the lay faithful are encouraged to play active roles. They are needed to assist the priest in the apostolate of impacting catechesis[470] on the young people, holding Sunday instructions, and organising moral instructions in various schools. They are to help in teaching the young couples preparing for marriage, as well as, instructing the new converts or the fallen Catholics who wish to return to the church.[471] So, in the spirit of Vatican II, the church in Igboland practices inclusivism of the lay faithful in the exercise of her mandate to evangelize the people.

Sometimes, what the church experiences from these lay collaborators turns out not to be satisfactory. At the Eucharistic celebration, for instance, some of the lay readers

---

468 A A, nos. 1 and 6.
469 Mendes, Heil für die Welt, 23.
470 All in all, it can be taken here that catechesis is an education of children, young people and adults in the faith, which includes especially the teaching of Christian doctrine imparted, generally speaking, in an organic and systematic way, with a view to initiating the hearers into the fullness of Christian life. Accordingly, while not being formally identified with them, catechesis is built on a certain number of elements of the church's pastoral mission that have a catechetical aspect, that prepare for catechesis, or that spring from it. These elements are: the initial proclamation of the Gospel or missionary preaching through the kerygma to arouse faith, apologetics or examination of the reasons for belief, experience of Christian living, celebration of the sacraments, integration into the ecclesial community, and apostolic and missionary witness. Nevertheless, the specific aim of catechesis is to develop, with God's help, an as yet initial faith, and to advance in fullness and to nourish day by day the Christian life of the faithful, young and old. It is in fact a matter of giving growth, at the level of knowledge and in life, to the seed of faith sown by the Holy Spirit with the initial proclamation and effectively transmitted by baptism. Catechesis aims therefore at developing understanding of the mystery of Christ in the light of God's word, so that the whole of a person's humanity is impregnated by that word (Cf. Catechesi tradendae, 18 and 20).
471 Angelika Mendes holds a similar view in describing the functions of the catechists in the following words: "Sie unterrichten die Menschen vor Ort im Glauben und in der kirchlichen Lehre, führen sie zum Verständnis der Bibel, lehren sie Gebete und liturgische Antworten, bereiten Interessente auf Taufe und Ehe vor, besuchen die Kranken, beerdigen die Toten, halten Wortgottesdienste und bauen kleine christliche Gemeinschaft auf" (Mendes, Heil für die Welt, 113).

are not audible enough for the participants to understand them. In some other situation, the reader is loud enough but could hardly pronounce any word well. Even most of the lay collaborators who help in moral instructions or catechetical apostolate often lack the depth knowledge of the church's theology, and as a result, they could not attend to certain theological questions should such questions come. Stressing further on these problems Angelika Mendes writes: "An vielen Stellen kamen die Laien zur Sprache. Sie seien in den meisten Ländern unvorbereitet,ungenügend ausgebildet und unzureichend religiös gebildet [...] wenn die Kirche die Laien nicht verlieren will, muss sie ihren Bedürfnissen mehr Aufmerksamkeit schenken und Strukturen schaffen, die Zusammenarbeit erleichtern, Klerikalismus vermeiden und die Laien gut vorbereiten".[472] First of all, these lay collaborators should be properly disposed in order to be efficient. What do I mean by this ? Necessary assistance that would help them to be more efficient should be provided. We should not, for example, be contempted that someone has volunteered himself to be reading at Mass. Instead, a formal school for lay readers should be founded and through proper certification should one qualify to read in the church as a lector. In order to obtain qualified moral and catechetical instructors too, the local church should invest in training such personnels by establishing a theological institute where these lay faithful are educated in the church's theology for effectiveness in their teaching apostolate. Similar suggestion was made by Anyanwu C.C.U when he proposed the establishment of liturgical institution in Igbo dioceses.[473] The importance of proper training for the lay collaborators is also emphasized by Angelika Mendes because "Als bestes Mittel und erster Schritt der Evangelisierung in unserer Zeit wird die Katechese gennant. Dementsprechend wichtig sei die gute Ausbildung von Katechisten, die in manchen Ländern als erste Glaubensverkünder unersetzlich seien".[474] I hereby commend the effort of one of the Igbo Bishops, Dr Hilary Okeke of Nnewi diocese, who has already thought in this direction and has established "St Paul's theological institute" in his diocese to satisfy this need.

St Paul's School of Theological Studies, Nnewi, is an initiative of our Local Ordinary, Most Rev. Dr. Hilary Okeke, to respond to a prevailing religious situation in our area. Presently in our country, Catholic Christians are being subjected to a very aggressive proselytism by the Evangelical and Pentecostal denominations. Armed with the power of American Dollar, these religious groups bombard average Catholics with their anti-Catholic doctrines at any available opportunity, in the market places and social gatherings. This has drawn away no small a number from the Catholic faith. In fact, a recent survey reveals that seven out of every ten new adherents of these groups are either catholics who maintain double religious affiliation or ex-catholics who have completely left the church. In addition, some practicing catholics often backslid into traditional religious practices in the face of some life challenges. The christian doctrine they learnt in their early years while preparing

---

472 Mendes , Heil für die Welt, 43 and 44.
473 Cf. Anyanwu , The rites of initiation, 378.
474 Mendes , Heil für die Welt, 42.

for the Sacraments of Initiation often prove inadequate to sustain them in the face of bigger life challenges. They grow in knowledge in other areas while remaining infants in the Faith. The School which is affiliated to the Catholic Institute of West Africa (CIWA), Port Harcourt offers Diploma in Theology as well as Certificate in Theology and Certificate of Attendance. It is a four-year-weekend (Saturdays only from 9am to 4pm) Programme. Graduates from this School can also be gainfully employed as Moral Instruction teachers in primary and secondary schools as well as in various church institutions in the country. The school took off in September 19, 2009 with 153 (one hundred and fifty three) students. The number was restricted to the space available. The official opening and maiden matriculation was held on 23rd January, 2010. The picture of the Bishop, with some of the staff and students is enclosed. The professors are made up of mainly Priests from within and outside the Diocese who are specialists in their various fields. We have about 20 [Twenty] of these Resource Persons. This school affords us the much desired opportunity to carry out formative and developmental programmes designed for our children and youths. The School of Theology is in session only on Saturdays from 9am to 4pm, from the Middle of September to June, while July to the middle of September is holidays, thus Mondays to Fridays as well as the holidays period are for the following youths' and children's programmes:

* Regular Secretarial and Computer Studies for young people to prepare them for job market especially those who have no means of University education.
* Evening Catch-up lessons for primary school pupils who are slow in learning.
* Catechism classes for kids preparing for various Sacraments.
* Seminars and Workshop for youths
* Computer programming
* Career discernment & choice
* Skill acquisition
* Responsible Citizenship and Leadership Training
* Sex, drugs, dressing, traffic codes etc.
* Youth and Evangelization
* Extramural Classes on key Subjects
* Conventions for various children and youth associations in the Diocese, like the Block Rosary Children, Boys Scouts, Altar Severs etc.

This is a step in the right direction and I wish other Igbo Bishops will soon emulate this.

5.12.2 Specific areas of inculturation

There are certain important areas that demand urgent attention so that Igbo words can effectively perform in the hearts and minds of Igbo christians. Below are few of these areas.

5.12.2.1 Prayer books

There is a great percentage of illiteracy in Africa, including Igboland.[475] This is a great hindrance, especially in the hinterland. Since most of the prayer books are written in foreign languages, and priests have familiarized themselves with praying in foreign languages right from formation houses, there arises the need of praying for the people and with the people in the language they understand.

In the spirit of Vatican II Council, attempts have been made in translating certain official prayer books including some parts of "Breviary". These attempts have got a very high record of failure because the translators did not take note of the people's speech genre which we enumerated in chapter three of this work. Not only that, most of the prayers lack Igbo originality in terms of the terminologies involved. For example, when the purgatorians gather to pray, the translated version of their prayer book maintains the word "purgatory" when encountered in the cause of the prayer. We are still too blind to see that our poor Igbo christians need to understand what purgatory means in Igbo word. Another example, when marian group prays, one notices that the word "virgin" associated with our mother Mary is equally maintained, and most of the pious men and women who pronounce this word, at times badly, do not even understand the meaning: Are there no proper Igbo words for purgatory and virgin? It will be of a great help if these official prayer books and all their contents are properly translated into the native language, and all the various aspects of the people's speech

---

475 It could be recalled that establishment of schools was the most successful strategy which the early missionaries adopted to win converts among the Igbo natives. Any study of the development of western deucation n south-east Nigeria that denies this fact should be considered as not sincere. The church had played a leading role in the struggle to entrench her influence and participation in education in this part of the country. So, with acts of charity on one side and western education on the other side, the early missionaries were able to gather around them a group of converts comprising freed men and slaves, adults and children. These categories of people formed the pioneer of the first catholic school in Igboland. Initially, certain factors prevented the western education from spreading to the hinterland. These factors included the inviting facilities provided at Onitsha at that time by the presence of the trading companies which made communication with the outside world much easier and penetration into the interior would result in a loss of these advantages. There was as lack of personnel resources. More important perhaps was the hostility of the Royal Niger Company to the catholic missionaries and to the riverrine people. Of course, we do not ignore the frequent wars between neighbouring Igbo communities and the difficulties and dangers of travelling in the interior before 1900. With the arrival of Joseph Shanahan in the opening years of the 20th century the school apostolate reached its distinctive feature and advancement through the introduction of what was known as 'Bush Schools', which was synonymous with Church-schools or Catechuminate schools. Part of the reason among other reasons for the movement into the interior was that the missionaries discovered that the densely populated interior held vast potentialities for a rich missionary harvest. (Cf. Abernethy D.B., Church and State in Nigerian Education, Ibadan 1966; Afigbo A.E., "The Mission, the State and Education in South-eastern Nigerian" in Fashole-Luke E. (ed.), Christianity in Independent Africa, London 1978; Fajana A., Education in Nigeria 1842–1939, Ibadan 1978; Isichei E., A History of the Igbo People, London 1976; Abernethy D.B., The Political Dilemma of Popular Education, Califonia 1969).

genre taken into account, so that our people can benefit from them. By translating, for example, the words "purgatory" or "virgin" into Igbo they (the words) would in turn impact a meaningful influence on the local christians who pronounce them whether at prayer or at christian instructions, at catechesis or at various occasions in which they are mentioned. This influence that the interpreted version of "purgatory" or "virgin" has on Igbo christians by which they totally embrace these entities and are motivated by them should be considered in the light of the J.L.Austin's three senses whereby saying something is doing something or in saying something or by saying something an act is performed.[476]

5.12.2.2 Liturgical books

Apart from "Usoro Emume" (Meßbuch), Sunday missal, the New Testament and the book of rituals that are already translated into Igbo language, certain other liturgical books need to be translated into the native language of the people. Even the above mentioned translated liturgical books could not be properly or completely translated, and this is a problem in liturgical celebrations. Where the translations are not properly done, it becomes difficult to grasp what the translator is actually saying. Anyanwu C.C.U cautions:

> There is need for a uniform translation of all liturgical texts for use in the dioceses of Igboland. This will not only enhance liturgical education but equally promote active and full participation in the life of the church as the liturgical celebrations unfold it.[477]

Because the weekday missal is not yet translated, both the priests and the lay leaders have no other alternative than to engage in direct personal translation.[478] The consequences of such free and personal translations is outlined by Anyanwu C.C.U in the following way:

> Where different texts are used for the celebration of the sacraments of initiation among people of the same language group, the result could be a communication of confusion rather than the experience of the biblical Pentecost where all heard the same message being proclaimed simultaneously in their own language.[479]

Again, Anyanwu C.C.U emphasizes on the use of a uniformed liturgical texts by saying: "The use of the uniform liturgical texts within a cultural area of the same language will protect individual officiating ministers at liturgical celebrations from seeking to privatize the liturgy".[480]

The translated book of rituals tries to provide solution for celebrations of various sacraments and blessings at various occasions in the native language, but again, it limits itself with those occasions that are contained in the foreign version without

---

476 Cf. Austin, How To Do Things With Words, 12.
477 Anyanwu, The rites of initiation, 329.
478 Anyanwu, The rites of initiation, 262.
479 Anyanwu, The rites of initiation, 329.
480 Anyanwu, The rites of initiation, 329.

including those occasions and events that are traditionally Igbo, for example, New Yam Festival. Again, priests make up by spontaneous prayer which naturally may be inconsistent, and the choice of words may be ridiculous. This is very serious. Translations will often be either beautiful but unfaithful to the original, or faithful but ugly and irrelevant. The insufficiency of translation is now accepted as a matter of fact, especially in non-western countries. The fuse of the vernacular has made the liturgy intelligible but not closer to the heart of the people. Beneath every translation is a message originally communicated to another people. A translation, even in paraphrase form, cannot adequately transmit this message to the people of this age and culture without breaking away from its original mode of expression. Inculturation of the liturgical texts, therefore, may necessarily lead to recomposition of the already existing foreign texts in a befitting local language of the people without offending the church's guidelines on liturgy.[481] In affirmation, the Council Fathers conclude: "provision shall be made, when revising the liturgical books, for legitimate variations and adaptations to different groups, regions and peoples, especially in mission countries".[482] A commission of Igbo experts should be set up and charged with the task of producing approved versions of native liturgical books of rites and rituals that accommodate various local festivals in which christians are encouraged to participate, and such that the wordings of these versions are properly chosen and theologically approved: "Free translations of liturgical texts have to be avoided".[483] Again, while trying to avoid the wrong interpretation of J.L.Austin's concept of performative word to mean "native language", we should at the same time understand that native language as language offers utterances opportunities to perform. Therefore, authentic translations and effective use of liturgical books lead to proper sowing of the christian faith on Igbo soil and in the hearts of the Igbo faithful, and in which case J.L.Austin would be interpreted to be saying: the utterance of the sacred words in the liturgical books would perform by leading to effective evangelization and active native Christians.[484]

5.12.2.3 Use of Igbo names and titles

In chapter three of this work, we discussed how Igbo names and titles influence the actions of the bearers. So, these names and titles are action-oriented, and are much appreciated by both the giver and the bearer. Because they are rich in meanings, and because they are not against the christian principles, the native bearers prefer them to foreign names which in most cases are difficult to be pronounced and to be understood.[485]

---

481 Cf. S C, nos. 37–40.
482 S C, no. 38.
483 Anyanwu, The rites of initiation, 329.
484 Cf. Austin , How To Do Things With Words, 12.
485 Cf. Austin, How To Do Things With Words, 276; see also canon 855.

It would be more beneficial if native names and titles which are accepted by christianity should be widely embraced by the local church at the celebration of the sacraments of Baptism and Confirmation.[486] I said widely because experience shows that instances where Igbo names are used for Baptism are very few, and it is as if to say that it is a taboo even to adopt Igbo names in Confirmation. To clarify on this point further, Anyanwu C.C.U gives a sympathetic account of past experiences on this issue, and he writes: "There have been reported incidences of clerical ministers who refuse to administer Baptism to parishioners because they were not ready with a name after a saint for their children as they present them for Baptism not minding that the vernacular names they preferred to call their children were quite in line with true christian sentiments".[487] The late Archbishop of Onitsha in Igboland, Stephen N. Ezeanya, did make a compilation of Igbo christian names, but proper implementation of these names is still lacking. The same implementation should be extended to ecclesiastical titles. Authentic Igbo version to these titles should be applied, and this would be more impressive on the natives, and at the same time not harming the christian values associated with these titles. I propose the following Igbo versions to these ecclesiastical titles : Pope (Nna Ora); Archbishop (Eze Nnukwu Ukochukwu); Religious sister (Nwa Ada Uka). It is really very surprising and disappointing that after a hundred years since the advent of christianity in Igboland, there is yet no Igbo versions to these and similar ecclesiastical titles, and our Igbo people, most of whom are not literate continue to practice their faith on borrowed words.[488]

Until the native names and titles are properly incarnated in the native culture, the impact of the foreign names and titles we bear may not achieve the desired effect in the hearts of many Igbo christians who do not even understand what they mean. I am not trying to sound anti-foreign names and titles but instead I am trying to expose the same difficulty J.L.Austin had when considering how to define the performative

---

486 In order to show how the use of local names for Baptism or Confirmation would be appreciated, Anyanwu C.C.U narrates a past experience: "It once happened in the 1990s that a seminary rector forced English christian names on some candidates to be admitted into the seminary because the candidates were bearing only vernacular names without supplementary English names after the saints in the Roman Canon of saints. Such students who have had names of patron saints forced on them whereas such names names have no relevance to their particular circumstances in life, have stayed all through life fighting the imposition by rejecting being addressed by those names. The result is that such candidates accommodate these names during the school periods for fear of the school authority, but afterwards they are ready to fight it out with anybody who dared to address them with these names outside the school premises" (Anyanwu, The rites of initiation in Christian liturgy and in Igbo traditional society, 329).

487 Anyanwu, The rites of initiation, 329.

488 Other ecclesiastical titles that have yet no Igbo version include seminarian, religious brother, nun, monk, deacon, ecolyte, lector, and so on. What we have been doing so far has been simply borrowing these foreign titles as they are and imposing them on our people, and most of these natives could neither pronounce them well nor understand their meaning. They simply accept them as an act of faith. How then should we expect that these borrowed words would in any way influence them in a meaningful way?

more clearly.[489] J.L.Austin suggested a list of performative verbs that should help to define when an utterance is performative even though he acknowledged the limitations of such a list of performatve verbs.[490] Likewise, I propose the use of Igbo names in baptism and confirmation even though a comprehensive list of such names may be difficult to achieve because I mentioned earlier in chapter three that Igbo society is marked with various dialects.

5.12.2.4 Use of local compositions

Songs appeal to the hearts, minds and emotions of the Igbo. While discussing traditional songs in chapter three of this work, we came to the conclusion that every occasion has its proper songs in which the wordings are suitably chosen and properly arranged to offer the best explanation of what is being celebrated, and thereby motivating the audience to act accordingly. We must recognize the fact that Igbo traditional songs have their own peculiar melodies, rhythms and styles of composition in which the various aspects of Igbo speech genre like proverbs, idioms and riddles play great roles. The problem with our today's Igbo liturgical hymns is their lack of these speech genre, and this makes them to remain foreign to the ears of the Igbo. In view of this, Fathers of Vatican II Council issue the following directive:

> In certain countries, especially in mission lands, there are people who have their own musical tradition, and this plays a great part in their religious and social life. For this reason their music should be held in proper esteem and a suitable place is to be given to it, not only in forming their religious sense but also in adapting worship to their native genius.[491]

Our local composers have a very big responsibility of composing songs that appeal to our people both in terms of employing the Igbo speech genre and the Igbo melodies and rhythms. They should always bear in mind that "the importance of music in African religious life is that it gives expression to the deepest feelings, but it is not only feelings, for it points to belief in the life force that underlies religious thought".[492] Analizing the importance of suitable music in christian liturgy we read: "sie ist als Kommunikationsbrücke zu sehen, oder – wenn man so will – als Kommunikationskrücke. Man kann sich auf sie stützen, man kann auf ihr gehen, man kann sich auch auf ihr ausruhen [...] sie kann die Gefühle wecken und Kommunikation in Gang bringen".[493] The songs must be theological , and this means, „the texts intended to be sung must always be in conformity with Catholic doctrine.[494] This is in the understanding that "der Lauf des Evangeliums vollzieht sich auf dem Zwillingsweg des

---

489 Cf. Austin , How To Do Things With Words, 67.
490 Cf. Austin, How To Do Things With Words, 67 and 83.
491 S C, no. 119.
492 Parrinder , Religion in Africa, 77.
493 Arbeitskreis für Gottesdienst und Kommunikation (ed.), Liturgische Nacht: Ein Werkbuch Jugenddienst, Wuppertal 1974, 164.
494 Arbeitskreis für Gottesdienst und Kommunion (ed.), Liturgische Nacht, 121.

Singens und Sagens".[495] These songs must be at the same time rich in the Igbo speech genre, and an attempt to Igbonize any foreign rhythm or melody will be detrimental. A mere carry-over or translation of the musical notes and tones of the west into Igbo christian liturgy does not encourage active participation in liturgy since such musical texts and tones are not natural but foreign to the people. Such translations cannot be described to be original Igbo. Music is a language, a way of expressing oneself. The religious sensibility of the Igbo, therefore, can best be aroused by using the Igbo musical language since the mother tongue is best understood in its wealth and abundance of expression better than any other language. Those songs, for instance, that traditionally express the significance of initiation and which is not against the doctrine of the church should be inculturated in the christian liturgy. Likewise, in celebrating death, the Igbo traditionally manifest in their hymns that death is a transformation or a passage into another life. Perhaps such Igbo traditional songs could be incorporated into the christian liturgy to form the locus of encounter between the Igbo and christian spirits in the frame-work of religious experience. I said locus of encounter because traditionally the Igbo, unlike the Christian religion, believe that death has no finality. This locus of encounter could be established based on the common ground that death is a ritual of process "rite de passage": "Lord, for your faithful people life is changed, not ended".[496] The two experiences of reality, Igbo traditional religion and christian religion, merge in the African faith in terms of mutual affirmation, confirmation and transformation.

Music should not only arouse and inspire the people to profess the faith and cultivate piety, but it is also a welcome and important help to the church in carrying out its apostolic ministry and celebration of the sacraments more effectively. Music is a language. It is an effective means of expressing oneself. It is a means of expressing people's culture. Suffix it to say, therefore, that music as a verbal language is performative in its effect. Igbo music as part of the global music should be accorded this performative character. When the effectiveness of the Igbo songs are recognized in terms of its ability to ignite an active participation in the local worshippers, among others, then, one would not be left in doubt about the relationship between the local compositions and the J.L.Austin's concept of performative word.[497] The vitality and vibrancy of christian worship in Igboland would be most heightened when in a liturgical celebration a song coming from Igbo experience of reality is intoned and accompanied by instruments communicative of the Igbo grasp of rhythm. One needed to watch how the native christian worshippers would dance to the tune of the songs which are often accompanied by clapping of hands, tapping of the foot, and sometimes, some local instruments. This would always make the christian liturgies to be ever lively on Igbo soil. H. Weman puts it more clearly by saying: "Anyone who has had the privilege of witnessing at close quarters the inherent vitality and artful

---

495   Block, Johannes, Verstehen durch Musik: Das gesungene Wort in der Theologie: Ein hermeneutischer Beitrag zur Hymnologie am Beispiel Martin Luthers, Tübingen 2002, 25.
496   The Weekday Missal, A New Edition, London 1975, 363.
497   Cf. Austin, How To Do Things With Words, 12.

expressivity of African Music dreams of the time when this music will be given its full right and recognition, its opportunity of reforming and recreating the worship and the service of christian church in Africa".[498] In songs, words unite with movements to arrive at faith-experience in which the worshipper is able to display his or her emotion.

The importance of Igbo native songs in christian worship is obvious. That such native songs lead to active participation among the native faithfuls and make the christian religion lively on Igbo soil cannot be over-emphasized. Igbo theologians should, therefore, work closely with local composers to popularize those native compositions that are doctrinally sound. Otherwise, singing only in foreign languages or igbonization of foreign notes and tones will be detrimental and will make the christian liturgy lack the vitality and vibrancy that it needs most.

5.12.2.5 Use of local symbols

Symbols have a lot of performative effects in Igbo traditional society, "and for that reason holy Mother Church has always been the patron of the fine arts and has ever sought their noble ministry, to the end especially that all things set apart for use in divine worship should be worthy, becoming and beautiful signs and symbols of things supernatural".[499] In chapter three, we saw the place of symbols in Igbo worldview, and we have come to understand that symbols speak very clearly and convincingly to the hearts of the Igbo. It is, therefore, surprising and difficult to believe that most of these native symbols are almost ignored in the Igbo christian liturgies. In order to make the Igbo respond most effectively to the Gospel, it is necessary that this response be on the platform of their cultural values among which are the local symbols, particularly, linguistic symbolism. For example, when an Igbo responds "ise" after the elder has finished prayer over kolanut, what it implies is complicity to the prayers said, and that means, let it be so. This is equivalent to "Amen". Most of the Igbo cannot explain the meaning of "Amen" because it is foreign. They simply take it as what a christian should respond at the end of every christian prayer. The point I am trying to establish is that "ise" which the Igbo understand very well, and which carries some motivations with it and is not contrary to christianity, can be an alternative to "Amen" in the celebration of Igbo christian liturgies. At the same time, I am not saying that "Amen" is not performative. The point I am trying to establish is that within the local setting, the use of "ise" will serve the immediate need of the word performing in the people because its meaning to them is very much understood, even though when judged under the two forms of J.L.Austin's performative word, one would say that it performs implicitly, meaning that "ise" may appear ambiguous, equivocatious or vague as a primitive language, and in which case it needs further clarifications.[500]

---

498 Weman, Henry, African Folkmusic in Christian Churches in Africa, Nairobi 1974, 2.
499 S C, no. 122.
500 Cf. Austin, How To Do Things With Words, 72.

Suffice it to mean that in relation to religion, symbolic language appears to be the ideal. To ascertain the intended meaning of the symbolic languages, the Vatican II Council's document on Divine Inspiration, *Dei Verbum*, stresses the need to pay attention to the customary patterns of perception and communication, and the established conventions peculiar to the people of that particular time and place. This is because all communication is historically conditioned and culturally shaped.[501] For the gospel to be effective, it must apply the human language, incarnating itself in the historical condition and understanding of the people to whom it is addressed. Only on this basis does it have the chance of influencing the lives and destiny of the people. So, linguistic symbols are important vehicles of communication and expression of people's world-view. Linguistic language as part of human language, therefore, helps man in his effort to grasp the divine realities. It is a way of defining rules and means that relate to God. That means that symbolic language helps to convey the mystery of God who is the object of theology. It is a vehicle of expression of a people's thought pattern, feelings and affiliations. The proclamation of the gospel message, therefore, requires the use of the linguistic language of a particular people among whom the gospel is being proclaimed. The importance of symbolic language in the work of evangelization is based on the truth that no true conversion will be achieved outside some inherited symbol system which not only mediates the person's experience of reality but also provides the identity and prescribes the conduct of each one. Symbolic language offers an easy access to a people's cultural world and thereby making conversion much more easier and sincere and total. So, evangelization must focus on human persons within their socio-cultural context. The christian liturgy must not neglect the Igbo symbolic language if it desires to make out of the Igbo, a sincere and dedicated christians. The church's celebration of the eucharist, for example, should make use of the native symbolic languages.

5.12.2.6 Use of traditional narratives

Jesus Christ distinguished himself as a great teacher, remarkable for his great wisdom (Lk 2,46–47). He taught with a great authority and conviction in such a way that no one before him had ever done. His words were full of wisdom that a great number of people were attracted to him. These same words were full of power that through them those held under the satanic bondage were freed; the sick became healed; the dumb could speak; the lame could walk; the blind could see; and the dead came back to life.

As a great teacher, Jesus adopted various methods to make his message be properly understood by those who listened to him. Prominent among his teaching method was the use of narratives known as parables: "indeed he said nothing to them without a parable. This was to fulfil what was spoken by the prophet, I will open my mouth in parables, I will utter what has been hidden since the foundation of the world'"(Mt 13,34–35). Jesus hardly delivered any major teaching without the use of parables. The people he spoke to, naturally, were people with a culture and tradition. They were

---

501   Cf. D V, no. 18.

people with a common experience and a particular world-view. Jesus Christ himself, of course, was not far away from their situations and perceptions because he was one who came from among them. Naturally, Jesus could not have made use of strange elements in his parables. For example, in trying to explain how our faith grows into maturity, he introduced the parable of the mustard seed.[502] This seed which is the smallest of all the seeds grows into the biggest of all the trees and produces enough branches for the birds of the air to make nests (Mt 13,31–32). The highlight is on the word "mustard seed". Of course, Jesus' application of mustard seed for the people he was talking to was because this seed was popular in this area, and that the people he was talking to were familiar with this seed. The people knew the seed and knew how, though it was considered the smallest of the seeds, eventually grew into the biggest of all the trees. They also knew how the birds of the air found homes on its branches. So, this parable could go down well with the people. They could clearly understand its application in their present situation. This means, this parable could perform in the hearts and minds of the people that Jesus was speaking to. This does not, however, make mustard seed universal. In Igboland, mustard seed is strange to the Igbo natives. This is because this seed is not known to have existed within the Igbo tropical region, and therefore, has never been known among the local people. To apply this seed in instructing the Igbo people in faith definitely will be fruitless because as we know, one goes from the known to the unknown. It is necessary to use elements that are familiar to a people in explaining the biblical parables. In other words, the biblical parables would be more meaningful to a particular people if these same parables are re-casted within the people's cultural milieu. I am not in any way suggesting a re-writing of the biblical parables but properly situating them within a context in our missionary efforts of evangelization of peoples. Peter Nlemadim Domnwachukwu was right by saying:

> Igbo Bible teachers should endeavour to understand Biblical concepts and symbols as they were originally and culturally conditioned and then draw suitable comparisons between their Igbo counterparts. If this is done, and with the leadership of the Holy Spirit, Igbo audiences will gain a deeper meaning of Biblical affirmations and respond to them appropriately and with deeper commitment to the christian faith.[503]

In Igboland, there is a seed called "oji"-Iroko seed. This is very much similar to mustard seed in terms of form and operations. Like mustard seed, the iroko seed is

---

502 The word seed is from Hebrew zera' . We can of course remember that the Bible talks of seed right from Old Testament, in the first book, Genesis: "I will put enmity between you and the woman, and between your seed and her seed" (Gen 3,15). The use of the word seed in the Bible can be applied in a symbolic way as a spiritual material or as an influence. As a symbolic concept, seed can be evocative or suggestive. In the Hebrew world-view, seed is an incontestable and an important element in the beingness of man. This is the reason why every individual is considered as an actualized seed. The categorization of seed into good and bad explains why we have good and bad men in existence. Seed can further be highly spiritualized to surpass the human realm and be associated with angels as "holy seeds", and because there are equally fallen angels,there are "unholy seeds".
503 Domnwachukwu, Authentic African Christianity, 172.

the smallest of all the seeds in Igboland, and when planted, it grows into the biggest of all the trees and provides branches on which the birds of the air nest. If the Igbo missionary, therefore, is able to re-cast the parable of the mustard seed in the light of the Igbo "iroko" tree, there will be no doubt that the parable of the mustard seed will then be able to perform in the Igbo christians since the "iroko" seed is something that they are familiar with.

One may be wondering whether narratives have any relationship with the Austin J.L's concept of performative word. In what way can we associate narratives with performative word? At a direct approach, narratives may seem not to be connected to our topic. Narratives seem to be descriptive in nature and not performative. Yet, as J.L.Austin himself puts it: "It has come to be seen that many specially perplexing words embedded in apparently descriptive statements do not serve to indicate some specially odd additional feature in the reality reported, but to indicate (not to report) the circumstances in which the statement is made or reservations to which it is subjected or the way in which it is to be taken and the like". [504] When descriptions are not taken to be "reports", but instead are considered as "indications", of the situations in which an utterance is made or reservation it is subjected under or the way this utterance is to be taken, it then implies that these descriptions have passed beyond being passive and have become active and effective, and in which case they are performative in character. This explains why the use of narratives in the situation in which I discuss them (narratives) is related, at least indirectly, to J.L.Austin's concept of performative word. The translation of the "mustard seed" into "iroko", and its narration should not be understood merely as a description but it is meant to make this biblical narrative more active, more effective, and therefore more performative in the hearts of the local christians.

5.12.2.7 Use of traditional proverbs

Jesus came from a certain culture and tradition, a Jewish culture and tradition. As a people, Jews have their peculiar proverbs, and Jesus the Jew, did not hesitate to make use of these proverbs in his teachings. A typical example of such application is the question about who is the greatest in the kingdom of God. Jesus answered this question by presenting a little child and demanding a such child-like purity or innocence of heart from anyone who wishes to enter the kingdom of God. What immediately follows this demand is the point I am trying to highlight. Jesus admits that whoever receives such a child in his (Jesus) name receives him (Jesus). Subsequently, Jesus was proverbial concerning whoever causes any of such children to sin, and Jesus warns: "it would be better for him to have a great millstone fastened round his neck and be drowned in the depth of the sea" (Mt 18,6). Hanging a great millstone round the neck and be drowned in the depth of the sea is proverbial. This proverb is regional, at least not peculiar to Igbo people. When a missionary applies this biblical proverb to the Igbo natives without relating it to its Igbo equivalent, there is the danger that it may not perform in the Igbo

---

504 Austin , How To Do Things With Words, 3.

people he intends to evangelize. The reason is very simple. The millstone is strange to the Igbo society and this makes the comprehension of this proverb in the minds of the natives very difficult, and because it is not understood, its ability to perform is far removed. In order not to be exclusive in our use of performative word, and as a solution to the situation we are discussing, and similar circumstances, J.L.Austin himself advices that "the term performative will be used in a variety of cognate ways and constructions".[505] The use of traditional proverbs in reference to J.L.Austin's concept of performative word forms part of these cognate ways and constructions.

In accordance to the above directive from J.L.Austin, therefore, a traditional Igbo proverb that is very similar to the Mt 18,6 above exists in the Igbo traditional society. For example, the Igbo say: "Isi kote ebu ogbaa ya". This means "every evil act has an evil reward"; "okuko nyuo ahuru ani achuba ya oso". This means "when a hen pollutes the air she is pursued around by her environment". These and similar proverbs are popular within the Igbo traditional society, and as it were, they are equivalent to the biblical proverb of Matt.18,6. So, the ability of the biblical proverb of Mt 18,6 to perform among the Igbo depends on how well the missionary has explained it in the light of the above-mentioned Igbo proverbs and their like.

This same process can be said of the biblical proverb of Mt 18,8–9: "And if your hand or your foot causes you to sin, cut it off and throw it from you; it is better for you to enter life maimed or lame than with two hands or two feet to be thrown into the eternal fire. And if your eye causes you to sin, pluck it out and throw it from you; it is better for you to enter life with one eye than with two eyes to be thrown into the hell fire". Jesus was talking about the consequences of temptation. Sins are the consequences of temptation. The cutting off of hand or foot in order to avoid sin is proverbial, likewise is the plucking off of eye. Such a radical proverb does not exist in Igbo world-view. To talk of a man with one hand or foot, or with one eye is a bad omen within the Igbo context. Such a man would not be considered good but rather evil. It would be believed that he suffers such incapacity from gods because of the evil he has committed. So, instead of such a biblical proverb being performative within the Igbo traditional society, it suffers rejection. But the Igbo has a similar proverb or proverbs that is or are milder, more attractive and more acceptable. For example: "kama m ga anuchaa mmanya dachie uzo kam ha kam ha". This means "better be humble and remain good than be proud and remain doomed"; "okeke nwanyi di nti njo". This means "good rewards and evil destroys". The Igbo are familiar with these Igbo proverbs and they are synonymous with the Mtt 18,8–9, and when the missionary applies them to explain what the Mt 18,8–9 means, he is sure of achieving some performance in the Igbo adherents because the proverbs are native and very much understood.

5.12.2.8 Use of traditional folktales

Igbos by nature are story tellers as well as story lovers. This aspect of their tradition keeps life going, and makes life enjoyable. There are people who are endowed with

---
505 Austin, How To Do Things With Words, 6.

the art of fabricating stories and make them to be imaginable and to appear interesting. These stories are fabricated because they are not real, and that is the reason why they are identified as folktales. Although they are folktales, they are very important in the traditional life because of their performance in the life of the traditional Igbo man. They are fabricated and told, according to their content, to perform such roles as warning, proclamation or pronouncement, judgement, command, absolution, and so on. However, one needs to listen properly in order to learn the above messages that the folktale passes across because these messages, be it warning or command or absolution and so on, are not explicit and we have earlier on in chapter three mentioned that folktales do not even have titles. When properly understood, these messages are meant to influence and direct the listener in events and endeavours in his life. Because these messages are inherent in the folktales and not explicitly identified and still perform in the individual listener, we may be right in associating them with the implicit form of the J.L.Austin's concept of performative word.[506] Experiences show that the Igbo learn better and faster and highly motivated when the teaching method is closely linked or supported by similar traditional folktales.

Bible, as we know, are full of stories about God's relationship with his people. Such stories deal with essential facts about the earthly life and life here-after. They teach about the basic principles of man's existence, and how these principles influence man's destiny. The church's theology is an expansion and extension of the foundation that the Bible has already laid. The church's doctrines, therefore, are not in isolation with the basic teachings of the Bible. Betram Stubenrauch, a professor of dogmatic theology in München university highlights this points while commenting on the church's doctrine of the Blessed Trinity: "Die Rede vom dreifaltigen Gott ist eine Fortsetzung der Rede vom liebenden Gott Jahwe vor dem Hintergrund der Jesusgeschichte. Die Spitzensätze der alt. Gottesoffenbarung rekurrieren auf das Thema 'Lieb' (Dt 1,31; 4,7f; 4,31; 4,37; 7,7; 6,4f; 7,9; Hos 11,1f; 14,6f; 2,21). Die Liebe Gottes zu seinem Volk provoziert umgekehrt die Liebe des Volkes zu Gott. Das ist Voraussetzung für das Bekenntnis zum dreifaltigen Gott seitens der frühen Christinnen".[507] In the missionary efforts to evangelize the Igbo natives better, the missionary would find it more helpful to make the Bible stories more meaningful to the traditional Igbo by explaining these divine stories in alliance with similar Igbo folktales. All I am trying to say is that Igbo folktales can guide the Igbo christian towards understanding the biblical stories as they are being narrated and explained. For example, the Bible teaches that God created the earth and everything therein. The Bible narrates that God made the creation in stages and in different days. A similar story of creation is not lacking in Igbo traditional society. According to Igbo tradition, Eri was sent by Chukwu-Supreme Being from the sky to the earth. On arriving, Eri was hindered from his mission because the earth surface was full of water. Eri complained to Chukwu, and Chukwu sent a blacksmith who came and dried up the earth. As a

---

506 Cf. Austin, How To Do Things With Words, 72.
507 Stubenrauch, Bethrand, Gotteslehre, unpublished Lectures on "Der Gott der dreifaltigen Liebe II: Grundlegung im NT", Sommer Semester, no.8, 2009.

reward for the work well done, the blacksmith was honoured with a staff of authority for his smithing profession. Eri was fed with manner from above. The creation of crops and palm produce was as follows: Shortly after the death of Eri, the heavenly manner stopped, and Nri the son of Eri complained to Chukwu for food. Nri could not obtain this request without some conditions which included the sacrifice of his first son and his first daughter, who were to be buried in separate graves. It happened that after three Igbo weeks, which is 12 days, yam grew from the grave of the son and cocoyam from that of the daughter. A similar experience happened when Nri made another sacrifice of a male and a female slave, and from their graves grew palm oil and bread fruit respectively, and after three Igbo weeks too.

I am not suggesting that the two creation accounts are the same. But the basic truth that regulates these two creation accounts is that God is presented as the creator who cannot be isolated from the world that he has created, and as Thomas Sartory would put it: "Es geht immer um ein und die gleiche Wirklichkeit, welche wir ebensogut ‚Welt in Gott wie Gott in Welt' nennen können [...] Wer es mit dieser Welt zu tun hat, mit dieser durchdas wirklich diesseitigen Welt, hat es letztlich mit Gott zu tun [...] Wer es mit Gott zu tun hat, hat es mit der Welt zu tun". [508] Igbo have known this basic fact from the much their folklore is able to inform them. Capitalizing on this pre-knowledge about creation, it is left for the missionary to renovate this folktale and to throw the divine light upon it so that the Igbo christian will be able to be led from the schackles of false belief to the true account of the divine creation contained in the Bible, because: "whenever they (missionaries) used the image of God as creator, they usually referred, whether explicitly or implicitly, to accounts in the opening chapters of Genesis". [509] So the missionary effort will be more effective in Igboland when it is neither in isolation from nor in opposition to the traditional folktale.

5.12.2.9 Use of traditional terminologies

The Bible is full of certain terminologies that are regional in nature and may appear foreign in the wider world. Let us pause briefly and take a closer look at some of these terminologies. An instance in Mt 12,22–28 is all about Jesus' healing of a demoniac who was blind and dumb: "And all the people were amazed, and said, ‚can this be the son of David?' But when the Pharisees heard it they said, ‚it is only by Be-el'zebul, the prince of demons, that this man casts out demons'". Of course, Jesus Christ vehemently opposed this false accusation and denounces this claim by teaching that Satan cannot divide against itself and still stand. My contention in this episode, however, is on Be-el'zebul. This is a terminology that is very much known to the Jews. Be-el'zebul in Jewish tradition is the prince of the demons. This name has a performative effect among the Jews but to what extent is this performance universal? How can it

---

508 Sartory, Thomas., Interpretation des Glaubens: Ein ökumenischer Beitrag zum Gespräch über die Zukunft der Kirche und der Christen, München 1966, 114–115.
509 Minear, Paul Sevier, Christians and the New Creation: Genesis Motifs in the New Testament, Kentucky 1994, 1.

perform where it's meaning is very much foreign? This is one of the challenges that face the missionary efforts. Certainly, Be-el'zebul is not an Igbo word, and no one should expect an ordinary Igbo man in the village to be influenced by a terminology that does not fit into his world-view. Of course, J.L.Austin himself suggests that as a performative force, the performative word itself must be a noun action.[510] So, the missionary can make this foreign terminology (Be-el'zebul) a noun action within the Igbo cultural milieu and make it perform even among the Igbo natives. How can he do this?

Igbo language is rich in its nature and scope. It is a language in which every concept and thought has its representation and interpretation. Because the Igbo people are highly religious, their Igbo language is equally very much religious, and as a result, does not lack terminologies to quantify and qualify its religious values and elements. So, when we talk of the prince of demons the Igbo refer to him as "ekwensu". Between Be-el'zebul and Ekwensu is a difference in name and not in operation. Because these two terminologies are the same, the biblical or rather the Jewish Be-el'zebul can perform in Igbo traditional society, and indeed in Igbo man, should the missionary be able to inter-change these terms and thereby making the gospel message original to Igbo people, as well as making this terminology to perform in the Igbo.

5.13 Conclusion

This chapter gives pastoral relevance to our discussions and channel them to an end that will be a great benefit in the work of evangelization in Igboland. Along this line of thought, this chapter begins by focusing on the impact the concept of performative word has on the use of Igbo language for effective evangelization in Igboland. It goes on to highlight the various infelicities in the light of Igbo traditional society and thereby giving them pastoral interpretations. It discusses explicit form of performative word and stresses its pastoral relevance. It enumerates the various concrete situations where word performs among the Igbo of our time. Because the whole issue of giving pastoral relevance to our key concept hinges on evangelization, we took a step further to analyse the term "evangelization". Evangelization, according to our discussion, is a biblical term rooted in both Old Testament and New Testament. The term evangelization could, therefore, be understood to mean proclamation of the Gospel message. To be an evangelizer is synonymous with being a proclaimer of this Gospel message, and the evangelized is taken to be all the nations and peoples everywhere. Our present chapter goes further to explain that the goal of evangelization is conversion. To arrive at this conversion, the evangelizer must adopt certain methods that he considers most suitable to any given circumstances. This chapter listed some of these methods to include christian witness, person to person encounter, catechesis, mass media, proclamation, and most importantly, the proper use of the local language.

---

510   Cf. Austin, How To Do Things With Words, 6.

The early missionaries in Igboland applied most of the above mentioned methods including the introduction of "christian village". But their most profound method became the "school method". Ours is a changing world and the church must introduce a new vision in its evangelizing mission. Thus, this chapter proposes a new vision that should be totally disposed to all cultures. In this new vision, the language of the evangelized should play a leading role in order to make the Gospel message original to the evangelized. This means, inculturation should be an essential aspect of evangelization. Proper evangelization cannot be achieved when the Gospel message is not incarnated in the people's culture. The process of inculturating the Gospel is not a matter of choice since Christ himself has commanded it (Mt 28,19; Mk 16,15; see also Acts 15,1–33). Inculturation should be based on the very principles that God wills that all men should be saved; and that Christ himself though he was inform of God accepted to take a human nature and be born into a culture. Therefore, various obstacles that might be encountered in the process of inculturating the Gospel message, namely: the system in formation houses, western-oriented nature of the church's doctrines and rites, more rationalizations, the dependent nature of the church, among others, should not frustrate this process. Instead, they should be overcomed through sincere dialogue. This dialogue would boost the relationship between gospel and culture and make the light of the gospel be more far-reaching to certain areas that urgently need attention. Our present chapter lists these areas where inculturated type of evangelization is needed, and at the same time, offers some recommendations, they include: right disposition of the agents of evangelization, prayer books, liturgical books, use of Igbo names and titles, use of local compositions, use of Igbo symbols, use of traditional narratives, use of traditional proverbs, use of traditional folktales, use of traditional terminologies, to mention but a few.

Although the context in which J.L.Austin discussed performative word is not limited within a native language (Igbo language), the fact remains that my contributions are as a result of my interest in showing how our key concept (performative word) can pastorally be relevant within the Igbo society. My desire, therefore, to translate this interest into a way that it will be beneficial in the work of evangelizing the Igbo people of south-east Nigeria gave birth to this research work whereby the performance of Igbo word in the pastoral work of the church is most experienced in concrete situations, namely: Prayer ministry, Crusade, Family ministration, Parish annual retreat, Parish weekly adoration, Charismatic renewal prayer group, Homily, Catechism classes, school apostolate and Counselling. From what we have earlier discussed about these concrete pastoral situations, we come to conclusion that proper use of Igbo language can be effective instrument and a necessary guide in the work of making the gospel message to perform among the Igbos. What this would mean to the Igbo christians is that they could then be motivated by the word of God as it is being presented to them in their original Igbo language either by proclamations or by songs or by any other verbal means.

Evaluation and General Conclusion

It could be said that this research work is an attempt at portraying how philosophy is at the service of theology: how philosophy is the handmaid of theology, whereby the J.L.Austin's philosophical concept "performative word" is given a theological interpretation, and through what may seem as a comparative religious studies, sacramental theology and Igbo traditional religion are brought to the search-light in order to show how this J.L.Austin's philosophical concept can be relevant within religious realms. One may ask: why are we seeking for the relevance of our concept "performative word" to sacramental theology and to Igbo traditional religion? It is because our subject matter is the Igbo natives and how best to present the gospel message to them in such a way that this message should properly be proclaimed within the context of their language and circumstance so that it could perform.

The philosophical treatise of J.L.Austin on "performative word", therefore, offers a philosophical basis to what theology has been teaching about the efficacy of ritual words. J.L.Austin in his treatise on "performative word" teaches that statement not only describes a situation or states some facts but is solely used to perform a certain kind of action.[511] In other words, J.L.Austin presents "performative word"is an utterance whereby to say something is to do something; or in saying something we are doing something; or by saying something we are doing something.[512] This is indeed a deviation from the traditional way in which philosophy had used word only for descriptive purposes. Instead, J.L.Austin insists on performative functions of word, and cautions that the validity of an utterance is not judged based on whether it is true or false but on whether it is happy or unhappy.[513] Although J.L.Austin would be acknowledged for introducing a new dimension in the way human language should be perceived for performative purposes, one might still criticize him for allowing his concept of performative word to be speaker-centered. He was interested in the speaker alone so much so that he failed to recognize the contributions the listener has to make in the communication. In other words, J.L.Austin failed to understand that communication is a dialogue and not a monologue. The dialogical nature of human communication gives each participant equal opportunity to contribute to the performance of the words uttered. By giving priority only to the speaker, the listener is made a passive partner. This dialogical nature of communication, indeed, is lacking in the way J.L.Austin has conceived performative language.

Again, the three senses in J.L.Austin's concept of performative word could not but be associated to his earlier teaching about the three acts of speech to mean:

---

511 Cf. Austin, How To Do Things With Words, 12.
512 Cf. Austin , How To Do Things With Words, 12.
513 Cf. Austin, How To Do Things With Words, 1.

saying something (locution); in saying something (illocution); by saying something (perlocution).[514] He teaches that illocutionary act is based on convention while perlocutionary act is not. For example in saying: "glory be to the Father and to the Son and to the Holy Spirit", one's mind is immediately directed to christian belief (illocution and conventional), and the effect may be, for example, devotion (perlocution and non conventional). The effect is not conventional because it does not necessarily follow that the above christian ejaculatory prayer must arouse act of devotion in the heart of the christian believer. After all, in uttering the christian doxology a different effect might as well be actualized. The meaning of any utterance should be open to multiple interpretations. It could be that the listener's past experience or future aspiration can determine the way he reacts to an utterance. At the same time, one might criticize the teaching on the conventionality of illocutionary act as being "a posteriori".[515] I consider this as presupposition. So, our judgement of illocutionary act should rather be "a priori".[516]

The church's highlight on the performative character of its ritual words could be said to have been prefigured in philosophy, precisely, in J.L.Austin's treatise on "performative word". The church's teaching about the intimate relationship between word and sacrament, which is irreversible and dynamic, is a proof of the great extent the J.L.Austin's "performative word" could be interpreted within the context of sacramental theology. The church's magisterium teaches that the action of the word constitutes the sacrament. In other words, the words employed in the celebration of the sacraments are efficacious, and therefore, performative. So, in the celebration of sacraments, it is the sacramental word that brings about the sacramental reality. This means, sacramental words lead to sacramental actions,viz: the words of consecrating bread and wine at the eucharistic celebration changes the bread and wine into the body and blood of Jesus Christ; the words of absolution over the penitent at the celebration of the sacrament of penance forgive sins. However, some critics may say that sacramental words do not always have precedence action, and that there are situations when both sacramental words and actions synonymously lead to another action or to a sacramental reality. This may seem to suggest that sacramental action is an integral part of sacramental word, and that word and sacrament are one concept. In other words, that the sacramental action cannot be separated from the sacramental word. In the sacrament of baptism, for example, the minister utters the sacramental words: "I baptise you in the name of the Father and of the Son and of the Holy Spirit" and at the same time pours the baptismal water at the fore-head of the catechumen. The minister cannot pronounce the words of baptism and later performs the act of pouring the water on the fore-head; at the Eucharistic celebration, the imposition of

---

514 Cf. Austin, How To Do Things With Words, 94.
515 "a posteriori" is implied when knowledge depends for its authority upon the evidence of experience. „a posteriori" is concerned with contingent truths.
516 "a priori" literally means prior to experience. It is implied when knowledge does not depend for its authority upon the evidence of experience. One must not, however, confuse "a priori" with "innate" because they are quite different concepts. "A priori" is concerned with necessary truths.

hand over bread and wine at "epiclesis" happens at the same time with the prayer of the invocation of the Holy Spirit; at confirmation, the Bishop anoints the candidate at the fore-head while saying, "receive the gift of the Holy Spirit ...". These same critics argue even further that in some cases, action takes precedence over word, and together, they lead to a sacramental reality. For example, at ordination of a new priest, the imposition of hand comes first before the prayer of consecration.

Again, we might say that the dialogical nature of communication which J.L.Austin failed to implement in his treatise is well represented in the way the church handles the efficacy of its words. For example, in the theology of incarnation, it is not only the angel's message to Virgin Mary was required for the conception of Jesus Christ to take place, but Virgin Mary's consent was highly necessary. It is the Mary's verbal acceptance of the divine message about being the mother of Jesus Christ that constitutes the conception of Jesus in her womb (Lk 1,38; Jn 1,14). This does not in any way mean that the efficacy of any sacramental word depends on the hearer, but at the same time, the church emphasizes that the response from the hearer helps to make the sacramental word accomplish its goal. Certain conditions are necessary to enable the hearer allow the sacramental word to achieve the desired end. Andreas Wollbold summarized these conditions into two groups, namely, external and internal conditions:

> Wie kann eine Gemeinde sich zum Hören lassen? Dazu sind zunächst die äußeren Bedingungen zu klären: Hörgewohnheiten, herkömmliche Erwartungen an die Predigt, Motivation zum Gottesdienst, auch akustische Gegebenheiten, Durchlüftung des Raums und Tageszeit. Noch mehr ist an den inneren Bedingungen zu arbeiten. Ist die Gemeinde geistlich wach? Will sie und jeder in ihr sich von Gott etwas sagen lassen, gerne und liebend gerne? Wozu braucht und gebraucht sie Gott? Was weiß sie von ihm? Was will sie von ihm wissen? [517]

The pastoral ministry of proclaiming the word of God, administering the sacraments and pasturing the children of God by the ordained ministers of God, together imply a living, concrete and functional sacramental reality which should cause the seed of the word of eternal life to germinate in the souls of the children of God, and through a sincere cooperation with the word of God sown in their hearts, the salvific works of Jesus Christ will attain the desired purpose, that is, the bringing of God to the children of God.

One could equally notice an existing relationship between J.L.Austin's performative word and the performative character of ritual words in Igbo traditional religion. The performance of ritual words in Igbo traditional religion is closely related to the Igbo worldview. The Igbo worldview, of course, cannot be separated from its religion which is tied to various rites and rituals. In Igbo rites and rituals, spoken words present events believed to have the power to effect meaningful transformations. In Igbo traditional religion, spoken words, therefore, are considered more sacred than the written words. Hence, the ritual ceremonies such as initiation, purification, healing, installation of a priest, marriage, oath-taking, covenant making, breaking of kolanut and sacrifice, are all performed with ritual words. To act contrary to a verbal word is one of

---

517 Wollbold, Handbuch der Gemeindepastoral, 192.

the greatest felonies in Igboland because the verbal word is performative and sacred. Despite the strong ties linking the Igbo ritual words to the J.L.Austin's performative word, one may still argue that in certain circumstances the Igbo ritual words are performative in so far as they are uttered in the context of certain actions. The traditional marriage ceremony may serve as an example, and Akogu Peter correctly writes: "Die Heiratszeremonie gipfeln in Igba nkwu nwanyi, dem Umtrunk von Palmwein aus Freude über die Braut, einem üppigen Fest, das vom Bräutigam gegeben warden muss. Die zukünftigen Ehepartner geben einander während dieser Feier ihre Einwilligung zur Eheschließung durch den Austausch von Palmwein. Hiermit bekommen sie den Heiratsstatus".[518] It is in the ceremony of "Igba nkwu nwanyi", Umtrunk von Palmwein aus Freude über die Braut, that marriage is sealed, and in them one may observe a certain action and words being performed at the same time, and which lead to a certain effect ,and in this case, to a union of man and woman as husband and wife. Uchendu Victor clarifies this further, and in his words:

> Before the father takes the bridewealth, he gives his daughter a cup of palm liquor and asks her to show her husband to the audience by giving him the liquor. The shy girl walks with faltering steps to her husband, sips the liquor, and as she gives it to him, tells her shouting audience: "This is my husband. Father may take the bridewealth". As the money is counted and an agreement is made out [...] a lavish refreshment is served. The festivity which marks the rest of the evening is disturbed by the weeping which marks the separation of the bride from her lineage. The elderly women console the bride and her mother by reminding them that what is involved is journey and not death.[519]

The above citation from Uchendu Victor makes it clear that in marriage ceremonies words have no precedence over action but both unite as they are being performed simultaneously to give birth to another action, viz: union of man and woman as husband and wife. There may also be another version to marriage ceremony whereby a marriage is sealed only with action. In this case, an action leads to an action and no utterance is needed in this sacred union of man and woman as husband and wife. Patrick Chibuko describes how this is carried out in certain Igbo traditional society:

> She goes to her father, receives the wine of marriage bond, or covenant, seeks out her husband in the midst of the crowd, sips the wine, with one knee on the ground (as sign of respect not only to the husband but to all present) still on her knee offers the glass of wine to the husband-to-be, who then accepts it lifting her up with one hand, drinks the wine amidst clapping and cheers from the assembly, marking the exchange of consent, sealed by sharing one cup of wine from the same cup.[520]

From the above description, Patrick Chibuko made it clear that the exchange of consent is done simply by the bride and the bridegroom sharing from the same cup. This act alone unites a man and a woman as husband and wife. No word is needed. It is not only that action suffices in this situation and leads to further action which is union of man and woman as husband and wife, but the service of word is not needed in making

---

518 Akogu, Leben und Tod, 78.
519 Uchendu, The Igbo of Southeast Nigeria, 53.
520 Chibuko, Igbo Christian Rite of Marriage, 51–52.

the union. It is necessary to understand that despite the fact that J.L.Austin's performative word is interpreted within the context of sacramental theology and Igbo traditional religion to be strongly related, one must not equally deny the truth that there are some differences when one considers the level to which this concept is related to each of these religious ideologies. For example, in sacramental theology, every performative word is sacred because it is uttered within the context of ritual ceremonies. The Igbo cosmology does not totally agree to this because of its inseparability of cultural, social and religious life of the people from one another. It may, therefore, not totally be correct to say that all the performative words within the context of Igbo traditional rituals are sacred. Again, the teachings of sacramental theology implies that performative word is scripture-oriented, sacrament-oriented and theology-oriented. Bible, of course, is the major source upon which the teachings and practice of sacramental theology is based. Likewise, the word constitutes the sacrament through its performance within the context of sacramental celebrations. The actions of the word is geared towards realization of sacraments. Again, in sacramental theology, performative word has a defined theology that sustains it, which, as it were, may be referred to as the theology of the word.[521] It is this theology of the word that compliments the theology of the sacrament. On the contrary, Igbo traditional religion is not a religion of the book, and therefore, there is no association of performative word to any written source within Igbo traditional religion. Although there are some sacramental realities in Igbo religious rites and rituals, it will be totally wrong to say that performative word in Igbo traditional religion is sacrament-oriented. It may not be logically accepted that performative word in Igbo traditional religion is theology-oriented. This is because Igbo traditional religion itself has not yet got a commonly defined and standardized theology of its own. Sacramental theology in its doctrine of incarnation, personifies performative word to be Jesus Christ, whereas, there is no such personification in Igbo traditional religion. Furthermore, the teaching of sacramental theology on "ex opere operato" is in sympathy with J.L.Austin's concept of performative word, whereas, the "ex opere operato" has no place in Igbo traditional religion. Whereas sacramental theology operates within the framework of the explicit form of performative word, Igbo traditional religion associates itself as well to the implicit form, for example, in its proverbs and idioms. Performative magic is totally unacceptable in sacramental theology, whereas, in Igbo traditional religion, perforemative magic is encountered in the ritual incantations.

---

521 The theology of the word is fundamental to the very basic teaching of the church because it studies the primary and fundamental reality of the christian faith, namely, the revelation or word of God addressed to human family. The theology of the word is the decisive and the principal event of christianity, that which conditions and justifies our christian faith. Establishing, thus, the fact of the word of God to the human family and the factum of the church as the transmitter of this word, apologetics fulfills an indispensable function. The church by addressing itself to human persons has to establish in a certain way that the word by which it speaks is not a human word but a divine word meant to be reflected upon and be communicated to all peoples and to all generations.

The interpretation of J.L.Austin's performative word in the context of sacramental theology and Igbo traditional religion alone would not be an interest to pastoral theology when we fail to outline the pastoral relevance such interpretation has. The last part of our research work, therefore, discusses the pastoral impact our key concept "performative word" would have in evangelization. Evangelization, then, is seen as the connecting factor between J.L.Austin's performative word, the way it is interpreted in both religions, and pastoral theology. Whereas the interpretation of J.L.Austin's performative word makes it relevant to sacramental theology and to Igbo traditional religion, its application makes it relevant to pastoral theology. Evangelization, therefore, is a strong player in this field because we are talking about the Igbo natives and how to proclaim the gospel message to them in such a way that the message would perform.

Along the line, we mentioned that Igboland records a high level of illiteracy. This factor makes it imperative that in order to make the gospel message perform, the use of Igbo language is inevitable because language is always the key to the heart. The Igbo language needs to open the heart of the Igbo people to allow the gospel message to enter. This was most probably the error of the early missionaries who came and not only that they did not make effort to learn the language of the people and preferred to use interpreters most of whom interpreted very badly[522] but were immediately interested in teaching Latin prayers and hymns to the illiterate natives. Later missionaries attempted to correct this error, and according to Obi Celestine:

> The era of Father Lejeune also witnessed the first stride in the promotion of Igbo culture. Language is the vehicle of culture. These missionaries put the Igbo culture on the world map by the publication of an English-Ibo-French Dictionary by Father Ganot, as well as a manual of Catholic Doctrine called "Katechisma nke Okwukwe Nzuko Katolik" by Father Vogler. Before this time the missionaries had had no books of any kind written in the vernacular. To help them in hearing confessions, they had a list drawn up in Igbo of mortal and venial sins. This list was later incorporated into the Katechisma under the headings: "Ndia buga nnukwu Njo" and "Ndia buga obele Njo." Apart from these lists, they depended entirely on the Onye Nkuzi Uka or the catechist-teacher interpreter as the link between them and the vast population to be Christianized.[523]

These efforts by the later missionaries to apply the local language as a vehicle of spreading the gospel message is qualified with the word "attempted" because it was not integral but limited only to the production of dictionary and manual of catholic doctrine. Nevertheless, it was a step in the right direction. The insistence on the use of vernacular in the missionary work of evangelizing the Igbo, however, should not in any way be detrimental to Latin language which is the traditional language of the church, nor should it be aggressive to any other foreign language. There must

---

522 "Bishop J.C Anyogu disclosed that these pioneer missionaries had a better knowledge and a greater disposition to learn the local languages. However, he stated that none had such a sufficient grip on the language as to be able to preach in Igbo. None of the people interviewed could recollect having heard any of the early missionaries preached fluently in Igbo" (Obi, A Hundred years of the catholic church in Eastern Nigeria, 81–82).
523 Obi, A Hundred Years of the catholic church, 81.

be opportunities whereby the natives, as part of the universal church, celebrate the Holy Mass in Latin. It may not be reasonable to insist that every word must be proclaimed in Igbo language, on the one hand because there are certain words that their meanings are best conveyed in their original languages, and on the other hand because inadequate translations may endanger the actual performance of such words. The strong message remains that evangelizing in the new vision of the church today, the language of the evangelized should play a leading role in order to make the gospel message original to the evangelized. This means, inculturation should be an essential aspect of evangelization. Inculturation is necessary because faith cannot be inseparable from culture, and between faith and culture there should be give and take process. One reviews in pain the attempts by the early missionaries in Igboland to deculture their converts. Tearing people away from their cultural surroundings is nothing but alienating them from their home. In the words of Eugene Igboaja:

> Missionaries lost their patience and resorted to an elimination method. They aimed at erasing, obliterating, phasing out whatever existed before their arrival. They termed them pagan, devilish, and idol-worship. Everything was condemned; burial ceremonies(ikwa ozu nkwa n'abo), masquerading(iti mmanwu), dancing(igba egwu), local cosmetics(igbu uli), title-taking (ichi ozo, ime oha etc.), outings(ipu afia, iwa-na-ogbo).[524]

Proper evangelization cannot be achieved when the gospel message is not incarnated in the people's culture. The major problem with the christianization of Igboland is that the Igbo culture was not understood or given serious consideration by many of the missionaries. Consequently, many who came under the influence of the missionaries paid lip-service to the foreign faith and stayed superficially committed because of certain benefits. There were some others who refused to accept the christian faith because of its flagrant neglect of, and sometimes attack on traditional customs and institutions. The process of inculturating the gospel is not a matter of choice since Christ himself has commanded it (Mt 28,19; Mk 16,15; see also Acts 15,1–33). Inculturation should be based on the very principles that God wills that all men should be saved; and that Christ himself though he was inform of God accepted to take a human nature and be born into a culture. Inculturation neither endangers the divine value of christianity nor under values human culture. Rather, they interact in such a way that each retains its identity or essential features in the process of mutual enrichment. This mutual enrichment guarantees progress and deepens the understanding of each other. It does not cause mutual extinction. Through inculturation, the gospel message is assimilated in the people's thought, language, value, ritual, symbolic and artistic pattern. In other words, the gospel and culture share the same values. In short, the gospel is inserted into the culture, history and tradition of the evangelized. The gospel, therefore, begins to speak and perform according to the local cultural pattern. Anything less than this implies that the gospel message would remain at the periphery of our people's cultural experience. We tried to give certain concrete instances where the performance of the gospel message is portrayed through

---

[524] Igboaja, Eugene, "From Uka Fada to Uka Anyi", Centinary Celebration Lecture, Enugu 1985, 3.

an inculcated liturgy, namely, prayer ministry, charismatic prayer group, family ministration, homily, catechism classes, school apostolate, counselling, to mention but a few. Although prayer ministry has added a new vigour to the performance of God's word among our people, there are equally numerous abuses associated with the way certain ministers and lay individuals go about it. Some ministers do and say a lot of things that have raised some serious questions contrary to the traditional teaching and beliefs of the church. Some of the prayer ministers, for example, create the impression that a child of God is not supposed to suffer hardship of any type, and anything contrary to this, the client is declared to be without faith. Other unorthodox practices found within some of the prayer ministries include demanding heavy amount of money for Mass or consultation, exclusive claim of the Holy Spirit, less emphasis of the role of medicine and medical care, inappropriate use of sacramental such as burying of the crucifix on the ground as part of prayer rituals and other practices and methods contrary to the church's teaching. Another worry is the interpretation of the Bible done in most of these prayer houses, especially among the so called lay Bible instructors. Many of those who teach the Bible as lay instructors in most of these prayer grounds have little or no theological training. We believe that the Holy Spirit is the interpreter of God's word in people's minds and hearts but Jesus Christ himself taught his disciples what to preach before sending them out to preach. Jesus Christ also in his humility did not hesitate to receive instructions from his heavenly Father when he spent many hours alone in prayer. He was knowledgeable in Jewish law and the scriptures to the admiration of all who listened to him. The aberrations associated with some of the prayer ministries, therefore, have become so intense and the situation so chaotic that they have led to the break down of discipline and abuse of the sacraments and liturgy. It became necessary that the National Theological and Pastoral Seminar on Healing Ministry be held at Enugu from 12th-14th February 1992 in order to address this problem. This was followed by an issuance of some Pastoral Guidelines for the Healing Ministry by the Bishops' Conference of Nigeria in 1997. Thereafter, subsequent seminars and conferences were organized in this regard. These efforts are directed towards giving prayer ministry it's proper place in the church's holistic ministry of salvation. Therefore, various obstacles that might be encountered in the process of inculturating the gospel message should be overcomed through sincere dialogue. This dialogue would boost the relationship between gospel and culture and make the light of the gospel be more far-reaching to certain areas that urgently need attention.

In conclusion, I decided to write on this J.L.Austin's concept of performative word because of my interest in investigating how much relevance it has to the church's teaching on the sacraments, as well as its relevance to the beliefs and practice of Igbo traditional religion, and through this to highlight the pastoral importance of our key concept in the use of Igbo language for effective evangelization in Igboland. It is my contention that for the Igbo to understand christianity and its demands, the christian message must be delivered to the Igbo in their socio-cultural context. The christian faith should be presented to the Igbo in such a way that they feel an indigenous sense of belonging to the faith. For christianity to become meaningful to the Igbo, the Igbo must be allowed to interprete the gospel message in Igbo conceptual metaphors and practice their faith within their cultural milieu, including those of their traditional systems and institutions which do not conflict with biblical affirmations. Pure christianity does not exist but always appears as a synthesis between the revelation of Jesus Christ and a cultural context. Authentic Igbo christianity would always seek a better and more active involvement of Igbo values. As we can see from our discussions, J.L.Austin's concept of performative word has exposed us to discussing these various ways through which this christian faith can be made to perform as an authentic Igbo faith. This hinges on the fact that proper use of Igbo language is performative within the context of Igbo religious rituals, and therefore, can be effective instruments and necessary guide in the work of evangelizing the Igbos. What this would mean to the Igbo christians is that they could then be motivated by the word of God as it is being presented to them in their original Igbo language either by proclamations or by songs or by any other verbal means. A careful implementation of the recommendations proposed at the last part of the final chapter, chapter five, would, therefore, bring the aim of this research to its fulfilment.

Abbreviations

i. Conciliar and Post Conciliar Documents

SC	Sacrosanctum Concilium
OT	Optatam Totius
NA	Nostra Aetate
LG	Lumen Gentium
GS	Gaudium et Spes
EN	Evangelium Nuntiandi
ES	Eucharistiae Sacramentum
DV	Die Verbum
CD	Christus Dominus
AG	Ad Gentes Divinitus
AA	Apostolicam Actuositatem
DH	Dignitatis Humanae

ii. Other Abbreviations

Can.	Canon
Ca.	Around
Cf.	Confer
Vgl.	Vergleich (confer)
ed.	(s) Editor (s)
e.g.	For example
et.	Et alii (and others)
f&ff.	Following (s)
i.e	That is
ibid.	Ibidem (in the same place)
Loc cit.	Loco Citato (in the place cited)
id.	Idem (the same)
Op.cit.	Opere citato (in the work cited)
S J	Society of Jesus
St	Saint
Vol. (s)	Volume (s)
NT	New Testament
OT	Old Testament
n.&nn.	Number(s)
p.&pp.	Page(s)
trans.	Translated
v.&vv.	Verse(s)

viz.	Videlicet (namely)
Is	Isaiah
Dt.	Deutronomy
Gen	Genesis
Judg	Judges
Jn	John
Js	James
1Th	1 Thesselonica
1Th	2 Thesselonica
Acts	Acts of the apostles
Heb	Hebrew
1Cor	1 Corinthians
2 Cor	2 Corinthians
Mt	Matthew
Mk	Mark
Lk	Luke
1Kg	1 King
2Kg	2 King
1Pt	1 Peter
2Pt	2 Peter
1Tm	1 Timothy
2Tm	2 Timothy
Ex	Exodus
Jer	Jeremiah
Ezek	Ezekiel

Bibliography

A) Primary sources

Sacred Scriptures

The Holy Bible, Revised Standard Version Containing The Old And New Testaments, Catholic Edition, Westminster 1966.

Tradition

Flannery, Austin, (ed.), Vatican Council II, The Conciliar and Post Conciliar Documents, Redised Edition, Republic of Ireland 1988.
Katechismus der katholischen Kirche, Kompendium, Übersetzung aus dem Italienischen im Auftrag der Deutschen Bischofskonferenz, Bonn 2005.

Vatican Council II Documents

Ad gentes divinitus, Decree on the church's missionary activity, 7 December, 1965.
Apostolicam actuositatem, Decree on the apostolate of lay people, 18 November, 1965.
Christus dominus, Decree on the pastoral office of Bishops in the church, 28 October, 1965.
Dei verbum, Dogmatic constitution on divine revelation, 18 November 1965.
Dignitatis humanae, Declaration on religious liberty, 7 December 1965.
Eucharistiae sacramentum, On Holy Communion and the Worship of the Eucharistic Mystery Outside of Mass S.C.D.W, 21 June 1973.
Evangelium nuntiandi, Evangelization in the modern world, 8 December 1975.
Gaudium et spes, Pastoral constitution on the church in the modern world, 7 December, 1965.
Lumen gentium, Dogmatic constitution on the church, 21 November, 1964.
Nostra aetate, Declaration on the relation of the church to non-christian religions, 28 October, 1965.
Optatam totius, Decree on the training of priests, 28 October, 1965.
Sacrosanctum concilium, The constitution on the sacred liturgy, 4 December, 1963.

Papal Encyclicals and Addresses

John Paul II, Christi Fidelis Laici, Dec. 30, 1998.
John Paul II, Fidei Depositum, October 11, 1992.
John Paul II, On Extraordinary Synod of Bishops 1985, IIB, 4.
John Paul II, Redemptoris Missio, Dec. 7, 1990.
Paul VI, Address At The Opening Of The Second Session Of The Second Vatican Council, September 1963.
Paul VI, Gravissimun Educationis, October 28, 1965.

Rites and Ritual Texts

Schott-Messbuch, Originaltexte der authentischen deutschen Ausgabe des Meßbuchs und des Meßlektinars mit Einführungen herausgegeben von den Benediktinern der Erzabtei Beuron, Freiburg 1984.
The Pocket Ritual. Rituale Parvum, Collected and edited by The National Lizurgical Center, Bangalore 1988.
The Weekday Missal, A New Edition, London 1975.

B) Secondary sources

Dictionaries and Encyclopediae

A Dictionary of Philosophy, U.S.A. 1988.
An Encyclopedia of Philosophy, London 1988.
Encyclopedia of Christian Theology, vol. 3, New York 2005.
New Catholic Encyclopedia, second edition, Washington D. C 2003.
The Concise Encyclopedia of Western Philosophy, third edition, U.S.A. and Canada 2005.
The Dictionary of Historical Theology, U.K 2000.
The Encyclopedia of Christianity, vol. 1, Köln 1999.

Bulletins

Bishops of Eastern Africa, art. Report on the Experiences of the church in the work of Evangelization in Africa, in: AER, 17/1, 1975.
Hilfsaktion Märtyrerkirche (HMK), Wir müssen mit einer Stimme sprechen, in: Stimme der Märtyrer, no.38, 2006.

Hilfsaktion Märtyrerkirche (HMK), Verprügelt und allein gelassen, in: Stimme der Märtyrer, no. 41, 2009.
Otunga, Martin, art. African Culture and Life-Centered Catechesis, in: AER, 20/1, 1978.

Books

Achebe, Chinua, Arrow of God, Ibadan 1989.
Achebe, Okey Patrick, The Social – Religious Significance of the Igbo Prenatal, Natal and Puberty Rates, unpublished doctoral thesis, Austria 1972.
Ackey, John, The church of the word: a comparative study of word, church and office in the thought of Karl Rahner and Gerhard Ebeling, New York 1993.
Aguwa, Jude, The Agwu Deity in Igbo Religion, A Study of the Patron Spirit of Divination and Medicine in an African Society, Enugu 1995
Akers, Regina Dawn, The Holy Spirit's Interpretation of the New Testament: A Course in Understanding and Acceptance, London 2007.
Akmajian, Adiran, Demers R.A., Farmer A.K. and Harnish R.M., An Introduction to Language and Communication, third edition, London 1990.
Akogu, Peter, Leben und Tod Im Glauben und Kult der Igbo, München 1984
Akwaranwa, Emmanuel, A Politico – Cultural History of Ngwa and Ukwa people of Imo State of Nigeria from pre – colonial times to 1984, Owerri 1988.
Allain, Paul, The Routledge companion to theatre and performance, London 2006.
Alston, Willian, Philosophy of Language, USA 1964.
Alyeshmerni, Mansoor, and Taubr P., Working with Aspects of language, second edition, New York 1975.
Amalorpavadass, D.S., Gospel and Culture: Evangelization and Inculturation, Bangalore 1978.
Ammon, Ulrich, (ed.), Status and Function of Languages and Language Varieties, New York 1989.
Anderson, Stephen, The Language Organ, Linguistics as Cognitive Physiology, London 2002.
Andersson, Jan, How to define Performative, Sweden 1975.
Antal, Laszlo, Questions of Meaning, Budapest 1963.
Anyanwu, Cyprain chima Uzoma, The rites of initiation in Christian liturgy and in Igbo traditional society: towards the inculturation of Christian liturgy in Igboland, Frankfurt am Main 2004.
Aphek, Edna and Tobin, Yisay, The Semiotics of Fortune – Telling, Amsterdam 1990.
Aquinas, Thomas, Summa Theologica, v., part 3.
Arbeitskreis für Gottesdienst und Kommunikation (Hrsg), Liturgische Nacht: Ein Werkbuch Jugenddienst, Wuppertal 1974.
Arinze, Francis, Sacrifice in Igbo religion, Ibadan 1970.
Arinze, Francis, The Church and Nigerian Culture, Onitsha 1973.

Austin, John Langshaw, How To Do Things with Words, second edition, Massachusetts 1975.
Austin, John Langshaw, Philosophical Papers, Oxford 1961.
Austin, John Langshaw, Sense and Sensibilia: Reconstructed from the manuscript notes by G.J. Warnock, Oxford 1962.
Awolalu, Joseph, Yoruba Beliefs and Sacrificial Rites, London 1979
Back, Kent and Harnish Robert, Linguistic Communication and Speech Acts, London 1979.
Ballmer, Thomas and Brennenstuhl Waltrand, Speech Act Classification, A study in the Lexical Analysis of English Speech Activity Verbs, New York 1981.
Barry, Fredrick, Eastern Nigeria, London 1969.
Barth, Karl, Das Wort Gottes und die Theologie, gesammelte Vorträge, München 1924.
Barth, Karl, Die Lehre vom Wort Gottes: Prolegomena zur kirchlichen Dogmatik, zweiter Halbband, Nördlingen 1938.
Basden, George, Niger Igbos, London 1966.
Beedham, Christopher, Language and Meaning, Amsterdam 2005.
Bernard, Cooke, Ministry to Word and Sacraments: history and theology, Philadelphia 1980.
Bevan, Edwin Robert, Symbolism and Belief, The Gifford Lectures, 1933 – 4, London 1962.
Birdsong, David, Metalinguistic Performance and Interlinguistic Competence, New York 1989.
Biser, Eugene, Glaubensbekenntnis und Vaterunser, eine Neuauslegung, Düsseldorf 1994.
Black, Elizabeth, Pragmatic Stylistics, Edinburgh 2006.
Blakemore, Diane, Understanding Utterances, Oxford 1992.
Block, Johannes, Verstehen durch Musik: Das gesungene Wort in der Theologie: Ein hermeneutischer Beitrag zur Hymnologie am Beispiel Martin Luthers, Tübingen 2002.
Bloomfield, Louis, Language, USA 1961.
Bolinger, Dwinght, Aspects of Language, New York 1968.
Bonhoeffer, Dietrich, Christologie, mit einem Nachwort von Eberhard Bethge und Otto Dudzus, München 1981.
Bonhoeffer, Dietrich, Sanctorum Communio: Eine dogmatische Untersuchung zur Soziologie der Kirche, Dritte erweiterte Auflage mit Register, München 1960.
Broeder, Peter, (ed.), Language and Thought in Development, Croo – Linguistic Studies, Tübingen 1999.
Bryant-Jefferies, Richard, Counselling for death and dying: Person-centred dialogues, Oxon 2006.
Butler, Judith, Excitable Speech, A politics of the performative, New York and London 1997.
Butterworth, Brian, (ed.), Language Production, vol. 1, New York 1980.

Caldecott, Stratford, The Seven Sacraments: Entering The Mysteries Of God, New York 2006.
Carleton, Christensen, Language and Internationality: a critical examination of John Searle's later theory of speech acts and intentionality, Würzburg 1991.
Carrell, Patricia, A Transformational Grammar of Igbo, Cambridge 1970.
Carter, Edward, ed., Shepherds of Christ Newsletters, vol. 2, New York 2002.
Chao, Yuen Ren, Language and Symbolic Systems, London 1970.
Chauvet, Louis Marie, The Sacraments, The Word of God at the Mercy of the Body, Minnesota 1997.
Cherry, Colin, (ed.), Pragmatic Aspects of Human Communication, USA 1974.
Chibuko, Patrick, Igbo Christian Rite of Marriage, A Proposed Rite for Study and Celebration, Frankfurt am Main 1999.
Chigbo, Kingsley, Catholic Healing Ministry on Fire, Abakaliki 1997.
Chukwuma, Helen, Igbo Oral Literature, Theory and Tradition, Abak 1994.
Clark, Hebert and Clark, Eve, Psychology and Language, An Introduction to Psycholinguistics, New York 1977.
Clark, Hebert, Using Language, Cambridge 1996.
Cole, Peter, (ed.), Radical Pragmatics, New York 1981.
Cooke, Bernard, Ministry to word and sacraments: History and Theology, Philadelphia 1977.
Cooke, Bernard, Sacraments and Sacramentality, Mystic, Connecticut 1987.
Cooper, David, Philosophy and the Nature of Language, London 1973.
Cribb, Tim, (ed.), The Power of the Word: The Cambridge Colloquia, New York 2006.
Cruse, David, Meaning in Language, An Introduction to Semantics and Pragmatics, New York 2000.
Crystal, David, Introducing Linguistics, London 1992.
Dascal, Marcelo, Pragmatics and The Philosophy of Mind I, Thought in language, Amsterdam 1983.
David, Holdcroft, Words and Deeds: the problems in the theory of speech acts, Oxford 1979.
Davis, Steven, Philosophy and Language, Indianapolis 1976.
Dawson, Christopher, Religion and Culture, London 1949.
Deese, James, The Structure of Associations in Language and Thought, Baltimore 1965.
De Napolis, George, Inculturation as communication, in: De La Cruz Aymes, Maria (ed.), Effective inculturation and ethnic identity, Roma 1991.
Dijk, Teun Adrianus Van, Studies in the Pragmatics of Discourse, New York 1981.
Dirven, Rene and Verspoor, Marjolijn, Cognitive Exploration of Language and Linguistics, Amsterdam 1998.
Dobrovol'skij, Dennis and Piirainen, Emmanuel, Figurative Language: Cross-Cultural and Cross – Linguistic Perspectives, Amsterdam 2005.
Domnwachukwu, Peter Nlemadim, Authentic African Christianity: An Inculturation Model for the Igbo, New York 2000.
Drummey, James, Catholic replies, Norwood 1995.

Dupuis, Jacques, Towards a Christian Theology of Religious Pluralism, New York 2002.
Dyson, Henry, (ed.), Augustine: The City of God Against The Pagans, Cambridge 1988.
Echema, Augustine, Anointing of the Sick and the Healing Ministry: The Nigerian Pastoral Experience, Frankfurt am Main 2006.
Edie, James, Speaking and Meaning, The Phenomenology of Language, London 1976.
Ehusani, George, A Prophetic Church, second edition, Ibadan 2003.
Ejizu, Christopher, Cosmological Perspective on Exorcism and Prayer-Healing in Contemporary Nigeria, Enugu 1992.
Ejizu, Christopher, Ofo, Igbo Ritual Symbol, Enugu 1986.
Ernest Johnson, Freder, (ed.), Religious Symbolism, New York 1969.
Esterhammer, Angela, The romantic performative: language and action in British and German romanticism, Stanford 2000.
Faber, Eva-Maria, Einführung in die katholische Sakramentlehre, Stuttgart 2002.
Fabian, Johannes, Power and Performance, ethnographic exploration through proverbial wisdom and theater in Shaba, Zaire, London 1990.
Fillmore, Charles, Studies in Linguistic Semantics, New York 1971.
Fitzsimmons, James, Called to Serve, Pastoral Notes and Practical Suggestions for the lay ministries, London 1985.
Flynn, Errol, Why Believe? Foundations of Catholic Theology, Franklin 2000.
Fodor, Jerry and Katz, Jerrold, The Structure of Language, Readings in the Philosophy of Language, New Fersey 1964.
Forde, Daryll and Jones, Gwilym Iwan, The Ibo and Ibibio speaking peoples of South-East Nigeria, London 1967.
Forgas, Joseph, (ed.), Language and Social Situations, New York 1985.
Francois, Recanati, Meaning and Force: the pragmatics of performative utterance, Cambridge 1987.
Fried, William, Evangelization, Culture and Catholic identity: proceedings of a symposium for catholic leaders, Florida 1996.
Gelpi, Donald, Charism and Sacrament, London 1976.
Gerd, Heinz-Mohr, Lexikon der Symbole, Bilder und Zeichen der christlichen Kunst, Köln 1983.
Gratsch, Edward, Principles of Catholic Theology, A synthesis of Dogma and Morals, New York 1981.
Green, Georgia, Pragmatics and Natural Language Understanding, New Jersey 1989.
Grunder, Jack, Elgin S.H., Guide to Transformational Grammer, History, Theory, Practice, New York 1973.
Grundy, Peter, Doing Pragmatics, New York 1995.
Guardini, Romano, Das Bild von Jesus Dem Christus im Neuen Testament, Freiburg 1961.
Guder, Darrell Likens, (ed.), Missional Church: A vision for the sending of the Church in North America, Michigan 1998.

Hallencreutz, Carl Fredrick, Christ is the Mountain, art. in Scripta Instituti Donneriani Aboensis x, Religious symbols and their functions, based on papers read at the symposium on religious symbols and their functions held at Abo on the 28th – 30th August 1978.
Heralds, Biezais (ed.), Sweden 1979.
Halliday, Michael, (ed.), Learning, Keeping and Using Language, vol 1, Amsterdam 1990.
Harley, Trevor, The Psychology of Language, From Data to Theory, UK 1995.
Hart, Trevor, ed., The Dictionary of Historical Theology, U.K 2000.
Hasan, Raqaiya, Linguistics, Language and Verbal Art, New York 1989.
Hawkins, John, (ed.), Explaining Language Universals, New York 1988.
Hayakawa, Samuel, Language in Thought and Action, New York 1949.
Häring, Bernard, Evangelization Today, England 1974.
Hebblethwaite, Peter, Paul VI: The First Modern Pope, New York 1993.
Henk, Haverkate, Speech Acts, Speakers, and Hearers: reference and referential strategies in Spanish, Amsterdam 1984.
Hick, John, (ed.), Truth and Dialogue in World Religions: Conflicting Truth-Claims, Philadelphia 1974.
Hillis, Müller Joseph, Tropes, Parables, Performatives: essays on twentieth – century interature, New York 1990.
Hodgson, Peter Craft, editor, Readings in Christian Theology, London 1985.
Holmes, Bernard, The Word of God: Mark's version, Toronto 1962.
Honderich, Ted, (ed.), The Oxford Companion to Philosophy, second editon, New York 2005.
Horn, Laurence, (ed.), The Handbook of Pragmatics, USA 2007.
Hospers, John, An Introduction to Philosophical Analysis, Fourth edition, London 1997.
Huxley, Renira,(ed.), Language Acquisition, Models and Methods, London 1974.
Hyman, Larry, (ed.), Language, Speech and Mind, London 1988.
Igboaja, Eugene, "From Uka Fada to Uka Anyi", Centinary Celebration Lecture, Enugu 1985.
Igwe, Georgewill and Green Margaret, Igbo Language Course, Igbo Language Study, Ibadan 1967.
Ikeobi, Godwin, Catholic Response to the challenge of 'Prayer Houses'-Origin of the 'Tuesday Prayer' in Onitsha, in: Nwosu Vincent (ed.), The Catholic Church in Onitsha, People, Place and Events (1885–1985), Onitsha 1985.
Ikeobi, Godwin, Towards the purification of the Igbo Ozo title in Onitsha Archdiocese, unpublished doctoral thesis in theology, Rome 1970.
Ikeobi, Godwin, "What I think God is doing in and through me", Enugu 1992.
Isichei, Elizabeth, A History of the Igbo people, London 1973.
Iwe, Nwachukwu, Igbo Deities, art in: The Igbo Concept of the Sacred, papers presented at the 1988 Ahiajoku Lectures (Onugaotu) colloquium, no.4, Owerri 1989.
James, Packer, "Fundamentalism" and the Word of God: some evangelical principles, London 1965.

Jassy, Perin, Basic Community in the African Churches, translated by sister Jeanne Marie Lyons, New York 1973.
Jernigan, Robert, (ed.), The Role of Language in Problem Solving 1, New York 1984.
Kalu, Ogbu, Under the Eyes of the Gods: Sacralization and Control of Social Order in Igboland, art. In: The Concept of the Sacred, papers presented at the 1988 Ahiajoku Lecture (onugaotu) colloquium, no.4, Owerri 1989.
Kearns, John, Using Language: the structure of speech acts, Albany 1984.
Kedar, Benjamin, Crusade and Mission: European approaches toward the muslims, New Jersey 1984.
Kirchhoff, Hermann, (Hrsg.), Ursymbole und ihre Bedeutung für die religiöse Erziehung, München 1985.
Kirk, Andrew, What is mission? Theological Explorations, Minneapolis 2000.
Klöckner, Stefan, Sakrament im Wort: Christologische Fundamentierung, Eschatologische Ausrichtung und Ekklesiale Vermittlung Wortsakramentalen Geschehens als Gegenstand Ökumenischer Konvergenzbestrebungen: Inauguraldissertation zur Erlangung der theologischen Doktorwürde an der Katholisch-Theologischen Fakultät der Eberhard-Karls-Universität Tübingen, Tübingen 1991.
Koch, Günter, Sakramentale Symbole: Grundweisen des Heilshandelns Gottes, Regensburg 2001.
Kpiebaya, George, Dagaaba Traditional Marriage and Family Life, London 1992.
Kurzon, Dennis, It is hereby performed ... : explorations in legal speech acts, Amsterdam 1986.
Lacoste, Jean-Yves, editor, Encyclopedia of Christian Theology, vol. 3, New York 2005.
Lambourne, R.A., Community, Church and Healing: A study of some of the corporate aspects of the church's ministry to the sick, London 1963.
Lanigan, Richard, Speech Act Phenomenology, Belgium 1977.
Lartey, Emmanuel Yartekwei, Pastoral counselling in inter-cultural perspective: A study of some African (Ghanaian) and Anglo-American views on human existence and counselling, Frankfurt am Main 1987.
Laver, John, (ed.), Communication in Face to Face Interaction, Australia 1972.
Lawler, Michael, Symbol and Sacrament: A Contemporary Sacramental Theology, New York 1987.
Lea, Henry Charles, A History of Auricular Confession and Indulgences in the Latin Church, London 1896.
Leeming, Bernard, Principles of Sacramental Theology, London 1956.
Lehmann, Winfred, Historical Linguistics, An Introduction, second edition, New York 1962.
Lennart, Annemarie, Performatives and Verifability by the use of Language: a study in the applied logic of indexicals and conditionals, Uppsala 1972.
Levinson, Stephen, Pragmatics, Great Britain 1983.
Lieber, Joachim, Ibo village communities, Ibadan 1971.
Lochhead, David, The Dialogical Imperative: A Christian reflection on Interfaith encounter, faith meets faith series, New York 1988.

Lock, Andrew, (ed.), Language Development, London 1984.
Louise, Pratt Mary, Toward a speech act theory of literary discourse, Bloomington 1977.
Makozi, Alexius and Afolabi Ojo, The History of the Catholic Church in Nigeria, Lagos 1982.
Marmaridou, Sophia, Pragmatic Meaning and Cognition, Amsterdam 2000.
Marthaler, Berard, New Catholic Encyclopedia, second edition, Washington D. C 2003.
Martos, Joseph, The Catholic Sacraments, Wilmington, Delaware 1985.
Mats, Furberg, Locutionary and Illocutionary Acts: a main theme in J.L Austin's philosophy, Göteborg 1963.
Mats, Furberg, Saying and Meaning: a main theme in J.L. Austin's philosophy, Oxford 1971.
Mautner, Thomas, A Dictionary of Philosophy, U.S.A 1988.
Maxim and Bryan K., Language of the Elderly, A clinical perspective, London 1994.
Mbefo, Luke, Priests and Healing Ministry in the Nigerian Church, Enugu 1992.
Mbiti, John, Bibel und Theologie in afrikanischen Christentum: Übersetzung von Bernard Ferrazzini; Herausgegeben von Gudrun Löwner mit einer Übersichtskarte, Göttingen 1986.
Mbiti, John, Introduction to African Religion, London 1975.
McCarthy, Dennis, Growing points in theology: Old Testament Covenant; a survey of current opinions, Oxford 1972.
McGuckin, John Anthony, The Westminster Handbook to Patristic Theology, London 2004.
Mendes, Angela, Heil für die Welt: Kriterien eines gegenwärtigen Missionsverständnisses, entwickelt aus den Diskussionen der Bischofssynode von 1974 über die Evangelisierung: Diplomarbeit zur Erlangung des Diploms in Katholischer Theologie an der Katholisch-Theologischen Fakultät der Ludwig-Maximilians-Universität München 2005.
Metu, Edmond Ikenga, African Religions in Western Conceptual Schemes: The problem of interpretations (studies in Igbo religion), Ibadan 1985.
Metz, Johann-Baptist, Schillebeeckx, Edward (ed.), World Catechism or Inculturation?, Edinburgh 1989.
Mey, Jacob, (ed.), Pragmalinguistics: Theory and Practice, New York 1979.
Mey, Jacob, Pragmatics, An Introduction, USA 1994.
Meyendorff, Paul, Reflections on Russian Liturgy, art. in St Vladimir's Theological Quarterly, a continuation of St Vladimir's Seminary Quarterly published by the Faculty of St Vladimir's Orthodox Theological Seminary, edited by John Beck, New York 1989.
Meyer, Hans, Thomas Von Aquin, Sein System Und Seine Geistesgeschichtliche Stellung, zweite erweiterte Auflage, Paderbonn 1961.
Minear, Paul Sevier, Christian and the New Creation: Genesis Motifs in the New Testament, Louis, Kentucky 1994.

Moore, Timothy, (ed.), Cognitive Development and The Acquisition of Language, New York 1973.
Müller, Gehard Ludwig, Katholische Dogmatik, für Studium und Praxis der Theologie, Freiburg 2005.
Ndiokwere, Nathaniel, The African Church Today and Tomorrow, vol. 11, Ibadan 1986.
Nemeth, Eniko, Pragmatics and The Flexibility of Word Meaning, Amsterdam 2001.
Neuner, Peter, Der Streit um den katholischen Modernismus, Frankfurt am Main und Leipzig 2009.
Neuner, Peter, Kleines Handbuch der Ökumene, Düsseldorf 1984.
Neuner, Peter, Ökumenische Theologie: Die Suche nach der Einheit der christlichen Kirchen, Darmstadt 1997.
Niemeier, Susanne, (ed.), The Language of Emotions, Amsterdam 1997.
Noveck, Ira, (ed.), Experimental Pragmatics, Great Britain, 2004.
Nwaoru, Emmanuel, Another look at magic in African culture, article in Chakana, vol.3, edited by missionswissenschaftliches Institut Missio e.V (MWI), Frankfurt/M 2005.
Nwosu, Vincent, (ed.), The Catholic Church in Onitsha: People, Places and Events,Onitsha 1985.
Nzeako, Tagbo, Omenala Ndi Igbo, Ibadan 1986.
O'Neil, Colman, Sacramental Realism: A General Theory of the Sacraments, Theology and Life series 2, Delaware 1983.
Oakeshott – Taylor, John, Acoustic Variability and its Perception: the effects of context on selected acoustic parameters of English words and their perceptual consequences, Frankfurt am Main 1980.
Obi, Celestine, A Hundred Years of the Catholic Church in Eastern Nigeria 1885 – 1995, Onitsha 1985.
Oborji, Francis, Concepts of mission: the evolution of contemporary missiology, New York 2006.
Oborji, Francis, Towards a Christian theology of African religion: issues of interpretation and mission, Nairobi 2005.
Ogbalu, Felix, Igbo Institutions and Customs, Onitsha 1992.
Okonkwo, Emmanuel, Marriage in the Christian and Igbo traditional context: towards an inculturation, Frankfurt am Main 2003.
Onoyima, Thaddeo, Attention Please, Enugu 1996.
Onwubiko, Alozie Oliver, Christian Mission and Culture in Africa, vol. I, African Thought, Religion and Culture, Enugu 1991.
Onwubiko, Alozie Oliver, Echoes from the African Synod: The future of the African Church from present and past experiences, Enugu 1994.
Onwubiko, Alozie Oliver, Missionary Ecclesiology: An Introduction, Enugu 1999.
Onwubiko, Alozie Oliver, The Church as the family of God (Ujamaa): In the light of Ecclesia in Africa, Nsukka 1999.
Onwuejeogwu, Angulu, The Social Anthropology of Africa: An Introduction, London, 1975.

Opoku, Kofi Asare, West African Traditional Religion, USA 1978.
Osborne, Kenan, Sacramental Theology: A General Introduction, New York 1988.
Osei-Bonsu, Joseph, The inculturation of christianity in Africa, Frankfurt am Main 2005.
Ott, Hans, Dialogue-Ecumenical Context, article in The Encyclopedia of Christianity, vol. 1, Köln 1999.
Otunga, Martin, African Culture and Life-Centered Catechesis, art. In: AER,20/1, 1978.
Oulton, John, Holy Communion and Holy Spirit, a study in doctrinal relationship, London 1954.
Parkinson, George, General editor, An Encyclopedia of Philosophy, London 1988.
Parret, Herman, (ed.), Meaning and Understanding, New York 1981.
Parrinder, Geoffrey, Religion in Africa, London 1969.
Partridge, John Geoffrey, Semantic, Pragmatic and Syntactic Correlates, An Analysis of Performative verbs based on English Data, Tübingen 1982.
Pelikan, Jaroslav., The Christian Tradition, A History of the Development of Doctrine, Chicago and London 1978.
Phan, Peter, In our own tongues: Perspectives from Asia on mission and inculturation, New York 2003.
Phan, Peter, Mission and Catechesis: Alexandre de Rhodes and Inculturation in seventeenth-century Vietnam, New York 1998.
Pinchin, Calvin, Issues in Philosophy, an Introduction, second edition, New York 2005.
Price, Betsey, Medieval Thought, An Introduction, USA 1992.
Principe, Walter, The Theology of the Hypostatic Union in the Early Thirteenth Century, vol. 2, Alexander of Hales' Theology of the Hypostatic Union, Toronto 1967.
Rahner, Karl und Eicher, Peter, editors, Theologie in Freiheit und Verantwortung, München 1981.
Rahner, Karl, Kirche und Sakramente, Freiburg 1960.
Ramsey, Ian, Religious Language, An Empirical Placing of Theological Phrases, London 1973.
Ree, James and Urmson, James, The Concise Encyclopedia of Western Philosophy, third edition, U.S.A. and Canada 2005.
Richard, Yann, Language and Utterance: an advanced resource book, London 2008.
Rieber, Robert, (ed.), Dialogues on the Psychology of Language and Thought, New York 1983.
Rieber, Robert, The Psychopathology of Language and Cognition, New York 1994.
Rist, John, Augustine: Ancient Thought Baptized, Cambridge 1994.
Robeck, Cecil, The Holy Spirit and the unity of the church: The challenge of Pentecostal, Charismatic, and Independent Movements, in: Donnelly, Doris,(ed.), The Holy Spirit, The church and christian unity: Proceedings of the consultation held at the monastery of Bose, Italy (14–20 October 2002), Leuven 2005.
Robinson, Douglas, Introducing Performative Pragmatics, New York and London 2006.

Robson, Mark, Language in theory: a resource book for students, London 2005.
Rommetveit, Ragnar, (ed.), Studies of Language, Thought and Verbal Communication, London 1979.
Ronald, Cox, By the same word: creation and salvation in hellenistic judaism and early Christianity, Berlin 2007.
Rosseau, Richard, (ed.), Interreligious Dialogue: Facing the next frontier, vol. one, modern theological themes: selections from the literature, United States of America 1981.
Ruhlen, Merritt, On the Origin of Languages, Studies in Linguistic Taxonomy, USA 1994.
Rui, Linhares-Dias, How to show things with words: a study on logic, language and literature,Berlin 2006.
Sadock, Jerrold, Toward a Linguistic Theory of Speech Acts, New York 1974.
Samartha, Stanley Jedediah, (ed.), Dialogue between men of living faith, papers presented at a consultation held at Ajaltoun Lebanon, March 1970, Lausanne-Switzerland 1970.
Sato, Chie, The Synthax of Conversation in Interlanguage Development, Tübingen 1990.
Scherer, James, Bevans, Stephen, New directions in mission and evangelization: Faith and Culture, New York 1999.
Schillebeeckx, Edward, Christus Sakrament Der Gottbegegnung, Mainz 1960.
Schilling, Klaus, Symbole erleben: Glauben erfahren mit Hand, Kopf und Herz, Stuttgart 1991.
Schmemann, Alexander, Introduction To Liturgical Theology, The Library Of Orthodox Theology, no. 4, translated by Asheleigh E. Moorhouse, New York 1975.
Schneider, Theodor, Zeichen der Nähe Gottes, Grundriß der Sakramententheologie, Mainz, 2005.
Searle, John, Foundations of Illocutionary Logic, New York 1985.
Searle, John, Speech Act, An Essay in the Philosophy of Language, Cambridge 1970.
Sharma, Savita, Early Indian Symbols, Numismatic Evidence, Delhi 1990.
Shorter, Aylward, African Culture and the Christian Church, an introduction to social and pastoral anthropology, Dublin 1973.
Shorter, Aylward, Prayer in the religious traditions of Africa, Nairobi 1975.
Shorter, Aylward, Towards a Theology of Inculturation, New York 1988.
Sigmund, Mowinckel, translated by Reidar B.Bjornard, The Old Testament as Word of God, Oxford 1960.
Sigo, John, Sharia: Blessing in Disguise, Enugu 2001.
Smith, Damian, Crusade, Heresy and Inquisition in the lands of the crown of Aragon (c.1167–1276), Boston 2010.
Smith, Frank and Miller, George, (ed.), The Genesis of Language, A Psycholinguistic Approach, London 1966.
Smith, Linda, Effecctive counselling: A groupwork manual on interpersonal skills for pastoral teams, England 1995.
Smock, David, Interfaith Dialogue and Peacebuilding, Washington D.C 2002.

Sridhar, Shikaripur, Cognition and Sentence Production, A Cross – Linguistic Study, New York 1988.

St Germans of Constantinople on the Divine Liturgy, The Greek Text with Translations, Introduction and Commentary by Paul Meyendorff, New York 1984.

Stilz, Gerhard, (ed.), Colonies-Missions-Culture in the English-speaking world: General and comparative studies, Tübingen 2001.

Studdert – Kennedy, Michael, (editor), Psychology of Language, London 1983.

Stump, Eleonore, (ed.), The Cambridge Companion To Augustine, Cambridge 2001.

Suenens, Leon Joseph, Introduction in Theology of Renewal, vol.ii, edited by Shook L.K., Montreal, 1968, 7; quoted by Donovan,in: The Church As Idea and Fact, Minnesota 1990.

Sykes, Stephen, editor, The Study of Anglicanism, Revised Edition, Minnesota 1988.

Sykes, Stephen, (ed.), Karl Barth: Centenary Essays, Cambridge1989.

Tannen, Deborah, Talking Voices, Repetition, Dialogue and Imagery in Conversational Discourse, New York 1989.

The Pocket Ritual. Rituale Parvum, collected and edited by The National Liturgical Centre, Bagalore 1996.

Thomas, Jenny, Meaning in Interaction: An Introduction to Pragmatics, London and New York 1995.

Thurian, Max, (ed.), Churches respond to BEM, vol. iv, official responses to the "Baptism , Eucharist and Ministry" text, Switzerland 1987.

Torrance, Thomas, Divine Meaning: Studies in Patristic Hermeneutics, Edinburgh 1995.

Torrell, Jean-Pierre, Aquinas Summa: Background, Structure, Reception, translated by Benedict M. Guevin, Washington D.C 2005.

Turner, Victor Witter, The Forest of Symbols, Aspects of Ndemba Ritual, Ithaca and London 1994.

Uchendu ,Victor, The Igbo of Southeast Nigeria, New York 1965.

Ukaegbu, John Ofoegbu, Igbo Identity and Personality vis – a – vis Cultural Symbols, Madrid 1990.

Umeasiegbu ,Rems, Words are Sweet, Igbo Stories and Storytelling, Sttutgard 1982.

Umoren, Anthony, Jesus and Miracle Healing Today, Ibadan 2000.

Uzondu, Celestine Chibueze, The hypostatic union as the principle of the eucharist, a systematic-theological investigation, Rome 2000.

Uzukwu, Eugene, A listening Church: Autonomy and Communion in African Churches, New York 1996.

Uzukwu, Eugene, Inculturation and Liturgy (Eucharist), in: Gibelini, R. (editor), "Paths of African Theology", London 1994.

Vanderveken, Daniel, Meaning and Speech Acts, Vol.1 and 2, Principles of Language Use, New York 1990.

Verschueren, Jef, On Speech Act Verbs, Amsterdam, John Benjamins, 1980.

Vorgrimler, Herbert, Sakramentalen theologie, Düsseldorf 1987.

Waardenburg, Jacques, Symbolic Aspects of Myth, art. in: Alan Olso (editor), Myth, Symbol and Reality, London 1980.

Walter, Funk Robert, Language, Hermeneutic, and Word of God: the problem of language in the New Testament and contemporary theology, New York 1966.
Weman, Henry, African Folkmusic in Christian Churches in Africa, Nairobi 1974.
Wilks, Yorick, Grammar, Meaning and the Machine Analysis of Language, London 1972.
Wodak, Ruth and Schulz, Muriel, The Language of Love and Guilt, Amsterdam 1986.
Wollbold, Andreas, Handbuch Der Gemeindepastoral, Regensburg 2004.
Wollbold, Andreas, Kirche als Wahlheimat, Studien zur Theologie und Praxis der Seelsorge (32): Beitrag zu einer Antwort auf die Zeichen der Zeit, Würzburg 1998.
Wollbold, Andreas, Pastoraltheologie, Homiletik, Religionspädagogik, Paderborn 2001.
Yokoyama, Olga, Discourse and Word Order, Amsterdam 1986.